Manuscripts and Medieval Song

The manuscript sources of medieval song rarely fit the description of 'songbook' easily. Instead, they are very often mixed compilations that place songs alongside other diverse contents, and the songs themselves may be inscribed as texts alone or as verbal and musical notation. This book looks afresh at these manuscripts through ten case studies, representing key sources in Latin, French, German, and English from across Europe during the Middle Ages. Each chapter is authored by a leading expert and treats a case-study in detail, including a listing of the manuscript's overall contents, a summary of its treatment in scholarship, and up-to-date bibliographical references. Drawing on recent scholarly methodologies, the contributors uncover what these books and the songs within them meant to their medieval audience and reveal a wealth of new information about the original contexts of songs both in performance and as committed to parchment.

HELEN DEEMING is Senior Lecturer in Music at Royal Holloway, University of London. She has taught medieval music at the University of Cambridge, King's College London, the University of Southampton and Royal Holloway, University of London and won several teaching prizes. She is the editor of *Songs in British Sources, c.1150–1300*, Musica Britannica, vol. 95 (2013) – a scholarly edition that makes many songs available in print for the first time.

ELIZABETH EVA LEACH is Professor of Music at the University of Oxford. Her publications include *Guillaume de Machaut: Poet, Secretary, Musician* (2011), *Sung Birds: Music, Nature and Poetry in the Later Middle Ages* (2007), *Citation in Medieval and Renaissance Musical Culture* (co-edited with Suzannah Clark, 2005), and *Machaut's Music: New Interpretations* (editor, 2003). In 2013 she was awarded the Dent Medal of the Royal Musical Association; she was also winner of the 2012 Phyllis Goodhart Gordan Prize of the Renaissance Society of America, and the 2007 Outstanding Publication Award of the Society for Music Theory.

MUSIC IN CONTEXT

Series editors:

J. P. E. Harper-Scott
Royal Holloway, University of London

Julian Rushton
University of Leeds

The aim of Music in Context is to illuminate specific musical works, repertoires, or practices in historical, critical, socio-economic, or other contexts; or to illuminate particular cultural and critical contexts in which music operates through the study of specific musical works, repertoires, or practices. A specific musical focus is essential, while avoiding the decontextualization of traditional aesthetics and music analysis. The series title invites engagement with both its main terms; the aim is to challenge notions of what contexts are appropriate or necessary in studies of music, and to extend the conceptual framework of musicology into other disciplines or into new theoretical directions.

BOOKS IN THE SERIES

SIMON P. KEEFE, *Mozart's Requiem: Reception, Work, Completion*

J. P. E. HARPER-SCOTT, *The Quilting Points of Musical Modernism: Revolution, Reaction, and William Walton*

NANCY NOVEMBER, *Beethoven's Theatrical Quartets: Opp. 59, 74 and 95*

RUFUS HALLMARK, *'Frauenliebe und Leben': Chamisso's Poems and Schumann's Songs*

ANNA ZAYARUZNAYA, *The Monstrous New Art: Divided Forms in the Late Medieval Motet*

HELEN DEEMING and ELIZABETH EVA LEACH, *Manuscripts and Medieval Song: Inscription, Performance, Context*

Manuscripts and Medieval Song

Inscription, Performance, Context

Edited by HELEN DEEMING and ELIZABETH EVA LEACH

CAMBRIDGE
UNIVERSITY PRESS

CAMBRIDGE
UNIVERSITY PRESS

University Printing House, Cambridge CB2 8BS, United Kingdom

One Liberty Plaza, 20th Floor, New York, NY 10006, USA

477 Williamstown Road, Port Melbourne, VIC 3207, Australia

314-321, 3rd Floor, Plot 3, Splendor Forum, Jasola District Centre, New Delhi-110025, India

79 Anson Road, #06-04/06, Singapore 079906

Cambridge University Press is part of the University of Cambridge.

It furthers the University's mission by disseminating knowledge in the pursuit of
education, learning and research at the highest international levels of excellence.

www.cambridge.org
Information on this title: www.cambridge.org/9781107642645

© Cambridge University Press 2015

First published 2015
First paperback edition 2017

A catalogue record for this publication is available from the British Library

Library of Congress Cataloging in Publication data
Manuscripts and medieval song : inscription, performance, context / edited by Helen
Deeming and Elizabeth Eva Leach.
    pages   cm. – (Music in context)
Includes bibliographical references and index.
ISBN 978-1-107-06263-4 (Hardback)
1. Music–Europe–500–1400–Manuscripts.   2. Music–Europe–15th century–
Manuscripts.   3. Manuscripts, Medieval.   4. Paleography, Musical.   5. Musical
notation–History–To 1500.   I. Deeming, Helen, editor.   II. Leach, Elizabeth Eva,
editor.
ML172.M36 2014
782.409′02–dc23   2014034732

ISBN 978-1-107-06263-4 Hardback
ISBN 978-1-107-64264-5 Paperback

Contents

Figures

Music examples

Tables

Contributors

SAM BARRETT

Sam Barrett is Senior Lecturer in Music at the University of Cambridge and Fellow and Director of College Music at Pembroke College, Cambridge. He has published widely on the sources and notations of the early medieval Latin lyric and co-edited with Francesco Stella a collection of fourth- to ninth-century accentual Latin poems with music. His two-volume study and transcription of melodies for Boethius' *De consolatione philosophiae* was recently published by Baerenreiter as part of the subsidia series of the Monumenta monodica medii aevi.

GUNDELA BOBETH

Gundela Bobeth studied Musicology, Medieval and Modern History, and Latin Philology at the Universities of Hamburg and Basle. In 2004, she received her PhD from the University of Basle with a monograph on musical settings of classical verses (Virgil, Stace, Lucan, and Terence) in the Middle Ages, which was published in the subsidia series of Monumenta monodica medii aevi. Having held the position of Assistant Professor at the Institute of Musicology at the University of Vienna, she is currently working on a comprehensive research project on Viennese song culture around 1800. The project is funded by the Swiss National Science Foundation and associated to the Institute of Musicology of the University of Zurich.

SEAN CURRAN

Sean Curran is a Junior Research Fellow at Trinity College Cambridge. His dissertation on the manuscript **F-Pn n.a.f.13521** (University of California, Berkeley, 2013) was supported by the Alvin H. Johnson AMS-50 Fellowship from the American Musicological Society, and the Grace Frank Dissertation Award from the Medieval Academy of America.

HELEN DEEMING

Helen Deeming is Senior Lecturer in Music at Royal Holloway, University of London with research interests in medieval music, the history of the book, and the history of musical notation. Her scholarly edition, *Songs in British Sources, c.1150–1300*, appeared as volume 95 of Musica Britannica in 2013, making a large repertory of early songs available in print for the first time.

RACHEL MAY GOLDEN

Rachel May Golden is Associate Professor of Musicology in the School of Music at the University of Tennessee, where she is also Co-Chair of the Medieval and Renaissance Studies Interdisciplinary Program. She earned the PhD in musicology from the University of North Carolina at Chapel Hill. An author of work on both medieval and twentieth-century topics, her research appears in *The Journal of Musicology*, *Music & Letters*, *Opera Quarterly*, and *Musical Quarterly*, among others. Her work has been supported by an American Council of Learned Societies Fellowship and through the NEH Summer Institute program.

HENRY HOPE

Following Masters degrees from the Hochschule für Musik Franz Liszt Weimar/Friedrich-Schiller-Universität Jena and the University of Oxford, Henry Hope obtained his doctorate from the University of Oxford with a study of the musicality of *Minnesang*. Expressly interdisciplinary, his work aims to bridge the gap between Germanist and musicological considerations of medieval German song repertories and is informed by a passionate historiographical interest in the construction of the modern academy. Further interests include GDR musicology, the music aesthetics of Johann Gottfried Herder, and early polyphony. Hope currently holds an appointment as stipendiary lecturer in music at Magdalen College, Oxford. More information and current research is available on his public blog: henryhopemusicology.wordpress.com.

ELIZABETH EVA LEACH

Elizabeth Eva Leach is Professor of Music at the University of Oxford and a Fellow of St Hugh's College. Leach has published extensively on medieval song and was the recipient of the Dent Medal of the Royal Musical Association in 2013. Her monograph on Machaut (Leach 2011) received the Phyllis Goodhart Gordan Prize of the Renaissance Society of America. Leach blogs about her research and makes most of her publications freely available at eeleach.wordpress.com.

JEREMY LLEWELLYN

Jeremy Llewellyn is Professor of Music at the Schola Cantorum Basiliensis-FHNW, having studied music as organ scholar at the University of Cambridge, medieval musicology under Wulf Arlt at the University of Basle, and worked at the interdisciplinary research centre devoted to the 'Cultural Heritage of Medieval Rituals' at the University of Copenhagen. He has published on medieval chant, song, and conductus, served as Vice-President of the IMS research group *cantus planus*, and as a member of Council of the Plainsong and Medieval Music Society.

Acknowledgements

For assistance and comments on various parts of this book, the contributors would like to thank Jessica Berenbeim, Catherine Bradley, Katherine Butler, Richard Crocker, Emma Dillon, Lawrence Earp, Steven Justice, Guido Kraus, Mary Ann Smart, Richard Taruskin, and Matthew Thomson.

A note on manuscript sigla

There are multiple ways of referring to individual manuscripts of music. Usually the sigla used for manuscripts containing a certain kind of repertory are well known to those who work on that area, but may be opaque or even confusing to those outside. Manuscript sources with generically mixed contents typically have a different identity for each area of scholarship in which they are referenced. Since this book is designed to treat the manuscript organization and mixing of genres as a positive item of study, it has been simpler to rely on the standardized sigla codified by RISM. Not only can these be unscrambled readily in a handy online resource but they have the advantage of simply reflecting the fact of the current location and shelfmark of the manuscript, without committing it, by siglum chosen, to being part of a particular subfield of scholarship.[1] Thus **GB-Ob Douce 308** is not forced into belonging to the scholarship on the trouvères (*I*), on motets (*D*), or even on Richard de Fournival, *Bestiary of Love* (*O*). What follows here, however, gives a listing of the manuscripts referred to in this book, summarizing the different titles and abbreviations by which they have been known in order to facilitate cross-reference with other scholarly work. This list includes, where present, links to a URL of digital surrogates for each manuscript. Since the visual and organizational features of the manuscripts themselves are so fundamental to the arguments pursued in this book, we strongly encourage readers to use these links – which will also be hosted and kept updated on the website associated with the book at Cambridge University Press – and then to navigate to the folio numbers given in the text.[2] Footnotes with links to the relevant folios are given in the text itself: in the e-book version, these are directly clickable.

[1] See www.rism.info/en/community/development/rism-sigla-catalogue.html.
[2] www.cambridge.org/9781107062634

List of manuscripts cited (with links to online surrogates where present)

A-LIs 324 (formerly Cc III 9)

B-Br 8860-8867

B-Br IV-319 = *Méliacin* MS *E*

B-Mbu 330-215

CH-BEb 389 = trouvère MS *C*

CH-EN 1003: www.e-codices.unifr.ch/en/bke/1003

CH-EN 102: www.e-codices.unifr.ch/en/list/one/bke/0102

CH-SGs 383: www.e-codices.unifr.ch/en/list/one/csg/0383

D-BAs Lit.115 = motet MS *Ba*; 'the Bamberg MS': http://nbn-resolving.de/urn:nbn:de:bvb:22-dtl-0000002752

D-DO 882

D-DO A.III.22

D-DS 3471 = motet MS *Da*: http://tudigit.ulb.tu-darmstadt.de/show/Hs-3471

D-EF Amplon. Oct. 32

D-F Fragm.lat.VI.41

D-HEu Cod.Pal.germ.848 = the 'Manesse Codex' or 'Große Heidelberger Liederhandschrift', usually given siglum *C*: http://digi.ub.uni-heidelberg.de/diglit/cpg848

D-Ju Ms.El.f.101 = the 'Jenaer Liederhandschrift', usually given siglum *J*.

D-Mbs Clm 716: http://daten.digitale-sammlungen.de/~db/bsb00007356/images/ (black-and-white images only)

D-Mbs Clm 4598

D-Mbs Clm 4660-4660a = 'Codex Buranus', 'Carmina Burana MS': http://daten.digitale-sammlungen.de/0008/bsb00085130/images/

D-Mbs Clm 5539: http://daten.digitale-sammlungen.de/0007/bsb00079147/images/

D-Mbs Clm 18190

D-MÜsa ms.VII 51

D-Sl HB I 95 = the 'Stuttgart Cantatorium': http://digital.wlb-stuttgart.de/purl/bsz339701315

D-Sl HB XIII 1 = the 'Weingartner Liederhandschrift', usually given siglum *B*; http://digital.wlb-stuttgart.de/purl/bsz319421317

D-W Guelf.628 Helmst. = motet MS *W1*: http://diglib.hab.de/mss/628-helmst/start.htm

D-W Guelf.1099 Helmst. = motet MS *W2*: http://diglib.hab.de/mss/1099-helmst/start.htm

E-Bac Ripoll 116

E-BUlh = motet MS *Hu;* 'Las Huelgas Codex'; MS without shelfmark

E-E Z.II.2

E-Mn 288

E-Mn 289

E-Mn 20486 = motet MS *Ma*

E-SAu 226

F-AIXm 166: selected images via http://toisondor.byu.edu/dscriptorium/aix166/index.html

F-AL 26

F-AN 403

F-CHRm 223

F-EV lat.2: images via DIAMM at www.diamm.ac.uk/jsp/Descriptions?op=SOURCE&sourceKey=3868

F-EV lat.17: images via DIAMM at www.diamm.ac.uk/jsp/Descriptions?op=SOURCE&sourceKey−276

F-EV lat.39

F-G 4413

F-LG 2 (17)

F-LPbd A V 7 009 (library formerly 'Bibliothèque du Grand Séminaire')

F-MO H196 = motet MS *Mo*; the 'Montpellier Codex': http://manuscrits.biu-montpellier.fr/vignettem.php?GENRE%5B%5D=MP&ETG=OR&ETT=OR&ETM=OR&BASE=manuf

F-O 149:

F-O 303

F-O 305

F-O 341

F-Pa 227: http://gallica.bnf.fr/ark:/12148/btv1b55005681f

F-Pa 2741

F-Pa 3517: http://gallica.bnf.fr/ark:/12148/btv1b55006913x

F-Pa 6361

F-Pm 942 (formerly 1002)

F-Pn fr.146 = 'the interpolated *Fauvel*'; the *Roman de Fauvel*: http://gallica.bnf.fr/ark:/12148/btv1b8454675g

F-Pn fr.372 = *Renart le Nouvel* MS *C*: http://gallica.bnf.fr/ark:/12148/btv1b90589327 (black-and-white microfilm images only)

F-Pn fr.412: http://gallica.bnf.fr/ark:/12148/btv1b84259980

F-Pn fr.837: http://gallica.bnf.fr/ark:/12148/btv1b9009629n (black-and-white microfilm images only)

F-Pn fr.844 = trouvère MS *M*; motet MS *R*; troubadour MS *W*; 'Chansonnier du Roi': http://gallica.bnf.fr/ark:/12148/btv1b84192440

F-Pn fr.845 = trouvère MS *N*: http://gallica.bnf.fr/ark:/12148/btv1b6000955r

F-Pn fr.846 = trouvère MS *O*; 'Chansonnier Cangé': http://gallica.bnf.fr/ark:/12148/btv1b6000950p

F-Pn fr.881 = Machaut MS *H*: http://gallica.bnf.fr/ark:/12148/btv1b8449041w

F-Pn fr.1455

F-Pn fr.1569: http://gallica.bnf.fr/ark:/12148/btv1b6000327c

F-Pn fr.1581 = *Renart le Nouvel* MS *L*: http://gallica.bnf.fr/ark:/12148/btv1b60009654

F-Pn fr.1584 = Machaut MS *A*: http://gallica.bnf.fr/ark:/12148/btv1b84490444

F-Pn fr.1585 = Machaut MS *B*: http://gallica.bnf.fr/ark:/12148/btv1b8449032x

F-Pn fr.1586 = Machaut MS *C*: http://gallica.bnf.fr/ark:/12148/btv1b8449043q

F-Pn fr. 1587 = Machaut MS *D*: http://gallica.bnf.fr/ark:/12148/btv1b8451101h

F-Pn fr.1589 = *Méliacin* MS *B*: http://gallica.bnf.fr/ark:/12148/btv1b8447872k

F-Pn fr.1593 = *Renart le Nouvel* MS *F*; trouvère MS *g*: http://gallica.bnf.fr/ark:/12148/btv1b6000803p

F-Pn fr.1633 = *Méliacin* MS *A*: http://gallica.bnf.fr/ark:/12148/btv1b9058840f (black-and-white microfilm images only)

F-Pn fr.1802: http://gallica.bnf.fr/ark:/12148/btv1b90076209

F-Pn fr.2165–66 = Machaut MS *P*: http://gallica.bnf.fr/ark:/12148/btv1b8449052p and http://gallica.bnf.fr/ark:/12148/btv1b84490496

F-Pn fr.9221 = Machaut MS *E*: http://gallica.bnf.fr/ark:/12148/btv1b6000795k

F-Pn fr.12469

F-Pn fr.12565

F-Pn fr.12615 = trouvère MS *T*; Motet MS *N*, 'Noailles chansonnier': http://gallica.bnf.fr/ark:/12148/btv1b60007945

F-Pn fr.12786 = trouvère MS *k*: http://gallica.bnf.fr/ark:/12148/btv1b60003511

F-Pn fr.20050 = trouvère MS *U*; troubadour MS *X*; 'Chansonnier de Saint-Germain-des-Prés': http://gallica.bnf.fr/ark:/12148/btv1b60009580

F-Pn fr.22545 = Machaut MS *F*: http://gallica.bnf.fr/ark:/12148/btv1b60007997

F-Pn fr.22546 = Machaut MS *G*: http://gallica.bnf.fr/ark:/12148/btv1b6000793r

F-Pn fr.24406 = trouvère MS *V*: http://gallica.bnf.fr/ark:/12148/btv1b84386028

F-Pn fr.24432: http://gallica.bnf.fr/ark:/12148/btv1b90075147 (black-and-white microfilm images only)

F-Pn fr.25532 = Gautier de Coinci, *Miracles* MS XV (or *N*): http://gallica.bnf.fr/ark:/12148/btv1b90631786 (black-and-white microfilm images only)

F-Pn fr.25566 = trouvère MS *W*; motet MS *Ha*; *Renart le Nouvel* MS *V*: http://gallica.bnf.fr/ark:/12148/btv1b6001348v and http://gallica.bnf.fr/ark:/12148/btv1b54002413d

F-Pn lat.5: http://gallica.bnf.fr/ark:/12148/btv1b85301526 and http://gallica.bnf.fr/ark:/12148/btv1b8530347k

F-Pn lat.778: http://gallica.bnf.fr/ark:/12148/btv1b84262695

F-Pn lat.903: http://gallica.bnf.fr/ark:/12148/btv1b9068069f (black-and-white microfilm images only)

F-Pn lat.1085: http://gallica.bnf.fr/ark:/12148/btv1b8432277r

F-Pn lat.1120: http://gallica.bnf.fr/ark:/12148/btv1b84323135

F-Pn lat.1139: http://gallica.bnf.fr/ark:/12148/btv1b6000946s

F-Pn lat.1153: http://gallica.bnf.fr/ark:/12148/btv1b90778858 (black-and-white microfilm images only)

F-Pn lat.1154: http://gallica.bnf.fr/ark:/12148/btv1b84324798

F-Pn lat.1240: http://gallica.bnf.fr/ark:/12148/btv1b6000528g

F-Pn lat.1720: http://gallica.bnf.fr/ark:/12148/btv1b8427235p

F-Pn lat.1897: http://gallica.bnf.fr/ark:/12148/btv1b8530357z

F-Pn lat.3545

F-Pn lat.3549: http://gallica.bnf.fr/ark:/12148/btv1b90660885 (black-and-white microfilm images only)

F-Pn lat.3719: http://gallica.bnf.fr/ark:/12148/btv1b52502489w

F-Pn lat.9449: http://gallica.bnf.fr/ark:/12148/btv1b8422992k

F-Pn lat.13388 = 'Libellus Turonensis'

F-Pn lat.15139 = motet MS *StV*; 'Saint-Victor MS': http://gallica.bnf.fr/ark:/12148/btv1b8432457p

F-Pn Moreau 1715–1719

F-Pn n.a.f.1731

F-Pn n.a.f.13521 = 'La Clayette': http://gallica.bnf.fr/ark:/12148/
    btv1b530121530

F-Pn n.a.lat.1235: http://gallica.bnf.fr/ark:/12148/btv1b8432301z

F-RS 1275

F-ROU 666 (A 506)

F-SEm 46

F-T 1742

GB-Cccc Ferrell 1 = Machaut MS *Vg*: images via DIAMM at www.diamm.
    ac.uk/jsp/Descriptions?op=SOURCE&sourceKey=3774

GB-Cgc 240/126

GB-Cjec QB 1

GB-Cmc 1594 = Machaut MS *Pe*: images via DIAMM at www.diamm.ac.
    uk/jsp/Descriptions?op=SOURCE&sourceKey=309

GB-Cu Ff.I.17 = the 'later Cambridge Song Book'; foliation given in text is
    from J. Stevens 2005

GB-Cu Gg.V.35 = the 'earlier Cambridge Songbook'

GB-H P.IX.7 = the 'Hereford breviary'

GB-Lbl Add.36881: images via DIAMM at www.diamm.ac.uk/jsp/
    Descriptions?op=SOURCE&sourceKey=919

GB-Lbl Arundel 248: images via DIAMM at www.diamm.ac.uk/jsp/
    Descriptions?op=SOURCE&sourceKey=411

GB-Lbl Egerton 274 = motet MS *LoB*; trouvère MS *F*: www.bl.uk/manu-
    scripts/FullDisplay.aspx?ref=Egerton_MS_274

GB-Lbl Egerton 2615: selected images at www.bl.uk/catalogues/illumina-
    tedmanuscripts/record.asp?MSID=6666&CollID=28&NStart=2615

GB-Lbl Egerton 3307: selected images at www.bl.uk/catalogues/illumina-
    tedmanuscripts/record.asp?MSID=8678&CollID=28&NStart=3307

GB-Lbl Harley 978 = Motet MS *LoHa*: www.bl.uk/manuscripts/FullDis-
    play.aspx?ref=Harley_MS_978

GB-Lbl Harley 4972: selected images at www.bl.uk/catalogues/illumina-
    tedmanuscripts/record.asp?MSID=8583&CollID=8&NStart=4972

GB-Lbl Royal 12.B.XXV

GB-Lma Cust.1

GB-Ob Add. A.44 = 'The Bekynton anthology'

GB-Ob Ashmole 1285

GB-Ob Auct. 6Q3.17

GB-Ob Douce 165: selected images at http://bodley30.bodley.ox.ac.
    uk:8180/luna/servlet/s/2o5m78

GB-Ob Douce 308 = trouvère MS *I*; motet MS *D*; 'the Oxford chanson-
    nier', 'the Lorraine chansonnier': selected images online at http://

bodley30.bodley.ox.ac.uk:8180/luna/servlet/view/search/what/MS.
+Douce+308/?&q=%22MS.%20Douce%20308%22

GB-Ob Laud lat.118

GB-Occ 59: selected images at www.diamm.ac.uk/jsp/Descriptions?
op=SOURCE&sourceKey=558

I-CFm Cod.CI

I-Fl Plut.29.1 = motet MS *F*; the 'Florence MS': http://teca.bmlonline.it/
TecaViewer/index.jsp?RisIdr=TECA0000342136 [requires Java]

I-Ma R71 sup.

I-MOe R4,4 = trouvère MS *H*

I-Pc C55

I-Pc C56

I-Rss XIV L3

I-Rvat Reg.1490 = trouvère MS *a*

I-Tr vari 42 = motet MS *Tu*; the 'Turin MS'

IRL-Dtc 432

US-NYpm Glazier 52

Abbreviations

AH   Analecta hymnica Medii Aevi. 1886–1922. 55 vols., ed. Guido
           Maria Dreves, with Clemens Blume and Henry M. Bannister.
GMO   Grove Music online. Available via www.grovemusic.com.
MGH   Monumenta Germaniae Historica. Available via www.dmgh.de.
MV   Motet voice with number as listed in van der Werf 1989.
PL   Patrologia Latina. Available via http://pld.chadwyck.com.

The book designates notated pitches using the letter-names of the Guidonian
gamut in italics; pitch classes are given in upper-case Roman letters.

Introduction

HELEN DEEMING AND ELIZABETH EVA LEACH

The traces of the medieval European song tradition lie scattered in hundreds of lyric collections. The verbal texts of this tradition have been surveyed a number of times, but the music, mediated by few and partial traces, has posed challenges of interpretation that scholarship has been slow to address. *Manuscripts and Medieval Song: Inscription, Performance, Context* contends that a fuller account of the role played by music within the history of medieval song is possible, and – in order to facilitate this – the surviving manuscript witnesses need to be read again with an eye to a wealth of previously overlooked evidence. Previous scholarship has typically removed songs from their manuscripts into editions organized by entirely different criteria. At the heart of this book lies the conviction that close attention to the way songs (whether musically notated or not) were gathered onto the page, specifically their layout, organization, and alignment with other texts, not only yields new insights into the musical culture of the medieval lyric, but challenges assumptions that have underpinned existing scholarship.

Some recent work on songs has adopted a similar approach, but to date studies have been limited to particular categories of manuscripts (especially those containing French and Occitan lyrics), and thus have done little so far to unravel the specific disciplinary preoccupations of the modern academy in relation to medieval song.[1] Taking as paradigmatic the 'monumental' collections of vernacular song compiled in the later Middle Ages, literary scholarship has tended to conceive of medieval song in monoglot groupings, and with a focus on named authors and rigidly taxonomized genres, categories which – as the contributions to this volume show – are not reflected in the majority of manuscripts that preserve song. This approach is apparent in perhaps the most recent book-length study of manuscripts of medieval song, in which Marisa Galvez notes at the outset that 'the songbooks most relevant to the development of Western poetry, in their typical qualities and conscious intention to establish literary

---

[1] Huot 1987; Bent and Wathey 1998; Nichols and Wenzel 1996.

traditions, are the monumental manuscripts compiled from the thirteenth century onward, such as the chansonniers of troubadour and *trouvère* poetry and *Liederhandschriften* of German *Minnesänger*'.[2] Moreover, scholarship on song has suffered particularly from the lack of attention devoted to one of its defining features: its musicality.[3] Where music has been considered at all, it has tended to be subject to similar disciplinary divisions that do not correspond to its medieval transmission. These have included the artificial separation of monophony from polyphony, and an interest in the latter (as the supposed distinguishing feature of a 'Great Western Tradition') that has far exceeded the former, as well as a concern with authorship and the 'work concept', both enquiring principally into compositional process. For medieval song, however, there is very little surviving evidence about the production or composition of songs. Sketch materials do not exist as they do for later music, and in most cases it is not known who provided the music for a song. The various and varied notational formats in manuscripts provide the sum of the evidence, but tend to be considered under-prescriptive or even inadequate from the perspective of more recent expectations of musical scores. The very variety of manifestations of a single song, or the different texting of related versions of what might broadly be considered the 'same' underlying melody, frustrate the idea of an authorial work and make it clear that a focus on the mediation of music to audiences through its performance constitutes a subject more germane to the nature of the repertory. That said, the only evidence that we have for performance and reception is the same as the evidence that proved inadequate for the study of poiesis: the books with songs in them.

Manuscripts and Medieval Song addresses the issue of how to read performative and reception meanings from an examination of the manu-script traces of songs. In particular, the other content of books containing song texts and notations can provide contextual evidence for audience and use, even to the extent of showing the length of use of a particular book and its changing functions over time. It is often unclear to readers reliant on modern editions that a manuscript juxtaposes a particular song copy with other non-song items, such as sermons, narrative poems, florilegia,

---

[2] Galvez 2012, 2.

[3] Again, Galvez perpetuates this tendency, in the process setting up a false dichotomy between manuscripts which 'preserve lyric texts rather than musical notation, include prose texts, and are large-format, costly objects of parchment' and 'performance manuals of traveling singers' (Galvez 2012, 4).

bestiaries, and scientific or theological works, yet these medieval habits of compilation stimulated associative reading practices, enhancing the appreciated meaning of songs. Existing studies have already examined the material contexts of late-medieval French manuscripts of song in this way, but *Manuscripts and Medieval Song* expands the geographic and chronological purview to uncover comparable and equally thought-provoking insights into books containing song from across Europe and throughout the Middle Ages.

This book is organized around a series of ten case-study manuscripts, each forming the subject of an individual chapter. By including a range of famous but surprisingly little-studied manuscripts this book is able both to represent the widely varied nature of the medieval song tradition and also to propose surprising connections between traditions that have been studied separately. Treating these 'songbooks' as bibliographic wholes ensures that the historical narrative is not exclusively predicated on any of the traditional divisions by language or thematic concern of the song text, type of notation, or polyphony versus monophony. Some of the manuscripts chosen here have been neglected in recent musicological scholarship, whereas others have assumed a degree of prominence that is based on a partial or skewed perception of the importance of some of their contents, while disregarding other contexts both within and beyond the book. Each chapter typically offers an account of the entire contents of the manuscript; an outline of the modern reception history of the book, including details of its presence in scholarship; a consideration of the specifically musical context (by noting the stylistic and repertorial contexts which the music in the manuscript engages and/or by reading the particular manuscript from its music outwards, rather than the other way around) sometimes focused through a discussion of individual songs; and an analysis of the issues arising from the presence of such songs in such a book.

The individual chapters

The opening chapter, by Sam Barrett, considers **F-Pn lat.1154**, which is frequently regarded as a songbook, but is in fact a varied collection comprising a litany of saints, a collection of prayers, an extract from Isidore of Seville's *Synonyma*, and some thirty Latin songs (including hymns, Boethian metra, early sequences, as well as moral-didactic poems, poems on recent political events, several laments for prominent individuals, and *versus* by leading Carolingian authors such as Gottschalk and

Paulinus of Aquileia). Eighteen of the songs are notated in this manuscript and many others are found with notation in other witnesses. Reading the *versus* collection alongside the contents of the book as a whole immediately shows what can be gained from a consideration of the whole book, since some of the other contents of this book offer a revision to the currently accepted provenance and dating, reviving a forgotten suggestion from 1930 that the manuscript is from St Martial in Limoges on account of the saints included in its Litany of Confessors. Barrett's careful palaeographical study of the main notator does not preclude remarks about the other hands in the book, which show a function in teaching. But Barrett carefully refrains from ascribing a single use to the whole: the book has a multiplicity of simultaneous functions within a monastic institution, including most importantly private prayer, a use which is confirmed not only by the other contents of the volume, but by the addition of Amens to some of the *versus*, and by some of the slightly later additions, which show the persistence of this function.

In Chapter 2 Jeremy Llewellyn considers **GB-Cu Gg.V.35**, which also seems to have had teaching as one of its uses. This collection of songs has acquired the title of the Cambridge Songs or the 'Earlier Cambridge Songbook'. Compiled on the cusp of the Norman Conquest at St Augustine's Abbey, Canterbury, the manuscript presents a dazzling array of poetic materials whose historical and geographical origins ultimately span several centuries and a fair portion of Western Europe. The book contains music-theoretical texts, glosses, and passages of neumation. Llewellyn draws out the ways in which the book itself addresses the singer in an admonitory manner, thrusting the figure of the 'cautious' or 'prudent' cantor to the fore, and thereby reflecting epistemological shifts in ideas of *musica* from the philosophically speculative to the technically practical.

In Chapter 3 Rachel May Golden looks at the small, twelfth-century Aquitanian *versarium* **GB-Lbl Add. 36881**, which shares repertory with three earlier manuscripts from the library of St Martial, Limoges. Golden argues that the diverse contents of this manuscript have been ill served by musicological study that divides polyphony from monophony, since the manuscript integrates both. In addition, the modern desire to separate the liturgical from the non-liturgical has contributed to the relative neglect of this music in favour of the more clearly liturgical Parisian repertories of a similar date. Golden's exploration of the songs of **GB-Lbl Add. 36881** as 'monastic inspiration, theological exploration, and instances of devotion to the Virgin within the context of the twelfth-century Marian cult' shows them to be indicative of the text–music relationships that are typical of the new song genres of twelfth-century Occitania. The new songs of the Aquitanian *versaria* show formal, thematic, and even linguistic interaction with the contemporary and geographically proximate repertory of troubadour song, in poetry, music, and the interaction of the two. As a manuscript that collapses several binaries that have become enshrined in later scholarship, **GB-Lbl Add. 36881** makes an especially clear case for reconsidering songs in their material context.

Gundela Bobeth's consideration of the 'Codex Buranus', **D-Mbs Clm 4660,** in Chapter 4, details how the reception history of this famous manuscript in the twentieth century, most notoriously in the setting of a selection of its texts by Carl Orff in 1936, has given prominence to some parts of its contents while obscuring its extreme variety as a whole. Its contents have been published in separate volumes of poetry, and this has added to the fragmentation of a repertory that is best considered wholesale. Again, the key issue is eclecticism: jostling within its covers may be found Latin lyrics ranging from the devotional to the frankly erotic, liturgical plays, German poems, and a 'Gamblers' Mass'. This chapter considers the way in which such a compilation points to the existence of smaller collections of songs behind this larger assembly and the role of the geographical provenance of the book in bringing these collections together. As a whole, the themes and older song genres are still present in the 'new song' preserved here, but they are subject to stylistic transformation. The musical notation in this manuscript is sparse but concordances exist for many songs, although not all; this chapter therefore raises similar issues to those in **GB-Cu Gg.V.35** (Chapter 2), but for a much later period. Like the Cambridge Songbook, too, the songs of the Carmina Burana are self-conscious about being sung: their texts reference singing and songs. This chapter establishes and discusses a repertorial context for these songs, taking into account both the well-known and the neglected material in the book.

In Chapter 5 Helen Deeming examines **GB-Lbl Harley 978**, which contains the famous Sumer canon (or 'Reading rota'). This six-part piece has a celebrated canonic role in the history of early music and is frequently performed and recorded, but its fame has obscured both the other music in the manuscript's single musical gathering (some of which has not been published in modern editions) and its wider non-musical contents, which provide valuable information on issues of use and transmission. Among its very varied contents are the earliest complete copy of the *Lais* of Marie de France, Latin narrative poetry, formulas for ecclesiastical letters, and oddments of practical things for monastic use. The complete book speaks of a routine communication between abbeys both within the British Isles and across the Channel, and of the ways that songs moved alongside the transmission of other kinds of practical knowledge. Deeming thus places **GB-Lbl Harley 978** within a hitherto unrecognized context of Latin, French, and English song cultivated within the cloister walls of thirteenth-century England and its Norman neighbours.

Deeming's second chapter, Chapter 6, takes **GB-Lbl Egerton 274** as its focus to provide a series of snapshots of a book's continued use, through preservation, adaptation, alteration, obliteration, amplification, and substitution. In its original state **GB-Lbl Egerton 274** challenges received assumptions of repertory, genre, and provenance, but its complexity is further heightened by numerous additions showing that its contents were not only keenly preserved by its later medieval owners but also that some of them were put to new use by the substitution of their secular French texts for liturgical Latin ones. Considering the whole book in the state bequeathed to us by these fourteenth-century recyclers allows us a rare insight into the continued use of a songbook whose peregrinations through northern France and Flanders caused it to be bound with a processional from Ghent alongside its already curious mélange of Latin and French lyrics, liturgical items, and two long narrative poems. By peeling back the layers of later accretion, the book can be viewed as if through the eyes of its original compiler, whose eclectic tastes in song can be seen to signify previously unremarked musical connections across repertories and genres.

In Chapter 7, Henry Hope examines **D-HEu Cod.Pal.germ.848**, the so-called Codex Manesse, one of two manuscripts considered in the present volume whose significance to musicology has been overlooked by their lack of explicitly musical notation (the other is **GB-Ob Douce 308**, considered in Chapter 9, but the same problem also affects some of the song contents in many of the other case-study manuscripts). Hope argues that the Codex Manesse represents evidence of *musical* Minnesang reception, despite its usual exclusion from the status of music manuscript. Its full-folio author illustrations enable music, musicians, and performance to be figured in the absence of explicit musical notation.

In Chapter 8, Sean Curran discusses the so-called La Clayette manuscript, **F-Pn n.a.f.13521**, dating from around 1300. The manuscript contains a rich mixture of contents; only 22 of the 419 parchment folios contain music. Curran notes that the music's place among Old French literary texts of a devotional or didactic nature suggests a single reader engaged in a practice akin to Joyce Coleman's idea of literary 'praelection', reading the musical pieces to other, non-reading singers who listened so as to learn their parts.[4] In this context he reads two of the motets from La Clayette as ritualizing moments, whether inside the liturgy or as part of lay devotion.

Such flexibility of role for the motet is noticeable also in its multiple places within **GB-Ob Douce 308**, considered by Elizabeth Eva Leach in Chapter 9. This manuscript's nearly 300 folios contain three courtly narratives in French (two in poetry, one in prose), plus two eschatological–allegorical works, between which is a large collection of anonymous French lyrics arranged into eight genre sections. Like all of the songs in **D-HEu Cod.Pal.germ.848** and many in **GB-Cu Gg.V.35** and **F-Pn lat.1154**, **GB-Ob Douce 308** is entirely without musical notation; it is nonetheless complete, since there are no empty staves. Leach argues that these songs were well enough 'notated' for the purpose of singing simply by having their texts copied, since their audience would have known the tunes (which were most likely simple, syllabic, and monophonic), or would easily have learnt them aurally from those who already knew them. The organizing principle for the lyrics is generic, with separate poetic genres named in the index, rubrics, and initial miniatures. Nonetheless motet texts and refrains associated with motets pervade the entire lyric collection and even reach the manuscript's other contents. Leach briefly discusses two examples as a means of noting how the motet's generic adaptability and fitness for the generation of intertextual networks collapses and conflates the devotional, the courtly, and the violent.

Generic organization is also found in the final manuscript considered here, **F-Pn fr.1586** ('Machaut MS *C*'). Leach's second chapter argues that as the first poet-composer to oversee the copying of his own complete works into a single book, Guillaume de Machaut signals a watershed in the history of song. As a composer whose works coincide with a change in musical style, the increased use of polyphony, the development of the *formes fixes*, a marked change in notation, and an increasingly literate culture for music-making, Machaut occupies an important place in the history of music. His attention to book-making and his training as a secretary made him highly attuned to how meaning could be created from the ordering of books, through which an authorial persona could be projected. **F-Pn fr.1586** is the earliest surviving of the collected works manuscripts for his work, and evidence from the copying suggests it may have been the first large book of Machaut's work ever attempted. Leach

---

[4] Coleman 1996.

traces how important evidence has been lost to scholarship on account of the manuscript's misdating in a library catalogue and subsequent exclusion from serious consideration in the modern collected editions of text and music.

The concluding chapter of the volume, jointly authored by Deeming and Leach, offers a synthesis and summation of the issues arising from the ten preceding chapters of *Manuscripts and Medieval Song*. In particular it presents a new overview of the roles of books in the beginning of the European song tradition. Books act as pivotal material because they are both retrospective – they serve to collect songs that have already been sung and are now being written down – and enduring – they provide a repository of song for continuing performance and a material context in which to record present and future repertory. Books both textualize and contextualize songs, by transforming their aural traces into material records, and setting those records alongside those of other songs and non-song items. As mediating vehicles, books point to the audience context and use for song, placing it in a general sphere of related social and private activities. This concluding chapter therefore aims to reveal, in a more extensive and nuanced fashion than has been attempted before, the multiple significances of the inscription of song in a wide range of medieval books, the functions of such books in the performance, delivery, transmission, and transformation of the medieval song tradition, and the material and social contexts that formed an inescapable part of the experience of song in the Middle Ages.

1 | New light on the earliest medieval songbook

SAM BARRETT

Previous studies of **F-Pn lat.1154** have emphasized its importance as a songbook standing at the very beginning of the tradition of medieval lyric collections, forming a counterpart to the predominantly liturgical contents of the musical manuscripts collected together at the Abbey of St Martial of Limoges.[1] A few scholars have gone into further detail by observing that the penitential theme of the *versus* collection is consistent with the contents of the earlier sections of the manuscript.[2] The manuscript has most recently begun to attract attention as a prayerbook within a tradition of *libelli precum* that flourished from the ninth century onwards.[3] This chapter will continue the trend towards contextual interpretation of the song collection by assessing its place within traditions of Carolingian prayer and Aquitanian notation. New evidence will be adduced to argue that the main body of the manuscript was copied and notated at the Abbey of St Martial, most likely in the late ninth century, and that the compilation served a distinct purpose as a book for private devotion.

The physical structure of the manuscript

In its current state **F-Pn lat.1154** is a compact volume measuring 210mm x 160mm. Its modern binding dates from the eighteenth century, shortly after the sale of the manuscript in 1730 as part of the collection of the Abbey of St Martial of Limoges to the Bibliothèque du Roi in Paris.[4]

---

[1] The most substantial studies of the *versus* collection emphasizing its distance from liturgical song traditions are Coussemaker 1852, 83–121, for whom the songs are lyrical compositions forming a link with antiquity and intended for the lettered classes, and Spanke 1931, who emphasized structural proximity to later vernacular song traditions. The songs are discussed under the heading of lyric and more or less explicitly aligned with later Aquitanian *versus* collections in Stäblein 1975, 51 and J. Stevens 1986, 48–52. For a digitized version of **F-Pn lat.1154**, see http://gallica.bnf.fr/ark:/12148/btv1b84324798.

[2] Chailley 1960, 73–6; Barrett 1997, 55–96.

[3] Black 2002, 25; Waldhoff 2003, especially 281n36.

[4] It is no.76 in the catalogue of manuscripts received from the Abbey reproduced in Delisle 1895, 46. 'LXXVI' appears at the head of f.1r alongside 'XCVII', which has been crossed out.

Table 1.1 Contents of **F-Pn lat.1154**

Part	Folios	Summary of contents
I	ff.i^v–25^v	Litany
II	ff.26r–65v	Prayers and Collects
III	ff.66r–97v	Isidore of Seville's *Synonyma* (Book I and Book II to chapter 19)
IV	ff.98r–143r	*Versus* collection

Although there are distinct parts within the manuscript, there is consistency in its manufacture: sixteen lines are ruled throughout, with all parts except the third ruled in two columns of similar widths, and the ruled space is similar in different parts of the manuscript (*c*.140mm x 100mm). Seven equally spaced sewing holes are found in all four parts. This material continuity underpins changes in content and scribe, which are briefly summarized in Table 1.1.

There is at first sight a consistency to the scripts of Parts II–IV. The Caroline minuscule forms are fluently executed, including a range of 'a' forms with uncial, alpha, and minuscule shapes. The visual similarity of Parts II and IV is reinforced by the double-column layout, the use of red ink for rubrics and most initials, and green highlights for incipits and refrains. The colouring-in of capitals at the beginning of new units of text is also common to Part I, whose script is nevertheless set apart by letter forms that are thicker and more erect, lacking the uncial 'a', using a more rounded 'g' with a completed upper loop, and featuring almost no ligatures. A further distinctive feature of Parts II and IV is the occasional placement of a rubric across both columns (ff.61v, 99v, and 106r),[5] which interrupts the continuous text layout through single columns and indicates that the same individual was both rubricator and text scribe. The initials are also remarkable for incorporating contractions and occasionally complete short words within their design.[6] The immediate impression is that one main scribe was responsible for all aspects of the writing and *mise-en-page* of Parts II and IV.

---

[5] http://gallica.bnf.fr/ark:/12148/btv1b84324798/f134.image, http://gallica.bnf.fr/ark:/12148/btv1b84324798/f210.image, http://gallica.bnf.fr/ark:/12148/btv1b84324798/f223.image.

[6] The running together of multiple letters in initials, whether by joining together letters or by placing letters inside those with internal spaces such as 'D' and 'O', is found also in **F-Pn lat.1240** (see http://gallica.bnf.fr/ark:/12148/btv1b6000528g). Compare, for example, the joining of letters in the initials on ff.95r and 96r of **F-Pn lat.1240**, and the use of contractions and shorter words as part of initials on ff.26r, 32r, and 45r of **F-Pn lat.1154**.

Part III differs slightly in its appearance, employing fewer textual ligatures, a more regular spacing of letters within words, and a more highly regulated heighting of ascenders and descenders. The pattern of decoration differs from Parts II and IV in so far as green highlights are used only to shade individual capitals in the incipit of book I of the *Synonyma*. Rudimentary decorative initials featuring vegetal forms in the shape of the palmette or acanthus leaves appear at the opening of book I of the *Synonyma* (coloured in brown, red, green, and yellow ink) and at a new section within the same book (on f.82v, which remains in brown outline).[7] As observed by Gaborit-Chopin, the design is reminiscent of both the work of the scribe and illuminator Bonibertus in the first Bible of St Martial of Limoges (**F-Pn lat.5**) and of a homiliary of similar date and provenance (**F-Pn lat.1897**).[8] The initials in **F-Pn lat.1154** are nevertheless less well formed (compare the simple 'h' on its f.82v with that on f.2r of the Bible),[9] implying the work of an imitator or pupil of this scribe.

Assigning dates and origins to this set of manuscripts is complicated by the fact that no comprehensive palaeographical study of the manuscripts collected at St Martial of Limoges has been undertaken.[10] The earliest manuscript that can be said with confidence to have been written at the abbey is **F-Pn lat.1240**, the first part of which was compiled *c*.932–5 for use at the basilica of the Holy Saviour within the abbey.[11] This manuscript stands at some distance from the first Bible of St Martial of Limoges, which is most reliably dated to the second half of the ninth century.[12] The similarities in decoration identified by Gaborit-Chopin nevertheless suggest the possibility of an active early scriptorium at St Martial, which would by necessity have to be placed after the foundation of the abbey as a Benedictine monastery in 848 and perhaps after the Norman invasions and temporary relocation of 888.

---

[7] http://gallica.bnf.fr/ark:/12148/btv1b84324798/f176.image.

[8] Gaborit-Chopin 1969, 45, 188; for images of the homiliary **F-Pn lat.1897** see http://gallica.bnf. fr/ark:/12148/btv1b8530357z. Similarities are particularly evident when comparing the 'A's on f.84r of the first Limoges Bible (**F-Pn lat.5**; see http://gallica.bnf.fr/ark:/12148/ btv1b85301526) and f.66v of **F-Pn lat.1154**, both of which display interlacing in a rhomboid right-hand shaft of the initial, a cross-bar filled with decoration, and a left-hand shaft that spreads in a triangular fashion towards its lower end, with further decoration including vegetal lobes attached to outer extremities of the capital letter.

[9] http://gallica.bnf.fr/ark:/12148/btv1b85301526/f13.image.

[10] For an instructive preliminary assessment of scribal hands in the notated St Martial manuscripts, see Aubert 2011, 1:245–54.

[11] See Emerson 1993, 193.

[12] Most authoritative datings of the Bible agree on the ninth century, but without providing palaeographical evidence: see Avril 1970; Samaran and Marichal 1962, 525.

Placing the initials of Part III of **F-Pn lat.1154** among a set of early
manuscripts decorated at the abbey accordingly leads to a probable late
ninth- or early tenth-century dating. While it remains possible that the
self-contained gatherings of the *Synonyma* that break off mid-sentence
were inserted into the manuscript at a later date, there are several indications that Part III was copied in the same environment as Parts II and IV.
Besides the continuity in ruling and basic appearance of the script cited
above, the colours used in decorating the initials are the same as those used
in Parts II and IV for highlights, namely bright yellow, orange, violet,
brown, and red, with a dominant green that sometimes becomes turquoise.

Bernhard Bischoff was reluctant to be more specific than 'West
Frankish' in assigning an origin to this manuscript on the basis of its
scripts, dating Parts II–IV to the late ninth or early tenth century, and
assigning a tenth-century date to Part I.[13] The latest internally verifiable
dates within each Part are consistent with this palaeographical assessment.
There is a *terminus post quem* of at least 874 for the litany in Part I if the
'Salomon' in the series of Martyrs is indeed King Salomon of Brittany.[14]
The *versus* collection must have been copied after the death of Hugh,
Abbot of St Quentin in 844, which forms the material for the lament
Hug, dulce nomen.

What may now be added to Bischoff's assessment is that a number of
different hands can be discerned in Parts II and III. The work of the main
scribe in Part II is interrupted several times by a less steady script that is
more upright, but less consistent in its formation of individual letters.
Changes of scribe happen at least three times in the middle of sentences,
indicating that at least one other less skilled scribe was working closely
alongside the main scribe.[15] One other confident script is identifiable in

---

[13] See Bischoff 1965, 203, his catalogue description for the exhibition 'Karl der Grosse' held in
Aachen in 1965. Bischoff vacillated between dates of ninth to tenth century and the late ninth
century in his published comments on this manuscript: 'etwa 9./10. Jh.' is given in his catalogue
description, Bischoff 1965; 's. ix-x' is assigned in Bischoff 1951, 121–47, reprinted in Bischoff
1966–81, 1:154n14. The manuscript is described in more general terms as ninth century in
Bischoff 1960, 61–8 (repr. Bischoff 1966–81, 2:28). Bischoff's unpublished notes held in the
Bayerische Staatsbibliothek date the litany (ff.1–25) to the tenth century, while the main body of
the manuscript is signalled as 'wahrscheinlich' (probably) ninth century.

[14] As suggested in Duine 1923, 60.

[15] A thinner and inconsistent script can be seen on two occasions taking over from the main
scribe in mid-sentence: f.45r, (column 2, l.13) through to f.49r (end of the first column), and
f.49v (the whole folio). This script is set apart by a 'g' in which the upper circle is joined up
and the lower stroke is more rounded; nevertheless, the curve of the lower stroke of the 'g' is
written at varying angles. The 'x' is also distinct from that of the main scribe in having a tick to
the left at the end of its long descender, and the cedilla placed under the 'e' to indicate 'ae' is

this section: the Antiphon for All Saints on f.61r was added by a fluent hand writing in a similar style to the main scribe, albeit with a distinctive diagonal descent rather than curved finish to the 'g'.[16] Part III also features a number of scripts of varying neatness. At the top of f.75v,[17] for example, a messier script takes over; intriguingly, the two short statements lower on the same folio that serve as the basis for the synonyms that follow (i.e. *Nichil enim bonum agis* and *Cotidie peccas*) are copied much more neatly in a script consistent with that of the main scribe. The change in scribe is made even more explicit by the fact that the main scribe writes *Nichil*, and the unsteady scribe writes *nihil*. The main scribe also corrects the work of the less well-formed scribe, changing *residit* to *resistit* using the more upright 's' consistent with the neater script. At other points, it is less clear whether distinctions in the grade of script represent two scribes working closely together or variations in the work of one scribe. At the opening of book II of the *Synonyma*, the impression is of a new hand writing less neatly, with a flatter execution of the lower curve of the 'g', but over several folios the writing becomes gradually neater, approaching almost typographic regularity on some folios, while at other places it descends into irregularly formed and inconsistently disposed letters.

Parts II and III therefore witness not only competent scribes working alongside less skilled ones, but also individual scribes executing their own work to varying standards. The pattern of master scribes working along-side pupils has been observed in the copying of texts used for teaching, as well as in another of the major Carolingian *versus* collections.[18] A similar interweaving of the work of a less formed script with that of a fluent scribe was observed by Emerson in the copying of the rite for Extreme Unction in **F-Pn lat.1240**.[19] This practice suggests a text produced for an immediate end rather than manufacture of an object for display or presentation. At the same time, the varying standard in execution implies differing degrees of attention and by extension status accorded to the separate parts of the collection. The *Synonyma* is a copy of a relatively widespread text whose

---

formed with a rising stroke from its base rather than with a hook mid-way up. The same features are also visible in the hand that copied the second column of f.42r through to the end of f.42v, although here the writing is neater and the individual forms slightly thicker in appearance.

[16] http://gallica.bnf.fr/ark:/12148/btv1b84324798/f133.image.

[17] http://gallica.bnf.fr/ark:/12148/btv1b84324798/f162.image.

[18] See, with reference to the Carolingian poetic collection **B-Br 8860-8867** and further examples, Barrett 2012, 131–4.

[19] Emerson 1993, 199n27.

layout poses few difficulties. By contrast, the *versus* section that has proved of such interest to musicologists and philologists is an unparalleled collection whose varied forms posed problems that were solved in a range of inventive ways by the main scribe.

The compilation of the manuscript

The multipartite construction of **F-Pn lat.1154** raises questions about when the parts were brought together and whether they were designed to serve a single purpose. The manuscript was evidently a single codex at the time of the mid-seventeenth-century catalogue drawn up by Montfaucon.[20] The chronological notes of Bernard Itier on f.i[r] place at least the litany at the Abbey of St Martial by the thirteenth century.[21] The closest match among the four medieval catalogues of the library of St Martial is to be found among the terse entries of the first, which dates from the twelfth century: '119 Orationes et synonima Isidori, in uno'.[22] If this volume is indeed **F-Pn lat.1154**, then at least Parts II and III were joined together by the twelfth century. Further insight into the compilation of the manuscript may be gained through an assessment of the contents and their co-ordination.

The litany

The litany, which was copied sometime in the tenth century, is remarkable for its length; indeed, the list of just over a thousand separately named entries, which is carefully marked out every one hundred names by a roman numeral, renders it substantially larger than ninth-century litanies. It is most likely that such an extended litany served as a compendium from which selections could be made rather than a list to be recited with any regularity.[23] Comments on the structure of the litany have tended to be restricted to the sequence of Breton saints within the list of Confessors.[24]

---

[20] Montfaucon 1789, 1034. Item number 40 reads: 'Litaniae plurium SS. 2. Collectae plures et orationes, 3. Plures preces seu versus deprecatorii, 4. Lib. S. Isidori continens lamentum animae poenitentis, 5. Versus in idem tendentes, in 4°'.

[21] Duplès-Agier 1874, XXXVII, 239.   [22] Delisle 1895, 492.

[23] Compare, for example, the litany in **F-Pn lat.1153**, whose over 600 entries are assigned for recitation on different days of the week in the *Officia per ferias*, PL 101, cols. 592–6.

[24] For the sequence of Breton names, see Jubainville 1876–8, 449–450. Duine's observation about regional groups is given in Duine 1923, 60. A full list of Breton saints in **F-Pn lat.1154** is provided in Loth 1890, 136–8.

Table 1.2 Limoges saints within the list of Confessors

Pardulfus	Patron of Saint-Pardoux de Guéret in the Limoges diocese
Valericus	Confessor of Limoges
Leonardus	of Limoges, Patron of Léonard de Noblat
Gonsaldus	Bishop of Clermont, who founded a hermitage at St Goussaud in the Limoges diocese
Iustus	of Bourges (?), Patron of Saint Just, Cosnac in the Limoges diocese
Austriclinianus	legendary companion of St Martial
Alpinianus	legendary companion of St Martial
Amasius	Confessor, whose relics were kept in church of Sainte-Marie in Limoges
Iustinianus	Confessor of Limoges
Celsus	early Bishop of Limoges, whose relics were translated to Roth in 861
Lupus	Bishop of Limoges, whose relics were held in the church of St Michael
Cessator	early Bishop of Limoges
Elegius	of Noyon, Founder of St-Pierre de Solignac, a suburbium of Limoges
Aredius	Patron of Saint-Yrieix la Perche in the Limoges diocese
Iunianus	Patron of Saint-Junien in the Limoges diocese

What has been overlooked is a series of obscure Limoges saints embedded within the same category (f.6r-v; see Table 1.2).

Only Gonsaldus may be securely identified in Astrid Krüger's compilation of early litanies, and several names are almost unheard of, strongly implying that the litany was drawn up in the vicinity of Limoges.[25] Of further note is that this sequence of Limoges saints is immediately followed by a number of regional saints, including Amandus of Genouillac (near Guéret), Frontius (whose legend is based on that of St Martial), Eparchius of Angoulême and Severinus of Bordeaux. Most importantly, almost all of these saints specific to the town of Limoges, its diocese and region, are found in probably the oldest surviving calendar from the Abbey of St Martial, transmitted in **F-Pn lat.1240**.[26]

The ordering and re-ordering of saints within the litany provides further clues as to its destination. Martin's name is highlighted in capitals and

[25] Krüger 2007. It is unclear which St Just is meant in this list. One possibility is St Just of Bourges, a third-century confessor and companion of St Ursinus, also known as St Just of Chambon, which lies in the far north-east of the Limoges diocese: see Sollerio, Pinio and Cupero 1723, 647–8. A church in Cosnac, lying to the south-east of Brive within the Limoges diocese, was dedicated to St Just before the end of the ninth century: see Aubrun 1981, 314.
[26] Emerson 1993, 201 and 204, from which most of the descriptions of local saints given here are taken.

placed at the head of the list of Confessors (f.5v).[27] His unusual promotion above Hilary assumes particular significance given the latter's pre-eminence in Frankish missals and litanies, prompting several commentators to assign the manuscript as a whole to an institution dedicated to St Martin.[28] Equally striking and previously ignored is Saint Valérie's appearance at the head of the list of Virgins, where she was placed above the usual hierarchy of early female saints beginning with Felicity. Valérie (Valeria) was a holy woman whose relics were placed alongside those of St Martial and were translated in 985 to Chambon when the tomb was threatened. An expanded version of her legend in the mid-tenth-century *Vita prolixior* of St Martial tells how she was Martial's first convert in Limoges and thereafter refused to marry Duke Stephen of Central Aquitania, who ordered her decapitation.[29]

Further clues as to provenance are found in alterations to the litany. The addition of St Martial's name to the list of Apostles and Evangelists has been well documented by Chailley.[30] The promotion of St Martial's companions Austriclinian and Alpinian to near the head of the Confessors (see below) presumably occurred at the same time. In all probability, these alterations took place in the wake of the extended campaign to promote St Martial as an Apostle that came to a dramatic head in the interrupted festivities of 3 August 1029.[31] What has remained unexplained is where Martial's name was in the litany before he was added to the list of Apostles. The 'Marcialis' listed among the Martyrs in **F-Pn lat.1154** cannot be St Martial of Limoges since he was not a martyr.[32] The possibility that the patron saint of the Abbey at Limoges was originally omitted from a litany containing a series of obscure saints of Limoges with Valérie placed at the head of the female saints is highly unlikely. **F-Pn lat.1240** again provides an instructive model because a number of

---

[27] http://gallica.bnf.fr/ark:/12148/btv1b84324798/f22.image.

[28] The earliest association of **F-Pn lat.1154** with an institution dedicated to St Martin is to be found in the catalogue entry for this manuscript, Lauer 1939, 422. Chailley 1960, 422 attributed the manuscript to either St Martial or St Martin of Limoges, but doubts have been cast on his frequent ascription of manuscripts to the modest institution of St Martin of Limoges; see Becquet 1979, 384. Huglo 1988, 26 specified the chapter of St Martin of Brive, in the south of the Limoges diocese, without providing supporting evidence.

[29] See Gauthier 1955, 35–80, and the summary in Emerson 1965, 31–46, especially 37–8.

[30] Chailley 1960, 75.

[31] For the now familiar story, see Landes 1995, 197–250; and, with particular reference to Adémar's musical contributions, Grier 2006, 25–34.

[32] Chailley 1960, 75 erred in referring to this entry as placed among the Confessors. He may have been confused by the fact that the appropriate rubrics follow rather than precede each group of saints.

entries in its *litania maiore* were similarly updated, albeit erased without being subsequently replaced. The original entries nevertheless remain visible and were transcribed by Jean Leclercq (the names under erasure are given in italics).[33]

S. Michahel
S. Johannes
S. Petre
S. Paule
S. Andrea
S. Simphoriane
S. Leodegari
S. Dionisi
S. Maurici
S. Marcialis
S. Martine
S. Elari
S. Gregori
S. Valeria
S. Felicitas
S. Perpetua
S. Agnes
S. Agatha

Two aspects of the original litany in **F-Pn lat.1240** are remarkable in this context. First, it includes the exceptional promotion of Valérie to the head of the female saints, something which is to my knowledge otherwise found only in **F-Pn lat.1154**. Second, Martial was initially placed at the head of the Confessors. This raises the question whether he was originally placed there also in **F-Pn lat.1154**. Although at first sight unlikely, there are palaeographical grounds for such a claim. Inspection of the list of Confessors on f.5v of **F-Pn lat.1154** reveals a number of smudged entries alongside those that have remained in their original state.[34] The entry 'Martine' is smudged from the 'r' through to the 'e' and includes a number of idiosyncrasies in its formation of capital letters: the 'T' appears as an enlarged 't', the 'N' is substantially elongated, and the final 'E' has a curved upper stroke as well as a middle bar that curves downwards. It seems that the original entry was updated. If the original entry was 'MARCIALIS',

[33] Leclercq 1929.   [34] http://gallica.bnf.fr/ark:/12148/btv1b84324798/f22.image.

then 'MAR' could remain as before, in transforming the 'C' a curve would appear at the base of the 'T', the letter 'N' would have to expand to replace three letters ('ALI'), and a transformed 'S' could retain the upper half of the form.

If Martin replaced Martial at the head of the Confessors, then the question that follows is where was Martin in the original layer of the litany? The following entry for Hilary appears unchanged, whereas the subsequent 'Benedicte' is watery and slightly smudged in appearance throughout in comparison with neighbouring entries. It is possible that the entry for Benedict replaced a name in the original layer, the most likely candidate for which is Martin, whose name usually follows immediately after Hilary in Frankish lists of Confessors. The set of proposed changes to the opening of the list of Confessors may be seen by comparing the first two columns of Table 1.3 (interlinear entries are signalled by italics).

This proposal would explain apparent alterations to the first and third entries in the list and provide a reason for the otherwise perplexing absence of St Martial from the original list of Confessors. The one issue that remains unresolved is where Benedict's entry was in the earliest layer of the litany. Although his name does not always appear near the head of the list of Confessors, it is frequently found there in early litanies and it would be surprising if he had been omitted from the litany as a whole. A possible explanation is that the scribe of the earliest layer had a standard ordering either in mind or to hand as a model, but that in elevating Martial to the head of the list and moving Martin to the third place Benedict was overlooked, an omission corrected at the point of altering the litany (see the third column in Table 1.3).

The new evidence assembled in this section suggests that the litany in **F-Pn lat.1154** was originally compiled not for an institution dedicated to St Martin, as often assumed in previous scholarship, but for St Martial of Limoges. The obscure sequence of Limoges saints and the promotion of

Table 1.3 Proposed changes to the opening of the list of Confessors

Earliest layer	Alteration	Standard model
MARCIALIS	MARTINE	Hilary
Hilari	Hilari	Martin
Martine	Benedicte	Benedict
Gregorii	*Austricliniane / Alpiniane*	Gregory
Silvester	Silvester / *Gregorii*	Silvester
Leo	Leo	Leo

Valérie are both held in common with **F-Pn lat.1240**, and there are grounds for assuming that Martial's name rather than Martin's likewise originally stood at the head of the Confessors in **F-Pn lat.1154**.

The prayers

The four prayers that open Part II are followed by the rubric *Incipiunt orationes*, implying that an earlier rubric signalled them as belonging to a different genre, most likely as collects given their combination of invocation and petition on behalf of gathered supplicants. A series of prayers follows, including two by Alcuin (*Miserere domine* and *Adesto lumen*), one attributed to St Gregory that includes a further litanic series (*Dominus exaudi orationem meam quia iam cognosco tempus*) and an established set of prayers to God in the person of Father, Son, and Holy Spirit, as well as to the Virgin Mary.[35] Several confessions of various types were copied next, beginning with Alcuin's *Deus inestimabili misericordiae*, elsewhere described as being composed for Charlemagne himself.[36] The tone within this series of prayers shifts from the public invocations of the collects to penitential confession expressed in heightened rhetoric in the first person, all of which indicates that the transition between Parts I and II of the manuscript is not as smooth as the ALIA rubric at the opening of Part II implies.

The prayers continue in a similar confessional vein with the series of seven penitential psalms, each of which is followed by a *Kyrie eleison*, *Pater noster*, a chapter (comprising verses drawn from other psalms) and collect (based on the present psalm), and then seven further uses for particular psalms cited by incipit alone. The occasions given for reciting particular psalms range from times of tribulation through to praise, the whole set of eight psalm uses corresponding in general terms to those specified in a short text preface (often called *De laude psalmorum*) to *De psalmorum usu*, a tract on praying for personal needs using the psalms.[37] The treatise itself is no longer widely considered to be by Alcuin, but the preface that prescribes specific psalms listed by incipit for eight distinct uses is generally

---

[35] The prayer attributed to Gregory is not found among published collections of ninth-century prayerbooks, but is in Otto III's prayerbook and several other eleventh-century collections of prayers: see Hamilton 2001a, 286 (no. 25). The prayers to the Godhead are drawn from a set which can be traced back to a Tours collection of *c*.805 (**F-T 1742**: see Wilmart 1940, nos. 7–9 and 11).

[36] For further discussion of this prayer, Bullough 1991, 170.

[37] See the commentary on this text and new edition in Black 2002, 1–60.

thought to be his work.[38] The filling out of the Alcuinian pattern in **F-Pn lat.1154** takes its place alongside six other manuscripts from the ninth century.[39] What is distinctive about the presentation in this manuscript is the way in which the established sequence of seven penitential psalms is expanded by *capitula* and *collecta* and presented alongside the Alcuinian sequence from the *De laude psalmorum*, albeit the remaining psalm uses are presented in a different order from those in the *De laude psalmorum* (2, 4, 6, 3, 5, 7, 8). This distinctive presentation may represent a later copy of an intermediary stage in the history of the amplification of Alcuin's pattern, standing between the bare list of incipits in the *De laude psalmorum* and the amplification of this pattern in strict order with additional material in six other manuscripts dating from the mid-ninth century onwards.

The prayer following the *De laude psalmorum* sequence hints at a context for the prayers in this section of the manuscript as it describes how to offer up private and secret prayers (*peculiaris* [...] *et furtivas orationes*) in order to obtain forgiveness of sins. To paraphrase: on rising from sleep the penitent should make a sign of the cross and say a short prayer to the Trinity. After satisfying the requirements of nature (!), the orator hastens silently, and in tears, to the church, and with head placed on the ground says the Sunday collect. Standing up again, the orator then recites the *versus* 'O Lord, open thou my lips' and the Gloria, then a sequence of thirteen psalms, the Kyrie eleison, and unspecified *preces*. The fascinating detail here is that this prescribed *ordo* is to be recited privately by an individual, but in a church.

A similar context might be imagined for the prayers that immediately follow, namely an antiphon for All Saints added neatly by a different hand and prayers for the Adoration of the Cross.[40] The feast of All Saints was established in the first half of the ninth century, largely under the influence of Alcuin, who seems to have brought the observance from England to the continent in the late eighth century and who composed several masses

---

[38] Alcuin's authorship of this treatise was first questioned by Wilmart 1936, 263–5, who nevertheless attributed to him the short text printed as the preface to this text in the PL edition. For Waldhoff 2003, 272–6, the *De laude psalmorum* was a secondary compilation based on Alcuin's prayerbook for Charlemagne discussed in more detail below. Black 2008, 772–4 restated the case for Alcuin's authorship of this short text in a review of Waldhoff's book, pointing to a reference in Alcuin's *Vita* and the appearance of material from the treatise in the prayerbook as reconstructed by Waldhoff.

[39] Black 2002, 25–35, from which the following summary of the place of **F-Pn lat.1154** in this tradition is drawn.

[40] While its overall aspect is similar, the 'g' of the hand that added the antiphon is notably less rounded in its stroke beneath the line than the main scribe.

and vigils for the festival.[41] The antiphon *Salvator mundi salva nos omnes* (CAO 4689) is found in many Antiphoners from the eleventh century onwards; to date, I have not been able to identify a comparably early witness.[42] The five prayers for the Adoration of the Cross include one of widespread circulation, the well-known invocations beginning *Domine Iesu Christe adoro te ascendentem in cruce* as found among other ninth-century witnesses in the prayerbook composed for Charles the Bald.[43] The sequence of prayers as a whole does not reproduce any of the emerging patterns in the ninth century as identified by Wilmart, but exceptionally all the prayers are found in almost the same order in **F-Pn lat.1240**, where they are recorded as part of the Adoration of the Cross on Good Friday.[44] The impression is therefore of a locally established series of prayers for this rite, further strengthening the association between these two manuscripts and the case for placing the earliest layer of **F-Pn lat.1154** at the Abbey of St Martial.[45]

The *Synonyma*

Isidore of Seville's *Synonyma*, also known in the Middle Ages as *De lamentatione animae peccatricis* ('Lamentations of a Sinful Soul'), falls into two books, the first focusing on the penitential confessions of *homo*, the second largely comprising the moral imperatives of *ratio*. Its guiding stylistic principle is the synonym: complaints or admonishments are first stated and then repeatedly paraphrased in a highly ornate prose style that relies on patterns of assonance, rhythm and rhyme for its cumulative effect. As argued by Fontaine, this classic example of the *stilus isidorianus* served to draw readers into prayer. Such indeed was the use to which it was put in *libelli precum* such as **F-Pn lat.1153**, where the *Synonyma* is found not

---

[41] See, principally, Wilmart 1914, 41–69, and Deshusses 1979, 281–302. A succinct overview of Alcuin's authorship of thirteen votive Masses with specific reference to All Saints and further bibliography is provided in Bullough 1991, 204–5.

[42] CAO number relates to the catalogue in Hesbert 1963–79.

[43] Munich, Schatzkammer der Residenz, ResMü Schk 4 WL, ff.39v–40r; see http://daten.digitale-sammlungen.de/bsb00079994/image_82.

[44] The prayers for the Adoration of the Cross are found on ff.61v–65v in **F-Pn lat.1154** and ff.26r–30r in **F-Pn lat.1240**. The sequence in **F-Pn lat.1154** is as follows: *Domine ihesu christe fili dei vivi qui regnas* (**F-Pn lat.1240**, i); *Signum nos dominici defendat ligni* (v); *Adoro te Domine ihesu christe in cruce ascendente* (iii), *Domine sancte pater omnipotens eterne deus* (vi); *Salve sancta crux quae in corpore christi dedicata es* (vii).

[45] The prayers in **F-Pn lat.1154** and **F-Pn lat.1240** share no concordances with the set of three prayers supplied for the ceremony of the Adoration of the Cross on Good Friday in the Romano-German Pontifical; see Vogel and Elze 1963, 91–2.

only alongside the pattern of daily prayer attributed to Alcuin, but also in the form of extracts presented explicitly as prayers.[46]

The reception enjoyed by the *Synonyma* in this manuscript may be deduced from two clues. First, the rubrics for book II were not formally entered and were completed by several different scribes working to a low standard of presentation, suggesting not only that interest in the copying process was waning, but also that younger scribes were taking the opportunity to practise writing when reading this book. The second clue is a prayer added to a blank space at the end of a folio between books I and II sometime in the eleventh century:

> Domine deus, qui in trinitate perfecta vivis et gloriaris, te rogo vultu supiniss[im]o, ut dones mihi perfectam sapienciam tibi conplacitam opus tale facere, ut ad te possim pervenire; etiam patri meo ac matri [et] omnibus meis parentibus timorem tuum, largitatem obtimam [et] conversationem bonam catinus obtineant tuam gratiam omnibus fidelibus tuis vivis et defuncti[s] requiem sempiternam. Qui vivis. . .

> O Lord God, you who live and glory in the perfect Trinity, I ask with most humble countenance that you might bestow upon me a perfect wisdom pleasing to you to do such work that I might be able to draw near to you; also, [I ask] for my father and mother, and all my relatives, fear of thee, outstanding benevolence and good relation, that they may obtain your favour for all your living faithful and eternal rest for the departed. You who live. . .[etc.]

The absence of any punctuation in the Latin text as originally copied, combined with the simple spelling mistakes ('supinisso' for 'supinissimo', 'defuncti' for 'defunctis'), suggests a scribe of incomplete training, while the form of the prayer offered on behalf of living parents suggests a young supplicant.[47] Its appearance here accords with Fontaine's view that in addition to leading readers into prayer, the *Synonyma* served an educational function as both a promoter of moral conscience and a model for rhetorical style.

The songs

Previous studies of the *versus* collection as a whole have been concerned mainly with thematic links between the texts.[48] No comprehensive study of

---

[46] See Elfassi 2006, 111–4.

[47] I would like to thank Leofranc Holford-Strevens for assistance in clarifying the text.

[48] Traube 1896, 721; Chailley 1960, 74–5, 123–35; Barrett 1997, 57–65.

the notation in this manuscript has been published, a significant *lacuna* given the place of this manuscript among the earliest layer of Aquitanian notations. As a first step towards understanding the rich set of surviving neumations, attention will be focused here on the work of the fluent notator (*A*), who added the majority of the notation to this collection.[49]

Before embarking on this notational study, two aspects of the way the *versus* are presented in this manuscript that have largely escaped previous comment are worth noting. The first is the opening rubric of the *versus* collection, which reads horizontally across the top of the first column of f.98r, *Versus Godiscalchi*, and descending vertically from the same point, *& oratio*.[50] No stronger indication of the intertwined traditions of song and prayer could be found. Second, a particular character is lent to the poems collected in **F-Pn lat.1154** by the addition of Amens that stand outside the regular strophic structure to twelve poems. In two cases, *Tocius mundi* and *Christe rex regum*, the poems are unique to this collection, thereby allowing no comparison with wider transmission. Seven further poems with closing Amens may be usefully compared: *Beatus homo, Mecum Timavi, Quique de morte, Tristis venit, Dulce carmen, Homo quidam* and *Concelebremus sacram*. In every instance the version in **F-Pn lat.1154** is the only version to include a final Amen extrinsic to the poetic structure. Concluding Amens are familiar from the hymnic tradition, echoes of which are found in the doxologies for final strophes unique to **F-Pn lat.1154** in *Beatus homo* and *Quique de morte*. Three more poems with final Amens entered into wider transmission as hymns: *Festiva saeclis, Nunc tibi Christe* and *Tellus ac aethra*. A full checking of manuscript witnesses is impractical in these latter cases, but it is instructive to note that the first two appear without a closing Amen in the Moissac hymnal (**I-Rvat Rossi 205**) and the last has no Amen in the version found in **F-Pn lat.1240**. In the absence of a consistent pattern even within the hymnic tradition, the writing out of final Amens in **F-Pn lat.1154** may be said to stand closer to the written tradition of prayers, in which closing Amens are routinely recorded.

Returning to notation, the pattern of a single, well-trained scribe adding the majority of the notation with several others of varying quality adding

---

[49] The following *versus* were notated by the main notator: *Ad caeli clara, Anima nimis misera, Tocius mundi, Fuit Domini, Christus rex vita, Mecum Timavi, O stelliferi, Bella bis, Quique de morte, Iudicii signum* and *Gloriam Deo. Anima nimis misera*, despite slight differences in neumatic formation, is included here since the slight differences in axis and dimension are consistent with the variations across this notator's work as a whole. For tables summarizing the different notators at work in **F-Pn lat.1154**, see Barrett 1997, 87, and Barrett 2000, 85.

[50] http://gallica.bnf.fr/ark:/12148/btv1b84324798/f207.image.

neumes alongside is one found in many contemporary *versus* collections.[51] The presence of work by a main scribe and several less skilled scribes also recalls the interweaving of scripts identified in Parts II and III of this manuscript. In this case, *A* was always the first to add neumes where they were added by more than one scribe to an individual *versus*, implying that this notator added the earliest layer of notation to the *versus* collection. A curious feature of the distribution of *A*'s work is the addition of neumes to poems in the first half of the collection, breaking off after *Gloriam Deo* and subsequently adding neumes only to the final *prosa, Concelebremus sacram*. This pattern may in part be explained by a desire to notate devotional *versus* without a place in the standard liturgical *cursus* as contained in the first half of the collection. It is also notable that opening lines of all but one of the *versus* left unnotated by *A* in the first half of the collection use contractions in their opening lines, making the addition of neumes problematic: *O D(eu)s misere, Ad te D(eu)s gloriose, Xpe rex regum, Spes mea Xpe,* and *Beat(us) homo qui paup(er) e(st) sp(irit)u;* the one exception is *Qui se volet*. It is therefore possible that *A* would have notated more items in the first half of the collection, but chose not to on practical grounds.

A's notational style is of further interest in itself. Distinctive features include a *tractulus* that tends to curve upwards as well as one that remains straight, and the use of both a semi-circle and a tick-shape as the second element of a *pes* with no discernible reason for the differentiation.[52] The sharp definition of the tick-shape sign is particularly notable with its consistent 45-degree angle and slight drawdown at the beginning (usually) and end (consistently) of the form. The second element of the *torculus* is similarly compact and angular in appearance with similar marks at the beginning and end of the shape. The 'm'-shaped *oriscus* is routinely drawn at a 45-degree angle of descent from the preceding neume, and an 's'-shaped *quilisma* is used (where the 's' is an 'f'-shape without the cross-bar). Remaining individual signs include a *cephalicus* in a curved '7' shape and a *porrectus* that resembles the '*ur*' abbreviation in the text (albeit with a straight diagonal ascender after the initial hump).

This set of features finds no precise match among the earliest notations in manuscripts from St Martial of Limoges. The notations in **F-Pn lat.1240**

---

[51] See Barrett 2013, ch. 3, 'Notators and Notation'.

[52] The prospect that the semi-circular *pes* was used by *A* to mark the half-step as in **F-Pn lat.903** is ruled out by its use in *Iudicii signum* at places where parallel melodic versions indicate no half-step; see http://gallica.bnf.fr/ark:/12148/btv1b9068069f (black-and-white microfilm images only).

provide few examples of similarly compact and defined neumes. Even the neume scripts on ff.22r–24r that are closest in overall appearance are substantially different in their range and use of signs, featuring as they do an isolated *virga*, an *oriscus* in a 'c' shape with a horizontally extended upper stroke, an 's'-shaped *quilisma* (where the 's' is as in this typeface) and a placement of the 'm'-shaped *oriscus* within the *pressus* alongside the preceding *punctum* rather than on a diagonal descent. Many of the notators in **F-Pn lat.1240** also use a conjunct *clivis* familiar from French scripts (for example, the scripts on ff.18v–20v, 30v–31r, and 33r), thereby distancing them even further from the work of the main notator in **F-Pn lat.1154**. Other neumes that have been dated to the tenth century in manuscripts of St Martial provenance survive only in fragments and even more distant in their morphology. The fine neumes in the palimpsest of **F-Pn lat.1085**, for example, which most likely date from the second half of the tenth century, employ a separate *virga* and use an enlarged 'm'-shaped *oriscus*, both of which features immediately set the script apart from the work of A.[53] The second elements in the *pes* forms are also distinctive: the semi-circular form begins with a long, near horizontal stroke leading to a rather squashed overall appearance; the other form uses a short, rather upright second element without separate drawdowns at the beginning and end of the form.

More compelling parallels with the work of A arise if attention is turned to early Aquitanian notations in manuscripts other than those later collected at St Martial of Limoges. A particularly intriguing comparison may be drawn with the neumes added by a late ninth-century glossing hand to the Muses' song in a copy of Martianus Capella's *De nuptiis Philologiae et Mercurii* written at a centre in the upper Loire region in the mid-ninth century, now **GB-Ob Laud lat.118**, ff.11v and 12r.[54] The neat, thin strokes are again in evidence with initial drawdowns at the beginning and ending of most of the second elements of the *pes*. The tall 's'-shape is used for the *quilisma* and the 'm'-shaped *oriscus* is similarly found at a falling diagonal axis when used as part of a *pressus*. The *tractulus* also features an occasional

---

[53] See, further, Aubert 2011, 194–8; **F-Pn lat.1085** is online at http://gallica.bnf.fr/ark:/12148/btv1b8432277r.

[54] For facsimiles, see Nicholson 1909, plates 10 (f.11v) and 11 (f.12r); also Steigemann and Wemhoff 1999, 729, Abb. 11 (f.11v), and Rankin 2000, 166 (f.12r). On the dating and origin of the manuscript, see Bischoff 2004, no. 3821. Nicholson 1909, xxii observes that the glosses are most likely ninth century, that the neumes were added in the same-coloured ink as the glosses, and that the interlinear glosses on f.12r are displaced by the neumes and so must have been added later. Rankin 2000, 165 follows Bischoff in dating the gloss scribe to the late ninth century and also identifies the gloss scribe with the notator.

curve upwards to the right at the end of an elongated form. Substantially more research needs to be undertaken on Aquitanian notations found in manuscripts from the upper Loire region (including institutions at Tours, Fleury-sur-Loire, Auxerre, and Ferrières-en-Gâtinais) before definitive characteristics for Aquitanian neumes as drawn in this area may be proposed.[55] What may be noted at this stage, however, is that a late ninth-century Aquitanian notation from the upper Loire region lies closer to the neumes in **F-Pn lat.1154** than any of the surviving neumes in manuscripts from St Martial.

Emboldened by this comparison, the intriguing prospect arises that *A*'s work might be dated to earlier than has previously been supposed, possibly even as early as the late ninth century. A certain amount of internal evidence can be found to support this hypothesis. The dots and dashes used in the punctuation, abbreviation signs, and the neumes are written in the same colour, with similar dimensions and thickness of stroke. In other words, the neumes of notator *A* are the same colour and size as the text, a feature that becomes more telling when it is observed that the work of the other notators immediately strikes the eye as different in size or ink colour. Such general similarities in appearance are supported by smaller-scale shared variations in shading: differences in ink colour, dimension, and size of shaft coincide. See, among many other examples, the variation in shading through *Fuit Domini*,[56] and especially the darker shades on f.112r,[57] or the darker ink of both text and neumes for *Bella bis quinis* on f.119v.[58] The shading used for incipits and refrains also serves to relate the work of the text scribe and main notator. At the opening of *Mecum Timavi* on f.116r,[59] the green shading used to highlight the incipit covers up some of the lower-placed neumes. This strongly implies that the neumes were added before the green shading was applied, since a later notator would have avoided placing the neumes on the edge of the green shading where they are almost illegible. It is most likely instead that the notator was adding neumes alongside the decoration in the earliest layer of the writing of this section of the manuscript.

---

[55] For an initial list of Aquitanian notations in manuscripts of Fleury provenance, see Corbin 1973, 385–92, at 390–2, a research report citing four manuscripts held in Orléans (**F-O 149**, **F-O 303**, **F-O 305** and **F-O 341**) and one in Paris (**F-Pn lat.1720**; see http://gallica.bnf.fr/ark:/ 12148/btv1b8427235p).

[56] http://gallica.bnf.fr/ark:/12148/btv1b84324798/f232.image.

[57] http://gallica.bnf.fr/ark:/12148/btv1b84324798/f235.image.

[58] http://gallica.bnf.fr/ark:/12148/btv1b84324798/f250.image.

[59] http://gallica.bnf.fr/ark:/12148/btv1b84324798/f243.image.

Several details of formal construction are also shared between the notator and the main text scribe. The small diagonal sign used as a contraction by the text scribe is identical in its construction to the second element in the rising two-note or *pes* neume. Compare the contractions on f.123r,[60] *signu(m)* (column 1, l.4) and *D(OMI)NI* (column 1, l.11), with the second element of the *pes* in the hand of the main, lower notator at the end of column 1, line 3 and at *terra* (column 2, l.1). As discussed above, the neat downward pulls at the beginning and end of the thin ascending diagonal are a distinctive feature of the notator's penmanship and are reproduced in the shape used by the text scribe. A second sign shared between the two systems is that used for the 'us' abbreviation and the *cephalicus*: these may be seen in close proximity on f.113v,[61] where the 'us' abbreviation is used for *ver(us)* (column 1, l.3) and the *cephalicus* is found over the word *iacet* (column 2, l.6). Most intriguing of all is that there are occasional moments that suggest a close relationship between the text scribe and main notator. Perhaps the clearest instance is on f.104r,[62] where the initial and opening two lines of *Anima nimis misera/Infelix scelestissima* were evidently written sequentially. The initial 'A' took up space on the second line, forcing the text scribe to place the 'In' under the cross-bar of the 'A'. The co-ordination is so neat at this point as to indicate that the initial scribe and text scribe were the same person. The text scribe took another precaution in placing the 'n' of 'In' significantly lower than the 'I'. The reason for this seems clear when the space above is considered: the text scribe was ensuring that there would be enough room to add a neume above the word 'In' and under the cross-bar of the 'A'.

There are therefore a number of indications that the main notator was the same person as the text scribe. This hypothesis, if accepted, would overturn the view that neumes were added at a later date to this manuscript. The argument for a significantly later dating was made most forcibly by Chailley, who agreed with Coussemaker in dating the *versus* collection to around the mid-tenth century on the grounds that it contains several pieces relating to the Last Judgement and its poetry makes no particular use of acrostics. Chailley was also of the view that the notation was added later, if not necessarily much later, largely on the grounds of what he perceived as frequent differences in ink colour and the fact that no attempt was made to plan for the addition of notation.[63] None of these arguments

---

[60] http://gallica.bnf.fr/ark:/12148/btv1b84324798/f257.image.

[61] http://gallica.bnf.fr/ark:/12148/btv1b84324798/f238.image.

[62] http://gallica.bnf.fr/ark:/12148/btv1b84324798/f219.image.   [63] Chailley 1960, 75–6.

carries much weight: several poems concerning the Last Judgement were written before the terrors associated with the turn of the millennium; many of the poems in **F-Pn lat.1154** do in fact contain structural patterns (the abecedary poems and the acrostic in the Sibylline *versus, Iudicii signum*) and many Carolingian poems anyway contain no acrostics. The differences in ink colour are a matter of contention, and given that neumes fit neatly between the lines there would have been no need to make special provision for neumatic notation.

The second important conclusion which follows from identification of the main notator with the text scribe is that an example of fluent Aquitanian notation may be placed at the Abbey of St Martial by the late ninth century or early tenth century. This would have significant repercussions for understanding the historical development of Aquitanian neumes, because it would place a controlled, fluent version of this notation at St Martial of Limoges significantly before the varied scripts in **F-Pn lat.1240**, many of which include traits familiar from more northern French notations, speculatively dated to the abbacy of Aimo (937–43) by Emerson.[64] While the hypothesis of an early dating for the neumes of the main notator remains to be proven, it raises the tantalizing prospect that Aquitanian neumes were being written at St Martial earlier than has been accepted, indeed contemporary with some of the early examples of neume scripts from St Gall and Laon, thus placing the Limoges abbey alongside the primary centres for the development of stylized neumatic notations.[65]

These proposals are not without precedent. Jacques Handschin anticipated them in a footnote to an article published in 1930, in which he turned aside from consideration of the early history of the sequence *Concelebremus sacram* to comment more widely on the notation in **F-Pn lat.1154**.[66] His view, given without supporting palaeographic evidence, was that the manuscript was copied in the ninth century at St Martial of Limoges. Moreover, the neumes were to his mind clearly written before those in **F-Pn lat.1240**, and were in some cases contemporary with the text: he cites in particular the neumes added to *Tocius mundi* and *Concelebremus sacram* as being written in the same colour as the text, and those added to *Fuit Domini* on f.110v as varying in both colour and

---

[64] Emerson 1993, 198. See also Evans 1970, 103–12, and Dubois 2012, 105–23.

[65] For a recent overview of the dating of the earliest St Gall and Laon manuscripts, including arguments for dating extant neumatic scripts to significantly earlier in the ninth century than previously considered, see Rankin 2011, 105–75, especially 173–5.

[66] Handschin 1930, 122n2.

thickness alongside the copying of the text. He also cites as a comparably early example of Aquitanian neumes those found in the ninth-century copy of Martianus Capella's *De nuptiis Philologiae et Mercurii*, now held in the Bodleian library (discussed above). The range of evidence newly cited here accords with Handschin's view, whose implications deserve to be further explored following their eclipse by Chailley's influential study.

Singing and praying

To understand the uses to which **F-Pn lat.1154** might have been put at the Abbey of St Martial of Limoges requires consideration of the function of parallel collections. Alcuin's instruction of Charlemagne as recorded in the *Vita Alcuini* written before 829 is particularly enlightening.

Docuit etiam eum per omne vitae suae tempus, quos psalmos poenitentiae cum letania et orationibus precibusque, quos ad orationem specialem faciendam, quos in laude Dei, quos quoque pro quacumque tribulatione, quemque etiam, ut se in divinis exerceret laudibus, decantaret. Quod nosse qui vult, legat libellum eius ad eumdem De ratione orationis.

He also taught him which psalms of penance to sing all his life with litany, collects, and *preces*; which psalms to sing for special prayer; which ones to sing in praise of God; which ones to sing for any tribulation; and which psalm to sing in order to occupy himself in divine praises. Anyone who wishes to learn about this should read his booklet on the conduct of prayer dedicated to that man.[67]

The correspondence with the contents of **F-Pn lat.1154** is significant as not only the types of text, but also their ordering and intentions are held in common. Alcuin reportedly instructed Charlemagne in a pattern of private devotion consisting of litanies, collects, prayers, and psalms for particular intentions, including three of the eight mentioned in the *De laude psalmorum*. In a letter of 801?–804, Alcuin stipulated a series of psalm verses and other formulae to be recited on rising in the morning as part of a daily set of hours apparently requested by the Emperor as a lay counterpart to observance of the Divine Office.[68] A similar pattern of private prayer to both these observations is described in a letter written by Hrabanus

---

[67] Arndt 1887, 193; translation after Black 2002, 4–5.
[68] The surviving letter contains only the beginning of a set of hours: see Alcuin's epistola 304, in Dümmler 1895, 462–3.

Maurus in 822 to Judith, second wife of Louis the Pious, in which he outlined a model for morning devotion:

Mane cum surrexeritis...confessionem quam beatae memoriae Alcuinus [domno Karolo] dedit, in exemplo illius secrete...faciatis. Et postea septem paenitentiae psalmos intente et devote cum letanie et suis capitulis atque orationibus domino decantetis.[69]

In the morning when you arise, you should make the confession that Alcuin of blessed memory dedicated to Lord Charles secretly, following his example. And afterwards you should recite intently and devotedly the seven penitential psalms with a litany and their chapters and collects.

The relation of these private devotions to prayerbooks that survive from the ninth century, especially from the mid-ninth century onwards, is a matter of debate. The booklet referred to in the *Vita* in all probability reflects the general pattern of devotion established by Alcuin rather than recording the observances recommended specifically for Charlemagne. Even so, Stephan Waldhoff has argued that a fully elaborated sequence of texts for daily offices as contained in Alcuin's booklet for Charlemagne may be reconstructed from later prayerbooks.[70] Whatever one makes of this proposal, the overall programme recommended by Alcuin of litanies, collects, chapters, individually prescribed psalms, and confessional prayers is mirrored in prayerbooks belonging to rulers from the later ninth century onwards. The prayerbooks of Charles the Bald and Otto III, as well as the Psalter of Louis the German, while differing substantially in contents and ordering conform in diverse ways with Alcuin's various stipulations, including confessional prayers, the seven penitential psalms and litanies, as well as prayers for the Adoration of the Cross. Additions to the Psalter of Louis the German in the later ninth century also include non-liturgical *versus* of broadly devotional intent, while daily devotions based on Alcuin's pattern in later ninth-century prayerbooks such as **F-Pn lat.1153** routinely include hymns.[71]

   F-Pn lat.1154 is certainly not of the same grade as the prayerbooks of rulers, but the contents of its first two sections accord with their pattern, raising the question whether the Paris collection reflects a similar programme of private devotion. The language of the prayers speaks against

---

[69] Wilmart 1922, 241.   [70] Waldhoff 2003, *passim.*

[71] On the notated Boethian *metra* in the Psalter of Louis the German, see Barrett 2013, 1: 64–5, 88–9, 143–50, and 227–9. Four hymns are included in the *Officia per ferias* as transmitted in **F-Pn lat.1153**: *Christe coelestis, Pange lingua, Crux benedicta nitet* and *A solis ortus cardine*; see PL 101, cols. 556–7, 562–3 and 609–11.

any idea that the manuscript was compiled for a layperson. The opening collect, for example, prays for a community of cenobites (*huius cenobii collegium*) and all varieties of cenobitic congregations joined in familiarity and consanguinity. Even more explicit is a later confessional prayer (starting *Confiteor tibi omnipotens pater qui filium tuum in terris misisti*, on f.49r) which admits to neglecting prescriptions of the Benedictine rule on liturgical observance, treating vessels and vestments of the church negligently, losing and breaking objects inside the monastery (*infra monasterium*) and being subject to excommunication by the prior. The obvious conclusion is that the prayer section was compiled with monastic use in mind, as indeed were the majority of early prayerbooks.[72]

The Benedictine Rule and its ninth-century commentaries provide precise instructions as to the place of private prayer and prayerbooks in Benedictine communities. Chapter LII, 'On the Oratory of the Monastery', states, 'if anyone wants to pray privately, let him just go in and pray, not in a loud voice, but with tears and fervour of heart'.[73] The wording resonates with the prayers gathered in **F-Pn lat.1154**, both with their overall tone of lamentation as signalled from the outset (*Incipiunt letanie de quacumque tribulatione*) and with the specific address to anyone who wishes to pray *secretius*. The place set aside for such private prayer was the oratory or monastic chapel. Occasions for private prayer in the oratory are left unspecified in the Rule, but are elaborated in Hildemar of Corbie's commentary on this chapter, where he specifies that if anyone becomes tearful during their normal schedule of reading or work they may go to the oratory to meditate (*causa contemplationis*).[74] He goes on to say:

In eo quoque loco, ubi dicit 'non in clamosa voce', manifestat, qua intentione hoc capitulum praeceperit; non enim dicit, ut ibi officium mortuorum non agatur, si generalitas est, similiter si duplicare vult officium, si generalitas hoc agit; verum non licet cuiquam, si non est generalis congregatio, in voce orare. Sciendum est enim, quia potest in oratorio ponere illum librum, qui ibi legitur, solummodo.[75]

Also in that place, where he says 'not in a clamorous voice', he shows with what intention this chapter should be taken; for he does not say that there the Office of

---

[72] Black 2005, 64.

[73] Si aliter vult sibi forte secretius orare, simpliciter intret et oret, non in clamosa voce, sed in lacrimis et intentione cordis: text from Vogüé and Neufville 1972, 610.

[74] Si enim contingit, cum quis habet contemplationem tempore lectionis vel laboris et reliq., non illi fraudavit lacrimas, sed ob hoc potest dimittere lectionem vel laborem et ire in oratorium causa contemplationis: Mittermüller 1880, 500.

[75] Mittermüller 1880, 500–501.

the Dead is not done, if it generally is; similarly, if anyone wants to duplicate the Office [of the Dead], if that is general practice, he may do this; what is in fact not allowed to anyone, if there is no general congregation, is to pray aloud. For it must be understood that it is possible to leave in the oratory only the book that is read there.

That a book might be read by a monk in the oratory for the purpose of private prayer during tearful contemplation is a fascinating detail. It is not the only place where we read of such a book being used in the oratory for private prayer. Gerhard of Augsburg recalls in his *Vita sancti Uodalrici* how St Ulrich (*c*.890–973) used to perform private prayers in Lent:

Prima vero expleta, fratribus solito more crucem portantibus, ipse remanens in aecclesia codiculum breviatum ex psalmis cum aliis orationibus interim decantavit, usque dum fratres cum cruce redirent, et missam sacrificationis caelebrare coepissent.[76]

When Prime had finished and it was the custom for brothers to carry the cross, he, staying behind in the church, would in the meantime recite psalms along with other prayers from a small handbook up to the point when the brothers returned with the cross and they began to celebrate Mass.

The combined reports of Hildemar's commentary for his oblates and a report of the practices of a Bishop suggest that the practice of personal recitation from a *libellus precum* in the oratory extended across all ranks within the monastic community. The contents of **F-Pn lat.1154** would seem particularly suited to the type of personal prayer that is always described in association with tears of compunction in the Benedictine Rule.[77] That music might form a part of personal prayer is further attested by the survival of private prayerbooks from the ninth century onwards, including hymns in the prayerbook of Reginbert (d.846), librarian of Reichenau, a notated Office of the Dead in a prayerbook copied *c*.900, and notated hymns, antiphons and responds in the *Portiforium* (or *Breviarium*) of Wulfstan (d.1095), bishop of Worcester.[78]

---

[76] Berschin and Häse 1993, chapter 4; 122, 10–14.

[77] See chapters IV.57, XX.3, XLIX.4, and LII.4.

[78] On the contents of Reginbert of Reichenau's prayerbook, which survives in two fragments copied in his hand, see Gamber 1985, 232–9, and Bischoff 2004, 2: no. 3644. A neumed Office of the Dead is found in a private prayerbook copied in Swabia, *c*.900: see Bischoff 1980, 223 and Bischoff 2004, 2: no. 3086. For Wulfstan's *Portiforium*, see Hughes 1958–60. On the musical notations in Wulfstan's manuscripts including the *Portiforium*, see Rankin 1996 and Rankin 2005.

Later additions to **F-Pn lat.1154** shed further light on the readers and users of this particular manuscript. A penitential confession entitled *Confessio pura* was added immediately after the *versus* collection by a hand that may be dated to no later than the early tenth century.[79] It takes the form of an extensive recitation of sins expressed in the first person before an altar in the presence of a priest (*sacerdos*), whose shorter prayer for forgiveness immediately follows. The opening formulae of both the confession and its response are found at an earlier date in a mid-ninth-century *libellus precum* from Tours, where the text is attributed to Saint Fulgentius and introduced by a rubric specifying its use for granting penitence, *Incipit confessio sancti Fulgentii episcopi ad penitentiam dandam.*[80] It also differs in content from versions found in the Poitiers pontifical and later in the Romano-German pontifical as part of the penitential rite for entry into penance on Ash Wednesday.[81] In the absence of a comprehensive study of this Confession, and given the poor state of the manuscript at this point, it is difficult to comment further on the version found here, but the fact that a Confession that circulated at an early date in Pontificals with a role for a *sacerdos* was copied in this manuscript raises the possibility that it might here have been of use to both the penitent and the bishop or priest involved in its enactment.

Closing remarks

A number of claims have been made about the origin and date of the manuscript, its notation, and its function that bear summary given the length and detail of this chapter. It has been proposed that the main body of **F-Pn lat.1154** – the prayers, the *Synonyma* and the *versus* collection – was copied at the Abbey of St Martial of Limoges in the late ninth or early tenth century, and that the litany was copied for the same institution during the tenth century. A strong case has also been made that the main scribe of the *versus* collection was the main notator.

---

[79] Bischoff dated the hand at the top of f.145v to 's. x in' in his notes, thus providing a *terminus ante quem* for the preceding *Confessio pura*.

[80] **F-Pn lat.13388** ('Libellus Turonensis'), Wilmart 1940, 65–7.

[81] For the prayer as it appears in the Pontifical of Poitiers, see **F-Pa 227**, ff.8v–11v; the manuscript images are online: http://gallica.bnf.fr/ark:/12148/btv1b55005681f. For the version in the Romano-German Pontifical, see Vogel and Elze 1963, 16–17 (nos. 50a–51). An overview of the whole rite for entry into penance on Ash Wednesday as it appears in the Romano-German Pontifical is provided in Hamilton 2001b, 108–17.

A specific role for **F-Pn lat.1154** as a prayerbook for use in the oratory to support private prayer has also been outlined. This does not rule out the possibility that the book was used for other ends within the abbey; indeed, it is likely that the manuscript was used in teaching given the number of less well-formed scripts and notations in the collection. This familiar explanation for the role within monastic communities of *versus* with no clear function within the standard liturgical round provides perhaps the simplest way of imagining the role of notation in the book. As skilled and less competent notations appear alongside each other, so might a master have used notation as a support for demonstrating melodies to students. To restrict the function of notated and sung *versus* to this one context is nevertheless to assume single functions for books within monasteries and to disconnect education from its cultural setting.

The case made here is that what has often been considered the earliest notated songbook can equally be considered a prayerbook. A corollary of this argument is that traditions of prayer could encompass song; indeed, the boundaries between the two were less stark than the distribution of notation in this manuscript suggests. The litany, for example, may well have been sung to a recitational formula, following the model of the notated litany in **F-Pn lat.1240** (f.32v). The penitential psalms, as well as their accompanying collects and chapters, were also likely chanted according to recitational patterns that remained unnotated; the antiphon for All Saints was also evidently suited to sung performance. The penitential *versus* of Part IV stand alongside these, as texts that might be sung or recited privately as a form of contemplative prayer, whether in the oratory in a low voice so as not to disturb others as highlighted here, or on other occasions set aside for either personal prayer or meditative reading in monastic communities.[82]

---

[82] In discussing comparable *libelli precum* of the eleventh and twelfth centuries, Susan Boynton has highlighted the time set aside in contemporary monastic customaries between Matins and Lauds in winter for personal prayer, as well as indications that individuals should withdraw from the choir in order to pray privately: Boynton 2007, 896–931. A useful summary of occasions for both private prayer and reading in the Benedictine Rule is provided in Stewart 2008, 201–21.

2 | The careful cantor and the *Carmina Cantabrigiensia*

JEREMY LLEWELLYN

It all seems so simple. Just six melodic *motus* or intervals are to be learnt in order to overcome any hindrances in singing chant. This, at least, is what the Benedictine monk Guido of Arezzo sets out in his *Regula ritmicae* written in the third decade of the eleventh century.[1] Guido was relentlessly interested in processes of learning and designing labour-saving devices to hone the efficacy of such processes in order that his wards may then have more time to devote to Holy Scripture.[2] Using self-proclaimed innovation for traditional ends, Guido draws on previous writings to redefine incrementally what it means to learn and think about music. At the crossroads between innovation and tradition he thus places the figure of the 'careful cantor' (*prudens cantor*), a figure charged with responsibilities, but also carrying ethical weight.[3] Guido did not call this personage into existence: the *prudens cantor* figures in earlier writings on music, including those by Aurelian of Réôme and Regino of Prüm.[4] In each case, prudence or carefulness is attached to specific matters of musical knowledge necessary for the successful performance of chant. Guido regards this newly refined body of knowledge, to be absorbed by the cantor, as important enough to displace the philosophical concerns of speculative music theory as represented by Boethius.[5] At the same time, however, the development of staff notation risked disabusing teachers in monastic and cathedral schools of their previously unquestioned monopoly in adjudging matters of right singing. Musical and moral authority seems to have been in a particular state of flux in educational circles of the early eleventh century, undoubtedly calling for especial prudence on the part of the *prudens cantor*.

---

[1] 'Moneo te, prudens cantor, hos [i.e. motus] perfecte discere/Nam qui hos plene cognoscit, nil in cantu dubitat' in Pesce 1999, 352–3.

[2] In his *Prologus in antiphonarium* Guido mocks those who would still be unable to sing a single antiphon after one hundred years, railing against the waste of time; see Pesce 1999, 408–9.

[3] The seemingly oppositional pairing 'innovation' and 'tradition' in relation to Guido has been carefully analyzed in Sachs 1989 and Barezzani 2000.

[4] For Aurelian, see Gushee 1975, 127 and 131 and for Regino of Prüm, LeRoux 1965, 26.

[5] This is most clearly elucidated at the end of Guido's *Epistola ad Michahelem*: '[Boethius] whose book is useful to philosophers only, not to singers' ('cuius liber non cantoribus sed solis philosophis utilis est') in Pesce 1999, 530–1.

There appears to be nothing particularly prudent about the layout of the batch of eighty-three songs tucked at the back of the substantial manuscript Cambridge, University Library, Gg.V.35 (henceforth **GB-Cu Gg. V.35**). The ten or so folios containing the songs follow on from over 400 folios of wide-ranging literary materials. The songs were obviously not prepared for a complementary form of musical notation – neumes – since no space was left above the song texts, although compromised bursts of neumes can be found sporadically in the collection.[6] Space in this section seems to have been at a premium: the texts themselves are unabashedly abbreviated which, again, militates against interlinear musical notation. Moreover, there appears to be no consistent policy when it comes to deciding where the ends of lines of particular verse forms – for example, hexameters – are to be put, which leads to lines running into each other. This concertinaed text is all the more unavoidable since, in contrast to the earlier portion of the manuscript, the song gatherings at the end of **GB-Cu Gg.V.35** are copied in double-column format. Even the number of lines of text per folio increases significantly. The general impression of calculated compression does not, however, conceal the less-than-pristine quality of the Latin, which has constantly preoccupied editors over the last century. These characteristics taken together – compression, double columns, irregular ends of verse lines – ironically define this section of the manuscript **GB-Cu Gg.V.35** as a codicological unity. These, then, are the *Carmina Cantabrigiensia*, also known as the 'Cambridge Songs', the 'Cambridger Lieder' or, in abbreviated form, the CC.

Although now in Cambridge, **GB-Cu Gg.V.35** was most probably copied around the middle of the eleventh century at St Augustine's Abbey, Canterbury, and stands as a startling testimony to the literary scope of Benedictine culture in pre-Conquest England.[7] Scholarly interest over the last three centuries has, however, largely been from German philologists and lexicographers drawn initially by a macaronic text in Old High German and Latin on a certain Henry of Bavaria (CC19).[8] Karl Breul

---

[6] Spanke 1942, 114 arrives at this conclusion but qualifies it by stating that the CC were nevertheless copied from an exemplar with 'melodies'; Bernhard 1989, 143 and Ziolkowski 1994, 237 cite the space left in copying CC21 'Diapente et diatesseron' as evidence that notation was originally envisaged. No amount, however, of horizontal space between words can make up for the lack of space above the text.

[7] On its Anglo-Saxon letter forms and insular practices of punctuation, see Ziolkowski 1994, xxxi and Rigg and Wieland 1975, 116–17. Towards the beginning of the manuscript a twelfth-century hand has written: 'Liber Sancti Augustini Cant.'.

[8] For an overview of scholarship on the CC from 1720 to 1914, see Breul 1915, 29–34.

Table 2.1 List of contents of **GB-Cu Gg.V.35** from Rigg and Wieland 1975

Part	Folios	Scribe/s	General description	Contents
I (a)	1–209	A, B	Late Antique Christian Latin poetry	including Sedulius *Paschale Carmen*; Prudentius, *Psychomachia*; Boethius, *De consolatione philosophiae*
I (b)	210–79*	A	Carolingian prose and verse texts	including Hrabanus Maurus, *De laude sancte crucis*
	*263–79	D	Writings on music	Hucbald, *Scolica Enchiriadis* (excerpts)
II	280–369	A, B	Anglo-Latin and continental prose and verse texts	including Aldhelm, *De virginitate*; Milo, *De sobrietate*; Hucbald, *Irrisio contra calvos*
III	370–431	A, B (E)	Miscellaneous Latin texts; Greek prayers	including Tatwine, *Enigmata*; Columban, *De bonis moribus observandis*; Bede, *De die iudicii*
IV	432–46	A (C)	*Carmina Cantabrigiensia* [CC]	

produced a facsimile edition of the CC with diplomatic transcription and individual studies in 1915, which was criticized by Karl Strecker in part for creating an artificial numbering system for the individual song texts.[9] Strecker produced his own edition of the CC, with introduction and commentaries, in 1926 and his numbering system, based on the ordering in the manuscript itself, has remained in use up to the present day.[10] The first detailed modern description of **GB-Cu Gg.V.35** and its contents appeared in a seminal article by Arthur G. Rigg and Gernot Wieland, published in 1975; Table 2.1 represents their listing.[11]

In 1983 Margaret T. Gibson, Michael Lapidge and Christopher Page reported the fortuitous rediscovery and return from Frankfurt of a single folio containing neumed Boethian *metra* which had been detached from **GB-Cu Gg.V.35** in the nineteenth century. Jan M. Ziolkowski's exemplary

---

[9] See Breul 1915 and the criticism in Strecker 1925, 209 of a 'totally arbitrary collocation [of the poems]' ('eine völlig willkürliche Anordnung').

[10] Strecker 1926; a further edition in pamphlet form, following Strecker's numbering system, is Bulst 1950.

[11] Supplementary details about the contents of **GB-Cu Gg.V.35** can be found in Dronke, Lapidge, and Stotz 1982.

1994 edition, translation, and commentary expanded the number of individual items in the CC from 49 to 83 by including the Boethian *metra*, as well as a handful of songs in another hand which spilt over into the next gathering of **GB-Cu Gg.V.35** but could nonetheless be reconsidered as part of the collection. In 2004 a reconstruction in sound or 'revocalization' of a selection of the CC was prepared by Benjamin Bagby and *Sequentia* for a recording entitled *Lost Songs of a Rhineland Harper (10th and 11th centuries)*.[12] Finally, 2009 saw the publication of a practical edition with translation into Italian by Francesco Lo Monaco in the series *Scrittori latini dell'Europa medievale*.

This thicket of modern editions testifies to the perennial fascination aroused by the CC, which has successfully traversed generations of scholars and national traditions of scholarship. It could be argued that the prime interest attached to the CC springs from the sheer diversity of subject matters and forms on display, from the fact that the CC do not represent a judiciously assembled repertory, stylishly arranged on parchment, but rather a somewhat unwieldy anthology or *florilegium*.[13] The macaronic poem that originally attracted attention to the collection is merely symptomatic of the variegated nature of the whole. Large-scale religious poetry jostles with ridiculous narratives, fairy tale-like fables with paeans of praise to the power of music, dirges on the deaths of temporal overlords with amorous verses, eulogies to springtime with moralistic admonitions.[14] The cast of characters includes she-asses, emperors, hermits, nightingales, sorcerers, lovers, and, for good measure, the devil.[15] The collection stands, therefore, as one of the most extensive miscellanies of medieval Latin poetry between the Carolingians and the *Carmina Burana* of the early thirteenth century, and has even been regarded as displaying certain features common to the early vernacular lyrical poetry of the Troubadours and Minnesang.[16]

---

[12] For an informative discussion about the reconstruction and performance of 'Lost Songs' see Bagby et al. 2012, and the texts on the website devoted to the project: www.sequentia.org/projects/lost_songs.html.

[13] Ziolkowski 1994, xviii comments on the size of the anthology while Strecker 1926, xxi draws a parallel with other medieval *florilegia*.

[14] See Breul 1915, 39, Spanke 1942, 120, Ziolkowski 1994, xix and Lo Monaco 2009, 4 for the various different categories, which broadly overlap between authors, as well as a statistical overview.

[15] Ziolkowski 1994, xl presents a more specific list of those groups of singing characters depicted in the CC.

[16] For the place of the CC within the history of early medieval verse, see Ziolkowski 1994, xviii; Spanke 1942, 124 and 142 posit a connection between the CC and Troubadour production

Given this vigorous diversity, historiographical debate concerning the CC has tended to coalesce around three principal concerns: geographical origins, manuscript organization, and performative function. None of these matters can be viewed entirely in isolation from the others but such a tripartite division can help to illuminate general tendencies in scholarship over the last hundred years. At the beginning of the twentieth century Breul drew the CC up into the broader sweep of the composition of medieval Latin poetry 'produced in Germany' and which, more specifically, 'would be of interest whether to laity or clergy living on the banks of the middle and lower Rhine in the first half of the eleventh century'.[17] This localization was based on the mention in certain poems of places along the Rhine (Trier, Cologne, Xanten) on the one hand, and on the dialect of the macaronic Old High German-Latin poems on the other.[18] That other poems may hail from France or Italy is a possibility entertained by Breul only in passing. His explanation for the poems crossing the Channel revolves around the enterprising initiative of an Englishman who may have acquired some form of *libellus* of the texts on the Continent which then found its way into the hands of the monks at Canterbury. Strecker was far more assiduous in sifting the concordances of poems in the CC for possible geographical origins. He thus discretely divides the 'German' poems numbering CC2–15 from a 'French' group CC35–47. The middle group CC16–CC34 exhibits traits that point to the 'probability' of Rhineland origins, but Strecker repeatedly stresses the necessity of separating the place of compilation from the place of composition.[19] Strecker's observations are taken further by Ziolkowski, partly on the basis of a more penetrating examination of concordant material including clusters of transmission, but principally because one would not necessarily expect a heterogeneous anthology such as the CC to present a homogeneous picture concerning origins. The CC are thus 'impressively multinational' while opening a window on literary production and culture in eleventh-century Germany, although 'the Germanness of the collection should not be

---

whereas Breul 1915, 36 sees in the CC 'the direct forerunners of the early Minnesong'. Moreover, scholarly fascination with the CC extends beyond the miscellaneous contents to what is not – or no longer – in the manuscript, since certain texts were excerpted and others even expunged by a prurient censor; see, for example, the commentaries in Ziolkowski 1994 and Lo Monaco 2009 to the songs CC27, CC28, CC39, and CC49 and the corresponding plates in Breul 1915, 438v, 440v, and 441v.

[17] Breul 1915, 39.   [18] Breul 1915, 23.

[19] See Strecker 1926, XVII ff. with the relevant quotation at XIX distinguishing between the place of 'Zusammenstellung' and the 'Entstehungsort' of the respective compositions.

overstated'.[20] In describing the CC as a 'raccolta europea', Lo Monaco caps this appreciation of the wider origins of the poems brought together in these song gatherings, reflecting a broader historiographical development in medieval studies in the latter half of the twentieth century away from national foci towards an investigation of processes of cultural exchange.[21]

Any overarching organizational principle concerning the contents of the CC remains a chimera. Breul swiftly recognized this and rearranged the texts thematically in his edition, beginning with the category of 'religious' poems and ending with 'some unconnected lines that appear to be nothing but metrical experiments'.[22] Strecker criticized this editorial rearrangement so effectively that all subsequent editions of the CC duly follow the manuscript ordering and adopt, in essence, Strecker's numbering scheme.[23] In distinguishing CC30 from CC30A, however, Strecker brought the question of verse introductions – or proems – to certain poems to the fore. Ziolkowski makes even greater use of this device, mining from Strecker's critical apparatus certain textual units which are then restored to the main edition as CC1A and CC14A; Lo Monaco dispenses with these last two sub-divisions, but unwillingly retains the numbering of CC30 and CC30A, even though he considers the former to be a self-contained text. There is thus a very real quandary at certain points of the CC concerning how apparently 'unconnected lines' are to be connected to their surroundings, if at all. Nevertheless, certain tendencies concerning organizational principles within the CC have been discerned, most notably in the contiguity of poetic form and presumed origins in the Germanic sequence section of CC2–15 or the French equivalent CC35–47. Patterns of concordances with other manuscripts at least suggest that handfuls of poems may have circulated together, regardless of the final ordering of the same poems in the CC.[24] Otherwise, more localized reasons for the arrangement of segments of the CC have been proposed, such as the use of refrains or a common thematic link, for example, revolving around springtime.[25] These glimpses of an organizing mentality can act as a spur to imagining the lost

---

[20] Ziolkowski 1994, xxxv.

[21] Lo Monaco 2009, 12; see also Ziolkowski 1994, xxxvii for a brief passage on historiographical trends away from the nationalism of the first half of the twentieth century, which are discussed more broadly in Kugler 2012.

[22] See Breul 1915, 39 for a list of his seven 'sub-divisions'.

[23] This includes the four poems that suffered the attentions of the censor, each of which received an individual number. In the same way, the two appearances of largely the same chunk of Statius' *Thebaid* acquire the separate numbers CC29 and CC32.

[24] For a survey on the scholarship of these smaller collections see Ziolkowski 1994, xxxiii ff.

[25] For further details and more examples of such miniaturized ordering, see Ziolkowski 1994, lv.

songs on the missing leaves of the CC which had become detached and scattered over the course of the centuries. Apart from the Frankfurt leaf, these others remain as intangible dotted lines in codicological descriptions of the physical structure of the final two gatherings of **GB-Cu Gg.V.35**. As Ziolkowski observed, however, the reconstruction of the original shape of these two gatherings, together with palaeographical analysis of scribal activity, suggest that scribe A continued copying past the end of gathering 44 into gathering 45, whereupon scribe C took over. This bridging of the gap is one reason Ziolkowski incorporates the poems copied by scribe C as part of the anthology, an editorial decision espoused later by Lo Monaco.[26] Thus it is possible to note an ever-growing fidelity on the part of the numerous editors of the CC towards presenting the contents of the collection as physically found in the manuscript source itself. As with the question of geographical origins, it is possible to detect a general historiographical trend away from coarse compartmentalization towards a greater appreciation of diversity and inclusiveness.

The historiographical arc concerning the performative function of the CC can be sketched with relative ease. Initially, the collection was regarded as mirroring the repertory of an itinerant cleric or scholar – the 'goliard' – who wandered between courts, both secular and ecclesiastical, performing a range of songs. Breul, indeed, emphasizes the 'versatility' of his goliard and imagines him deftly responding in performance to the penchants of the audience in front of him.[27] This is not simply a performative flight of fancy on Breul's part: he is careful to refer philologically to the way in which texts in the CC refer to themselves as 'ridiculum' (CC14 and CC35) or 'mendosa cantilena' (CC15), the last recommended for 'little boys' and thus for some form of instruction or entertainment at a monastery or cathedral school.[28] Only a small minority of songs in the CC advertise themselves in this way. Nevertheless, the image of the wandering singer has remained enthralling not least as a result of the chance survival of a description found of such performances in a satirical work of the mid-eleventh century by Sextus Amarcius Gallus Piosistratus, who was active in the Rhineland region. His description of a performance in a tavern by a 'iocator' ('jongleur'), accompanying himself on a stringed instrument, has

---

[26] The grounds for expanding the collection to 83 compositions – already presaged by Dronke – and thereby including the significant David song are given in Ziolkowski 1994, xlvi–xlviii.

[27] Breul 1915, 39, which also references the 'very heterogeneous audiences' of the performer.

[28] A 'fantastical depiction' ('phantasievolle Schilderung') is the criticism levelled at Breul in Strecker 1926, XII. See also the reference in CC10 to 'young scholars and their pastimes' ('ad scolares et ad ludos') in Ziolkowski 1994, 46–7.

been of particular interest to scholars of the CC as a result of the specific reference by Sextus Amarcius to four songs: 'how the sling of a shepherd laid low Goliath, how a sly little Swabian deceived his wife [...] how perceptive Pythagoras laid bare the eight tones of song, and how pure the voice of the nightingale is'.[29] Three of these songs appear in CC as traditionally constituted, and the fourth has been duly identified and incorporated. This lucky coincidence between song collection and a literary vignette of performance has generated much debate.[30] This can, perhaps, best be summarized by maintaining that the mode of performance sketched by Sextus Amarcius – a self-accompanied solo singer – is by no means implausible, whereas the context of performance – the boozy tavern – is more likely the result of satirical licence. Indeed, this critical perspective informs the 2004 recording of the *Lost Songs of a Rhineland Harper*, which explores the possible performing conventions of a 'bilingual harper/singer' of the tenth and eleventh centuries who was equally a 'sophisticated professional entertainer'.[31]

The wandering singer theory, however alluring, cannot account for the entire contents of the CC. Strecker's sticking point concerned the presence of numerous excerpts of longer poems, that is, the incomplete nature of the collection. This led him to surmise that the CC were compiled according to literary interests and tastes, gobbets and all; he was relatively dismissive of any attempt to place these songs sociologically in a context other than educated and cultivated circles.[32] This concept of an essentially literary collection would seem to chime in with the idea proposed by Rigg and Wieland that **GB-Cu Gg.V.35** represents a series of graded school books for use in the classroom, beginning with the elementary and progressing to the more taxing.[33] This would explain why the earlier poetic texts in **GB-Cu Gg.V.35** are often heavily glossed. Nevertheless, Ziolkowski queries whether the CC, unglossed and uncommented, were really the crowning glory of this educational programme. Rather, the multifarious references to 'musicality' displayed by the CC provide for Ziolkowski one of the most compelling explanations for the performative function – or

---

[29] For the Latin original and translation here see Ziolkowski 1994, xlv–xlvi.

[30] The possible connection between Sextus Amarcius and the CC was first mooted in the nineteenth century; for insights into the scholarly debates see Strecker 1926, XIV–XVI and Ziolkowski 1994, xliv–liii; for the new edition of Amarcius's text see Pepin and Ziolkowski 2011.

[31] See the accompanying CD booklet in Sequentia dir. Bagby 2004, 6.

[32] Strecker 1926, XVI   [33] Rigg and Wieland 1975, 129–30.

'suitability for performance' – of the collection as a whole.[34] First, there are
the numerous texts that allude, in one way or another, to musical terminology and classification, whether to the typology of musical instruments or
else to melodic intervals. Second, certain texts reveal explicit invocations of
performance situations such as the encouragement of the master to make
his lyre sound sweetly (CC43) or the skilled girl singing beautiful songs
(CC27). Third, it is possible to construe implicit performing conventions
on the basis of, for example, the use of refrains or the suggestion of
antiphonal singing. Fourth, neumes can be found sporadically in the CC
and, in one place, space is apparently left for them. Fifth, a number of
concordances of the texts in the CC are furnished with neumes in other
manuscripts, even though these songs bear no notation in the CC. Finally,
Ziolkowski sees a correlation between the copying of excerpts in the CC
and their possible mnemonic function as re-actualizing the melody of the
whole of that particular text. In this way, Ziolkowski makes a strong case
for revising Strecker's assertion that the collector or collectors behind the
CC were less interested in a wide array of texts than a wide array of songs.
The danger is, simply, of a circular argument: the indifferent Latin, abbreviations, Old High German, excerpting, and proems might suggest that the
parchment was ultimately the site of a garbled vocality, redeemed only by
melody. The texts would not have been so important for the eleventh-
century collectors; the melodies fired their interest. Melody would then
stand behind each and every song, binding them into a collection and
exculpating the texts from any formal or formative function. This argument in general is, therefore, less about the 'codical absorption of vocality'
in relation to, for example, normative liturgical texts than an immaterial,
contingent and melodious absolution of Latinity.[35] As with geographical
origins and manuscript organization, recent scholarly and, indeed, artistic
engagement with the performative function of the CC would appear to
have radically opened up new possibilities for interpretation.

Exactly how far these new possibilities concerning the form, shape, and
interpretation of the CC extend is a matter for future research. It should,
however, be noted that the very criteria deemed to convey a coherence upon
the CC as a song collection can also be applied to the earlier sections of

---

[34] For this and the following see the section 'The Musicality of the CC' in Ziolkowski 1994,
    xxxix–xliv.
[35] The phenomenon of 'die kodikale Absorption der Vokalität' was described by Andreas Haug
    in a paper presented at the seminar 'Codex und Geltung' in connection with the
    Mediävistischer Arbeitskreis meeting at the Herzog-August Bibliothek in 2010; it will appear in
    the conference proceedings. I am grateful to the author for an advance copy.

Table 2.2 Comparison of neumed portions in **GB-Cu Gg.V.35** and CC adapted from Hartzell 2006

Rest of manuscript (ff.1r–431v)		
83r	*A solis ortu cardine*	Abecedary by Sedulius; first strophe fully neumed
362r	*Cives celestis patrie*	Anonymous *versus* on precious stones; ll.1–2 + 'fundatio' neumed
367r	*Stridula musca volans*	Anonymous mockery ('irrisio') on baldness by Hucbald; first two-and-a-half lines neumed; sporadic neumes in l.5
CC (ff. 432r–446r + new leaf)		
434v	*Aurea personet* (CC10)	Nightingale song; beginning of l.8 ('Nemoro [sa]') neumed
438r	*Sponso sponsa* (CC25)	Homage to Archbishop Poppo of Trier (1016–47); neumes on first three syllables
439r	*Quisquis dolosos antiqui* (CC30A)	Tale of St Basil thwarting pact with the devil; sequence form; versicles 1a and 2a neumed
441v	*O admirabile Veneris* (CC48)	Love poem; first two strophes neumed
new leaf recto	*Carmina qui quondam* (CC50–CC54, CC56)	Boethian *metra* extensively neumed, including alternative marginal version of 'Nubibus atris'
444r	*Ut belli sonuere* (App.4)	Later addition; eight-line poem on battlefield exploits of Amazons; fully neumed

GB-Cu Gg.V.35. A comparison between the CC and the earlier sections of **GB-Cu Gg.V.35** immediately focuses attention afresh on those same working procedures – layout of the text, usage of neumation, textual aggregation – which informed the compilation of this weighty poetic anthology as a whole.

Most simply, this concerns the presence of neumes: Table 2.2 sets out a comparison of those texts that are neumed elsewhere in **GB-Cu Gg.V.35** and in the CC.[36] Furthermore, a handful of unnotated texts in the first sections of **GB-Cu Gg.V.35** have concordances in other manuscripts with musical notation; a comparison with the CC is presented in Table 2.3.

Most striking is the fact that **GB-Cu Gg.V.35** contains two redactions of Boethian *metra* from *De consolatione philosophiae*, both copied by scribe A.

---

[36] Hartzell 2006, 10–11 includes neumes used as reference signs on f.1 and ff.83–4, which are omitted in Table 2.2; his description does not include the neumes for *Aurea personet* (CC10) and *Sponso sponsa* (CC25), but see Ziolkowski 1994, 191.

Table 2.3 Comparison of unnotated texts in **GB-Cu Gg.V.35** and CC which have concordances elsewhere with musical notation

GB-Cu Gg.V.35, fols 1–431

Folio	Text incipit
81v	*Cantemus socii domino*[37]
148r	*Senex fidelis prima*[38]
170r	*Carmina qui quondam*[39]
369r	*Sum noctis socia sum*[40]
-	Hymns[41]

GB-Cu Gg.V.35, fols 432–46 + new leaf (= CC)[42]

Folio	CC no.	Text incipit
432r	1	*Gratuletur omnis caro*
433r	6	*Omnis sonus cantilene*
434v	10	*Aurea personet lira*
434v	11	*Magnus cesar Otto*
435r	12	*Vite dator, omnifactor*
435v	13	*O pater optime*
436v	18	*Audax es, vir iuuenis*
437v	22	*Salve festa dies*
438v	27	*Iam dulcis amica*
439r/v	29/32	*Huc adtolle genas*
439v	31	*O mihi deserte*
439v	34	*Tempus erat quo prima*
441r	42	*In gestis partum veterum*
441v	44	*Hec est clara dies*
441v	45	*Rota modos arte*
441v	46	*Miserarum est nec amori*
443v	82	*David vates*

---

[37] For a description of a musical – and choreographic – performance of this chant in terms of the carol see Page 2010.

[38] For a reference to an alphabetical notation of this Prudentius text with further literature see Hornby 2010, 60. I am grateful to Sinéad O'Sullivan for information about Prudentius manuscripts and to Nicolas Bell for consulting the Cleopatra manuscript *in situ*.

[39] The transmission and edition of notated Boethian *metra* in the Middle Ages is presented in Barrett 2013.

[40] Details concerning the transmission of this *versus* as well as a melodic reconstruction can be found in Gillingham 1993, 40–45.

[41] This hymnic material spread throughout the earlier parts of the manuscript is described and edited in Dronke, Lapidge, and Stotz 1982.

[42] Information about neumatic notation in concordant sources from Lo Monaco 2009, 15–17, 'Tabella 2' (excluding *Hec est clara dies*).

In the main body of **GB-Cu Gg.V.35** they are glossed as part of the full text, whereas in the CC a handful of excerpts are neumed. It appears that the scribe was using multiple exemplars since the textual redactions are different. For one *metrum*, *Nubibus atris* (CC56), the text is entered a third time in the margins with a different neumation.[43]

For the purposes of exemplification, it is now possible to place one of the *Carmina Cantabrigiensia* under the microscope: *Hec est clara dies* (CC44). This may appear to be a peculiar choice since the liturgically coloured text for Easter is, at first sight, unremarkable, and in a different realm from the more exotic compositions in the collection. Yet its outer propriety is deceptive; it reveals a variety of details concerning the compositional choices in the CC.

Hec est clara dies (CC44), or at least its final segment, falls into that category of texts in **GB-Cu Gg.V.35** that seem to have been copied twice: the final distich is based on the famous *Salve festa dies* which appears as CC22. The history of this Latin poem in elegiac distichs by the sixth-century poet, Venantius Fortunatus, has been carefully laid out by Michel Huglo.[44] Having started out life addressed to Felix, bishop of Nantes, and praising spring and the resurrection, the poem was subsequently trans-formed from Carolingian times onwards in myriad ways – extirpation of the opening lines relating to spring, discarding the closing lines for the addressee, introduction of a refrain form, contrafacta procedures – into a processional chant for the liturgy. In other words, the poem underwent a process of performative appropriation. That *Salve festa dies* (CC22) appears in CC in excerpted form is not surprising: scribe A had already copied excerpts of lengthy Christian poems, such as *O dee cunctipotens* from Prudentius' *Hamartigenia*, in the first sections of **GB-Cu Gg.V.35**. Scribe A had also copied the abecedary poem by Sedulius, *A solis ortu cardine*, which the scribe could well have known as an Office hymn and which was 'excerpted' in **GB-Cu Gg.V.35** in the sense that its first strophe was furnished with neumes. The redaction of *Salve festa dies* in the CC on folios 437v–438r amounts to only five chosen distichs of Venantius Fortunatus' poem. The first is the standard liturgical distich hailing the perennial reverence of the day on which God triumphed over hell and attained the stars (originally ll.39–40). The following four distichs, which revel poetically in this triumphant pose, comprise ll.31–38 of the original

---

[43] For a facsimile see Gibson, Lapidge, and Page 1983, Plate V.

[44] The poem actually begins *Tempora florida*, with *Salve festa dies* only appearing after the springtime description is over at lines 39–40; for a complete, annotated edition of the text, see Huglo 2006, 603.

Venantius Fortunatus poem. Scribe A thus stopped copying the text at the point where the distich beginning *Salve festa dies* had originally had its rightful place, before it had been uprooted and moved back for performative reasons. This coincidence raises the question whether scribe A was copying from an exemplar which only contained an excerpt of the whole poem – the liturgical 'libretto', as it were – or had access, materially or memorially, to the complete poem by Venantius Fortunatus. The evidence is not conclusive. To take the cue 'Salve': this appears in the CC only after the second distich and is absent thereafter. Other manuscripts, however, repeat this cue word after every distich and clearly signal thereby the refrain function of the opening line of text. In addition, the first distich is not separated into its constituent hexameter and pentameter lines by punctuation sign and capital letter in the CC; this only occurs in distichs two to five. Finally, the next poem, CC23, begins with the image of woodlands which 'clothe the slender shoots/of boughs, laden with fruits' before continuing on with an ornithological fixation on birdsong. This has been interpreted as picking up the implicit springtime subject matter of CC22; implicit, because the really lush description of vernal plenitude occurs in those earlier parts of Venantius Fortunatus' poem that are absent from the CC.[45] Taken together, these arguments admittedly only provide the slightest hint that scribe A was using multiple exemplars which laid out the text *Salve festa dies* in different ways. More significant is the information concerning transmission that Huglo provides. According to his tables, the solid majority of manuscript sources in medieval Europe transmitting *Salve festa dies* as a processional chant contain a version longer than presented in the CC, with further distichs from Venantius Fortunatus. Only one other group of manuscripts in Huglo's table present the same number of distichs in the same order as the CC, and they all hail from Aquitaine.[46]

This geographical orientation is similarly in evidence in the transmission of *Hec est clara dies* (CC44) with concordances from Nevers (**F-Pn lat.9449** and **F-Pn n.a.lat.1235**, collectively 'Nevers'), Sens (**F-SEm 46**), Beauvais (**GB-Lbl Egerton 2615**) and Le Puy (**F-G 4413** and **F-LPbd A V 7 009**; collectively 'Le Puy'). Table 2.4 lays out the concordances for the various segments of the text with the manuscripts placed in descending order of age, from the eleventh to the sixteenth centuries.[47]

---

[45] Ziolkowski 1994, xix.   [46] Huglo 2006, 605.

[47] The last two manuscripts are described in Arlt 2000, 324–6; I am immensely grateful to Wulf Arlt for access to the treasure trove of his materials and transcriptions. This list expands the collation of concordances found in Ziolkowski 1994, 298 and Lo Monaco 2009, 64.

Table 2.4 Concordances and order of segments for *Hec est clara dies* (CC44)

Manuscript (Provenance, Date)	Folio											
GB-Cu Gg.V.35 (Canterbury, mid-11thC)	441v			1		3	4				8	9b	10a
F-Pn lat.9449 (Nevers, mid-11thC)	34r–v	10	9a	1		3	4	5	6	7			
F-Pn n.a.lat.1235 (Nevers, mid-12thC)	76v–77r			1		3	4	5	6	7		9a	
F-SEm 46 (Sens, first half of 13thC)	201v–202r			1	2		4						10b
GB-Lbl Egerton 2615 (Beauvais, first half of 13thC)	2r–v			1	2	3	4						10b
F-G 4413 (Le Puy, 16thC)	151v–152r			1	2	3	4						10a
F-LPbd A V 7 009 (Le Puy, 16thC)	184r–v			1	2	3	4						10a

1   Hec est clara dies clararum clara dierum
2   Hec est festa dies festarum festa dierum
3   Hec est sancta dies sanctarum sancta dierum
4   Nobile nobilium rutilans diadema dierum
5   Ecce dies toto rutilat festivior anno
6   Qua Deus omnipotens superata morte resurgens
7   Traxit ab infernis captorum mille cavernis
8   Quid est hoc tam dure quod in vestro manet pectore
     amarumque ducitis animum
     de Iesu nobis est dure manet in nos mors eius
     et ipsa mors est incognita
9a Namque nostre abiere atque Iesum invisere
     Celi cives dicunt illum vivum iam regnare
9b Nostre quedam abiere
     sepulturam invisere
     celi cives illum visum
     dicunt iam regnare
10 Salve festa dies [processional chant]
10a Salve festa dies salve resurrectio/circumcisio sancta
     salve semper ave lux hodierna vale
     ['lux hodierna vale' repeated twice in **F-G 4413** and **F-LPbd A V 7 009**]
10b Salve festa dies toto venerabilis evo
     qua dies est ortus virginis ex utero

Two points immediately demand attention. First, the redaction of *Hec est clara dies* in the CC shares the most materials – segments 1, 3, 4, 9, and 10 – with the manuscripts from Nevers; indeed, **F-Pn lat.9449**, dated to the second half of the eleventh century, is closest in date to the Canterbury collection. Second, segment 8 in CC44 appears to be a *unicum*.

Returning to the text of *Hec est clara dies*, the opening line recalls the beginning of carmen 63 by the Carolingian grammarian and poet Sedulius Scottus: 'Haec est alma dies, sanctarum sancta dierum'.[48] This poem in elegiac distichs praising spring and the 'day that the Lord Jesus has made' ('Hic est namque dies, dominus quem fecit Iesus') is definitely inspired in form, content, and even vocabulary by the Venantius Fortunatus poem. Whereas the sixth-century poem was not composed for liturgical purposes, its ninth-century imitation seemingly draws idealized descriptions of liturgical performance up into its texture. This does not only pertain to the allusion to the Gradual chant for Easter, *Haec dies quam fecit dominus*. After the vegetative excrescences of springtime, the ornithological returns as 'varied fowl soften the air with their song/They raise the trophies [of Christ against death] heavenward on their little springtide instruments.'[49] Meanwhile back on earth, 'the alleluia multiplies its pitches a hundredfold' which is a startling reference to the practice of the purely melodic elaboration of the Alleluia chant in the form of the *iubilus*.[50] Rather than functioning as a trope to the Gradual of the Mass, this text – or its imitation in *Hec est clara dies* (CC44) – instead reveals the interest of Carolingian poets in ennobling central liturgical chant texts by integrating them into a poetic form.[51] In the later process of the performative appropriation of the Sedulius Scottus poem, the distichs were dismantled, leaving only the opening hexameter line, which was then immediately repeated. This innate predisposition to anaphora is taken even further in the later manuscripts with a third permutation of the 'Hec est [. . .] dies' line. In all

---

[48] The correspondence was noted in Breul 1915, 72 and picked up by subsequent scholars. A critical edition of Sedulius Scottus's poem can be found in Meyers 1991, 104.

[49] The 'tropaea' would seem to be an allusion to line 86 of Venantius Fortunatus, 'Belliger ad caelos ampla tropaea refers' ('The wager of war [against death] bringing back to heaven the honourable trophies').

[50] For a discussion of the poem see Iversen 2009, 236.

[51] In Strecker 1926, 102 the lines in CC represent the 'remains of a trope-like structure which is preserved here more completely' ('Reste eines tropenartiges Gebildes, das hier vollständiger erhalten ist'); the lines are taken up in Ziolkowski 1994, 298 as a possible 'Easter trope to embellish [. . .] the gradual', qualified in Lo Monaco 2009, 64. Another example of the poetic imitation of liturgical chants is 'Gloriam deo in excelsis hodie' by Paulinus of Aquileia, analysed in Llewellyn 2004.

Example 2.1: A unit consisting of three or four lines whose musical structure is shaped A^a [A^a] A^{cl} B, where A^a utilizes an *apertum* ending modally and A^{cl} a *clausum*

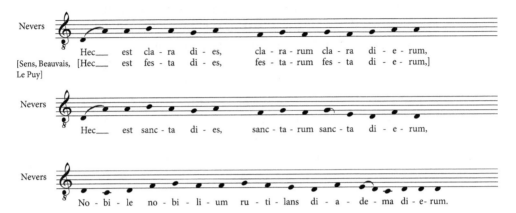

cases, this leads into a final hexameter line beginning 'Nobile nobilium'. The result is a unit consisting of three or four lines whose musical structure is shaped A^a [A^a] A^{cl} B, where A^a utilizes an *apertum* ending modally and A^{cl} a *clausum* (Example 2.1).

The transmission of segments 1 to 4, in both text and music, is remarkably stable. The additional 'Hec est...dies' line in the later manuscripts could be taken as a sign of the success of the original conception behind the unit as a whole. The Nevers manuscripts take this one step further and create a second, three-line strophe of hexameters (segments 5, 6 and 7), which uses the same melody as the first three-line strophe (segments 1, 3 and 4). Poetically, these new lines transform selected lines of the Venantius Fortunatus poem into rhyming leonine hexameters.[52] Given the stability of this opening unit, there is little chance to prise open the transmission by means of chronology or cultural exchange.

No such stability is in evidence with segment 9, 'Nostre quedam abiere' (to leave the *unicum* segment 8 'Quid est hoc' on one side). Transmitted only in the CC and Nevers manuscripts, the text is related to the biblical account from Luke's Gospel of the discussion between the two disciples and Christ on the road to Emmaus. Table 2.5 sets out the Bible text with the two versions of segment 9b.

---

[52] Line 39 'Salve festa dies, toto venerabilis aevo' becomes 'Ecce dies toto [toto dies in **F-Pn lat.9449**] rutilat festivior anno' (segment 5); l.40 'Qua deus infernum vicit et astra tenet' becomes 'Qua deus omnipotens superata morte resurgens' (segment 6); l.73 'Solve catenatas inferni carceris umbras' possibly becomes 'Traxit ab infernis captorum mille cavernis'.

Table 2.5 Synoptic comparison of Luke 24 with *Nostre quedem abiere* (segment 9b) in CC and Nevers

Luke, 24	CC	Nevers
22. Sed et mulieres quaedam ex nostris terruerunt nos	Nostre quedam abiere	Namque nostre abiere
ante lucem fuerunt ad monumentum	Sepulturam invisere	Atque Iesum invisere
23. et non invento corpore eius venerunt		
dicentes se etiam visionem angelorum videsse	Celi cives illum vivum	Celi cives dicunt
qui dicunt eum vivere	Dicunt iam regnare	Illum vivum iam regnare
24. et abierunt quidam ex nostris ad monumentum		
et ita invenerunt sicut mulieres dixerunt		

Ziolkowski characterizes the text in the CC as 'four rhythmic verses (8p + 8p + 8p + 6p)'.[53] The crucial difference with Nevers, however, would seem to be the placement of the word 'dicunt' in the transition of the third to the fourth lines: if syntax is followed, the lines would split 6p + 8p ('The heavenly citizens said/That He is now alive and reigns'), whereas a continuation of the 8p pattern from the first two lines would lead to a putative enjambment ('The heavenly citizens said that He/Is now alive and reigns'). This may seem a minuscule difference, but if processes of textual aggregation are central for understanding the compilation of the CC it is incumbent to probe further how and why such choices may have come about. Most obviously, it could be argued that the Nevers version of the text strays further from the biblical and, more specifically, Lucan account. 'Namque nostre' and 'Atque Iesum' in Nevers appear weak next to 'Nostre quedam' and 'Sepulturam' in the CC, although the reference to the experience of meeting the risen Christ is more Johannine than the revelation triggered by witnessing the empty tomb. Nevertheless, the sudden predilection for the enclitic in Nevers is suspicious, and could be explained by the context of 'Namque nostre' within the earlier Nevers manuscript, **F-Pn lat.9449**, which is contemporaneous to the CC.[54] Here 'Namque nostre' follows on

---

[53] Ziolkowski 1994, 299.

[54] For a colour reproduction of the folio in question (including the famous illumination of the two musicians) see http://gallica.bnf.fr/ark:/12148/btv1b8422992k/f76.item.

directly from the twelfth and final distich of *Salve festa dies,* performed with refrains. It seems, then, that the scribe of **F-Pn lat.9449** had already copied lines 33 and 34 of the Venantius Fortunatus poem which begin with 'Namque' and 'Undique'. This casts new light on the structuring of the text as 8p + 8p + 8p + 6p since *Salve festa dies,* with its elegiac distichs, operates on the basis of a hexameter line followed by a pentameter line which could be construed as a longer then slightly shorter line. Adding together the first and last two lines of 'Namque nostre' (16p + 14p) produces this effect. Moreover, this might explain the relative positioning of 'dicunt', which at first glance appears to be closer to the Bible text and thus renders the version in the CC at this point as the *lectio difficilior.* But the avoidance of enjambment in **F-Pn lat.9449** might be deliberate: it creates the illusion of the metrical caesura in the pentameter, the second half of an elegiac distich ('Celi cives dicunt | illum vivum iam regnare'). Thus, the version of 'Namque nostre' in **F-Pn lat.9449** would appear secondary as a result of being moulded on to *Salve festa dies.* This fusion was not a success: in the later Nevers manuscript from the twelfth century, **F-Pn n.a.lat.1235,** 'Namque nostre' appears in a different position entirely, preceded by the 'Hec est [. . .] dies' unit.

An alternative explanation would regard 'Namque nostre' in Nevers as representing an original version and the collectors behind the CC pluckily banging it into better rhythmical shape and trimming its text back more closely to the biblical language. But these Canterbury collectors also seemed to suffer from an urge for the elegiac since the segment copied directly after 'Nostre quedam' in the CC was inspired by Venantius Fortunatus: not a direct quotation from *Salve festa dies,* but an imitation of a distich which poetically greets in an almost tautological manner the feast-day, the Resurrection, and the Easter light. Scribe A had already copied *Salve festa dies* into the CC earlier (as CC22) and, inspired by the Easter subject matter, may well have decided to round off CC44 with a more freshly minted formulation: the repetitions of 'salve', 'ave' and 'vale' – the last two resulting in a rhymed pentameter – are reminiscent of the acclamation in anaphora of the holy day in the opening 'Hec est [. . .] dies' unit. This would astutely provide a frame surrounding the inner segments 8 and 9 of CC44, which deal with the Emmaus and Tomb narratives, while simultaneously charging the refrain function of the 'Salve festa dies' distich with a new force. From the perspective of transmission, this newer 'Salve festa dies' distich cannot be found in the Nevers manuscripts, either young or old, but it does occur following on from 'Hec est clara dies' in manuscripts from the twelfth century onwards in connection with the Office for

Example 2.2: 'Nostre quedam' and 'Salve sancta dies' reconstructed from concordances

the Circumcision.[55] The displacement liturgically from Easter to Circumcision must have been a later phenomenon, but this does not mean that the
knowingly repetitive 'Salve festa dies' formulation originated in the CC as
the earliest witness. Perhaps the Canterbury scribe was, indeed, inspired
associatively by the musicality of the texts being joined together, although
the evidence from the melodic version of 'Nostre quedam' and 'Salve
sancta dies' as reconstructed from concordances is ambiguous
(see Example 2.2).

It is difficult to try and discern historical priority between the versions
from musical analysis: the melodic language, essentially syllabic and reminiscent of antiphons, allows for flexibility in syntactic articulation. Thus in
the Nevers version the word 'dicunt' lands on the final *D*; there is no reason
why a modal articulation could not be made here. Indeed, the melody then
continues using a gesture already heard from 1.2 ('atque Iesum invisere')
except that this time a *clausum* ending on *D* is deployed, instead of an

---

[55] As laid out in the materials collated by Wulf Arlt; see fn47 above.

apertum on the lower second, *C*. Alternatively, the melody could articulate the hypothetical melodic reconstruction of the text in the CC supremely well in that the four-note gesture *D-C-D-F* on 'Celi cives' is then echoed on *E-D-F-G* at 'illum vivum' before leading into a four-note stepwise descent – heard previously on 'abiere' and imagined at 'invisere' – on 'dicunt iam reg-(nare)'. Thus the last two lines could be articulated after six syllables at 'dicunt' in Nevers, after eight syllables at 'vivum' in the CC or else without articulation as a single, long line of fourteen syllables. The flexibility is a facet of performance, not notation. This also seems to inform the musical dovetailing of the following segment, 'Salve festa dies', which circles around *F* and rises to *a* before falling to *E* which proves to be the final. The shift from mode 2 to mode 4 pragmatically re-designates certain pitches and demonstrates, again, how performance can convincingly paper over theoretical cracks. It is, therefore, no wonder that this flexibility also manifests itself in material form in the CC through the use of punctuation: the catchy rhythm and rhyme of 'Nostre quedam' is actually read by the insertion of *punctus* marks as two long lines, rather than four shorter ones; and, alternatively, the long line of 'Salve festa dies' is actually broken down into two by a mark after 'dies'.[56]

If the glue holding together the constituent elements of CC44 does not appear to be of an aesthetic consistency, the prime motivation behind the concoction would appear to be functional: Guido Maria Dreves noted in his edition of 'Nostre quedam' in *Analecta hymnica* that the text came 'presumably from an Easter play', a viewpoint taken up by subsequent scholars.[57] This was an inspired intuition since none of the concordant manuscripts reveal such a function for the text which otherwise appears either in a processional context for Easter (Nevers) or else in connection with the excessive festivities for the Office of the Circumcision (Sens, Beauvais, Le Puy). Nevertheless, the question-and-answer format of the *unicum* segment in CC beginning 'Quid est hoc?' coupled with change between second ('in vestro manet pectore [. . .] ducitis animum') and first person plural ('manet in nos mors eius') inevitably calls to mind the 'Quem

---

[56] This can be clearly seen in the photographic reproduction of folio 441v in Breul 1915, and Lo Monaco 2009, 238 actually edits 'Nostre quedam' like this (but without the helpful punctuation marks around the dialogue in Ziolkowski 1994, 122–3). In CC22, *Salve festa dies*, none of the lines is broken up into two in this way (Breul 1915, plates 437v–438r).

[57] 'Vermutlich aus einem Osterspiel', Dreves *AH* 50:80 in the critical apparatus to his edition of *Salve festa dies*, taken up by Strecker 1926, 102; Ziolkowski 1994, 298, 'this song, which is partly dramatic'; and Lo Monaco 2009, 64, 'molto probabilmente anche CC 44 doveva avere. . .una recitazione drammatica'.

quaeritis?' dialogue between the heavenly messengers and followers of Christ at the tomb on Easter Sunday, which assumed a number of forms and positions within the medieval liturgy.[58] The success of such ritualized dialogues led to newer compositions on other topics, such as the *peregrinus* play relating the story of disciples on the road to Emmaus.[59] In the case of 'Quid est hoc' in the CC, however, the scholarly critique has been withering. Strecker bemoaned the fact that the wording of the text was 'difficult to understand' whereas Spanke caustically characterized the Latinity as 'barbaric' and 'feral'.[60] Could this, too, have been the work of the notorious 'Zudichter', the 'bypoet' who composed additional segments of text in the CC to supplement what was before him? According to Spanke, he was responsible for the additional versicle 3c in the sequence CC14 which languished in the critical apparatus of the earlier editions until Ziolkowski restored it as CC14a.[61] Admittedly, the Latinity of the interpolated sequence versicle is far superior to the halting dialogue of 'Quid est hoc?', although, as Ziolkowski lucidly notes in his edition, there is some attempt to organize the prose of the latter poetically in the approximately equal line-lengths between question and answer and the prominent placement of 'dure' as the affective, rhyming heart of both. Moreover, both the additional versicle 3a in CC14 and 'Quid est hoc?' make recourse to Biblical language. What then ultimately saves 'Quid est hoc?' and its apparently execrable Latinity from being relegated to the critical apparatus, from being quarantined as CC44a? The simple answer would be the difference in form between a sequence and a trope. But this would presuppose a difference between the 'Zudichter' of the sequence and the 'Tropator'.[62] The results might vary in quality between the *Kunstprosa* of a sequence and the readier tropes and, of course, proems, but the urge to aggregate, supplement, and comment is surely the same.[63] Moreover, there is no reason necessarily in this case to make a 'Troubadour' out of the

---

[58] The literature on 'Quem quaeritis' is vast; for the latest study see Rankin 2008.

[59] See Mahone 1977. Her manuscripts begin in the twelfth century with Beauvais; the ritual dialogues comprise a liturgical 'compilation' of antiphons rather than new compositions and there are no concordances with the CC.

[60] Strecker 1926, 102, 'Der Wortlaut ist schwer verständlich' and Spanke 1942, 123, 'barbarisches Latein' and 124, 'verwildertes Latein'.

[61] For the reference to the 'Zudichter' see Spanke 1942, 115 and the edition of CC14a in Ziolkowski 1994, 68–9.

[62] The reference to the 'Tropator' and its putative etymological connection to 'Trobador' can be found in Spanke 1942, 124.

[63] The crucial term 'aggregate' is used in the typological description of poetic collections framed in Sannelli 2005.

'Tropator' since another explanation for the enigmatic Latinity of 'Quid est hoc?' presents itself; namely, that the text was meant to be enigmatic. Included in the earlier sections of **GB-Cu Gg.V.35** are a series of *Enigmata* or 'riddles' by Eusebius, Tatwine, Boniface, Simphosius and Aldhelm in whose copying scribe A participated. These supplied ideal materials for classroom teaching, as testified to by the frequent glosses in **GB-Cu Gg. V.35**. The connection between riddles and Easter plays celebrating the Resurrection is the staged acquisition of knowledge, through revelation, in the form of a dialogue.

The CC as a whole present a panoply of dialogues. Moreover, these dialogues manifest themselves across a dazzling diversity in both content and form and could thus be considered key to a fresh appreciation of the collection.[64] Across the parchment leaves of the CC Archbishop Heriger and the false man, the humble Swabian and his wanton wife, Abba John and his taller companion, Christ and Cleophas on the road to Emmaus each debate a single moral quandary and thus furnish plentiful materials for the contemplation of *exempla* or even for role-playing exercises. Even when the passages of direct speech are not clothed in dialogue form but are monologues – such as certain excerpts from the Classics (Vergil, Statius) and, by extrapolation, Boethius' first-person *metrum* opening the *De con-solatione philosophiae* – an audience is implied, if only by the passionate and pathos-laden content of the texts. Beyond content, the dialogical quality of the CC infuses an appreciation of form: in the strophe–antistrophe form of the sequence; in the amplificatory function of a trope; or in the introductory scene-setting of a proem. Moreover, performance indications such as cue words for refrains or imperative forms of words ('cane', 'pange', and so on) suggest the interaction between different groups or protagonists. Finally, there is a conscious dialogue between old and new – including with the materials from the earlier sections of **GB-Cu Gg.V.35** – whereby older texts can be taken up and transformed in some way: a dialogue between textual aggregation and performative appropriation.[65]

An appreciation of the richness of tradition and continuity between old and new marked out Benedictine culture in the Middle Ages. Morality – or

---

[64] See, however, the question of reciprocity addressed in Bayless 2005.

[65] Indeed, this process of transformation even forms part of the opening lines of CC42: 'In the deeds of the early fathers I read a certain amusing story. . .that I will tell you in rhythmic poem,' ('In gestis partum veterum quoddam legi ridiculum. . .quod vobis dicam rithmice') in Ziolkowski 1994, 118–19.

the concern for and cultivation of right living – underpinned the daily life of the community. This is reflected in the contents of **GB-Cu Gg.V.35** with writings on sobriety by Milo and on virginity by Aldhelm as well as in the poem by Columban on the 'observation of good morals'. However, morality was not only a matter of contents, but also a matter of form and performance. The dialogue form provided just such an arena for exploration of these issues, as did performance. In a text compiled by Lanfranc, archbishop of Canterbury, after the Norman Conquest, the singer who 'falls by the wayside' and 'deviates' in the performance of a chant is to be led back on to 'the path'.[66] The individual charged with carrying out this musical and moral task 'with foresight and preparedness' is the cantor. Only a couple of decades earlier in the CC, the character of the cantor is constructed before our eyes in the proem *Caute cane, cantor care* (CC 30).[67] An earlier attempt at such a construction at the end of *Gratulemur omnis caro* (CC1, thus *Caute cane, caute cane* as CC1A) had been aborted after a few words, but in an alliterative string of words commencing with the letter 'c', the cantor gradually comes to life in CC30. He should exercise caution or prudence, but is dearly cherished by the community. Above all, he should 'take the right path': right living and right performance go hand-in-hand in a text whose dialogical ambition is realized through accumulation, aggregation and association. In many ways, CC30 stands for the CC as a whole. Perhaps a later reader of this enlightening manuscript grasped the value of this one, small text, because at some point an individual entered a ruffed *manicula* above it, not finger-wagging in a moralistic manner, but pointing to the creative achievements of Benedictine culture.

---

[66] Knowles 1951, 118, 'ne eueniat neglegentia in quocunque obsequio' and 'si quis [...] iam bene incepto aliquo modo deuiauerit, ipse [the cantor] debet esse prouisus atque paratus'.

[67] Famous since every word in the poem begins with the letter 'c', just like the earlier poem in **GB-Cu Gg.V.35** by Hucbald which praises baldness; see Ziolkowski 1994, 98–9 for an edition of the text and 264–7 for the commentary.

3 | Across divides: Aquitaine's new song and London, British Library, Additional 36881

RACHEL MAY GOLDEN

The medieval manuscript London, British Library, Additional 36881 (hereafter **GB-Lbl Add.36881**) is a small, personal collection of twelfth-century Aquitanian song, one that preserves contemporaneous cultural expressions, new song forms, and traces of living performance. Featuring the new *versus* genre, the manuscript is known as a *versarium*, a twelfth-century term that persists in modern scholarship.[1] As such, **GB-Lbl Add.36881** shares characteristics and repertory with three other Aquitanian *versaria*: **F-Pn lat.1139**, **F-Pn lat.3545**, and **F-Pn lat.3719**, respectively. Although **GB-Lbl Add.36881** did not circulate with these other manuscripts, it maintains close relationships with them, exhibiting song concordances, likenesses in musical style, related literary themes, and the imprint of a similar monastic milieu.

The Aquitanian *versus*, newly cultivated in twelfth-century Occitania, feature Latin, rhymed, accentual, and strophic poetry, set to both monophonic and two-part polyphonic music. They reflect a preoccupation with the newly budding cult of the Virgin Mary: many *versus* contemplate and explore new ideas about theologies surrounding Mary, and her relationship to Christ – as mother, as bride, as *mediatrix*, and others – in a time when these roles were being reinterpreted. The pieces also present some ambiguities surrounding liturgical function, and they dynamically interact with their surrounding secular context.

But the contents and origins of the manuscripts that collect these *versus* prove more diverse than the phrase 'Aquitanian *versaria*' might imply. The *versaria* are not single entities, but rather comprise smaller manuscript books or libelli. While named for the preponderance of *versus* they contain, the manuscripts incorporate other genres too, often comparatively neglected in contemporary scholarship, such as Mass Ordinary tropes, Mass and Office proses, freestanding prayers, epistles, and liturgical drama. Featuring both polyphony and monophony, the *versaria* retain some of the earliest known examples of Western practical polyphony, representing

---

[1] Grier 1990, 6; Chailley 1960, 260–1.

sung liturgical and paraliturgical usages rather than purely theoretical examples. These pieces include instances of organal lines added to a pre-existing *cantus*, as well as two-voice settings in which both voices were newly composed. They also employ innovative polyphonic techniques, integrating both florid and discant styles. Collectively the *versaria* span the entirety of the twelfth century. With **GB-Lbl Add.36881** falling at the latter end, it is the youngest of the group.

GB-Lbl Add.36881 reveals an awareness of text–music relationships typical of the new song genres of twelfth-century Occitania. The manuscript indicates the close integration of monophonic and polyphonic composition, resisting the sharp divide between monophony and polyphony often adopted by evolutionary models of music history. Further, **GB-Lbl Add.36881** attests to the self-conscious cultivation of a novel polyphonic style, crossovers between secular and sacred spheres, and monastic musings on creative theologies, the Virgin Mary, and the meaning of Christmas miracles.

Originally held at the medieval library of the Abbey of St Martial under the connoisseurship of its head librarian, Bernard Itier (1163–1225), the three Paris *versaria* were sold to the Bibliothèque nationale (then the Bibliothèque du roi) in the eighteenth century. **GB-Lbl Add.36881**, in contrast, did not pass through Bernard's collection, and little is known of its history until the British Museum purchased it in 1904.[2] **GB-Lbl Add.36881** carries some old but uninformative shelfmarks that bear witness to stages of its journey prior to its purchase by the British Museum from one P. Birb.[3] Although Bruno Stäblein speculated that the manuscript derived from the Franco-Spanish border region, perhaps near Apt or Catalonia, more recent scholars trace the manuscript simply to Aquitaine or a nearby Occitanian province.[4] Similarly, earlier scholarship that posited St Martial as the specific musical centre of the Aquitanian *versus* (based on the presence of the *versaria* there) has since unravelled, as has the related notion of a 'St Martial school' of composition.[5] Sarah Fuller has instead repositioned the repertory as a less centralized and more broadly based Aquitanian body of music.[6]

Owing to a traditionally teleological tendency in musicology to emphasize Notre-Dame polyphony as the culminating compositional achievement of

---

[2] Grier 1990, 48–9.

[3] Ibid.; see also the images via www.diamm.ac.uk/jsp/Descriptions?op=SOURCE&source Key=919 (login required).

[4] Stäblein 1963, 344–6.

[5] See, for example, Spanke 1928–32; Dronke 1968, 288–94.   [6] Fuller 1979.

the high Middle Ages, Aquitanian manuscripts have often been neglected or misrepresented. Early scholarship on **GB-Lbl Add.36881** and related *versaria* reinforced a divide between monophony and polyphony, although they appear side-by-side in the same manuscripts. Two important dissertations were organized along these lines. Fuller's treatment of the *versaria* dealt exclusively with its polyphony, providing codicological source studies and establishing score editions.[7] On the other hand, Leo Treitler's work on the same manuscripts focused solely on monophony and especially treated melodic constructions.[8] While both scholars dealt with interactions between formal poetic structure and musical structure, neither, notably, discussed textual meaning. Since then, Treitler, Margaret Switten, James Grier, and others have more strongly stressed semantic content as an important consideration in understanding the *versus*, its significance and meaning.[9]

Along with Fuller's dissertation, three published editions present the polyphony: those of Bryan Gillingham, Theodore Karp, and Hendrik Van der Werf.[10] As evinced by their titles and contents, these editions treat the two-part works as a discrete subdivision of the Aquitanian repertory, not as part of an integrated whole that includes monophony. Karp further posited a sharp melodic and rhythmic differentiation between the polyphonic *versus* and the chant repertory. Focusing on contrapuntal combinations, notational patterns and performance-based perspectives, Karp unusually rendered the Aquitanian square notation in patterned rhythmic modes similar to those used in Notre-Dame organum. Most scholars, however, transcribe the polyphony in freer rhythms, as Fuller does, and my own transcriptions in the examples below follow this convention. Roughly contemporaneous with Karp's publication, Van der Werf offered an edition of Aquitanian polyphony with a more theoretical, rather than practical, bent, closer to a diplomatic transcription.

Grier's contributions to the scholarship are significant, offering an understanding of the codicological and stemmatic features of the *versaria* and meaningfully positioning the works in the context of monastic devotion in Aquitaine.[11] The latter strain of work has been particularly influential on my own research, which deals with the *versus* as monastic

---

[7] Fuller 1969.   [8] Treitler 1967.
[9] Treitler 1995; Grier 1994; Switten 1999. See also Golden Carlson 2003.
[10] Gillingham 1984; Karp 1992; Van der Werf 1993; see also Crocker 1994 and Karp 1999.
[11] See especially Grier 1985; Grier 1988; Grier 1990; Grier 1992; and Grier 1994.

inspiration, theological exploration, and instances of devotion to the Virgin within the context of the twelfth-century Marian cult.

The history of the *versus* proves intertwined with that of the Abbey of St Martial in Limoges. Even though **GB-Lbl Add.36881** was not collected there, its contents reflect the same environment, and many pieces it contains concord with the Paris manuscripts once housed at St Martial. This Benedictine abbey enjoyed a rich musical culture that included tropes, *sequentiae*, and proses, as well as Office and Mass Liturgies for St Martial. In the eleventh century, following substantial financial losses, the abbey was sold to Cluny, which significantly affected musical activities. The conservative Cluniac liturgy favoured straightforward psalmody, devoid of ornamentation or liturgical embellishment; accordingly, office manuscripts indicate that the abbey's liturgical individuality was suppressed under Cluny, since unique components of eleventh-century St Martial offices subsequently disappear.[12] Likewise, production of sequences and tropes at St Martial significantly decreased as Cluny approved only of melodic elaborations of the Alleluia as liturgical ornamentation.[13] Given these liturgical constraints, James Grier suggests that the *versus* was 'fulfilling a need, felt by both composer and listener, for a less formal medium in which to express ideas about the faith that they shared. [The] need to communicate about the substance of Christianity had outgrown the restrictions of the liturgy'.[14] Grier further submits that the primary motivation for *versus* composition and use was personal contemplation on the part of monks who were 'so pious [...] that [they] used their leisure time to create, perform, and listen to sacred songs of an informal nature'.[15]

This monastic environment animated the *versus* repertory and its integration with the twelfth-century Marian cult.[16] *Versus* in **GB-Lbl Add.36881** frequently express Marian devotion by referencing contemporaneous reinterpretations of the Song of Songs as pioneered by twelfth-century monks and theologians, including Honorius Augustoduensis, Rupert of Deutz, and Bernard of Clairvaux.[17] Theologically, the *versaria*'s focus on Mary's virginity and her role in Christ's Incarnation honours Mary as a vehicle for Christ's materiality, a force of physical and spiritual strength against demons and heathen enemies. In so doing, *versus* stress Mary's unaltered chastity and innocence, vividly depicting these ideas

[12] Grier 2000; Golden Carlson 2003, 530–1.
[13] Fassler 1993, 114–15; Grier 1994; Golden Carlson 2003, 30–31.
[14] Grier 1994, 1069.   [15] Grier 1994, 1047.
[16] Golden Carlson 2000, 9–21 and *passim*; Golden Carlson 2006.   [17] Fulton 2002, 351–404.

through reference to biblical allegories of flowering purity, including Gideon's fleece, Daniel's mountain, the burning bush of Exodus, and Jesse's rod.[18]

Free lyrical use of biblical motifs in the creation of the *versus* resonates with the practice of active reading known as *lectio divina*, by which monks internalized Scripture and incorporated it into their beings.[19] Monastic reading entailed not only looking with the eyes, but also pronouncing with the lips and listening to the articulated words with the ears, engaging multiple senses. In this way, reading is akin to *meditatio*, which, through contemplation of Scripture, combines speaking, thinking, and remembering as three aspects of the same activity in which one 'pronounce[s] the sacred words in order to retain them'.[20] The frequently employed and creatively recombined biblical themes in the *versus* represent manifestations of internalized Scripture; they substantiate the active practice of medieval *ars memoria* and some of its implications for music making.[21]

The pieces contained in the Aquitanian *versaria* are contemporary with, and arose in the same regions as, the troubadour culture of Occitania. The two genres enacted common interests, not only in their kindred adoption of large-scale formal structures and poetic themes, but also in their reflection of Occitanian cultural context and the aesthetics of new song composition.[22] Both genres express intense personal devotions or desires with a strong sense of self-reflection, self-consciousness, and new intellectual exploration, all qualities consistent with twelfth-century notions of individuality and subjectivity.[23] Further, both genres often articulate devotion to a feminine beloved.

Notably, both *versus* and troubadour song emblemize a kind of 'new song' or *nova cantica*, a phrase employed by Wulf Arlt in reference to the Aquitanian *versus*.[24] These new songs contrasted with older liturgical works such as hymns, sequences, and liturgical tropes by employing language in an integrally new way, featuring poetic texts with rhymed and syllabic accentual structures. Further, their music corresponded in kind, with 'balanced phrase structures and regular cadence patterns' that

---

[18] Golden Carlson 2000, 76–146.   [19] Golden Carlson 2003, especially 531–8.

[20] LeClercq 1982, 15–16.

[21] Important discussions of this topic include Carruthers 2008 and Busse Berger 2005.

[22] Studies on relationships between troubadours and *versus* include Spanke 1936; Chailley 1955; Treitler 1995. An extensive bibliography of such studies is given in Switten 2007, 92n2.

[23] Grier 1994; Golden Carlson 2003. On the troubadours see, for example, Kay 1990; Peraino 2011.

[24] Arlt 1986; Arlt 1992.

reflected the text and was conceived concurrently with it.[25] Fuller characterized *versus* poetry as '*poesia per musica*' that was 'evidently conceived from the beginning as song'.[26] While the troubadours accomplished this unity between text and music in the Occitan vernacular, *versus* explored similar possibilities in Latin. Margaret Switten notes, 'in a larger sense, the term "New Song" can be used to refer to the immensely creative outburst of song-making in Europe in the early twelfth century'.[27]

Intermittently, French and Latin languages even occur in combination within single *versus* or troubadour songs. Such cross-fertilization of Latin and vernacular language, and sacred and secular themes, rests at the very origins of new song. Many troubadours were steeped in learned Latin culture and Christian institutions; their work relied on Latin models, and even occasionally, as in Marcabru's *Pax in nomine domini*, contains insertion of Latin language. Conversely, the *versus* repertory incorporates elements of Occitan language, particularly in the earliest *versaria*. For example, the *versus O maria deu maire* (**F-Pn lat.1139**, ff.49r–50r)[28] employs Occitan rather than Latin in its entirety, and *In hoc anni circulo* (**F-Pn lat.1139**, ff.48r–49r)[29] alternates Latin and Occitan throughout. Such fluidity is also evident in the lives of troubadours, who crossed from the courtly arena into the monasteries, as did Bertran de Born and Folquet de Marseilles.[30]

An examination of the twelfth-century *versaria* reveals mingling between oral and written transmissions. Falling at the late end of this temporal spectrum, **GB-Lbl Add.36881** exhibits a greater concern for textual culture than earlier *versaria*. As Grier remarks, 'scribes were gradually increasing the specificity of that notation [the musical notation found in Aquitanian *versaria*], and thus were moving continually towards a literate tradition, a transition not fully achieved in the youngest manuscript witnesses of the repertory'.[31] This increased musical literacy is evident in regular use of clefs, indications of text–music alignment, and score notation that prescribes specific pitch locations and the polyphonic relationship between the voices.

Yet memory and orality also persist in **GB-Lbl Add.36881**. The small size of the manuscript precludes the possibility that it was used as a reading score during the moment of performance itself.[32] Rather, like many

---

[25] Switten 1999, 141.   [26] Fuller 1969, 1:10.   [27] Switten 2007, 93.
[28] http://gallica.bnf.fr/ark:/12148/btv1b6000946s/f105.image.
[29] http://gallica.bnf.fr/ark:/12148/btv1b6000946s/f103.image.
[30] See, for example, Schulman 2001; Paden, Sankovitch, and Stäblein 1986, 24–8.
[31] Grier 1990, 21.   [32] Ibid.; Treitler 1981.

medieval manuscripts, it must have functioned as a reference, and therefore represents only one of a complex set of tools employed in musical memory and singing. Yet, as discussed below, its role as a reference does not preclude its applicability to performance. On the contrary, markings in the manuscript suggest that it served practical purposes, such as clarifying voice coordination and phrasing.

The variations in concordant works among the *versaria* also speak to the continued importance of orality and the agency of the singer as he engaged in the act of performance. Grier describes the 'musical texts' of the *versus* as being in 'a constant state of change', with each individual copy of a song representing an individual 'aesthetic and musical sense' with a 'personal repertory of variants'.[33] Importantly, this situation parallels the transmission of the interrelated troubadour repertory. Circulating orally over the twelfth century, troubadour songs were committed to writing and musical notation only in the late thirteenth century in locations across Occitania, northern France, and Italy. The variable and collaborative acts of composition, copying, and performance (among composers, performers, and scribes) that characterized the repertory therefore involved a fundamental changeability, re-creation, or *mouvance*. This aesthetic is reflected in a spirit of improvisation and collective composition; aspects of spontaneity and variability emerge in various nuances of writing and of melodic and textual difference among multiple versions of troubadour chansons.[34]

Like the other Aquitanian *versaria*, **GB-Lbl Add.36881** is a composite manuscript. It contains two libelli, referred to in scholarly literature as DI and DII (by Fuller) or as 36881a and 36881b (by Grier). The two are copied by different scribes, but demonstrate similarities in layout and in format and likely emerged from the same, or nearby, scriptoriums in close temporal proximity to one another. The dating of **GB-Lbl Add.36881** as relatively late – to the end of twelfth century or c.1200 – is based on several features of the manuscript's presentation. Fuller has noted **GB-Lbl Add.36881**'s compressed hand, frequent use of textual abbreviations, and vertical strokes found on individual letters.[35] While **GB-Lbl Add.36881** preserves monophonic song, another aspect of its lateness is its particular interest in polyphonic settings: its musical notation carefully directs the relationship between the two voices by arranging them into generously spaced vertical alignment (score notation), and

---

[33] Grier 1988, 410.

[34] See, for example, Van der Werf 1972, 26–34; Van Vleck 1991, especially 71–90; Zumthor 1992.

[35] Fuller 1979, 20.

using vertical strokes to further guide how upper and lower parts fit together. Further, the note shapes of both voices are comparatively uniform and legible, square or oblong in shape and carefully heighted in relation to the C and F clefs.

GB-Lbl Add.36881 proffers a modest, personal collection of favourite pieces.[36] It is the smallest of the Aquitanian *versaria*, comprising only twenty-four folios, and humble in its physical dimensions, measuring 16cm x 10.5cm.[37] Uniquely among the Aquitanian *versaria*, **GB-Lbl Add.36881** contains only lyric-musical items, no prose pieces such as sermons, tracts, or letters. These contents further intimate that **GB-Lbl Add.36881** resulted from a mindful cultivation of a musical identity; the manuscript asserts an apparent self-consciousness as a songbook.

This emphasis on musical settings is reinforced by the manuscript layout, evidently devised to expedite the reading and writing of the musical notation: the layout of the polyphony is standardized, even across the two libelli, with a regularly sized page frame and consistently ruled dry point lines. These techniques, along with the unique score notation employed, should be understood as new scribal technologies designed for the repertory at hand: as Elizabeth Aubrey writes, 'scribes of the thirteenth century were caught among several musical traditions (plainchant, courtly monophony, sacred and secular polyphony), and they had to struggle to develop notations appropriate to each'.[38] Likewise, the manuscript features polyphonic pieces and intricate polyphonic techniques. Indeed, **GB-Lbl Add.36881** preserves a larger preponderance of polyphony than earlier manuscripts, witnessing the increasing popularity of practical polyphony over the course of the twelfth century.

In addition, the polyphonies of **GB-Lbl Add.36881** demonstrate an inventive and distinctive style of discant polyphony, one that employs pronounced contrary motion between the voices, sequences, palindromic gestures, symmetrical or mirroring motion, and voice exchange.[39] On the basis of these features, Treitler described **GB-Lbl Add.36881** as typified by the 'spirit [...] of the magic square and the palindrome', displaying the 'greatest preference for symmetry' in its counterpoint among the *ver-saria*.[40] These characteristics are not typical of the earliest Aquitanian polyphonies, which are freer in form, often with a more loosely conceived, quasi-improvisatory florid style. According to Jens Bonderup, the budding

---

[36] See Grier 1990, 56.   [37] Gillingham 1987, iv.   [38] Aubrey 1993, 2357.
[39] See Golden Carlson 2006, 637–8; Golden Carlson 2000, 44–7; Fuller 1969, 1:295–309.
[40] Treitler 1964, 38.

discant style such as that found in **GB-Lbl Add.36881** was marked by its incorporation of 'progressive elements'.[41]

The first libellus (hereafter DI) of the manuscript comprises ff.1r–16v. DI features well-circulated musical works, with 61 per cent of the compositions concordant with other *versaria*.[42] A number of works too appear in contemporary song manuscripts such as the Madrid Tropers (**E-Mn 288** and **E-Mn 289**, both from Sicily), **F-Pn lat.1120** (a St Martial troper-proser in Aquitanian notation), and **F-Pn lat.778** (a twelfth-century troper-proser from Narbonne), among others.[43] DI contains *versus*, tropes of the Sanctus, two Latin rondeau songs and *Benedicamus Domino versus* settings. Strictly defined, the latter pieces are tropes of the dismissal formula for the divine office, '*Benedicamus Domino Deo gratias*'. Fuller, however, calls these pieces *Benedicamus versus* rather than *Benedicamus* tropes because in music and text the *Benedicamus Domino* settings correspond closely with the ordinary *versus* that feature freely composed texts.[44] *Benedicamus Domino versus* occasionally carry the rubric *Benedicamus*, but mostly convey no distinguishing markings from other *versus* in the manuscripts, as is the case in **GB-Lbl Add.36881**.

This last point reinforces the fluid paraliturgical and liturgical functions of sacred *versus* within the liturgy. *Versus* exist alongside tropes of liturgical genres, such as, in DI, of the Sanctus and the *Benedicamus Domino*; pieces of differing genres are infrequently distinguished from one another. The similarity in style between ordinary *versus* and *Benedicamus Domino versus* further suggests blurring between liturgy, paraliturgy, and devotion. Along similar lines, Gillingham has argued for functional mutability at the core of the Aquitanian *versus* (some of which he refers to as conductus), positing that they arise from a 'natural creative penchant for hybridization', drawing on hymns, sequences, and twelfth-century polyphonic trends.[45] Additionally demonstrating synthesis between Latin and vernacular genres, DI contains two Latin rondeaux on f.16v, *Ave mater salvatoris* (discussed further below) and *Virga floruit/Virgo deum*.

The scribe of DI organized its contents by number of voices: pieces for two voices appear first on ff.1r–13v. Fuller cites this organization by number of voice parts, soon to become a predominant manner of organizing music manuscripts, as an important shift in conceptualizing

---

[41] Bonderup 1982, 26.   [42] Grier 1988, 262.
[43] See Fuller 1969, 2:399–402, for a catalogue of pieces and concordances.
[44] Fuller 1969, 1:22–5.   [45] Gillingham 1991, 66–9.

the arrangement of musical texts.[46] Some of DI's polyphonic works are re-settings of *versus* that appear in monophonic dress in earlier *versaria*. These adaptations reflect the late-twelfth-century vogue for polyphony and the high medieval tastes for elaboration, additive processes, and reuse of pre-existing melody. Further, *versus* recast as polyphony locate the 'newness' of some song in the process of revision and reinterpretation, rather than solely in the creation of new melodic foundations. The act of transformation involved in such adaptation recalls the parallel to the troubadour concept of *mouvance*.

Between DI and the second libellus (hereafter DII), an unknown number of folios are missing: the final piece of DI is incomplete at its end, while the first piece of DII is incomplete at its beginning.[47] DII comprises ff.17r–24v and contains *versus, Benedicamus Domino versus*, a partial prose, and a prayer to St Nicholas (*Ora pro nobis Sancte Nicholas*) for two voices.[48] Once again, polyphonic pieces precede monophonic ones, an organization that highlights the polyphonic works.

Several pieces at the end of DII were entered with text only, with no space allotted for music. These pieces appear intermixed among the monophonic *versus* that do have preserved melodies. The melodic omissions occur only in the monophonic section of the book, further establishing the scribe's particular emphasis on polyphonic pieces, whose musical settings he renders completely and often meticulously. To my knowledge these unnotated pieces are *unica*, but perhaps their melodies were well enough known or sufficiently remembered at the time of their copying to render their notation unnecessary.

For instance, the unnotated piece *Letetur orbis hodie* (a *Benedicamus Domino versus*) features twelve lines of text, with each odd line ending in the refrain 'Fulget dies', and each even line ending in 'Fulget dies ista'. The manuscript transmits the text of this song as heavily abbreviated, perhaps indicating that the song enjoyed enough currency to be known to its likely readers with only minimal cues; closely written, it fills out only six tightly spaced lines on ff.23r–23v.[49] One can imagine that this song, with a readily

---

[46] Fuller 1979, 23.   [47] Grier 1990, 49–50.

[48] Nicholas and Mary Magdalene are important secondary figures of devotion in the *versus*; their presence in these pieces suggests possibilities for locating more specifically the provenance of the *versaria* and may support further inquiry into regional Occitanian spiritual practices; see Grier 1990, 53–5.

[49] Images via DIAMM (login required): http://www.diamm.ac.uk/jsp/AnnotationManager?imageKey=40658 and http://www.diamm.ac.uk/jsp/AnnotationManager?imageKey=40659.

memorable text that relied on repetition, likewise carried a melody that lodged easily in the memory. Bruno Nettl emphasized repetitive elements, or 'recurring musical events or signposts', as key characteristics that 'hold an orally transmitted piece intact' in the memory.[50] Memory indeed held a central role in performance, especially in monophony, again replicating the situation in troubadour song, of which Aubrey reminds us: 'singers [of troubadour song] continued to sing from memory. Writing during that period [the twelfth and thirteenth centuries] served the function mainly of collecting and preserving the songs'.[51]

Following the final *versus* entered in DII – the short, notated, *Eya pueri*, a *Benedicamus Domino versus,* copied on f.24r – a full page of text follows on f.24v, carrying no musical notation and entered in an apparently later hand.[52] A unique inclusion within the libelli, this page presents a collection of short devotional texts, often in heavily abbreviated Latin. Its appearance and contents of the page correspond with presentations of medieval Christian charms found outside of the *versus* corpus.

This folio features frequent signs of the cross, a performative cue often included in medieval charm manuscripts that likely prompted readers of the book to make the sign of the cross on their own body.[53] A litany of holy figures, including the four evangelists and several Greek saints, specifically invokes the efficacy of these intercessors. Interspersed among these, one finds the Lord's Prayer, the apostolic blessing, and other similar benedictions, often truncated to only the first letter of each word. Among the prayers too is found a charm for eyes entitled *Ad maculum de oculo*, in keeping with the medicinal and bodily function that medieval Christian charms often performed.[54]

Like the *versus,* charms were sonic and performative expressions of private devotion. Lea Olsan explains that 'charms are unique in that performance is typically private; the audience is often only one person'.[55] In this respect, the inclusion of charms in **GB-Lbl Add.36881** reinforces its identity as a personal songbook. Further, it supports the interplay between orality and writing already inherent in the *versus* sections of the book.

---

[50] Nettl 1981, 140.   [51] Aubrey 1993, 2365.

[52] Images via DIAMM (login required): http://www.diamm.ac.uk/jsp/AnnotationManager?imageKey=40660 and http://www.diamm.ac.uk/jsp/AnnotationManager?imageKey=40661.

[53] Paden and Paden 2010, 314.

[54] Lea Olsan records and discusses a charm for cure of the eyes entitled "Ad oculi maculam," in the fourteenth-century **GB-Lbl Royal 12.B.XXV**, although its contents are different from the version in **GB-Lbl Add.36881**; see Olsan 1989, 124–5.

[55] Olsan 1992, 134.

Olsan emphasizes the orality of charms, and their interaction with text, memory, and performance: 'some charms [...] seem to have been recorded from aural memory, and others, although neatly textualized, are clearly meant to be performed orally', adding that 'charms, in fact, live only in performance'.[56] Although the charms carry no musical melodies, they functioned and gained efficacy as sonic entities or as sung-recited texts, as the root word 'carmen' indicates: '*Carmen* [...] in classical Latin meant, among other things, "a solemn ritual utterance, usually sung or chanted in a metrical form". [...] The word denoted [...] a religious hymn, or [...] a magical chant, spell, or incantation. [...] These words carry associations with magic due to the implications of chanting or incanting'.[57] In fact, many relied upon their sound patterns, such as alliteration, short units of meaning, repeating names of saints and apostles, and even on nonsense syllables.[58] This association between chant, charm, and song may have inspired the addition of this page of charms to the songbook.

An additional three leaves, ff.25–7, follow; these final folios are smaller in size than those of the main libelli and represent a tradition disconnected from the *versarium* portion of the manuscript. They transmit the sequence *Planctus ante nescia*, a lament of Mary at the foot of the Cross. Attributed to Godfrey of St Victor, this piece is known from its version in *Carmina Burana* and survives in over twenty manuscripts.[59] The melody found in **GB-Lbl Add.36881** adopts northern French notation on a four-line staff and differs in melodic detail from other known versions.[60] Likely, the rhymed poetry, syllabic melodic setting, and Marian content of this piece encouraged its binding with this *versarium*, which features Marian devotion, personal prayer, and rhymed poetic song. Its insertion into **GB-Lbl Add.36881** as an addendum typifies the placement of the song in other manuscripts too: Charles Brewer notes that this *planctus* normally appeared as an appendix to a main corpus and was never copied into a main body of a 'traditional medieval liturgical source'.[61]

Overall, DII transmits a repertory very distinct from DI. It emphasizes *unica*, with only a small 12 per cent of works concordant with other Aquitanian *versaria*.[62] This seems to indicate, as Grier suggests, that DII represents the repertory of a different locale that the compiler of DI wished to add to the collection.[63]

---

[56] Olsan 1992, 122–3.   [57] Olsan 1992, 116.   [58] Olsan 1992, 124.
[59] See J. Stevens 1986, 130–138; Brewer 2012, 72.   [60] Brewer 2012, 73.
[61] Ibid.   [62] Grier 1988, 272.   [63] Grier 1990, 51.

The two libelli display a number of similarities as well, causing Grier to characterize DII as an appendix to DI.[64] The precise heighting of pitches makes frequent use of C, F, and occasionally G clefs, and the pitch notation employs tidily drawn square and oblong shapes, many connected in conjoined neumes or ligatures.[65] Although copied in two different hands, both libelli feature a finely written, compressed text.[66] Further, the page layout is nearly identical in both sections of the manuscript, and was clearly designed to accommodate the careful presentation of musical notation. Both are consistent in the width of the writing frame and employ similar ruling. Uniquely among the *versaria*, **GB-Lbl Add.36881** regularly implements a vertical score notation for the polyphony. In contrast, **F-Pn lat.1139** employs successive notation, a style devised to accommodate polyphonic pieces with a strophic repetition structure.[67] DI and DII arrange polyphony in the same manner, with four or five lines of text per page, each of which has a wide space above to accommodate two musical voices vertically aligned in score notation. In both libelli, the organal voice sits above the principal voice, divided by a red line.

Some written conventions of the libelli preserve notational traces of the singers who used the books. For instance, DI and DII similarly employ vertical lines, written in the same colour ink, to help align the musical notation with the lyric texts. These lines testify to a practical purpose in music making; they apparently were added by performers to clarify ambiguous passages of text-setting and alignment.[68] The consistent score notation also speaks to the practical and performative functions of this manuscript. As Grier notes, 'it presents a much clearer visual indication of the relationship between the two voices and the text of the composition', and represents 'the increasing importance of the visual presentation of the music'.[69] This visual emphasis and its performance-oriented markings advance the above notion of this manuscript as a reference copy with practical use, including acting as a resource for pre-performance preparation or as an aid to post-performance reflection.

A more detailed analysis of selected examples from **GB-Lbl Add.36881** demonstrates the manuscript's negotiation of sacred and secular interests, as well as the dialogue between literacy and orality. The monophonic *Ave*

---

[64] This paragraph draws from Grier 1988, 272–3.   [65] Fuller 1979, 15.
[66] Fuller 1979, 20.   [67] See Grier 1992, 381–382; Fuller 1971.
[68] Grier 1990, 51.   [69] Grier 1992, 381–2.

Example 3.1: Text, translation, and transcription of *Ave mater salvatoris*, **GB-Lbl Add.36881**, f.16v (DI)[70]

I. Ave mater salvatoris	Hail Mother of the Saviour
nostri terminus doloris	*the end of our sorrow,*
virga Iesse cuius floris	the rod of Jesse of whose blossom
mater es et filia	you are mother and daughter.
nostri terminus doloris	*The end of our sorrow*
confert nobis gaudia	*bestows joys upon us!*
II. Moyses ardentem foris	Outside Moses saw
nostri terminus doloris	*(the end of our sorrow)*
vidit rubum sed ardoris	a burning bush,
non passum incendia	but it did not submit to the heat of the flame.
nostri terminus doloris	*The end of our sorrow*
[confert nobis gaudia]	*bestows joys upon us!*
III. Angelici verbum oris	The word of the angelic voice,
nostri terminus doloris	*(the end of our sorrow)*
de supernis missum oris	of the voice delivered from the heavens,
te replevit gratia	replenished you with grace.
nostri terminus doloris	*The end of our sorrow*
confert nobis gaudia	*bestows joys upon on us!*

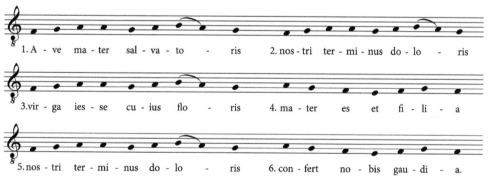

mater salvatoris, Example 3.1, DI, f.16v, helps to date DI, based on its concordance with the conductus *Decet vox letitie* in **I-Fl Plut. 29**, f.462. In fact this piece represents the only concordance with Notre-Dame from the Aquitanian *versaria*.[71] In keeping with the designation of DI as a collection of significant, personal pieces, the Notre-Dame concordance appears in the Florence manuscript as part of a collection of unique 'musical curiosities', according to Robert Falck.[72] Further, echoing the

---

[70] For full transcription details, see Golden Carlson 2000, 579–80.   [71] Fuller 1969, 1:65.
[72] Falck 1981, 127.

expressivity of the Aquitanian *versus*, John Haines describes the 'voice' referenced in the title *Decet vox letitie* as one of 'no restrained joy, but one that is fierce and even sensuous, eager for expression'.[73]

The melodies of *Decet vox letitie* and *Ave mater salvatoris* are identical, although *Ave mater* breaks off partway through. This piece is a three-strophe Marian salutation, which relies on several biblical motifs and allegories of Mary as virginal mother of Jesus. Each stanza runs six lines and features recurring textual-musical repetition typical of a rondeau, with the scheme aAabAB, where A and B are poetic-musical refrain lines. Here all As (both capital and lower case) are set to the same musical phrase and exhibit poetic rhyme; likewise all Bs exhibit this same relationship with one another, giving a controlled affinity between text and music typical of new song. In stanza 1, Jesus' birth is likened to the blossoming rod of Jesse; in stanza 2, a parallel is drawn between Mary's virginal purity and the burning bush of Exodus, which flared with fire but retained its wholeness without being consumed. The refrain lines (lines 2, 5, and 6 of each stanza) emphasize Mary's roles in spiritual transformation: by giving birth to Jesus she completes the old world of the Old Testament and ushers in the new; by acting as *mediatrix* between heaven and earth, she transforms sorrow into joy.

Of the three strophes, only the first carries musical notation, as is often the case in *versaria*. As in troubadour chansonniers, the subsequent stanzas follow the musically notated one, but are written in text only, using a compressed script and textual abbreviations. Strophic repetition of the melody is clearly implied.

This convention for notating strophic songs invites further contemplation of oral–written interactions in *versaria* (and troubadour) manuscripts, and highlights the mnemonic as opposed to the prescriptive role of notation. In a strophic song, the performed reiterations of the melody in the second and subsequent stanzas provide a space for variation and recreation. Further, the scribal choice to write the melody for only the first strophe suggests that the memory of the melody from one strophe to the next could be actively creative. Choosing not to write down each strophe encourages variation and acknowledges the performative tradition; thus, even in the act of creating a literate text, these manuscripts continued to participate in aspects of orality and performativity.[74]

---

[73] Haines 2010a, 71.

[74] Speaking of a strophic *versus*, Treitler writes: 'there is no reason to assume that the user of the manuscript would have taken care to sing each variant exactly as written'.

Ave mater relies on F as a pitch centre, a less common choice than D or G, which are the most typical modal centres for *versus*. The F modality is also a feature of the Notre-Dame concordance. *Versus* typically rely on small-scale melodic or motivic repetitions, in strophic and through-composed settings alike. A similar stress on structural repetition is found in *Ave mater*. *Ave mater*'s melody consists of two musical phrases, as is expected of a rondeau, with the A phrase ending with an open cadence on G, thus demanding continuation, and the B phrase providing a closed ending on the F final.

The musical setting reinforces the poetic structure and rondeau form. Its primarily syllabic melodic diction emphasizes the strong accentual and rhymed elements of the poetry; similarly, the use of oxytonic and para-oxytonic musical cadences support the correspondingly oxytonic and paraoxytonic poetic lines (ll.4 and 6) of each strophe.[75] The latter lines also coincide with the only points in the text where syntactical sentences end. Treitler characterizes the resulting musical–textual interplay as a 'balanced, configuration [that] depends [...] on the manipulation of phrases that relate to one another as question and answer, open and closed – in general, antecedent and consequent'.[76]

The use of the rondeau form for a Latin Marian piece and its presence within the *versarium* also demonstrates fluidity between sacred and secular works in twelfth-century Aquitaine. *Ave mater* evokes the sacred in its use of Latin language and its expression of Marian devotion. Simultaneously, secular aesthetics are evoked in the rondeau form's strong association with ring dancing, love song, and 'energetic, sensuous joy'.[77]

The polyphonic *unicum Quam felix cubiculum*, DII, f.21 (Example 3.2), also attests to the late twelfth-century cult of the Virgin Mary, particularly in its depiction of Mary as bride and lover of Christ. Such representations of Mary reflect contemporaneous interpretations of the Song of Songs and feature sensuality, gender ambiguity, and erotic allegory expressed through invocation of a bride and bridegroom, often uniting in a private marriage

---

(Treitler 1981, 485). Commenting on similar themes, Grier has remarked: 'when music is to be repeated as a reflection of the poetic structure of a piece, a number of factors may affect how exact the repetition is', including 'the result of variability in the oral performing tradition', and how this has 'penetrated the written tradition' (Grier 1994, 1064); see also Arlt 1986, 31–44.

[75] Treitler 1965, 79–80.   [76] Treitler 1965, 82.   [77] Haines 2010a, 68–70.

Example 3.2: Text, translation, and transcription of *Quam felix cubiculum,* **GB-Lbl Add.36881,** f.21r–v[78]

1. Quam felix cubiculum	How auspicious is the bedroom
2. in quo fiunt nupcie	in which the marriage was made,
3. in quo dedit osculum	in which the bridegroom gave a kiss
4. sponse sponsus hodie	to the bride today.
5. nec ibi periculum	There was no danger
6. fuit pudicicie	to her chastity there
7. Sed vis sancti spiritus	only the power of the Holy Spirit.

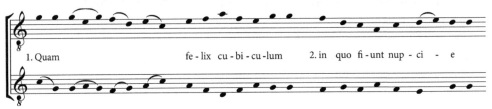

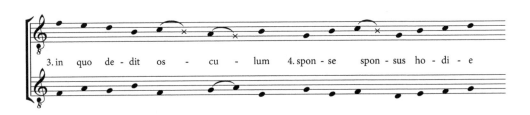

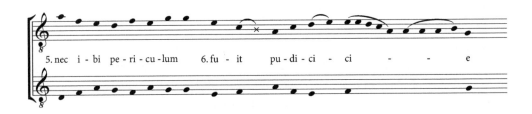

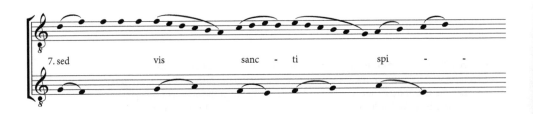

[78] For further information on the transcription, see Golden Carlson 2000, 589–91.

Example 3.2: (*cont.*)

chamber.[79] This set-up creates an evocative version of the Trinity, featuring Christ and Mary as lovers, plus the Holy Spirit, who oversees their union.[80]

[79] Golden Carlson 2003, 6–10, 18–20; Golden Carlson 2000, 204–32.
[80] Golden Carlson 2000, 269–76.

The piece comprises a single strophe with seven lines of seven syllables each, arranged in the rhyme scheme ababab.[81] Within this single-strophe framework, small-scale repetitions and varied repetitions occur, both in the poetic and musical settings. Lines 2 and 3, for instance, both employ the phrase 'in quo' at their openings. On a smaller scale, l.4 features two versions of the word 'sponsus' in immediate succession.

This polyphony is not based on a cantus firmus; both upper and lower voices are newly composed. The predominant texture is note-against-note discant, often accompanying syllabic text setting, but this is notably interspersed with florid passages (for example, 'pudicicie' in l.6, 'vis' and 'sancti' in l.7), as well as melismatic treatments of the text. Melismas occur on the opening syllable, at the cadence of l.6, and climactically throughout l.7. In the latter instance, this extended cadential elaboration on the poem's penultimate syllable – '-ri-' of 'spiritus' – fills out half the duration of the whole piece.

Melismas on the penultimate syllable occur frequently in the *versus* corpus, and the ones found in **GB-Lbl Add.36881**'s late repertory display especially elaborative tendencies. As I have discussed elsewhere, such extensive melismas in this repertory prove expressively powerful; transcending the limits of speech in favour of non-literal sound, they can function as rhetorical devices or as exclamations of emotional exuberance.[82]

Vertical octaves, particularly those on F and G, are used structurally in the polyphony, both at selected cadences and at other interior points, creating moments of contrapuntal tension and release. Sequences, pitch palindromes, and contrary motion are all prevalent. For example, immediately preceding the cadence of l.1 on G, one finds a short pitch palindrome in the lower voice: *a-F-D-F-a* ('felix cubiculum'). This coincides with a palindrome in the upper voice as well: *e-f-aa-f-e*. Further, the final line of the piece employs several sequences, including five-note melismas in the upper voice from *f* ('vis') and then *e* ('-ti'), accompanied by sequencing two-note neumes in the lower voice.

The musical setting, like that of *Ave mater*, reveals a concern for poetic rhyme and structure. While l.1, l.3, and l.5 all share the *a* rhyme ('-ulum'), l.1 and l.5 are more closely linked in that their final words – 'cubiculum' and 'periculum' – share not two but three syllables of rhyme. This relationship is reflected in the musical settings of l.1 and l.5, whose settings of the final three syllables are identical and which feature motion from a vertical F octave to a

---

[81] A standard construction in this repertory; see Fuller 1969, 1:179–209.
[82] Golden Carlson 2003, 541; Golden Carlson 2006, 642–3.

prolonged G octave. In a further parallelism, l.1 and l.5 both make use of a vertical twelfth, on *D-aa*, prior to this cadential formula. These two instances are the only times this interval occurs in the piece, with the pitch *aa* of the upper voice standing as the high pitch climax of the work. Indeed the entire melody of l.5 appears to be a shortened redaction of the melody of l.1.

In its text, *Quam felix cubiculum* focuses on a kiss ('osculum', l.3) exchanged between bridegroom and bride, or Christ and Mary, as an active theological principle. The kiss enacts a moment of spiritual transformation, reminiscent of the word made flesh: here a promise of love is made into a marriage, realized and consummated in the bedchamber, even as Mary's virginity and purity are preserved. Twelfth-century theologian Alain de Lille opened his explanation of the Song of Songs with a moment of such erotic and divine transformation, in which the kiss symbolized the mystery of incarnation and the powerful efficacy of verbal expression, thus:

Glorioso igitur Virgo sponsi optans praesentam, gloriosam conceptionem ad angelo nuntiatam, affectans divinam Incarnationem, ait sic: 'Osculetur me osculo oris sui'.

The glorious Virgin, therefore, hoping for the presence of the Bridegroom, desiring the glorious conception announced by the angel, eagerly wishing for the divine Incarnation, speaks thus: 'Let him kiss me with the kiss of his mouth'.[83]

The reference to a marital bedchamber is multivalent. Its interior domestic location suggests Mary's purity in the style of the common metaphor for Marian virginity of the enclosed garden ('hortus conclusus').[84] The image also resonates with the intersections between writing and memory so significant in the surrounding culture. Mary Carruthers explains that in medieval Christian contexts, the bedroom ('thalamus' or 'cubiculum') epitomizes a rich host of gendered, intellectual, and private interactions: 'while all the sexual associations of fertility and fruitfulness resonate in this bedroom mystery, its goal is cognitive creation, and its matrix is the secret places of one's own mind, the matters secreted away in the inventory of memory, stored and recalled, collated and gathered up, by the "mystery" or craft of mnemotechnical invention'.[85]

As *Quam felix cubiculum* expresses shifting attitudes toward religious representations, and encapsulates dynamic aspects of the memorial arts, **GB-Lbl Add.36881** itself also crosses many boundaries. While intimately related to the monastic culture of St Martial of Limoges, the manuscript negotiates between courtly and church spheres, freely combining formal

---

[83] Alanus de Insulis [Alain of Lille], *Elucidatio in Cantica*, in PL 210, col. 53. Astell 1990, 61.
[84] Rubin 2009, 310–12. [85] Carruthers 1998, 171.

and thematic ideas associated with each. It also challenges notions of liturgical and paraliturgical in its collection and presentation of devotional *versus* and other song genres that defy one-dimensional categorization. Many of these pieces experiment with newly emerging roles for the Virgin Mary at a time of her reinterpretation by twelfth-century monks and theologians. Fluidly exchanging roles of devoted mother and erotic bride, Mary is revealed as a polyvalent cult figure whose importance and potency can eclipse even that of the masculine divine.

GB-Lbl Add.36881 also stands at the nexus of oral and literate cultures, remaining embedded with traces of living practice. Refusing to categorize monophony and polyphony as fundamentally different, it mixes newly important varieties of polyphony, particularly the florid and discant styles that have been attributed historiographically to the later, northern Notre-Dame school. As polyphony emerges as an important expressive form, not only a theoretical exercise, **GB-Lbl Add.36881** evidences a delight in a playful, composerly, contrapuntal style. The scribes of **GB-Lbl Add.36881** preserved these works by writing in a newly conceived score form especially designed for the task. Meanwhile, the manuscript continues to value and preserve monophony with care.

Like other important medieval manuscripts of song, **GB-Lbl Add.36881** encourages the construction of a song multiply rather than singly, acknowledging the process of *mouvance*. Catherine Brown has discussed the activity of reading as a transformative process, one that crosses borders and arrives at mediating moments of transition, suggesting that, when we read 'performatively, *per artem* – in the middle [. . .] from the inside out – something wonderful happens. Our writers and texts are medieval and coeval at once. Time turns around on itself'.[86] By similarly traversing borders, **GB-Lbl Add.36881** invites an encounter with the manuscript as part of the experience of performance, a remembrance and re-enactment of the many modes of conception – in sound, in memory, on the written page – that create new song.

---

[86] Brown 2000, 566.

4 | Wine, women, and song? Reconsidering the *Carmina Burana*

GUNDELA BOBETH (TRANSLATED BY HENRY HOPE)[1]

Introduction: blending popular views and scientific approaches

By choosing the catchy title *Carmina Burana* – 'songs from Benediktbeuern' – for his 1847 publication of all Latin and German poems from a thirteenth-century manuscript held at the Kurfürstliche Hof- und Staatsbibliothek Munich, a manuscript as exciting then as now, the librarian Johann Andreas Schmeller coined a term which, unto the present day, is generally held to denote secular music-making of the Middle Ages in paradigmatic manner.[2] The *Carmina Burana* may be numbered among the few cornerstones of medieval music history which are known, at least by name, to a broader public beyond the realms of musicology and medieval history, and which have evolved into a 'living cultural heritage of the present'.[3]

Held today at the Bayerische Staatsbibliothek under shelfmarks Clm 4660 and 4660a, and commonly known as the 'Codex Buranus', the manuscript – referred to in what follows as **D-Mbs Clm 4660-4660a** – constitutes the largest anthology of secular lyrics in medieval Latin and counts among the most frequently studied manuscripts of the Middle Ages.[4] Yet the entity most commonly associated with the title *Carmina Burana* has only little to do with the musical transmission of this manuscript. Carl Orff's eponymous cantata of 1937, which quickly became one of the most famous choral works of the twentieth century, generally tops the list of associations. Orff's cantata relates to **D-Mbs Clm 4660-4660a** only in as much as it is based on a subjective selection of the texts edited by Schmeller; it does not claim to emulate the medieval melodies. The tremendous popularity of the *Carmina Burana* is thus nurtured not so much by a historically verified knowledge of the medieval repertory's sound and context, but by its eclectic artistic reception by a composer

---

[1] Unless otherwise noted, all translations of quotations from German in this chapter are also by Henry Hope.

[2] Schmeller 1847.   [3] Vollmann 1987, 905.   [4] Drumbl 2003, 323.

who is likely to have been unaware of the musical notation of **D-Mbs Clm 4660-4660a**.[5] Drawing on an obsolete image of the Middle Ages, in which itinerant scholars with unbounded sensuousness indulged excessively in wine, women, and song, Orff's setting – like its spectacular production and film adaptation by Jean Ponnelle in 1975 – offers a paradigmatic example of the modern usurpation of songs from **D-Mbs Clm 4660-4660a** as a reflective space for romantic visions of the Middle Ages.[6]

From the beginning, the popular imagination and academic study of **D-Mbs Clm 4660-4660a**'s songs shared a fascination for this repertory of unique scope, content, and design, which as an 'inestimable monument of the Latin Middle Ages and its love of poetry and song' promised far-reaching insights into the non-liturgical musical life of the High Middle Ages.[7] The remarkable combination of poems of a moralizing–satirical nature, criticism of the Church and Curia, blatant lovemaking, exuberant carousing, and pleasurable idleness soon after the manuscript's discovery earned **D-Mbs Clm 4660-4660a** a reputation as 'the most famous and important collection of "vagrant poetry"'.[8] In the context of a historically and philologically determined understanding of the Middle Ages in the nineteenth century, these features established the manuscript as infamous, especially since Schmeller's well-intended decision to suppress inappropriate passages from the texts and collate them on the final page of his edition helped to overemphasize the manuscript's frivolities.[9] The owners, makers and performers of such explicit poetry, it was then believed, must have been socially marginalized groups – an itinerant class of scholars and eternal students opposed to the Church, whose promiscuous lifestyle

---

[5] Since Orff is known to have worked exclusively with Schmeller's commentary-free edition – the only complete edition available in his day – he is unlikely to have been aware that neumatic notation existed for some of the texts he set to music; these were, in any case, irrelevant to his plans. More generally, Orff seems to have had only a vague idea of early thirteenth-century music, as a letter which he sent to his philological advisor Michel Hofmann during his work on *Carmina Burana* demonstrates: 'I want the text to be used in the truly *ancient* way. Double texts, including a mixture of Latin *and* German' (Frohmut Dangel-Hofmann, 1990, 19, original emphasis); Orff appears to be alluding to the later compositional practices of motets.

[6] See *Carl Orff, Carmina Burana: Cantiones profanæ cantoribus et choris cantandæ comitantibus instrumentis atque imaginibus magicis*. Dir. Jean-Pierre Ponnelle. With Lucia Popp, Hermann Prey et al., Chor des Bayerischen Rundfunks, Tölzer Knabenchor, Münchner Rundfunkorchester, with Kurt Eichhorn (leader). Gerhard Reutter (producer). Zweites Deutsches Fernsehen, Bavaria Film- und Fernsehgesellschaft, 1975. DVD release: RCA Red Seal, 2002.

[7] Bischoff 1970, 31.   [8] Hilka and Schumann 1930–70, II.1, 82*.

[9] Schmeller justified his censorship of a total of five songs with the notion of propriety, and recommended that his more sensitive readers cut out the final page of his edition, which contained the omitted passages in small print. See Düchting 2000.

of addictive gambling and drinking seemed to find vivid expression in the confession of the Archpoet contained in the **D-Mbs Clm 4660-4660a** (*Estuans interius ira vehementi* (CB191)). The precipitous adoption of such texts for the alleged realities of their poets – and, occasionally, also for those of the scribes of **D-Mbs Clm 4660-4660a**, which thus even became a 'vagrant's song book' – are the roots of the excessively Bohemian image of the *Carmina Burana* that cemented itself through the inclusion of its Latin drinking songs in student songbooks and other anthologies to be used for communal singing as early as the nineteenth century,[10] and which continues to exert its influence through Orff's adaptation.

The foundation for the academic scrutiny of the collection was laid in the 1930s by Otto Schumann with his comprehensive and critical complete edition of the *Carmina Burana* (encouraged by Alfons Hilka, and based on preliminary work by Wilhelm Meyer).[11] In contrast to the prevailing ideas of the *Carmina Burana*, Schumann critiqued the notion that the poets and users had been 'people [. . .] for whom drinking, gambling, and idleness was a way of life'.[12] Since then, the parameters for an objective scrutiny of the *Carmina Burana* have changed significantly. Following the critique of the rigid polarization between 'sacred' and 'secular' prevalent in nineteenth- and early-twentieth-century historiography, it is no longer inconceivable to image the creation and performance of Latin poetry of bold content within the context of a monastery, an episcopal court, or a cathedral school.[13] The concept of 'vagrant poetry' outside of any institutional context has also been brought into question: many of the alleged itinerants – among these, in all likelihood, even the Archpoet – are now known to have had at least temporary roles in reputable offices; and revision to the medieval concept of *vagantes* has shifted its focus from a notion of easy-going vagabonds to spotlight homeless or travelling clerics,

[10] Hilka and Schumann 1930–70, II.1:72*. See also Hüschen 1985, 46–53.

[11] W. Meyer 1901 managed to connect seven bi-folios to the manuscript's original corpus (**D-Mbs Clm 4660a**), and was crucial to the reconstruction of the original ordering of the leaves and gatherings (which had been obscured by Schmeller's numerous additional errors). The first two volumes of Schumann's edition, I.1 and II.1 were published in 1930; the second text volume (II.2) followed in 1941. The seminal text edition was concluded with volume I.3 only thirty years later by Bernhard Bischoff; see Bischoff 1970. The commentary associated with this editorial project remains unfinished.

[12] Hilka and Schumann 1930–70, II.1, 84.

[13] See Dronke 1996, 27: 'wherever a monastery or bishop's court, or later a cathedral school or university, had any pretensions to musical culture, it admitted to a greater or lesser extent songs intended for entertainment and for cult, songs performed in hall rather than in church or oratory, which were thus far less restricted in their choice of themes'.

who were nevertheless firm in their faith and loyal to the Church.[14] The ontology of *vagare* unquestionably implies neither the abandonment of social status and morals nor the membership of an hermetically seques-tered group, making the inference of a certain stratum of poets from the content of the poems obsolete: the social layer referenced by the term 'vagrant' is ambiguous at best, and it cannot be determined whether an alleged piece of 'vagrant poetry' was composed by a vagrant or whether this lyrical perspective is a literary construct only. In contrast to the long-standing interpretation of the scurrilous, bawdy scenarios in the *Carmina Burana* as a kind of *Erlebnislyrik*, more recent scholars have proposed an approach which begins by understanding such texts as experimentation with diverse idioms, stylistic registers, and literary topoi.[15]

The continued application of labels such as 'vagrant poetry' or 'poetry of itinerant scholars' for the characterization of the *Carmina Burana*'s contents is, consequently, of limited use, and even misleading.[16] Despite this anachronistic terminology, however, scholars have reached a broad consensus regarding the highly artificial construction and classical educa-tional background of the poems: the sources from which the redactors of **D-Mbs Clm 4660-4660a** drew their material and which include some of the most important poets of the Latin Middle Ages, such as Philip the Chancellor, Walter of Châtillon, Peter of Blois, Hilarius of Orléans, Godfrey of St Victor, and the Archpoet, circulated among cultivated clerics and university students.[17]

The large scope and elaborate preparation, including coloured initials and a number of pen drawings, point to a well-equipped scriptorium at a sacred centre for the production of **D-Mbs Clm 4660-4660a**, as do the sacred dramas in the final section of the manuscript, which escaped attention for a long time. In a recent study, the placement of the dramas CB227 and CB228 in the context of post-Christmas clerical celebrations as well as the observation of further features of the collection's contents led Johann Drumbl to what is currently the most tangible suggestion for the manuscript's localization: 'the *Codex Buranus* is designed for a user who was responsible for ascertaining the liturgical framework for a church, including the provision of texts for the *tripudia* of the sub-deacons'.[18]

---

[14] See, among others, Naumann 1969, 69–105, and Moser 1998, 11f. A quick overview can be gained from Bernt 1999.

[15] Another monograph of interest for this issue (though focused on a later period) is Irrgang 2002.

[16] See, for example, Vollmann 1995, 457.

[17] Among more recent publications, see Duggan 2000.

[18] Drumbl 2003, 353–5, 336.

Provenance and dating

The manuscript's comparatively secure dating to the first third of the thirteenth century (with individual additions over the course of the thirteenth and early fourteenth centuries) is generally accepted, as is the acknowledgement that the 'Codex Buranus' is very unlikely to originate from the Benedictine monastery at Benediktbeuern (Latin, 'Buria'), as had been assumed for a long time, and which led to Schmeller's labelling, which is still used today, its known inaccuracy notwithstanding.[19] It remains unclear when and how the manuscript came to Benediktbeuern, where it was found in 1803 when the monastery was dissolved. Linguistic idiosyncrasies and scribal traits point to a creation in the southern areas of the Upper German language region. At first, Carinthia or Styria were considered likely locales: Bernhard Bischoff and Walther Lipphardt suggested the Augustinian canons at the Styrian city of Seckau or the episcopal court at Seckau because of concordances with the contents of manuscripts from Seckau.[20] More recently, the South Tyrolian community of Augustinian canons at Neustift/Novacella near Brixen/Bressanone has been considered the 'favourite in the competition for the provenance of the *Codex Buranus*'.[21] Johann Drumbl has even more recently suggested a possible provenance at Trento, in the circles of Emperor Friedrich II; he combines this assertion with a potential designation of the codex for a church in Sicily, but concedes that, ultimately, 'all hypotheses regarding the provenance of the *Codex Buranus* were established by inference from external criteria' and leaves it to later studies to judge arguments for and against his theory.[22]

It is certain, however, that **D-Mbs Clm 4660-4660a** originated at a cultural nexus which guaranteed access to song repertories from across Europe. The collection's internationality – with songs coming from German, Austrian, French, Northern Italian, and Spanish traditions – and the extent to which the redactors interwove the most diverse repertories with each other became strikingly apparent in Schumann's edition. Thus, **D-Mbs Clm 4660-4660a** shares concordances with the large-scale Notre-Dame

---

[19] A seminal contribution to issues of dating is Dronke 1962. Newer publications which continue to assume the origin of the collection at Benediktbeuern in this respect reflect scholarly opinions of the 1960s; see, for example, Gillingham 2004, 105; or Galvez 2012, 20.

[20] Bischoff 1970; Lipphardt 1982.

[21] Knapp 1998, 300. A Brixen/Bressanone origin is supported in particular by the numerous indications of Italian influence outlined in a meticulously documented and interpreted linguistic study by Sayce 1992.

[22] Drumbl 2003, 353–5.

manuscripts, as well as with the St Martial repertory, the younger
Cambridge Song Book (**GB-Cu Ff.I.17**), **GB-Ob Add. A.44, CH-SGs
383**, and the Stuttgart Cantatorium (**D-Sl HB I 95**), to name but a few
of the most prominent. Moreover, the codex contains individual stanzas by
the Marner, Walther von der Vogelweide, Reinmar der Alte, Neidhart,
Dietmar von Aist, Otto von Botenlauben, and Heinrich von Morungen.
Some of these stanzas feature neumatic notation or are added to a notated
Latin poem with the same poetic form, making them the earliest layer
of musical transmission of German *Minnesang*.[23]

Ways into the music

By including the neumes contained in **D-Mbs Clm 4660-4660a**,
Schumann's seminal edition finally also provided the material for a consideration and evaluation of the manuscript as a 'song book'.[24] In addition
to a separate chapter on the manuscript's music scribes in the commentary,
the critical apparatus not only lists the – complete and incomplete –
examples of notation for 50 of the 254 pieces, but also indicates spaced
syllables or red placeholders – indicators of the musical connotation
of pieces which were not furnished with neumes in **D-Mbs Clm 4660-
4660a**.[25] Schumann collated the concordances for all of the texts and
melodies, allowing for a musical contextualization even of those pieces
not notated in the manuscript. For those songs with neumes, his work
provides a comparative framework that bears much potential information:
among the musical concordances, there are numerous diastematically
notated pieces, which give valuable evidence for the interpretation of
the adiastematic neumes of the German repertory, and can at times even
guide the reconstruction of such melodies.

Using a combination of concordances and the assertion of contrafacture
on the basis of parallel poetic structures, Walther Lipphardt proposed
melodies for nineteen partly notated, partly unnotated songs in **D-Mbs
Clm 4660-4660a**.[26] By 1979, René Clemencic and Michael Korth had

---

[23] Vollmann 1995, 457.

[24] The first to take on the challenge of studying **D-Mbs Clm 4660-4660a** from a specifically music historical perspective was Spanke 1930–31.

[25] Hilka and Schumann 1930–70, II.1, 63*f.

[26] Lipphardt 1955, 122–42, and Lipphardt 1961, 101–25.

increased the number of reconstructable melodies to forty-five.[27] Both are meritorious, pioneering attempts which undoubtedly contributed to generating an awareness for the 'original medieval melodies', as Ulrich Müller provisionally termed the notations in **D-Mbs Clm 4660-4660a** in order to distinguish them from Orff's omnipresent composition.[28] As apparent, however, are the problems associated with both methodologies. Lipphardt's diastematic, tonal, and rhythmical interpretations can be justified by the neumes only in part. This critique holds true even more strikingly for the transcriptions of notated songs provided by Bryan Gillingham in his *Anthology of Secular Medieval Song* (1993). His interpretations of the neumes by far surpass those of Lipphardt in their generosity, to the extent that they resemble new compositions inspired by source material.[29] The edition by Clemencic and Korth, in turn, intended for 'practical use' by non-musicologists, consciously refrains from any form of grounding in academic discourse. Its positivistic attitude and the resulting simplifications lead to a popularization of the repertory akin to nineteenth-century traditions, rather than to an understanding of the medieval transmission.[30]

Lipphardt, Clemencic and Korth, and Gillingham are united in seeing the reconstruction of the melodies as the ultimate and only goal of their endeavours. The central concern is the establishment of readable editions, not the specific evidence and context of the manuscript. In the case of Clemencic and Korth, the concentration on this 'reconstruction of the melodies' leads to an almost complete neglect of the neumatic variants in **D-Mbs Clm 4660-4660a**: relying on the musical appearance of the consulted concordant witnesses, their edition presents as '*Carmina Burana*' even rhythmicized, polyphonic settings without further comment.[31]

The habit of neglecting the genuine transmission of **D-Mbs Clm 4660-4660a** in the light of more easily usable concordant sources is already latent in Schumann's text edition. In contrast to what the choice of *Carmina Burana* as the title of Schumann's edition might suggest, he prints the texts not in their variants from **D-Mbs Clm 4660-4660a** – the *Codex Buranus* – but conjectures from a broad selection of concordances

---

[27] Clemencic and Korth 1979. It is not impossible that the three-voice setting of *Potatores exquisiti* (CB202) contained in **GB-Lbl Egerton 3307** might be based on an earlier monophonic version, even if Bryan Gillingham sees no way 'to reconstruct the original melody of the thirteenth-century original' (Gillingham 2004, 115).

[28] U. Müller 1988.   [29] Gillingham 1993.

[30] Clemencic and Korth 1979, 174; see also the review of this edition in Planchart 1991.

[31] Clemencic and Korth 1979.

a version which, according to his comprehensive philological experience, comes as close as possible to the 'original' wording. Although Schumann's meticulous commentary of variants documents the text versions of all manuscript witnesses, the setting found in **D-Mbs Clm 4660-4660a** can be distilled from these variants only with great effort, especially in the case of widely concordant texts.[32]

Schumann's editorial practice rests on the traditional philological assumption that every deviation from a manuscript witness that has been classified as authoritative must be the result of corrupted transmission, a poor exemplar, or grave copying errors. Even today, assertions akin to Schumann's critique of the 'text's poor state' or references to 'better versions' in the concordant sources count among the stock features of almost every description of **D-Mbs Clm 4660-4660a**.[33] It is beyond question that numerous pieces in **D-Mbs Clm 4660-4660a** have obvious mistakes or show traits of corrupted texts. The rigid emendation of all deviations in favour of the reconstruction of alleged archetypes, however, obstructs the possibility of understanding idiosyncratic features in the transmission as the result of deliberate editorial decisions made by those responsible for **D-Mbs Clm 4660-4660a** or its exemplars.

Aware of these issues, Benedikt Vollmann's 1987 edition of the *Carmina Burana* is the only complete edition to present the poems 'in the extent, form, order, and text of the Munich manuscript'.[34] Even in the short commentaries on the individual texts, Vollmann demonstrates the value of an approach that anticipates the intention on the part of the manuscript's redactors, 'to achieve new poetic meaning by collating poems which were originally unrelated'; his approach points out a new way of understanding the collection, which has so far been embarked upon only partially.[35]

The traditional philological denigration of the text variants in **D-Mbs Clm 4660-4660a** is matched by the musicological classification of the source's musical transmission as 'defective' or 'atavistic'. One reason for this assessment is found in the notation of German neumes, which remained indeterminate in both diastematic and rhythmic terms, when the notation of complex polyphonic music with fixed pitch and rhythm

---

[32] Without doubting Schumann's 'magisterial feat of textual criticism', Vollmann 1987, 916ff. also criticizes the lost opportunity to make immediately apparent the 'often idiosyncratic and interesting' variants of **D-Mbs Clm 4660-4660a**.

[33] Hilka and Schumann 1930–70, II.1, 73*–77*; Galvez 2012, 23.

[34] Vollmann 1987, 917.   [35] Vollmann 1987, 916.

had long been established in the West. It is, moreover, strengthened by the discrepancy between the monophonic or entirely lacking musical transmission in **D-Mbs Clm 4660-4660a** compared to the artful two- and three-voice polyphonic concordances from the Notre-Dame repertory. As Lipphardt demonstrated, the lower parts of the latter more or less match the neumatic melodies in **D-Mbs Clm 4660-4660a**, so that the melodies of **D-Mbs Clm 4660-4660a** are commonly viewed as 'reduced' versions, pruned back to the tenor voice. Such terminology not only evokes a clear directionality of the process of reception, but also a lessening of competence. On the one hand, this view correlates with the overarching music historical narrative of the 'atavistic nature' of the German-speaking countries, which sought to copy with limited musical and notational means those rays of artistry which shone through to the most provincial of 'peripheries' from the 'centre' of Paris. To propose this manuscript being 'most closely related to vagrants' as an additional reason for the mono- phonic layer of transmission in **D-Mbs Clm 4660-4660a** paradigmatically demonstrates the dense conflation of several antiquated historiographical concepts, persistent catchphrases, and unquestioned premises that confront the scholarly history of the *Carmina Burana*.[36]

Barriers to understanding generated by the neumatic notation and the alleged lack of musical complexity, artistry, and philological soundness of **D-Mbs Clm 4660-4660a** may provide the reason that its songs have, to date, become the object of in-depth musicological studies in only the most rudimentary of manners. Although **D-Mbs Clm 4660-4660a** is generally appraised as the most famous songbook of the thirteenth century, there is still no comprehensive study of the manuscript from a musical vantage point, which fully takes into account the specific textual and musical transmission of the manuscript without prejudice.[37]

Fundamentally new perspectives have been opened up for an assessment and evaluation of the songs of **D-Mbs Clm 4660-4660a** by the ideas of the New Philology, which raised the awareness of phenomena such as 'mouvance' and 'variance' in medieval text transmission, and by the ideas of cultural transfer developed in cultural studies. The consider- ation of performative contexts suggested by Paul Zumthor's concept of 'mouvance', and Bernard Cerquiglini's understanding of variance as the

---

[36] Quotation from Flotzinger 1981, 102.
[37] See David Fallows (with Thomas B. Payne), 'Sources, MS, §III: Secular Monophony, 2. Latin' via GMO. The first attempt at a comprehensive study of the entire musical notation in **D-Mbs Clm 4660-4660a**, Lammers 2000, remains unpublished.

'mobilité incessante et joyeuse de l'écriture médiévale' (joyous and inces-
sant mobility of medieval writing), make divergent transmissions of a song
comprehensible as the result of an inherent flexibility, and 'not, in fact, as
the result of a deficient transmission of a fixed text'.[38] This approach
engenders neither a smoothing out of all variants nor a complete disregard
for textual and philological criticism, but a methodology which takes
seriously the specifics of any given transmission and seeks to understand
these in the context of their transmitting medium.

Such an approach also ties in with the concept of 'cultural transfer'
developed by cultural studies in order to shift the attention from potential
loss, lack of skill, or misunderstandings of a transmission process to a
consideration of changes to objects of reception as deliberate, and as results
of the recipients' needs.[39] In the case of the *Carmina Burana*, this approach
means substituting an immediate judgement against the Notre-Dame
repertory with a study that interprets the notation of **D-Mbs Clm 4660-
4660a** from within its specific situatedness, and considers nuanced processes of acquisition, adaptation, and re-contextualization.[40]

The insights of such approaches to the *Carmina Burana* can be demonstrated in an example which is as simple as it is striking, and which in
essence goes back to an observation made by Friedrich Ludwig, although
the interpretative potential inherent in his observation has not yet been
exploited.[41] This example is *Gaude. Cur gaudeas vide* (CB22; f.2r),[42] which
was not furnished with neumes in the manuscript, and whose text-layout
does not suggest that the song was intended to be notated.[43] The song's
musical concordances point to the Notre-Dame repertory: a monophonic
setting in **E-Mn 20468**, a two-voice motet setting in **D-W Guelf.1099
Helmst.**, and three-voice motets in **D-W Guelf.1099 Helmst.** and **I-Fl
Plut.29.1**.[44] As the text given in Figure 4.1 shows, all concordances share
the text *Homo, quo vigeas vide*; **D-Mbs Clm 4660-4660a** alone features the
variant incipit *Gaude. Cur gaudeas vide*.

---

[38] First quotation Cerquiglini 1989, 114; second quotation Haug 2004, 67. See also Zumthor 1984.

[39] Middell 2001, 17.

[40] Initial studies of the conductus reception in the German-speaking countries, which scrutinized
the continuation of a number of Parisian conducti in the form of Marian tropes, have suggested
in what ways new insights into the motivations and competencies of transfer processes can be
gained by such queries; see Bobeth 2012 and Bobeth 2002.

[41] Ludwig 1910–61, 1:105.

[42] http://daten.digitale-sammlungen.de/bsb00085130/image_7

[43] Yet Spanke 1930–31, 241 emphatically proposed that the unnotated lyric songs of the *Codex
Buranus* were, without exception, intended for musical performance.

[44] Clemencic and Korth 1979, 26f. edit from **E-Mn 20468**.

D-Mbs Clm 4660-4660a, f.2r (punctuation/layout based on Vollmann 1987, 56ff.)	Notre-Dame sources (punctuation from Hilka and Schumann 1930-1970, I.1, 42f., lineated differently)
GAUDE. – Cur gaudeas, uide! Dei fidei adhereas, in spe maneas et in fide intus ardeas, foris luceas; turturis retorqueas os ad cellas.	Homo, quo vigeas vide! Dei fidei adhereas, in spe gaudeas, et in fide intus ardeas, foris luceas, turturis retorqueas os ad ascellas.
Docens ita uerbo, uita, oris uomere de cordibus fidelium euelles lolium. lilium insere rosae, ut alium per hec possis corripere.	docens ita verbo, vita oris vomere de cordibus fidelium evellas lolium, lilium insere rose, ut alium per hoc corripere
Spetiose ualeas uirtuti, saluti omnium studeas, noxias delicias detesteris, opera considera; quae si non feceris, dampnaberis.	speciose valeas. Virtuti, saluti omnium studeas, noxias delicias detesteris, opera considera, que si non feceris, damnaberis.
Hac in uia milita gratiae, et premia cogita patriae, et sic tuum cor, in perpetuum gaudebit.	Hac in via milita gratie et premia cogita patrie, et sic tuum cor in perpetuum gaudebit. Motet/clausula tenor: ET GAUDEBIT

Figure 4.1: Text of *Gaude. Cur gaudeas, vide* (CB22) compared to the textual transmission of the Notre-Dame repertory

The motets are based on a clausula on the passage 'et gaudebit' from the *Alleluia V. Non vos relinquam*. The eschatological promise 'et gaudebit cor vestrum' made in the alleluia verse text is mirrored almost verbatim at the end of the text of *Homo, quo vigeas vide*, which is notated almost identically in all manuscript sources: 'et sic tuum cor in perpetuum gaudebit', here phrased as the promised reward for the Christian lifestyle to which the text has previously called its recipients in admonitory imperatives. Thus the text of *Homo, quo vigeas vide* closes with an idea which is present in the motet from the very beginning through the use of the *ET GAUDEBIT* tenor. Long before the upper voices make it explicit, the proclamation of salvation is inherent in the piece – the promise of joy ('it [your heart] will rejoice') accompanies the text's numerous exhortations from the very beginning. However, this particular mode of intertextual wit, typical of polyphonic motets, can hardly be conveyed in a monophonic version. By placing the words 'Gaude. Cur gaudeas' at the very beginning (instead of 'Homo, quo vigeas'), however, the notion of joy is also present in **D-Mbs Clm 4660-4660a** from the outset. Thus, this version generates a similar effect to the Notre-Dame renditions by remarkably simple, yet successful means.

A traditional perspective might consider the transmission of CB22, with its unique text incipit, as 'apocryphal', or as 'reduced' in light of the lack of explicitly musical notation. Yet the knowledge of performances of *Homo, quo vigeas vide* as a motet in Paris makes it seem much more likely that the opening variant of **D-Mbs Clm 4660-4660a** is a deliberate reference to the tenor of the related motet. In the case of CB22, study of its purely textual transmission already illuminates far more facets of the reception process than the simplistic assumption of a 'reduction' from three-voice polyphony to monophony might suggest.

If the scenario outlined for *Gaude. Cur gaudeas* (CB 22) holds true, it would lead to the conclusion that those responsible for the textual variant in **D-Mbs Clm 4660-4660a** were familiar with a musical performance of the polyphonic version. On the basis of a written exemplar of the motet alone – the disposition of which has the tenor *follow* the upper voices – the crucial simultaneous performance of the *ET GAUDEBIT* tenor and the text of the upper voices would have likely been missed by users from the German-speaking areas, unfamiliar with this form of notational layout. The assumption that 'a Notre-Dame manuscript containing musical notation was one of the models for the *Codex Buranus*', voiced by Bischoff in the commentary to his facsimile edition of **D-Mbs Clm 4660-4660a**, would need to be extended in order to include an additional, performative dimension of transmission.[45]

Structure and content

One should assume the additional, *sounding* presence of transmitted materials also in the case of the other collections likely to have been used for the compilation of **D-Mbs Clm 4660-4660a**. It has long been accepted that the redactors drew their materials not from songs circulating

---

[45] Bischoff 1970, 26.

individually, but from pre-existing manuscripts or *libelli*. This is suggested not only by the partially identical or similar ordering of numerous songs in concordant sources such as **D-Sl HB I 95** or **GB-Ob Add. A.44**, but also by the presence of 'text clusters' by certain poets.[46] In light of the carefully planned design of **D-Mbs Clm 4660-4660a**, it is apparent that the aim was not simply to collect and copy haphazard sources for conservational purposes. Instead, the placement of the individual pieces within a remarkable overarching thematic design, unique in its extent, needs to be considered an original achievement of the responsible redactors of **D-Mbs Clm 4660-4660a**.

The clarification of the main collection's overarching design is among the central merits of the codicological studies undertaken by Wilhelm Meyer and Otto Schumann.[47] There is a wide consensus about the main tenets of the manuscript's four thematic sections: the opening group (CB1–55) of moralistic-satirical songs, transmitted incompletely at the beginning, is followed by a second (CB56–186), containing love songs, which, in turn, is followed by a section of drinking and gambling songs (CB187–226). Two extensive sacred dramas (CB227–228) close the main collection. Further possible subgroupings and thematic differentiations were discussed at length in earlier scholarship, though not always with unanimous conclusions.[48] In addition to considerations of content, formal criteria also played a role in the well-thought-out design of the manuscript (for example, the separation of sequences, strophic songs, and refrain songs), and verses in quantitative metres were inserted in order to structure the collection and to provide a layer of commentary. Introduced by rubrics as *versus* and generally interpreted as unsung elements within the otherwise rhythmic-accentual poetry aligned with sung performance, these sententious insertions constitute a '*unicum* in literary history', which additionally underlines the original design envisaged by the redactors of the *Carmina Burana*.[49]

Philologists have recently also considered whether the musical notation of selected pieces provided a further means for the redactors to demarcate thematic links or generate emphasis.[50] This consideration overlooks the various individual forms of neumatic notation in **D-Mbs Clm 4660-4660a**, which counter such claims: almost all notators involved make use of a

---

[46] See Vollmann, 1987, 902ff. and Traill 2006.

[47] W. Meyer 1901; Hilka and Schumann 1930–70, II.1, 31*ff., 41*ff.

[48] Hilka and Schumann 1930–70, II.1, 31*ff., 41*ff. Vollmann 1987, 907–9 suggests a modified structuring.

[49] Vollmann 1987, 911.   [50] Drumbl 2003, 336–40.

wide range of types, from the detailed notation of only the opening melisma, the notation of single lines and stanzas, to the complete notation of multi-stanzaic texts.[51] These varying notations all appear to be the result of specific reasons related to the differing needs for written presentation of these particular melodies, and thus propose an explicitly musical interpretation. Such an interpretation does not exclude a particular estimation of a given song having prompted the insertion of neumes. But considering the specific conditions of neumatic transmission, the effectiveness of which requires an additional oral transmission of the music, the lack of neumatic notation does not necessarily allow the reciprocal assumption of little value for unnotated songs, but might instead be a result of the wide-spread fame and firm know-ledge of any particular song making its written transmission superfluous.

Varying areas of responsibility can be made out between the different notators of **D-Mbs Clm 4660-4660a**.[52] In the manuscript's main corpus, Schumann distinguished a total of four main notators – labelled n1 to n4 by him – and considered whether n1 and n2 might be identical to the two main text scribes (h1 and h2).[53] The most clearly demarcated areas of responsibility can be discerned for n2 and n4: while n2 notated a majority of the songs in the first section which have polyphonic concordances in the Notre-Dame repertory, the bulk of notation for the Latin songs which conclude with an additional German stanza in the second section was provided by n4. Further songs with an additional German stanza, and individual other songs in the first two sections, were notated by n3. Notator n1, in turn, was responsible for a number of laments in the second section, for some drinking and gambling songs in the third section, and for the sacred drama CB227.

All notated songs of **D-Mbs Clm 4660-4660a**, as well as those songs for which musical concordances have been found, are listed in the Tables 4.1 and 4.2: Table 4.1 covers the main corpus of the manuscript, while Table 4.2 outlines the musical items among the later additions. In addition to the indication of musical notation, the tables also reference concor-dances, contrafacta, and include further remarks relevant to the songs' music historical contextualization.

The numbering of the *Carmina Burana* follows the edition by Benedikt Vollmann. It is largely identical to the numbering established by Hilka and Schumann, but does not emulate the common separation of German

---

[51] An exception is Schumann's notator 'n2', who is the only one to always notate all stanzas of a given song.

[52] A similar conclusion is also reached in Lammers 2004, 78ff.

[53] Hilka and Schumann 1930–70, II.1:63*–65*.

Table 4.1 The main corpus of **D-Mbs Clm 4660-4660a**

CB	Incipit	Folio	Comments	Musical concordances
3	*Ecce torpet probitas*	43r	not neumed	**GB-Cu Ff.I.17**, 2v–3r [foliation according to J. Stevens 2005]
8	*Licet eger cum egrotis*	45r–v	not neumed	**F-EV lat.2**, 4v–5r
12	*Procurans odium*	47v	not neumed	**D-Mbs Clm 5539**, 37r **E-Mn 20486**, 124r–v **GB-Cjec QB 1**, 1ar **I-Fl Plut.29.1**, 226r–v
14	*O varium Fortune lubricum*	47v–48r	fully neumed	**F-Pn fr.146**, 3v **I-Fl Plut.29.1**, 351v
15	*Celum non animum*	48r–v	stanzas 1–2 neumed	**D-W Guelf.628 Helmst.**, 15r (11r)–15v (11v) **I-Fl Plut.29.1**, 223v–224r
19	*Fas et nefas ambulant*	1r	fully neumed	**GB-Cjec QB 1**, 1av **I-Fl Plut.29.1**, 225r–v
21	*Veritas veritatum*	2r	not neumed	**I-Fl Plut.29.1**, 423v–424r
22	*Gaude. Cur gaudeas vide*	2r	not neumed	**D-W Guelf.1099 Helmst.**, 127r (3-part motet), 148v–149r (2-part motet) **E-Mn 20486**, 126r–v **I-Fl Plut.29.1**, 386v–387r (3-part motet)
26	*Ad cor tuum revertere*	3r	not neumed	**D-Mbs Clm 18190**, 1r **E-BUlh**, 161v and 167r **I-Fl Plut.29.1**, 420v–421v **I-Rss XIV L3**, 141r
27	*Bonum est confidere*	3r–v	not neumed	**E-BUlh**, 157r–v **E-SAu 226**, 100v **GB-Ob Auct. 6Q3.17**, 15ext.a **I-Fl Plut.29.1**, 430r–v
30	*Dum iuventus floruit*	4r	fully neumed	unicum
31	*Vite perdite me legi*	4r–v	fully neumed	**F-Pn fr.844** (with French text *A l'entrant du tens salvage* by trouvère Huc de St. Quentin), 81v **F-Pn fr.12615** (with French text *A l'entrant du tens salvage* by trouvère Huc de St. Quentin), 43r **I-Fl Plut.29.1**, 356r **I-Ma R71 sup.** (with Occitan text *Per dan que d'amor m'aveigna* by troubadour Peirol), 46r–v

Table 4.1 *(cont.)*

CB	Incipit	Folio	Comments	Musical concordances
33	*Non te lusisse pudeat*	5r–v	fully neumed	**I-Fl Plut.29.1**, 435r–v
34	*Deduc Sion uberrimas*	5v	not neumed	**D-W Guelf.628 Helmst.**, 159v (150v)–161r (152r) **D-W Guelf.1099 Helmst.**, 93r–96r **E-Mn 20486**, 83r–85v **F-Pn lat.15139**, 280v **GB-Cjec QB 1**, Dv (22v) **I-Fl Plut.29.1**, 336r–337r
36	*Nulli beneficium*	6r	not neumed	**D-W Guelf.628 Helmst.**, 117v (108v)–118v (109v) **E-Mn 20486**; 63r–65r **F-Pn fr.146**, 7v **I-Fl Plut.29.1**, 334r–335r
37	*In Gedeonis area*	6r–v	not neumed	**E-Bac Ripoll 116**, 101r
47	*Crucifigat omnes*	13r–v	not neumed	**D-Sl HB I 95**, 31r **D-W Guelf.628 Helmst.**, 78v (71v)–79r (72r) **D-W Guelf.1099 Helmst.**, 46v and 138v–139v **E-BUlh**, 97r–v **GB-Cjec QB 1**, 1Cr–1Cv **I-Fl Plut.29.1**, 231v–232r
48	*Quod spiritu David precinuit*	13v–14r	neumed except for German final stanza	unicum
52	*Nomen a sollempnibus*	17r	not neumed	**F-Pn lat.3549**, 164r–v **F-Pn lat.3719**, 41r–42r
63	*Olim sudor Herculis*	23v–24r	not neumed	**GB-Cu Ff.I.17**, 5r [foliation according to J. Stevens 2005] **GB-Ob Auct. 6Q3.17**, 16ext.b, 19ext.a, 21ext.a (fragments) **I-Fl Plut.29.1**, 417r–v
67	*E globo veteri*	26r–v	not neumed	**I-Fl Plut.29.1**, 446v
71	*Axe phebus aureo*	28r–v	not neumed	**D-EF Amplon. Oct. 32**, 89v, r [sic]
73	*Clausus Chronos et serato*	29r–v	not neumed	**CH-SGs 383**, pp.158–62 **F-Pn lat.1139**, 47v
79	*Estivali sub fervore*	34r–v	stanzas 1–3 neumed	unicum
80	*Estivali gaudio tellus*	34v	(=228.I)	unicum
85	*Veris dulcis in tempore*	36v	not neumed; copied again as CB159 (with neumes)	**E-E Z.II.2**, 287r
88	*Ludo cum Cecilia*	37r–38r	not neumed	**F-Pn lat.3719** (stanzas 9, 10, 13, 14), 28v

Table 4.1 *(cont.)*

CB	Incipit	Folio	Comments	Musical concordances
90	*Exiit diluculo*	38v	not neumed	**D-Mbs Clm 5539**, 35r–v **E-BUlh**, 93r
98	*Troie post excidium*	73v–74r	only incipit neumed	unicum
99	*Superbi paridis*	74r–75r	first stanza neumed	unicum
100	*O decus o Libie regnum*	75r–v	not neumed	**D-Mbs Clm 4598** (fully neumed), 61r
108	*Vacillantis trutine*	80r	fully neumed	**GB-Cu Ff.I.17**, 2r–v [foliation according to J. Stevens 2005]
109	*Multiformi succendente Veneris*	80r–v	fully neumed	unicum
111	*O comes amoris*	80v–81r	not neumed (neumed as CB8*)	unicum
116	*Sic mea fata canendo solor*	82r–v	not neumed	**F-Pn lat.3719**, 88r
119	*Dulce solum natalis patrie*	50r	fully neumed up to the last word of each stanza	**A-LIs 324**, 83r–v **F-CHRm 223**, 66v
128	*Remigabat naufragus*	53r–v	fully neumed	unicum
131	*Dic Christi veritas* (alternating with *Bulla fulminante*)	54r–v	neumed (without closing melismas in the *Dic Christi* stanzas; first stanza of *Bulla* neumed)	**CH-EN 1003**, 114v **D-F Fragm.lat.VI.41**, Ar–v **D-Sl HB I Asc. 95**, 31v–32r **D-W Guelf. 628 Helmst.**, 73r (66r)–73v (66v) **E-Mn 20486**, 114r–115r **E-SAu 226**, 100v **GB-Lbl Egerton 2615**, 88v–89r **I-Fl Plut.29.1**, 203r–204r
140	*Terra iam pandit*	58r–v	only beginning of first stanza neumed	unicum
142	*Tempus adest floridum*	58v–59r	only beginning of first stanza neumed	unicum
143	*Ecce gratum et optatum*	59r–v	first stanza and end of the German final stanza neumed	unicum
146	*Tellus flore vario vestitur*	60r	first stanza and German final stanza neumed	unicum
147	*Si de more*	60r–v	last Latin stanza and closing German stanza neumed	unicum

Table 4.1 (*cont.*)

CB	Incipit	Folio	Comments	Musical concordances
150	*Redivivo vernat flore*	61r	beginnings of both the first stanza and the German final stanza neumed	unicum
151	*Virent prata hiemata*	61r–v	stanzas 1–2 and the beginning of the German final stanza neumed	possible contrafact of *Quant je voi l'erbe* by trouvère Gautier d'Espinau in **F-Pn fr.20050**, 51r [suggested in Clemencic and Korth 1979]
153	*Tempus transit gelidum*	61v–62r	first stanza neumed	formal contrafact (that is, shares strophic form) of *Fulget dies celebris* (**F-Pn lat.3719**, 27r)
159	*Veris dulcis in tempore* (=85)	64r	fully neumed	**E-E Z.II.2**, 287r
160	*Dum estas inchoatur*	64r	fully neumed	unicum
161	*Ab estatis foribus* (=228.II)	65r	fully neumed	unicum
162	*O consocii quid vobis videtur*	65r–v	first stanza neumed	unicum
164	*Ob amoris pressuram*	66r–v	stanzas 1–2 and the beginning of the German final stanza neumed	unicum
165	*Amor telum est insignis*	66v–67r	first stanza neumed	unicum
166	*Iam dudum amoris militem*	67r–v	first stanza neumed	unicum
167	*Laboris remedium*	67v	first stanza neumed	unicum
168	*Anno novali mea*	67v–68r	first stanza neumed	unicum
169	*Hebet sydus*	68r	not neumed; similar versification to CB151	possible contrafact of *Quant je voi l'erbe* by trouvère Gautier d'Espinau in **F-Pn fr.20050** [suggested in Clemencic and Korth 1979]
179	*Tempus est iocundum o virgines*	70v	stanzas 1–2 neumed	unicum
180	*O mi dilectissima*	71r	first stanza and refrain neumed	unicum
185	*Ich was ein chint*	72r–v	not neumed	unicum; possible contrafact of *Ecce tempus gaudii* (**I-Fl Plut.29.1**, 468r) [suggested in Clemencic and Korth 1979]

Table 4.1 *(cont.)*

CB	Incipit	Folio	Comments	Musical concordances
187	*O curas hominum*	83r	only beginning neumed	**I-Fl Plut.29.1**, 424v
189	*Aristipe quamvis sero*	83r–v	only first word neumed	**F-Pn fr.146**, 29r **GB-Ob Auct. 6Q3.17**, 12ext.a (fragment) **I-Fl Plut.29.1**, 416r–417r
196	*In taberna quando sumus*	87v–88r	not neumed	possible contrafact of conductus *Congaudentes celebremus* from the *Ludus Danielis* (**GB-Lbl Egerton 2615, 103r–104r**) [suggested in Clemencic and Korth 1979]
200	*Bacche bene venies*	89r	not neumed	Contrafact of conductus *Jubilemus regi nostro* from the *Ludus Danielis* (**GB-Lbl Egerton 2615**, 95v)
202	*Potatores exquisiti*	89v–90r	not neumed	**GB-Lbl Egerton 3307**, 72v–74r (in 3 parts; connection to CB version unclear)
203	*Hiemali tempore*	90r–v	not neumed	**D-Ju El.f.100**, 143r (*Eckenlied*-Melodie (Bernerton))
211	*Alte clamat Epicurus*	92v	not neumed	**D-MÜsa ms.VII 51**, 1r–v (Palästina-Lied (Walther von der Vogelweide))
215	*Lugeamus omnes* (*Officium lusorum*)	93v–94v	extensively neumed	unicum
227	*Ecce virgo pariet* (*Benediktbeurer Weihnachtsspiel*)	99r–104v	fully neumed to f.102r; f.104r partially neumed	unicum

stanzas from the Latin songs to which they are attached by adding an 'a'. Instead, a piece made up of Latin and German stanzas is referenced by a single song number. This practice mirrors the visual presentation of the manuscript, in that the latter's use of initials, line breaks, and rubrics such as 'Item de eodem', 'unde supra', and similar suggest that the redactors of the songs wished these cases to be understood as coherent wholes, and transmitted them as such.[54]

---

[54] See U. Müller 1981, especially 88 and 95.

Table 4.2 The musical items among the later additions to **D-Mbs Clm 4660-4660a**

CB	Incipit	Folio	Remarks	Musical concordances
4*	*Flete fideles anime*	55r	fully neumed; also part of the Passion play CB16*	**D-DO A.III.22**, 2v–3r **D-Sl HB I 95**, 23r–24v **I-CFm Cod.CI**, 74r–76v **I-Pc C55**, 31v–36v **I-Pc C56**, 32r–36v
5*	*Furibundi cum acceto*	100v	fully neumed	unicum
8*	*O comes amoris dolor*	Iv	fully neumed; = CB111 (not neumed)	unicum
9*	*Mundus finem properans*	IIr	stanza 1 neumed	unicum
11*	*Ave nobilis venerabilis Maria*	IIIr	fully neumed	**D-DO 882**, 175v–177v [MS lost] **F-LG 2 (17)**, 282v–283r **F-Pa 3517**, 13v–14r **I-Fl Plut.29.1**, 363v–364r
12*	*Christi sponsa Katherina*	IIIr	fully neumed	unicum
14*	*Planctus ante nescia*	IVr	fully neumed; as incipit, also part of the Passion play CB16*	**F-EV lat.2**, 3v–4v **D-Mbs Cgm 716**, 150r **F-AL 26**, 113r–113v **F-EV lat.39**, 1v–2r **F-Pm 942**, 234r (235r)–237r; **F-ROU 666 (A 506)**, 94r–96v
15*	*Ludus Dominice resurrectionis*	Vr–VIv	fully neumed	many concordances with the Klosterneuburg Easter play, on which it is largely based
16*	Passionsspiel (*Primitus producatur Pilatus et uxor sua...*)	107r–110r	fully neumed	unicum (= *Großes Benediktbeurer Passionsspiel*)
19*	*Katerine collaudemus*	111v	not neumed	**CH-EN 102**, 149v and others (compare AH 52, 220ff.)
20*	*Pange lingua gloriose*	111v	not neumed	(compare AH 52, 224, 226)
21*	*Presens dies expendatur*	112r	not neumed	(compare AH 52, 224f.)
22*	*Hac in die laudes pie*	112r	fully neumed	(compare AH 55, 226f.)
23*	*Iesus, von gotlicher art* (*Cantus Ioseph ab Arimathia*)	112v	fully neumed	unicum

Table 4.2 *(cont.)*

CB	Incipit	Folio	Remarks	Musical concordances
26*	*Exemplum apparacionis Domini discipulis suis*	VIIr–v	fully neumed	unicum

* = *addenda* with musical transmission

Roman numerals for isolated individual folios now under the shelfmark **D-Mbs Clm 4660a**, whose link to the medieval state of **D-Mbs Clm 4660** was shown in Meyer 1901.

The phenomenon of the roughly 50 Latin songs contained in **D-Mbs Clm 4660-4660a** which are concluded by one – or, in a few cases, a number of – Middle High German stanza(s) has been much discussed particularly by Germanists, without however reaching any consensus beyond the most general issues.[55] Were the appended German stanzas, which include some from poems by famous *Minnesänger*, used as models for the preceding Latin ones, or are the German stanzas contrafacta of the Latin ones? Did the side-by-side presentation of Latin and German stanzas, unattested outside **D-Mbs Clm 4660-4660a**, function merely as the visualization of formal similarities, or did it imply a specific performance practice? Can the musical identity of the Latin and Middle High German stanzas be assumed in all cases?

Only an in-depth interdisciplinary scrutiny of the entire Latin-German transmission in **D-Mbs Clm 4660-4660a** could shed light on these questions. The multi-layered material suggests that one will need to expect various different answers. Thus, previous case studies of individual songs have been able to suggest convincingly both that Latin stanzas were generated as contrafacta of a German stanza as well as the inverted relationship of a Latin model for a secondary German stanza.[56] Concerning the possible motivations of **D-Mbs Clm 4660-4660a**'s redactors for the combination of Latin and German stanzas, earlier scholarship in particular proposed that the German stanzas were primarily used to facilitate

---

[55] A list of all songs with appended German stanzas (alongside further songs which feature linguistic mixtures) can be found in U. Müller 1981, 88–91; the entire Middle High German material contained in **D-Mbs Clm 4660-4660a**, including glosses, individual verses, and so on, is listed in Edwards 2000, 68–70.

[56] The former is argued explicitly on the basis of the notated melodies in Beatie 1965. For the latter, see, for example, Vollmann 1987, 136, 138f., 141, 170, 181.

understanding by recipients with insufficient Latin skills.[57] This notion is starkly contradicted by the localization of the manuscript within a genuinely multi-lingual context, accepted by current scholars.[58] More recent commentators have understood the German stanzas as indicators of formal parallels or as pointers to the melodies which are to be underlaid to the Latin texts.[59]

Even today, however, it is still is rarely considered that the transmission of Latin and German stanzas in **D-Mbs Clm 4660-4660a** might have been intended and performed as a single coherent song. An exception to this is Ulrich Müller, who has argued for a performance of the stanzas in the order transmitted by the manuscript, understanding 'the clearly marked units [...] as coherent songs or song versions'.[60] The montage of (newly created) Latin and (familiar) Middle High German stanzas into a new whole, based on the principle of barbarolexis, he argues, 'engendered a comic effect to the knowledgeable listener'.[61] The argument used against this suggestion, that the conjoined performance of stanzas in different languages would have left 'the change of language without function and the relation of content unconvincing', fails to take account of the additional semantic level provided by the music.[62] To take up one of Müller's central examples, if the Latin praise of an Epicurean lifestyle, gluttony, and drunkenness voiced in CB211 *Alte clamat epicurus* were sung to the melody of Walther von der Vogelweide's *Palästinalied* from the very beginning, such a grotesque re-contextualization of the familiar melody may indeed have had comic effect, which found its apex in the concluding performance of the actual German stanza – the content of which is then shifted from a pilgrim's perspective to that of the *venter satur* (sated belly).

It is obvious that this parodic technique can be applied only if the model German song was widely disseminated and familiar; it provides no explanation for pieces in which the concluding German stanza is a contrafact of the preceding Latin one. It is just as apparent, however, that the unusualness of a joint performance of Latin and German stanzas of differing origin in itself is not sufficient justification to discard such a possibility outright.

---

[57] See Spanke 1930–31, 246. See also Sayce 1982, 234–64.
[58] See Drumbl 2003, 349 and Sayce 1992.
[59] See, for example, Heinzle 1978, 160, or Wachinger 1985 2:300.
[60] U. Müller 1981, 95.   [61] U. Müller 1981, 97 and U. Müller 1980, 108ff.
[62] Wachinger 1985, 299.

These observations notwithstanding, the crucial importance of performance considerations for the redactors of **D-Mbs Clm 4660-4660a** is demonstrated, for example, by the neumatic notation of pieces such as *Si de more* (CB147). This song combines two topically contrasting texts (the German stanza is by Reinmar der Alte). While notator n4 usually provides neumes for the *first* Latin stanza, for *Si de more* it is the *last* Latin stanza and the immediately following German stanza that are furnished with neumes.[63] As the versification structures of the two combined texts in this rare example are not entirely congruent and their melodies can thus not have been exactly identical, it appears to have been a particular concern to securely ascertain the melodic adaptations to the differing texts by making them visible in direct comparison (the provision of neumes for the first Latin stanza and the German stanza would have required a page turn in order to compare the text settings directly). This observation need not necessarily indicate that the Latin stanzas and the additional German stanza were intended to be performed together, but at the very least it documents the concern for a careful coordination of text and music.

Case studies

The combination of stanzas from different pieces in **D-Mbs Clm 4660-4660a** is not limited to songs with an appended German stanza. A revealing example of the combination of two Latin songs can be found in *Dic Christi veritas* (CB131; see Figure 4.2). The three stanzas of Philip the Chancellor's *Dic Christi veritas* are presented in alternation with the three first stanzas of *Bulla fulminante*, another piece by Philip (see Figure 4.3).[64] All stanzas of *Dic Christi* are notated with neumes, but only the first of *Bulla*.

Beyond **D-Mbs Clm 4660-4660a**, *Dic Christi veritas* is transmitted as a three-voice conductus in all large-scale Notre-Dame manuscripts (**I-Fl Plut.29.1, D-W Guelf.628 Helmst., D-W Guelf.1099 Helmst., E-Mn 20468**), as well as in **GB-Lbl Egerton 2615**; *Bulla fulminante*, in contrast, is contained in a monophonic version in the French songbook **GB-Lbl Egerton 274**.[65] Both pieces are musically related insofar as they are among those conductus melodies which derive from the final melisma of a

---

[63] See f.60v.   [64] http://daten.digitale-sammlungen.de/bsb00085130/image_111.
[65] On the last of these manuscripts, see Chapter 6 below. For further information on the sources of CB131, see http://catalogue.conductus.ac.uk.

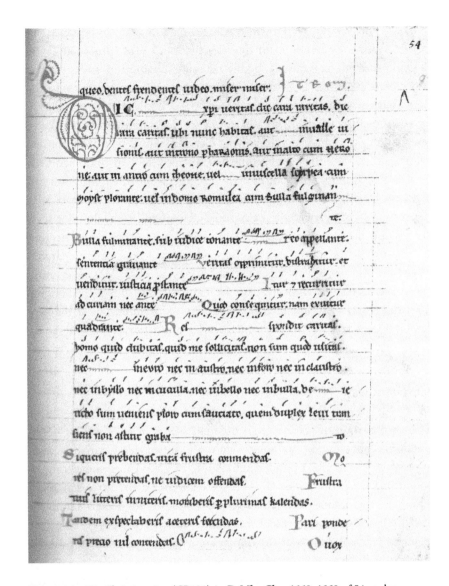

Figure 4.2: *Dic Christi veritas* (CB131) in **D-Mbs Clm 4660-4660a** f.54r-v; by permission of the Bayerische Staatsbibliothek Munich

pre-existent conductus: the melody of *Bulla* is the tenor line of the final melisma of *Dic Christi*, which begins on the penultimate syllable of the concluding words 'cum bulla fulminante'.[66] It appears that the text-only notation of *Bulla* in **I-Fl Plut.29.1**, where it follows directly after the three stanzas of *Dic Christi*, is a result of this relationship.

---

[66] See Payne 2007.

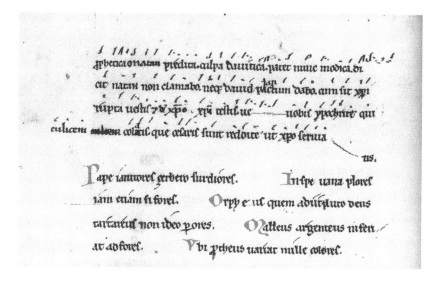

Figure 4.2: (*cont.*)

A consistent intermeshing of *Dic Christi* and *Bulla* with three stanzas each is found only in **D-Mbs Clm 4660-4660a**. Of the two other witnesses from the German-speaking areas, **D-Sl HB I 95** also combines notated versions of both pieces, but includes only two stanzas of *Dic Christi* with a single intervening *Bulla*-stanza; the text of the second *Bulla*-stanza was later added in the margin. A further notated setting in a manuscript from Engelberg (**CH-EN 1003**), which has so far largely escaped scholarly attention and which makes tangible a thread of early thirteenth-century reception of Parisian conducti, transmits only the first two stanzas of *Dic Christi*.[67]

The *mise-en-page* of *Dic Christi veritas* (CB131) on f.54r–v unquestionably presents the combined stanzas of *Dic Christi* and *Bulla* as a coherent unit, emphasized by the rubric *Item* (which appears only at the beginning of the song), the size and decoration of the initial of *Dic* [*Christi*], and the following continuous disposition of the text, interrupted only by larger gaps for melismas.[68] For early scholars, it nevertheless appears to have been inconceivable that stanzas of two different songs with their own melodies and poetic structures could have been performed

---

[67] For more information on **CH-EN 1003**, which was rediscovered only in 1963, see the commentary to Arlt and Stauffacher 1986, 67.

[68] http://daten.digitale-sammlungen.de/bsb00085130/image_111 and http://daten.digitale-sammlungen.de/bsb00085130/image_112.

I. [i.]   »Dic, Christi ueritas,
               dic, cara raritas
               dic, rara caritas:
               ubi nunc habitas?
           aut in ualle uisionis,
           aut in trono Pharaonis,
           aut in alto cum Nerone,
           aut in antro cum Theone?
               uel in uiscella scyrpea
                   cum Moyse plorante?
               uel in domo Romulea
                   cum Bulla fulminante?«

                                        II. [1.]   Bulla fulminante
                                                    sub iudice tonante,
                                                        reo appellante,
                                                    sententia grauante
                                                veritas opprimitur,
                                                distrahitur et uenditur
                                                iusticia prostrante.
                                                Itur et recurritur
                                                ad curiam, nec ante
                                                        Quid consequitur,
                                                        quam exuitur quadrante.

III. [ii.]   Resspondit caritas:
               »homo, quid dubitas?
               quid me sollicitas?
               non sum, quod usitas,
                   nec in evro nec in austro,
               nec in foro, nec in claustro,
               nec in bysso nec in cuculla,
               nec in bello nec in bulla:
                   de Iericho sum ueniens,
                       ploro cum sauciato,
                   quem duplex Leui transiens
                       non astitit grabato.«

                                        IV. [2.]   Si queris prebendas,
                                                    uitam frustra conmendas.
                                                        Mores non pretendas,
                                                    ne iudicem offendas!
                                                Frustra tuis litteris
                                                inniteris: moraberis
                                                    per plurimas kalendas.
                                                Tandem exspectaueris
                                                a ceteris ferendas,
                                                    Pari ponderis
                                                    precio nisi contendas.

V. [iii.]   »O uox prophetica,
               o Natan, predica:

Figure 4.3: Three strophes of *Dic Christi veritas* (CB131) alternating with three strophes of *Bulla fulminante*

culpa Dauitica

    patet n*on* modica.«

dicit Natan: »non clamabo,

neque Dauid planctum dabo,

cum sit Christi rupta uestis

et de Christo Christi testis!

    ue, uobis, ypochrite,

        qui culicem colatis!

    que Cesaris sunt, reddite,

        ut Christo seruiatis!«

VI. [3.]   Pape ianitores

        cerbero surdiores!

           In spe uana plores,

        iam etiamsi fores

        Orpheus, quem a*u*diit,

        Pluto, deus Tartareus,

           non ideo perores,

        Malleus argenteus

        ni fereat ad fores,

           Vbi Protheus

        uariat mille colores.

Large roman numerals denote the order of the stanzas in **D-Mbs Clm 4660-4660a**; small roman numerals in brackets give the order of the stanzas of *Dic Christi* as transmitted outside **D-Mbs Clm 4660-4600a**; arabic numerals in brackets give the order of the stanzas of *Bulla fulminante*.

Figure 4.3: (*cont.*)

in alternation, thus combining them into a new whole. Hilka and Schumann, for example, present as CB131 only the three stanzas of *Dic Christi* as transmitted in the Notre-Dame repertory; the four stanzas of *Bulla* from **GB-Lbl Egerton 274** (with the texts from **I-Fl Plut.29.1**) follow as CB131a. But how can this explain the textual layout in the *Codex Buranus*? Could its sole purpose have been to demonstrate the musical dependency of *Bulla* on the final melisma of the *Dic Christi* stanza, by attaching the former to the latter? Should *Bulla* thus be understood merely as a 'materialized' final melisma, especially since the final melisma of *Dic Christi* itself was not notated despite space being left for it? Or might the combination of the two pieces result from a misunderstanding on the part of the *Carmina Burana* redactors, who came to the wrong conclusions on the basis of the songs' musical relationship?

For a simple demonstration of the identity of the final melisma of *Dic Christi* and the melody of *Bulla*, it would have been sufficient to append *Bulla* as a whole to one of the *Dic Christi* stanzas, as is the case in the text-only notation of *Bulla* in **I-Fl Plut.29.1**.[69] The notion of a misunderstanding of the relationship between *Dic Christi* and *Bulla*, in turn, is rendered unlikely by the careful presentation, which uniquely involved a collaboration between notators n1 and n2: while the neumes of *Dic Christi* were provided by n2, the *Bulla*-stanza was notated by n1. Considering the specialization of the notators across the rest of the manuscript, it seems probable that this sharing of responsibility was a concession to the notators' divergent knowledge of the repertories: notator n2, who notated most of the pieces related to the Notre-Dame repertory in **D-Mbs Clm 4660-4660a**, was apparently more familiar with the melody of *Dic Christi*, whereas n1 was more familiar with *Bulla*. In any case, their respective notations suggest that they were very well aware of what they were doing: the neume patterns not only match the diastematically decipherable versions of *Dic Christi* (tenor part) and *Bulla* very closely, but also fit well with the neumatic practices seen in other manuscripts from the German-speaking countries, as the synoptic overview of neumatic notations in Examples 4.1 and 4.2 demonstrates.[70]

Large-scale agreement between the different versions of *Dic Christi* can be made out regarding melodic contours in the syllabic passages, cadential patterns at syntactic breaks, as well as the use of extensive melismas. The melismas themselves are less closely related, with **D-Mbs Clm 4660-4660a** and **D-Sl HB I 95** on the whole featuring more elaborate variants than the other manuscript sources. In light of the correlation of the other features, however, one may assume that these variants are individual 'workings out' of a melodic framework, the central notes of which correspond between the different settings. The divergences from the Notre-Dame settings in the melismas of the manuscript witnesses from German-speaking lands may also be related to the fact that the crucial musical features of the former – such as voice exchange, voice crossing, and rhythmic correspondence between different voices – could not be transferred into the monophonic settings, and that the recipients consequently saw themselves challenged to devise their own, modified musical solutions.

In **D-Mbs Clm 4660-4660a**, the long melismas were already planned during the disposition of the texts, the notation of which was provided for both *Dic Christi* and *Bulla* by the main scribe, n2. The melisma which apparently required the largest amount of space – the final melisma of *Dic*

---

[69] Bernt 1979, whose texts are based on Hilka and Schumann 1930–1970, also employs this mode of presentation.

[70] See also the three-voice conductus version of *Dic Christi* in **D-W Guelf.628 Helmst.** f.73r; transcription in G. Anderson 1986, 1:50ff.

Example 4.1: Synoptic overview of neumatic notations of *Dic Christi veritas*.
a) **D-Sl HB I 95**; b) **D-Mbs Clm 4660**; c) **CH-EN 1003**

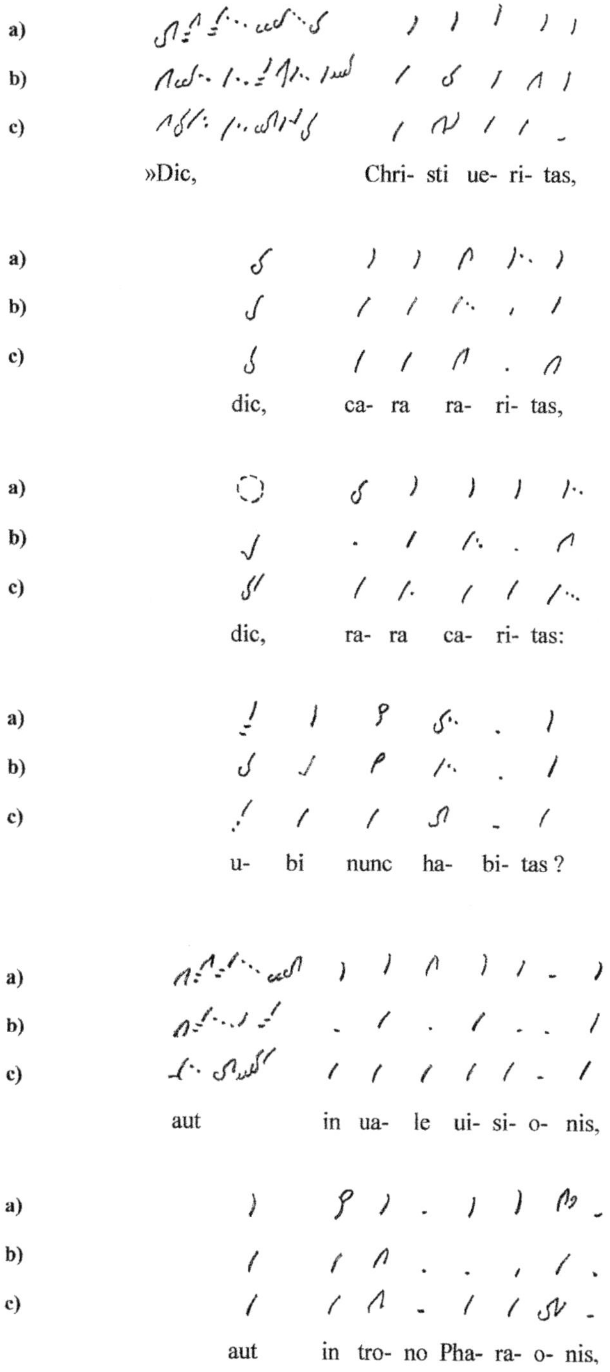

a)

b)

c)

»Dic,   Chri- sti ue- ri- tas,

a)

b)

c)

dic,   ca- ra   ra- ri- tas,

a)

b)

c)

dic,   ra- ra   ca- ri- tas:

a)

b)

c)

u-   bi   nunc   ha- bi- tas ?

a)

b)

c)

aut   in ua- le ui- si- o- nis,

a)

b)

c)

aut   in tro- no Pha- ra- o- nis,

Example 4.1: (*cont.*)

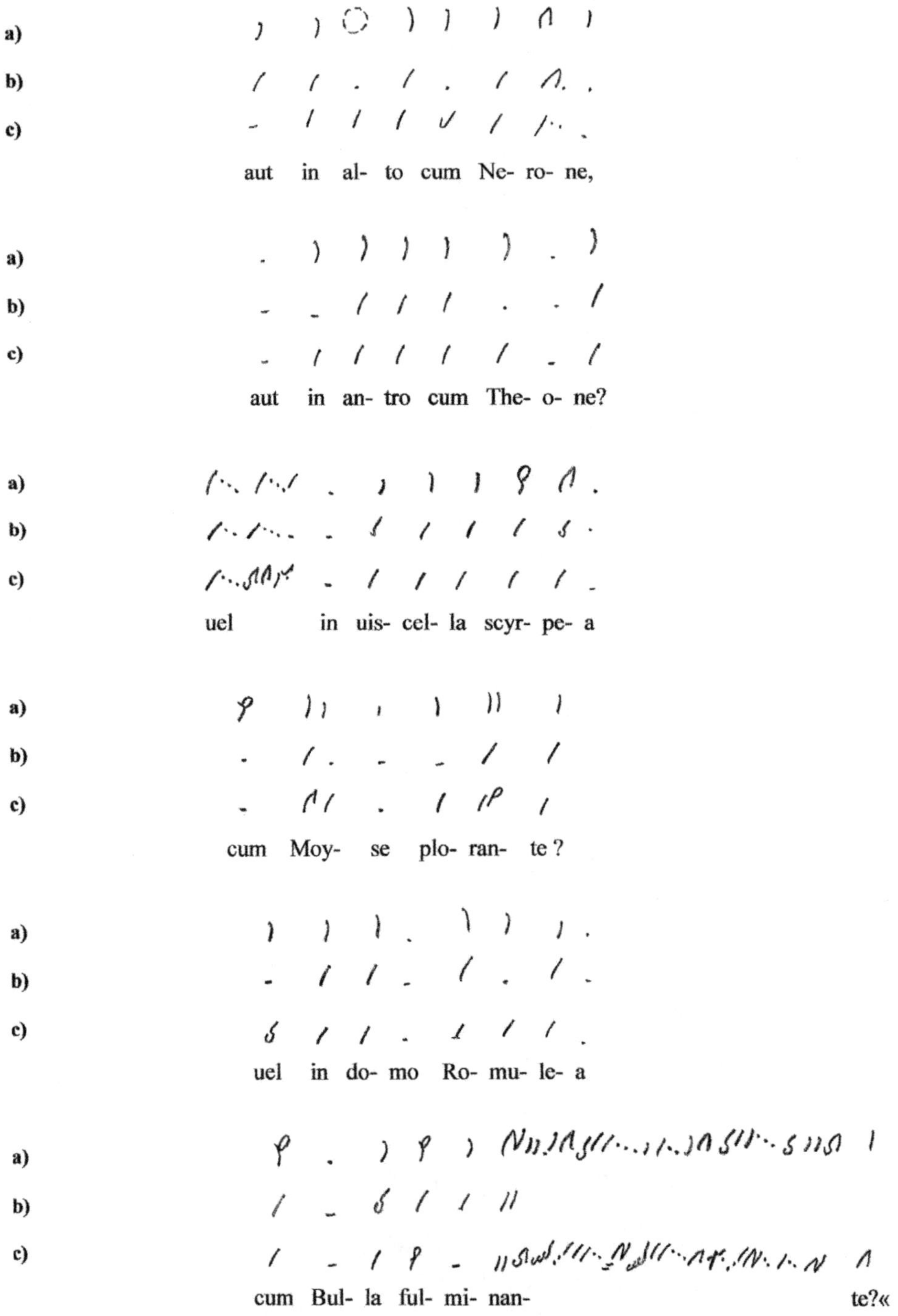

a)

b)

c)

aut in al- to cum Ne- ro- ne,

a)

b)

c)

aut in an- tro cum The- o- ne?

a)

b)

c)

uel in uis- cel- la scyr- pe- a

a)

b)

c)

cum Moy- se plo- ran- te ?

a)

b)

c)

uel in do- mo Ro- mu- le- a

a)

b)

c)

cum Bul- la ful- mi- nan-   te?«

Example 4.2: Synoptic overview of neumatic notations of *Bulla fulminante*. a) **D-Sl HB I 95**; b) **D-Mbs Clm 4660**; c) **GB-Lbl Egerton 274**

Example 4.2: (*cont.*)

a)

b)

c)

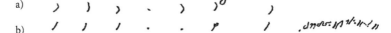

ius - ti - ci - a　　pro - stran - te.

a)

b)

c)

I - tur　et　re - cur - ri - tur

a)

b)

c)

ad　cu - ri - am,　nec　an - te

a)

b)

c)

Quid　con - se - qui - tur,

a)

b)

c)

quam ex - u - i - tur__ qua - dran - te.

Christi – was, however, never notated by n2, but indicated with no more than a red line which functions 'in the text as a sign for the activity of the voice', or a 'melismatic placeholder'.[71] More significantly, the scribe also left relatively large spaces after each pair of rhymes in *Bulla*, which were indeed used for notation by n1. Neither **GB-Lbl Egerton 274** nor **D-Sl HB I 95** features melismas following the rhymed verse endings 'tonante', 'gravante', 'prostrante', 'nec ante', and 'quadrante'. Setting aside a few small melismas, *Bulla* is consistently syllabic in both manuscripts, adequately reflecting its creation through the texting of *Dic Christi*'s final melisma.

One possibility of understanding the internal melismas interpolated into *Bulla* in **D-Mbs Clm 4660-4660a** is to suggest that they are the individual phrases from the final melisma of *Dic Christi* which remained unnotated: the latter was not notated in the space left for it, but was split into sections and added to the relevant phrases of *Bulla* instead. Such a procedure would have been comparable to the 'synoptic *mise-en-page*' typical of the older sequence type in the German-speaking areas, although this is commonly found in the margins.[72] This scenario could also explain why the interpolated melismas in *Bulla* are found not on the final syllables of any particular word, but *after* the individual passages of text. The use of identical melismas following the melodically identical phrases for ll.1–2 ('Bulla fulminante/sub iudice tonante') and ll.3–4 ('reo appelante/sententia gravante') might be seen as further evidence for such an argument. The various melismas in the following verses of *Bulla*, however, no longer allow for a reliable reading related to the preceding syllabic melodic phrases; the possibility that the melismas provide a doubling of musical information can, in these cases, be eliminated.

It is particularly crucial to an understanding of the melismas in *Bulla* that they were provided not by the notator of *Dic Christi*, n2, but by the notator of *Bulla*, n1, and also that they were envisaged in the relevant places in the following stanzas of *Bulla* already by the text scribe. Regardless of whether or not they transmit melodic material from the final melisma of *Dic Christi*, the interpolated melismas of *Bulla* can thus hardly have been intended as a mere exemplification of the musical origins of the *Bulla* melody, but appear to have formed an integral part of *Bulla*'s musical design as devised and presented by the redactors of **D-Mbs Clm 4660-4660a**.

On the basis of these observations, much seems to suggest that the function of *Bulla* was not limited to the materialization of the final melisma of *Dic Christi*, but was intended for *alternatim* performance with the stanzas

---

[71] Meier and Lauer 1996, 39.   [72] See Haug 1987, 15–19.

of its twin song. Interpolated, the texts of the two pieces would indeed generate a plausible message: interspersed into the dialogue of the *Dic Christi* stanzas, the *Bulla* stanzas become asides which illustrate the song's general moral critique through concrete examples and focus it into a biting critique of the Pope.[73] The insertion of the melismas in *Bulla* also connect the interwoven texts musically: like the melismas on the first 'Dic', 'aut', and 'vel' of *Dic Christi*, the individual melismas in *Bulla* separate the individual syntactic-formal segments; the alternation between melismatic and syllabic passages becomes a shared characteristic of both songs, and the connection of the two songs, transmitted separately in France, thereby merges into a new, meaningful whole – both textually and musically.

In its deliberate alternation of *Dic Christi* and *Bulla* stanzas, the notation in **D-Mbs Clm 4660-4660a** – and, to some extent, that in **D-Sl HB I 95** – documents an act of creative appropriation, in which the knowledge of the internal musical connection of two otherwise independent pieces has inspired their explicit combination, and which thus created a meaningful stanzaic design with its own textual and musical profile. The monophonic reception is an essential condition for this process: within a polyphonic context, the performance of the texted final melisma would not have been possible without further modification, since the text of *Bulla* is modelled specifically onto the tenor voice of the three-part conductus.

As in the case of *Gaude. Cur gaudeas* (CB22), the detailed findings regarding *Dic Christi* and *Bulla* as CB131 suggest more generally that the blanket devaluation of the text and music transmission in **D-Mbs Clm 4660-4660a** on the basis of a limited focus on textual variants, transmission errors, reduction of voices, and compositional or notational atavism does not do justice to the underlying receptive processes. Even though the settings in **D-Mbs Clm 4660-4660a** ultimately elude any diastematic reading because of their neumatic notation, they give sufficient indications of the fact that they result from very conscious, careful, and idiosyncratic processes of reception and adaptation.

A systematic analysis of all of the pieces in **D-Mbs Clm 4660-4660a** that have concordances in the Notre-Dame repertory and their comparison to the corresponding Notre-Dame versions would still be desirable. It is likely that this might further support the recognition of the songs of **D-Mbs Clm 4660-4660a** as realizations of individual, self-contained musical solutions. Finally, an unprejudiced approach would also allow for the possibility

---

[73] See Vollmann 1987, 1120.

that a given version from **D-Mbs Clm 4660-4660a** is not necessarily a
monophonic reception of a polyphonic piece, but conversely that the
Notre-Dame version is a two-part expansion of a pre-existing melody.
This seems plausible, for example, in the case of *Vite perdite* (CB31), which
shows an almost exact correlation between the neumatic notation in
D-Mbs Clm 4660-4660a and the tenor of the two-voice version in **I-Fl
Plut.29.1**.[74] Since the upper voice of the two-part version is restricted to
the purely accidental function of adding strength to the sound, it is likely
that the tenor of *Vite perdite* circulated in a monophonic version from the
very beginning, particularly considering that this melody is transmitted
also with French and Occitan texts.[75] It becomes clear from such examples
that closer scrutiny would open up the possibility both of shedding new
light onto broad issues regarding the relationship of Notre-Dame and
'peripheral' repertories, and also of contributing to a modification of
current music historical narratives.

Conclusion

As a document from a time in which extra-liturgical music-making only
exceptionally made its way into written sources and whose historical
accounts give only little information about the forms and content of secular
singing, the importance of **D-Mbs Clm 4660-4660a** can hardly be overesti-
mated. Its significance lies not only in its large scope and diverse contents,
which bring together sources from across Europe, but also in its carefully
designed and executed manner of presenting individual songs and groups of
songs. The manuscript's decorative programme also manifests the value that
those responsible bestowed upon the repertory included. **D-Mbs Clm 4660-
4660a** evokes the image of a rich, secular musical life at a clerical centre in
the German-speaking countries, which took up songs from diverse proven-
ances and repertories in a process of creative reception, adapting and re-
contextualizing the songs to its own needs and preferences.

It is impossible to discern whether a song variant in **D-Mbs Clm 4660-
4660a** was the result of an adaptation by the manuscript's redactors or
whether it already formed part of a source which served as an exemplar
for the production of this manuscript. For pieces from the Notre-Dame
repertory with a large number of concordances in manuscript witnesses

---

[74] **D-Mbs Clm 4660-4660a** f.4r–4v; **I-Fl Plut.29.1** f.356r.
[75] Transcription in G. Anderson 1979, 60.

from German-speaking countries in particular, it cannot be ruled out that the version found in **D-Mbs Clm 4660-4660a** (including any idiosyncratic features) was copied from model sources. Conclusive insights regarding this issue, however, could be made only on the basis of a systematic comparison of all traces of the Notre-Dame repertory in manuscripts from German-speaking countries, and only if certain characteristic changes to the transmission could be plausibly posited as unique features of the versions in **D-Mbs Clm 4660-4660a**.

The unique editorial achievement of **D-Mbs Clm 4660-4660a** is most apparent in its ordering. By placing the pieces within an original large-scale framework – in which the exuberant praise of wine and women represents only one of many thematic concerns, directly contrasted by serious, moralizing texts – those responsible for **D-Mbs Clm 4660-4660a** reveal themselves not only as collectors and recipients, but also as redactors who confidently held diverse, internationally wide-spread song repertories at their disposal.

A characteristic feature of **D-Mbs Clm 4660-4660a** is the combination of songs of varying origins into new, unified songs, as seen exemplarily (but not singularly) in the combination of *Dic Christi veritas* and *Bulla fulminante* in CB131. The sacred dramas included in the manuscript's fourth section and the later additions, only touched upon briefly in the preceding discussion, strengthen this impression through their discernible compilation character: they merge various liturgical elements, fragments from other plays, conducti and other Latin versified poetry – occasionally even from the earlier sections of **D-Mbs Clm 4660-4660a** itself – into new, unique dramas.[76] The most unusual fruit of this practice of combination is found in the comprehensive number of Latin songs with a concluding Middle High German stanza, located mainly in the second section of the manuscript. As yet, not a single of these numerous Latin-German collages has been found outside the *Codex Buranus*, suggesting that this specific form of song compilation – as an 'intellectual and witty play of at least bilingual music connoisseurs with a good education and corresponding knowledge' – could indeed be traced back to the redactors of **D-Mbs Clm 4660-4660a** or their immediate context;[77] if so, it would make this practice the 'fashion of a geographically very limited circle'.[78] In their rich

---

[76] The play CB228, for example, opens with two pieces which are already contained in the second section of the manuscript as *Estivali gaudio* (CB80) and *Ab estatis floribus* (CB161); see Binkley 1983 and the references provided in Drumbl 2003, 333n31.

[77] U. Müller 1981, 103.   [78] U. Müller 1981, 102.

documentation of attempts to create montages of new songs and generate intertextual links from material that was, in part, already available and specifically created in others, the Latin-German combinations of the *Codex Buranus* allow conclusions concerning the song practices of the High Middle Ages extending far beyond any potentially localized tradition.

The *Carmina Burana* have been problematic because of their adiastematic notation, their special textual variants, and the persisting open questions about their context, but there remains a unique opportunity to gain important insights from a focus on **D-Mbs Clm 4660-4660a** as a whole. Deriving the competencies, intentions, and performance practices of the redactors and users of **D-Mbs Clm 4660-4660a** from the interpretation of individual songs can, in the end, be achieved only through an approach – sketched in this chapter – which considers the individual observations in the context of a systematic study of the transmitted corpus as a whole, and supports this methodologically by a comparison with a wide range of analogous cases. In this respect, much remains to be done for the most famous songbook of the thirteenth century.

5 | An English monastic miscellany: the Reading manuscript of *Sumer is icumen in*

HELEN DEEMING

GB-Lbl Harley 978 occupies a special place in the history of English music.[1] Within its opening gathering, among thirteen other pieces of music (Latin, French, English and textless; monophonic and polyphonic), nestles *Sumer is icumen in* (often known by one of its modern sobriquets, the 'Cuckoo song', the 'Summer canon', or the 'Reading rota'). Regarded by nineteenth- and early twentieth-century readers as the first song in the English language, the song's rustic theme and quaint spelling has come to represent the very essence of 'Merrie England'.[2] Furthermore, the song is to be sung as a round, making it straightforward to learn and perform, and has provided countless hours of musical pleasure to generations of amateur musicians. The nostalgic reception of *Sumer is icumen in* continues today: in a recent 'pocket-sized' edition, the song is presented with elegant, medieval-inspired calligraphy and suitably spring-like illustrations of flora and fauna, and advertised by its publishers as 'an ideal present or stocking-filler'.[3]

The *Sumer* canon has been a fixation of musical scholars, too: as a four-part round, with a two-part 'pes' underpinning the harmony, it can generate six-part polyphony though from an era when music in as many as four parts was rare. To scholars intent on seeking out the roots and development of that 'great Western invention', polyphony, *Sumer is icumen in* provided valuable (if questionable) evidence for an all-but-lost English vernacular idiom. For these scholars, the polyphonic interest of the manuscript did not stop there: just as exciting was a list towards the

---

[1] The extensive historiography of the manuscript is explored and listed in Taylor 2002. Especially relevant to the present study are Kingsford 1890; Handschin 1949–51; Hohler 1978; Taylor and Coates 1998. Digital images of the complete manuscript are now available at www.bl.uk/manuscripts/FullDisplay.aspx?ref=Harley_MS_978.

[2] It appeared as the opening poem in Quiller-Couch 1900 and has fronted many other poetry anthologies since; see Taylor 2002, 76–9. Perhaps the earliest of several appearances of the song in film, Erich Korngold's score for the 1938 Errol Flynn film, *The Adventures of Robin Hood*, has Little John whistling the tune when he meets Robin Hood for the first time. I am grateful to Paul Harper-Scott for this reference.

[3] Hardman, Morris, and Castle 2006. Promotional material at www.tworiverspress.com/SumerIsIcumenIn/SumerIsIcumenIn.html.

end of the volume, purporting to be the contents of a lost book of liturgical polyphony.[4] Not only did this list seem to point to a significant, and previously undiscovered, cultivation of polyphonic music within the British Isles, but it had names attached: in short, this was the discovery of the very first English composers.

Over time, the historiography of **GB-Lbl Harley 978** has become less hidebound by these concerns, largely because the book has attracted the attention of literary and historical scholars on account of some of its non-musical contents. But the musicological study of the book – with a few notable exceptions – has continued to be dominated by disproportionate attention given to the manuscript's only English-language text and its list of lost polyphony, to the detriment of the other musical pieces and their non-musical companions in the manuscript. Moreover, within the land-scape of English music before 1300, otherwise dominated by fragmentary and lost sources, the manuscript has assumed singular importance.[5] This perception of the manuscript as monumental has been reinforced by its display for many years, open at *Sumer is icumen in*, in the British Library's permanent exhibition, resulting in damage to the spine of the book and its subsequent re-classification as one that may only be viewed with special permission. Along with the stone tablet mounted in 1913 on the wall of the ruined Chapter House at Reading Abbey, which displays a giant facsimile of the same page under the description 'the most remarkable ancient musical composition in existence', this treatment of **GB-Lbl Harley 978** publicly declares it to be special, even epic.[6]

Yet **GB-Lbl Harley 978**, as a miscellaneous collection of poetry, prose, and music, in three languages, and with both religious and secular con-cerns, is much less unusual than was once thought. In fact, some thirty-seven other 'musical miscellanies' survive from twelfth- and thirteenth-century Britain, although they have been all but completely ignored in musicological scholarship. This chapter aims to reintegrate **GB-Lbl Harley 978** into this context of musical transmission in medieval Britain, exploring new ways of

---

[4] The list is transcribed in Wibberley 1977, 180–1.

[5] For a guide to the types of musical source from Britain in this period, see N. Bell 2008.

[6] The unveiling of the stone tablet was accompanied by the publication of a booklet about the piece and its history by the historian of Reading Abbey, Jamieson Boyd Hurry (Hurry 1913, reprinted 'in response to a widespread demand' in London by Novello the following year). This publication has some similarities with the recent 'pocket-sized' edition (cited in fn3 above), in its use of medieval-style decorated initials and miniature illustrations; it further makes use of a typeface that includes the archaic long s and st ligature, imbuing its pages with a pseudo-antique appearance.

reading its contents against those of similar manuscripts. Above all, it seeks to apply a musicological perspective to the whole book, asking how its songs (some of which first appeared in print only in 2013) function within the complex dynamics of this particular collection, while also representing a musical tradition that is more than usually scattered among disparate sources.[7]

Contents and origins

GB-Lbl Harley 978 is a miscellany containing French, Latin, and English poetry (some with, but mostly without, musical notation), historical and medical texts, and a calendar of the use of Reading Abbey. In addition to its musical contents, some of which are unique to this manuscript, **GB-Lbl Harley 978** is both the earliest and the only complete source for the lais and fables of Marie de France, as well as being a significant repository of the satirical poetry of the so-called 'Goliards', and of a few historical texts, including two laments on the death of Thomas Becket and one description of his genealogy, and the *Song of Lewes*, which commemorates Simon de Montfort's victory over Henry III in 1264. It has been suggested that 'the entire manuscript [. . .] was compiled within [the] period 1261–5', since the calendar (near the beginning of the manuscript) contains an obit that can be no earlier than 1261, and the *Song of Lewes* (towards the end of the book) postdates the battle of 1264, but was probably copied before the death of Simon de Montfort at Evesham the following year.[8]

    GB-Lbl Harley 978 was not designed and executed in a single phase of copying. It is the work of several hands, some of which recur at more than one location in the book, and it does not adopt a uniform page-layout throughout.[9] Some portions of it are self-contained booklets, often ending with blank leaves. Twenty-two leaves disappeared from the book at some time in the seventeenth or early eighteenth century, but this did not cause

---

[7] The songs surviving in British sources between 1150 and 1300 are edited in Deeming 2013. See especially Deeming 2013, xxxi–xxxiv (for details of their manuscript contexts) and 167–224 (for the individual entries for each manuscript in the Textual Commentary).

[8] Taylor and Coates 1998; these authors argue that after 1265, a supportive scribe would be more likely to copy a lament commemorating Simon's death than one celebrating an earlier victory.

[9] Attempts to determine the precise divisions of the manuscript by scribal hands and gathering structure have encountered many difficulties: see the discussion in Kingsford 1890, xviii–xix, and the diagrammatic representations in Hohler 1978, 5 and Taylor 2002, 84. For the present purpose, however, what is significant is not the precise locations of the divisions but rather the clear overall sense of a sectional compilation.

any text to be left incomplete: this lost section too must therefore have formed one or more self-contained units.[10] The sections of the manuscript may have been brought together over time, if perhaps not a very long time, since no section has suffered the obvious wear of a long period spent unbound. This codicological evidence indicates that, far from being the work of a single scribe, consciously intended as a collection, the various contents of **GB-Lbl Harley 978** may have ended up together through the choices of several compilers. The full contents of the manuscript are listed in Table 5.1, with indications of the codicological divisions between separate sections: points at which obvious changes of hand occur are indicated in the table by X, and where these coincide with new quires, they are marked with Q. Changes of layout and blank leaves are also noted in boldface, as further indications of the *ad hoc* nature of the compilation.

As this list of contents shows, **GB-Lbl Harley 978** contains more French and Latin poetry than anything else, but exhibits a wide variety of forms and thematic concerns. Attention has tended to focus on a small number of the manuscript's contents: *Sumer is icumen in*, the *Song of Lewes* and the medical and hawking tracts tend to feature at the forefront of discussion of the book, but their significance in the collection as a whole is greatly outweighed by its clear bias towards poetry of the Latin moral-satirical and French narrative types. The interest in English political history of the recent past – evinced by materials relating to the Barons' Revolt and the martyrdom of Thomas Becket – has often been emphasized, but in fact seems marginal when these items are viewed as a proportion of the whole book. With all its codicological disruptions, and the variety of themes and concerns apparent in its poetic and non-poetic materials, **GB-Lbl Harley 978** does not readily lend itself to interpretation as the product of a single, conscious design, but rather – like many other English miscellanies discussed below – seems to be a more 'accidental' compilation, whose precise final arrangement was not necessarily envisaged by any of those involved in its production.

Within the scholarship on **GB-Lbl Harley 978**, a particular yearning to identify the book's first owner may be discerned. A book deemed so important to the history of English music and poetry needed, it seemed, a firm link with an identifiable reader, or at least with a defined

---

[10] Hohler 1978, 3–4. An extract that may have appeared in the missing section was copied by Richard James in the 1620s; it is interesting to note that it is a Latin poetic text adopting the thirteen-syllable line pattern of much of the Latin satirical (or 'Goliardic') poetry that remains in the manuscript; Hohler 1978, 33fn5.

Table 5.1 The contents of **GB-Lbl Harley 978**

Folios	Codicological divisions	Contents
1r–14v		Music
		Mainly monophonic songs in Latin, with one French, one English, and three textless pieces (for full list see Table 5.2)
14r–15r	X	Music-theoretical diagram, solmization piece, and didactic song
15v–21r	X	Calendar
		Commemorations filled in only for January and February; prognostic texts in external margins of 15v–19r (those on 17v– 19r **in a different hand**)
21v	X	Short Latin medical text
22r–37r	Q X	Medical tracts in French and Latin
		(in two columns and **in several hands)**
37v	**blank**	
Gap of 22 leaves (according to the oldest foliation)		
38r	X	Ecclesiastical specimen letters
38v	X	Latin satirical poem
38v–39v	X	Three short Latin texts on moral and biblical topics
40r–67v	Q X	Marie de France's translation of Aesop's fables **(in two columns)**
68r	**blank**	
68v–73v	X	Latin debate poem 'Noctis sub silencio' **(one column)**
74r–74v	**blank**	
75r–89r	Q X	Latin satirical poems **(two columns)**
89v–91v		Two Latin poems on the martyrdom of Thomas Becket
92r–102v		Latin poems on religious and moral themes
102v–104v		French moral poem
104v–106r		Latin poem on the angels
106r–107r	**X?**	French satirical poem
107r–114v	X	'Song of Lewes'
		(Latin poem on the Battle of Lewes, 1264)
114v–116r		Latin text on the marriage of Thomas Becket's parents, and **incomplete** French translation of the same
116v–117r	X	French treatise on hawking
117v	**blank**	
118r–160r	Q X?	Lais of Marie de France
		(with Prologue, and **titles in top margins)**
160v–161r	X	List of polyphonic music
		(headed 'Ordo libri W. de Wint.')
161v		pen trials (various dates)

geographical location. But the origins of the manuscript are not immediately obvious. It lacks any *ex libris* inscription or scribal colophon and its several hands offer no evidence of the house style of any particular scriptorium or workshop that might have been responsible for producing the book. Instead, the contents of the manuscript have been scrutinized for clues, leading some scholars to imagine an eccentric and colourful character for its first reader. Some have assumed that the 'W. de Wint.' (perhaps to be expanded as William of Winton, Wintonia or Winchester) whose name heads the list of pieces on f.160v was also the owner of **GB-Lbl Harley 978**.[11] The scandalous history of a Reading monk of this name has proved an enticing hook upon which to hang the manuscript's eclectic contents.[12] Others, drawing on both textual and codicological evidence, have sought to link the manuscript with the fledgling university at Oxford, one author proposing that an itinerant music teacher, who collected some of his materials at Oxford but eventually joined the monastic community at Reading, is a plausible candidate for the book's first owner.[13] Most, however, with greater caution and less speculation, have posited the manuscript's origin at Reading Abbey, an attribution based on a few scattered indications in the manuscript itself. The names of Reading monks appearing in the list of polyphony and as obits in the calendar have been crucial to this attribution, as has the liturgical affiliation of the calendar, which would have had no practical use except at Reading or one of its dependent priories, though its state of incompletion raises questions in any case over its use in monastic practice.[14]

The codicological make-up of the manuscript suggests that some of its sections may have originated in different environments. The section containing the Lais (ff.118r–160r),[15] for example, is written in a more practised hand with a two-column layout and running titles that may suggest the work of a professional scribe, perhaps from one of the workshops that had begun to spring up in Oxford, to serve the needs of the scholars.[16] Its eventual arrival at Reading Abbey, where it was most likely assembled with

---

[11] Ernest H. Sanders, 'Wintonia, W. de', via GMO. Taylor 2002, 93, 110–21, and 132–6; Coates 1999, 14–16, 73, 91, 101.

[12] See especially Taylor 2002 and Wulstan 2000.   [13] Hohler 1978.

[14] For the monks whose names feature in the list of polyphony, see Ernest H. Sanders, 'Burgate, R. de' and 'Wycombe, W. de', via GMO. On Wycombe see also Madan 1924, 169 (item 16) and Sharpe et al. 1996, list B76, pp.461–3. On the liturgical affiliation of the calendar, see Taylor and Coates 1998.

[15] www.bl.uk/manuscripts/Viewer.aspx?ref=harley_ms_978_f118r.

[16] Taylor 2002, 120–1.

the other components of the manuscript as now compiled, could have been facilitated by one of the monks of Reading who studied at Oxford in the thirteenth century, and who may have commissioned or purchased book-lets from the booksellers while they were there.[17] Though certain sections of it may have been produced outside the abbey, and the ultimate origin of some of its texts could have been even further afield, Jacques Handschin's 1949 assessment that the manuscript *as a collection* originated at Reading Abbey still has much to recommend it.[18]

The transmission of song in English miscellanies

Reluctance to accept a monastic origin for **GB-Lbl Harley 978** has partly resulted from a perception of its contents as unsuitable reading matter for Benedictine monks.[19] Yet numerous other manuscripts testify to an inter-est in secular poetry, both Latin and vernacular, among the religious orders in thirteenth-century England (as elsewhere on the Continent).[20] Some evidence suggests that clerical readers found ways to employ poetry and songs for mnemonic purposes and even as a source of quotations to illustrate and enliven their preaching and other forms of pastoral instruc-tion.[21] Poetry and songs regularly circulated alongside devotional texts and sermons, or with historical and liturgical materials, and – as this chapter will show – the circles in which they moved around were, like those of **GB-Lbl Harley 978**, religious houses and their members.

The networks of communication extending outwards from a community such as Reading are readily observable through the contents of **GB-Lbl Harley 978**. It contains the names of individual Reading monks, at least one of whom, William de Winton, probably travelled to Oxford to study. Both Winton and William of Wycombe (also named in the manuscript) spent time at the abbey's dependent priory at Leominster, where, according to an inventory dated 1248–9, Wycombe was active as a scribe and possibly

---

[17] Though there is no concrete evidence of Reading monks studying at Oxford until some time after **GB-Lbl Harley 978** was produced, Abbot Robert de Burgate (named in the list of polyphony in the manuscript) was involved in the attempt to establish a Benedictine house at Oxford in 1277, suggesting that Reading monks had connections to the university at least by this date; Coates 1999, 91; Taylor 2002, 121.

[18] Handschin 1949–51.   [19] Hohler 1978, 7; Taylor 2002, 136.

[20] See, for example, Wilmart 1941, Hunt 1961 and Pouzet 2004.

[21] Deeming forthcoming; on Middle English poetry in this context, see S. Wenzel 1986 and A. Fletcher 1998.

also a composer of liturgical music.[22] **GB-Lbl Harley 978**'s group of specimen letters on f.38r include one letter of introduction for a monk travelling from one house to another:[23] such letters must frequently have been required, since Reading monks were in close contact not only with dependent priories and other houses in the British Isles but also with Cluny, the mother house from which Reading itself was founded.[24]

Similar networks are apparent in other thirteenth-century musical miscellanies. **F-EV lat.17** was made at Wareham Priory, but moved early in its history to the priory's mother house at Lyre in Normandy. The book shares no concordances with **GB-Lbl Harley 978**, but similarly includes gatherings of songs, in comparable styles and forms.[25] Another Lyre manuscript, **F-EV lat.2**, contains contributions made by a scribe who went to England in 1246 and two musical pieces with predominantly English transmission histories. The cross-Channel connections of Lyre Abbey extended to four other dependent priories besides Wareham, and close links with Hereford Cathedral, in the form of prayer agreements and reciprocal visiting rights. The music-theory song *Est tonus sic* (discussed further below) is found in **GB-Lbl Harley 978**, **F-EV lat.2**, and the Hereford Breviary, **GB-H P.IX.7** and – although the connection between these three sources should not be overstated – this fact would seem to typify the circulation of songs between religious houses and their members on both sides of the Channel.

Evidence that books, including miscellanies preserving poetry and songs, circulated between religious houses and their members in thirteenth-century England is plentiful: to name just a few examples, the thirteenth-century portions of **IRL-Dtc 432** were owned by Belvoir Priory and later by brother Henry of Dunstaple; **GB-Ob Ashmole 1285** was apparently given to Southwark Priory by brother Hugh of Wendover; and **GB-Occ 59** appears in an early library catalogue of Llanthony Secunda, but may at one time have been the property of the priory's schoolmaster.[26] In all of these cases and many more, songs moved between individuals and communities in tandem with other kinds of written material, much of it serving practical functions in the life of a religious community. Manuscripts like these have seldom been contemplated as whole books, but – as for **GB-Lbl Harley**

---

[22] Madan 1924.

[23] www.bl.uk/manuscripts/Viewer.aspx?ref=harley_ms_978_f038r.

[24] Coates 1999, 6–7; Gillingham 2006, 91–5.

[25] See Deeming 2006, 16–17 and Deeming 2005, 1:62–80. The connection between **GB-Lbl Harley 978** and the Lyre manuscripts was first suggested by Hohler 1978.

[26] See Deeming 2005, chapter II, 3.

978 – such an approach brings us closer to understanding the modes of transmission of song which, along with the specifically musical dimension to be explored in the next part of this chapter, is crucial to the present reassessment of these song gatherings.

The songs and their contexts

Table 5.2 lists the items to be found on ff.2–15 of **GB-Lbl Harley 978**, the musical portion that opens the book.[27] Only one attempt has been made to explore these anonymous songs together as a collection: John Stevens' article uncovering this 'neglected context' for *Sumer is icumen in* was the first to catalogue all the songs, trace their concordances, and produce critical editions of their texts.[28] Despite his work, inaccurate descriptions of the songs still abound, and the music for four of the songs remained unpublished until 2013.[29] Moreover, because Stevens limited his scope just to the songs on ff.2–13v, these pieces have still yet to be considered in the light of the music-theory material that immediately follows, and in relation to the remaining contents of the whole book.[30] Most significantly, the music of **GB-Lbl Harley 978** may now be placed in the context of other English miscellanies containing music, revealing that its styles and organization are much less individual than has been thought.

There is a clear preponderance of Latin, monophonic songs, and a preference for sacred topics, overwhelmingly the Blessed Virgin Mary. Eight songs and the three textless pieces use a musical form based on progressive repetition (AABBCC, in its simplest kind). The form is associated with a number of medieval genres, including the liturgical sequence, the lyric lai, and the instrumental estampie. Generic distinctions, especially between the sequence and the lai, can be difficult to draw, as John Stevens' work on the songs showed, and it makes sense therefore to consider all these formal types together. Only two songs appear in languages other than Latin, *Sumer is icumen in* and *Duce creature*, and it is striking that both of

---

[27] www.bl.uk/manuscripts/Viewer.aspx?ref=harley_ms_978_f002r.

[28] Stevens 1996.

[29] Deeming 2013: the songs in **GB-Lbl Harley 978** are nos. 79–88 there; those unpublished before are nos. 80 *Regina clemencie*, 84 *Felix sanctorum*, 86 *Eterni numinis*, and 87 *Ante thronum*.

[30] The didactic song *Est tonus sic* was not included in Deeming 2013 and is edited for the first time in Example 5.3 below. The text of the theoretical items on ff.14r–15r, with reproductions of their notations from the manuscript, is edited in *Thesaurus musicarum latinarum* (www.chmtl. indiana.edu/tml/13th/ANOINT_MLBLH978.html).

Table 5.2 The music preserved in **GB-Lbl Harley 978**

Folios	Incipit	Language	Musical setting	Musical form	Textual topic
2r–4v	Samson dux fortissime	Latin	monophonic	progressive repetition	Samson
4v–6r	Regina clemencie	Latin	monophonic	progressive repetition	BVM
6r–7r	Dum Maria credidit	Latin	monophonic	progressive repetition	BVM
7r–8v	Ave gloriosa virginum	Latin	monophonic	progressive repetition	BVM
8v–9r	[3 textless estampies]	–	2 parts	progressive repetition	–
9v–10r	Ave gloriosa mater / Duce creature	Latin / French	3 parts	through-composed	BVM / BVM
10v–11r	Felix sanctorum	Latin	monophonic	progressive repetition	Apostles
11r	*Petrus romanis*	*Latin*	*unnotated poem*		*Apostles*
11v	Sumer is icumen in / Perspice christicola	English / Latin	4-part round with 2-part pes		Spring / Easter
12r–13r	Eterni numinis	Latin	monophonic	progressive repetition	BVM
13r	Ante thronum regentis omnia	Latin	monophonic	progressive repetition	St Thomas
13v	Gaude salutata virgo	Latin	monophonic	progressive repetition	BVM
13v	*Deus qui beatam virginem*	*Latin*	*unnotated prayer*		*BVM*
14r	*diagram of the gamut* and solmization exercise	Latin	monophonic	–	musical intervals
14v–15r	Est tonus sic ut re ut	Latin	monophonic	–	musical intervals
15r	further demonstrations of musical intervals	Latin	monophonic	–	musical intervals

Items in italics are not notated; the double horizontal line indicates a change of hand.

them are copied in **GB-Lbl Harley 978** with an alternative Latin text. Though the section containing the songs is predominantly a musical gathering, two unnotated texts appear within it, one (*Petrus romanis*) copied by the same hand as the music, and the other (*Deus qui beatam virginem*) added somewhat later to the space remaining at the end of f.13v.[31]

---

[31] www.bl.uk/manuscripts/Viewer.aspx?ref=harley_ms_978_f013v.

Among the songs based on progressive repetition, Stevens identified lais, sequences, and several pieces that were difficult to classify as either. The problems of generic definition begin with the absence of any functional indications in the manuscript: the nature of their preservation here, as in similar miscellaneous collections, gives us no information about the occasions (liturgical or otherwise) on which they were sung. Since function cannot contribute to the repertory of generic markers for these pieces, we must rely solely on the technical, communicative and presentational information encoded within the manuscript witnesses, though these indications are frequently at variance with one another. Most obviously, the definitions of 'sequence' and 'lai' tend to rely on both poetic and musical parameters: a constant syllable-count and regular pattern of musical repetition is most likely to signify a 'sequence', as opposed to the greater variety of the 'lai'. But both within **GB-Lbl Harley 978** and in the English song repertory more generally, there are songs with constant syllable-counts but irregular musical repetition and vice versa, and a complete spectrum of degrees of 'constancy' and 'regularity'. For example, *Regina clemencie* (Example 5.1) could hardly be more constant in poetic terms: every one of its forty-four lines has thirteen syllables, with a caesura after the seventh; moreover, only two rhyme sounds are employed throughout the text ('-ata' for lines 1–20 and 41–4, and '-isti' for lines 21–40).[32] Yet its music is much less predictable: sometimes two thirteen-syllable lines form a versicle whose music is then repeated; elsewhere the repetition occurs after four lines. Some versicles are not repeated immediately, but their music returns later in the song.[33] Perhaps the strangest feature of all is that the change of rhyme (from '-ata' to '-isti') occurs between the two versicles of a musical repetition, the music thus cutting decisively against the grain of the poetry.[34]

---

[32] In the examples included in this chapter, double underlay and numbering of versicles 1a/1b, etc, are editorially supplied to draw attention to passages of music that are repeated to different phrases of text, but in the manuscript itself the musical repetitions are all written out in full, with the exception of *Ante thronum regentis omnia* (discussed below). Differences between repeated passages are shown on the ossia staves above the main stave. An English translation of *Regina clemencie* may be found in Deeming 2013, no. 80.

[33] The unique and complex patterning of this song explains why Stevens' numbering of the versicles (in Stevens 1996, 314–15) differs from mine in Example 5.1 below.

[34] In some manuscripts, the section beginning 'Primum fuit gaudium' is preserved as a separate poem, a reading that is understandable poetically but nonsensical musically: the music, however, is uniquely preserved in **GB-Lbl Harley 978**. See Stevens 1996, 314. This section is, however, highlighted with an enlarged initial at 'Primum' in **GB-Lbl Harley 978** (on f.5v: www.bl.uk/manuscripts/Viewer.aspx?ref=harley_ms_978_f005v).

The reverse situation is represented by *Ante thronum regentis omnia* (Table 5.3): here, the versicles of text begin as three monorhymed lines of ten syllables, then increase to four monorhymed decasyllables; the third stanza shifts to three decasyllables plus a final four-syllable line with contrasting rhyme, and the final stanza involves five lines (of eight, seven, eight, eight and seven syllables respectively, rhyming abacb). The music, though, maintains a stable pattern of repetition of versicles throughout, a

Example 5.1: *Regina clemencie* (**GB-Lbl Harley 978**, ff.4v–6r)

Example 5.1: (*cont.*)

regularity that has allowed the scribe to economize by copying the music for each versicle only once, with both versicles of text underlaid beneath.[35]

[35] See www.bl.uk/manuscripts/Viewer.aspx?ref=harley_ms_978_f013r. For an edition of the music (also unique to this manuscript), see Deeming 2013, 130–1, where the song is edited both

Example 5.1: (*cont.*)

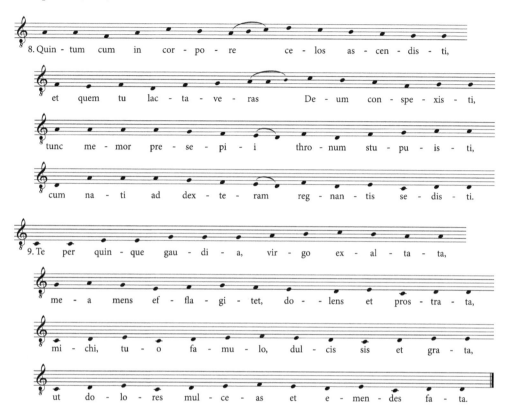

8. Quin - tum cum in cor - po - re ce - los as - cen - dis - ti,

et quem tu lac - ta - ve - ras De - um con - spe - xis - ti,

tunc me - mor pre - se - pi - i thro - num stu - pu - is - ti,

cum na - ti ad dex - te - ram reg - nan - tis se - dis - ti.

9. Te per quin - que gau - di - a, vir - go ex - al - ta - ta,

me - a mens ef - fla - gi - tet, do - - lens et pros - tra - ta,

mi - chi, tu - o fa - mu - lo, dul - cis sis et gra - ta,

ut do - lo - res mul - ce - as et e - men - des fa - ta.

This layout procedure for songs based on progressive repetition is unique among the songs in **GB-Lbl Harley 978**, and found in only one other British song manuscript from before 1300.[36] Double and multiple underlay is occasionally found for other reasons, such as when two alternative texts are provided for the same music – as in *Ave gloriosa mater / Duce creature* and *Sumer is icumen in / Perspice christicola* in **GB-Lbl Harley 978** –[37] or, just as rarely, for strophic songs, but on the whole scribes seem to have

non-rhythmically (as no. 87a) and mensurally (as 87b): as explained in the Textual Commentary (208) and Editorial Notes (lii), the notation of this song – in a different hand from the remaining songs in the manuscript – is capable of mensural interpretation, which makes it unique in this respect among all the songs in British sources before 1300.

[36] The other source is **GB-Cgc 240/126**, dating from the end of the thirteenth century, in which five out of six songs of this form are copied with double underlay; see Deeming 2013, 80–8 (songs), 194–5 (commentary).

[37] See www.bl.uk/manuscripts/Viewer.aspx?ref=harley_ms_978_f009v and www.bl.uk/manuscripts/Viewer.aspx?ref=harley_ms_978_f011v.

Table 5.3 The text of *Ante thronum regentis omnia* (**GB-Lbl Harley 978**, f.13r)

Versicle	Text	Poetic pattern	Translation
1a	Ante thronum regentis omnia,	10a	Before the throne of the one reigning over all,
	festivatur Thome presentia,	10a	the presence of Thomas is celebrated,
	tonat hympnis celestis regia:	10a	the kingdom of heaven resounds with hymns:
1b	organizat triplex ierarchia,	10a	the triple hierarchy sings polyphony,
	Christi decor, transcendens omnia,	10a	the glory of Christ, transcending all things,
	mentes rapit et desideria.	10a	seizes minds and desires.
2a	Christus Thomam benigne respicit,	10a	Christ looks upon Thomas kindly,
	Thomas, Christum cernens, se	10a	Thomas, seeing Christ, remakes himself,
	reficit,	10a	the wound of Christ thus bestows on Thomas
	Christi vultus Thomam sic afficit	10a	what he wishes – he has what he does not fail
	quod vult, habet nec velle deficit:		to wish for:
2b	de coronis Thome lux emicat,	10a	from the crowns of Thomas light gleams out,
	Christus lucem Thome multiplicat,	10a	Christ multiplies the light of Thomas,
	meritorum coronas triplicat	10a	he makes triple the crowns of the deserving
	et in terris glebam santificat.	10a	and sanctifies the clay throughout the lands.
3a	Gleba felix cum gemmis rutilans,	10a	The happy clay glowing red with gems,
	ornat aurum gemmas irradians,	10a	illumining the gems it shows off gold,
	nova luce noctes illuminans	10a	illuminating nights with new light
	desperatis:	4b	for the desperate:
3b	uva merum fundens letitie,	10a	grape pouring out the wine of happiness,
	magne martir mire clementie,	10a	great martyr of marvellous mercy,
	regnum nobis impetra glorie	10a	secure the kingdom of glory for us
	cum beatis.	4b	with the blessed.
4a	Rosa rubens rosario,	8a	Rose blushing with rosiness,
	sanguinei ruboris,	7b	with the blood of redness,
	sub tue laudis pallio	8a	under the cloak of your praise
	nos foveas et vestias	8c	may you shelter us and clothe us
	rubore tui floris:	7b	with the redness of your flower:
4b	O Thoma, tui pretio	8a	O Thomas, by the price
	salvifici cruoris,	7b	of your salvific blood,
	a peccati contagio	8a	from the contagion of sin
	nos eruas et statuas	8c	may you release us and set us up
	a dextris salvatoris.	7b	by the right hand of the saviour.
	Amen		Amen

eschewed the economy of such strategies in favour of writing out musical repetitions in full.[38] When they did so, there are invariably slight

[38] Double underlay of alternative texts is found only for these two song-pairs in **GB-Lbl Harley 978** and two further pairs, one preserved in **GB-Lbl Arundel 248** (Deeming 2013, 96–7, nos. 70a–70b (songs), p.199 (commentary)) and the other in **GB-Lma Cust.1** (Deeming 2013,

differences between the repetitions, and it is therefore difficult to avoid the conclusion that these apparently minor variants (such as those shown on the ossia staves in Examples 5.1 and 5.2) were deemed significant and worthy of preservation. This layout of *Ante thronum regentis omnia*, so unusual in its own chronological and geographical context, anticipates scribal practices of the following century, in which an increasing fixity of form in the vernacular lai was accompanied – especially in the manuscripts of Machaut's works – by a customary adoption of double underlay (or text stacking) of the two parallel versicles.[39]

In the wider repertory of songs preserved in English miscellanies, around half use forms based on progressive repetition, and some 40 per cent of these have constant syllable-counts and regular musical repetition.[40] Scarcely fewer (35 per cent) have a changing syllable-count with regular repetition, and smaller proportions (15 per cent and 8 per cent respectively) involve changing syllable-counts with irregular repetition, or constant syllable-counts but irregular repetition. In this sense, then, the Harley songs are representative both of the preference for forms based on progressive repetition among thirteenth-century English songs, and also of the range of possible approaches to the form. The desire to accord generic labels to these pieces is a modern preoccupation that seems not to have been important to thirteenth-century scribes: only a tiny handful of songs in miscellanies (and none in **GB-Lbl Harley 978**) are labelled in their sources, and Stevens noted that 'in the end it perhaps does not much matter how we label [them]. The question is unlikely to have worried contemporaries'.[41]

Several songs in **GB-Lbl Harley 978**, like many in the contemporary English and Continental repertories, exhibit an active control over the successive introduction of higher melodic peaks, so there is a sense of the overall range being stretched upwards during the course of the piece. In *Felix sanctorum chorus* (Example 5.2) the compass of the first three stanzas increases from a seventh (1: *F-d*), to an octave (2: *D-d*), to a ninth (3: *D-e*); thereafter, the top of the range continues to rise (to *f* in stanza 4 and *g* in

---

135–7, nos. 92a–92b (songs), pp.211–12 (commentary)). Multiple underlay of strophic songs is found twice in **GB-Lbl Arundel 248**, including the strophic song-pair nos. 70a–70b already mentioned and the single-texted no.71 (Deeming 2013, 98 (song), 199–200 (commentary)), and in one further instance, in **F-EV lat.2** (Deeming 2013, 42–3, no.23 (song) and pp.177–8 (commentary)).

[39] See Elizabeth Eva Leach's discussion of this feature in Chapter 10 below.

[40] Fuller discussion of the musical and poetic characteristics of the broader English repertory may be found in Deeming 2013, xxxvii–xlv.

[41] Stevens 1996, 324–5.

Example 5.2: *Felix sanctorum chorus* (**GB-Lbl Harley 978**, ff.10v–11r)

Example 5.2: (*cont.*)

stanzas 5 and 6), while the lowest notes (*D* and *E*) are abandoned. These factors contribute to the strong sense of the melody becoming more expansive as the song progresses. *Ante thronum regentis omnia* not only introduces successively higher peaks in each of its four stanzas (*e, f, g, aa*), but also opens each stanza with a different note (*G, b, d, g*), tracing out the triad above the final and its octave. A strong sense of tonal focus, particularly around the final and its upper triad, is widely apparent throughout the songs and is often complemented by a counter-sonority that contrasts with but draws the melody back towards the final. This can be seen in the first stanza of *Felix sanctorum chorus*, which begins by circling around *G, b*, and eventually *d* (at 'apostolorum'), but then switches to an emphasis on the alternative triad of *F-a-c* (throughout the words 'duodenarius / per quos ecclesia'), returning to the final *G* only at the cadence-point.[42]

---

[42] For an English translation of *Felix sanctorum chorus*, see Deeming 2013, no. 84.

In poetic techniques as in musical ones, there are similarities between the Harley songs and their contemporaries in other miscellanies. The structures rely heavily on end-rhyme, and in forms with progressive repetition the two versicles sung to repeated music are often additionally wedded with a shared end-rhyme. *Regina clemencie*'s striking use of only two rhymes throughout is unique, but its dense patterning of verbal sounds within the lines is highly typical. The play on similar sounding words in versicle 2a ('Tu virga, tu virgula, tu virgo signata') and in 5b ('Purum pura puerum'), as well as the long anaphora (thirteen consecutive lines begin with 'Tu') are emblematic of a concern for the phonic aspects of language found widely throughout the repertory. The poetic and musical techniques of the songs are characterized more by small-scale patterning than by sophisticated, long-range discourse, although Stevens was right to note that **GB-Lbl Harley 978**, with its inclusion of the ambitious compositions *Samson dux fortissime* and *Ave gloriosa virginum* (the latter attributed to one of the most renowned Latin poets of the thirteenth century, Philip the Chancellor), seems to reflect the interests of a particularly intellectual group of readers and singers. The impressive geometrical metaphor that closes *Felix sanctorum chorus* (stanza 6 in Example 5.2) appears geared to an audience likely to revel in allusive and complex wordplay, and the whole text of *Ante thronum regentis omnia* (Table 5.3) fits in with this cerebral culture. Its dazzling images in the third and fourth stanzas – difficult to pin down in translation – contribute to what I characterize as a deliberate ambiguity over which St Thomas forms the subject of the poem. While the references to martyrdom would surely have evoked an association with St Thomas Becket in the mind of a thirteenth-century English reader or listener (particularly as other texts relating to Becket occur in the manuscript), the allusion in the second stanza to Christ's wound and Thomas' desire in relation to it seems to be drawn instead from the story of St Thomas the Apostle. An intellectual game – of setting the two saints into close juxtaposition in order, perhaps, to inspire devotional reflection on their association – seems to be behind the poetic intent of this complex piece.[43]

The notation of the songs in **GB-Lbl Harley 978** has attracted attention, because a subsequent hand has altered some note-forms in some of the songs: this has usually been interpreted as an attempt to render the originally

---

[43] Denis Stevens includes *Ante thronum regentis omnia* in his list of music devoted to St Thomas Becket (D. Stevens 1979, 322–3); John Stevens discussed the ambiguity of the imagery in this poem without referring explicitly to the question of which Thomas was the intended subject (J. Stevens 1996, 336–8).

unmeasured notation rhythmic, and – as in other respects – *Sumer is icumen in* has featured at the forefront of this discussion.[44] Detailed analysis of the notational revisions across all the music in **GB-Lbl Harley 978**, however, points to a different conclusion.[45] With the exception of *Sumer is icumen in*, whose notation probably contained some rhythmic indications from the outset which the later reviser tried to clarify, in the other songs, the notational changes do not lend themselves to interpretation as mensuralizing, but rather seem to involve replacing one note- or neume-form with an equivalent one, written in a different way. For example, a three-note descending group was written by the original scribe using the traditional *climacus* neume-form, but has been routinely replaced by the reviser with the so-called 'English *coniunctura*' (with a sloping tail to the left of the first note-head, instead of a straight tail to the right).[46] This has no effect on the rhythmic or melodic reading of the notes, but apparently serves the purpose of replacing a perhaps out-dated notational form with a more current one. Nevertheless, the first music-scribes who worked on **GB-Lbl Harley 978** were apparently familiar with some methods of rhythmic notation. Modal ligatures are employed for the block-written tenor at the end of *Ave gloriosa mater / Duce creature*, and for the untexted pieces on ff.8v–9r.[47] In the rest of the music, syllabic declamation prevented use of the modal system, though some knowledge of mensural ways to notate syllabic melodies is apparent in *Sumer is icumen in* and *Ante thronum regentis omnia*.[48] The range of approaches to rhythm and its notation exhibited both by the original notators and the later reviser is striking but not unique; what deserves more thorough investigation in manuscripts of medieval song is the spectrum of different musical intentions (rhythmicizing and otherwise) to be observed in later notational revisions.[49]

---

[44] For a summary of the literature on this topic, along with an interpretation with which the present author largely concurs, see Duffin 1988.

[45] In his study of this aspect in *Samson dux fortissime*, Stevens remained convinced that the reviser's intentions were mensuralizing, although he noted numerous examples of phrases and passages where the later notator's work appears inconsistent or incompetent in this respect; J. Stevens 1992.

[46] This alteration can be clearly observed on f.8r above the syllables 'oracu*lum*' on the third line and 'umbracu*lum*' on the fifth; www.bl.uk/manuscripts/Viewer.aspx?ref=harley_ms_978_f008r.

[47] See www.bl.uk/manuscripts/Viewer.aspx?ref=harley_ms_978_f008v, www.bl.uk/manuscripts/Viewer.aspx?ref=harley_ms_978_f009r and www.bl.uk/manuscripts/Viewer.aspx?ref=harley_ms_978_f010r. For discussion of *Ave gloriosa mater / Duce creature* and its different versions, see Deeming 2006, 22–6 and Deeming 2013, 205–6. One of these versions is also analysed by Sean Curran in Chapter 8 below.

[48] See Deeming 2013, 207–8.

[49] These matters are given closer consideration in relation to **GB-Lbl Egerton 274** in the following chapter.

The production of the second quire of **GB-Lbl Harley 978**, which opens with further musical materials and continues with a calendar, involved different scribes and a change in decoration style from the first. In this quire, the red and blue inks of the first gathering are supplemented by yellow and green (found in the gamut diagram on f.14r and in the calendar),[50] and some of the larger initials are elaborated with pen-work flourishing, including the letter E at the start of the solmization song *Est tonus sic* (ff.14v–15r).[51] The elegance of the presentation on these folios, especially the careful alternation of descriptions and musical examples of varying lengths in the demonstrations of musical intervals on f.15r,[52] is somewhat undermined by apparent scribal misunderstanding of the text and music of *Est tonus sic*. Example 5.3 lays out the song with line-breaks and capital letters to show its sense-divisions; in the Harley manuscript, however, the sections demonstrating the semitone, ditone and semiditone are differently punctuated, with enlarged letters at 'Personat', 'Ditonum', 'Diatessaronque'. It could be argued that the scribe was paying more attention to melodic than to textual sense here, being reluctant to regard the close on e at 'mi fa fa mi' as a phrase-ending, and preferring to continue until the more likely-looking cadence on a at 'cernis'. But the result mangles the text in this part of the song, undermining its value as a didactic resource to accompany the gamut diagram and the intervallic exercises that follow it. Both concordances of the song (in **F-EV lat.2** and **GB-H P.IX.7**, mentioned above) avoid the mistakes of the Harley scribe, indicating that rather than generally circulating in corrupt copies, the song was misunderstood in its copying into the Harley manuscript.

Conclusion: networks within and beyond GB-Lbl Harley 978

Though there are some shared poetic and musical techniques among the Harley songs, their arrangement in the manuscript does not seem to constitute a fully coherent grouping. The secular, vernacular nature of *Sumer is icumen in* stands out against the primarily sacred Latin context. Some of the Latin songs have concordances in liturgical sources, indicating their use in the contexts of formal worship, and the music-theory materials

[50] See www.bl.uk/manuscripts/Viewer.aspx?ref=harley_ms_978_f014r and www.bl.uk/manuscripts/Viewer.aspx?ref=harley_ms_978_f015v.

[51] www.bl.uk/manuscripts/Viewer.aspx?ref=harley_ms_978_f014v.

[52] www.bl.uk/manuscripts/Viewer.aspx?ref=harley_ms_978_f015r.

Example 5.3: *Est tonus sic* (**GB-Lbl Harley 978**, ff.14v–15r)

Example 5.3: (*cont.*)

- *The tone is thus:* ut re ut, *or* re mi re, *or* fa sol fa sol la sol *should sound as here.*
- *The semitone is always sounded thus:* mi fa fa mi.
- Ut mi *or* fa la *you discern as sounding always the ditone [major third].*
- *And the semiditone [minor third] sings the notes* re fa *or* mi sol, *these sweetly.*
- *In a harmonious voice the diatessaron [fourth] sounds in the notes of holy citharas,* ut fa *or* re sol *and equally* mi la *this sounds.*
- *The diapente [fifth] runs through five strings:* ut sol, *or* re la *it sounds and moves from* mi *to* mi *or jumps from* fa *to* fa, *often falling.*
- *The diapason [octave] holds eight notes, from* c *to* c, *or* d *to* d, *and thus singing all the elements it climbs to itself.*

(including *Est tonus sic*) would most often have found a use in ecclesiastical schools. The use made of all of this musical material by the thirteenth-century monks of Reading, though, can only be conjectured. Though it has been shown that the entire manuscript probably came together without an overall design, there are some links between the musical portion and the rest of the book. The music itself is not uninterrupted: two unnotated texts are interposed, both of them connected thematically to the adjacent songs. An interest in good poetry, especially in Latin, is clear both from the songs and the satirical poems later in the manuscript; equally, a reader interested in the disposition and quality of musical intervals (evinced by the materials at the start of the second quire) may have been well placed to appreciate the tonal and triadic organization of many of the songs in the first, and their control over musical compass. A discussion of the music in the manuscript cannot escape the phantom of the polyphonic pieces whose incipits are listed at the end.[53] Though we can know little of their musical style, it is clear from the list, partly arranged in calendar order, that they were designed for liturgical use and, as in the calendar near the start of **GB-Lbl Harley 978**, someone took care to record the names of Reading monks responsible for them.[54]

The songs of **GB-Lbl Harley 978** include several that were widely transmitted in British and Continental witnesses (*Samson dux fortissime* and *Ave gloriosa virginum*, the latter attributed elsewhere to Philip the Chancellor, including in **GB-Lbl Egerton 274**, considered in the next chapter), and some of more limited transmission (*Eterni numinis*, which appears in a few British, Irish, and Spanish liturgical manuscripts, and *Gaude salutata virgo* and *Est tonus sic*, each found in only two other insular witnesses).[55] Five of its songs are *unica* (*Dum Maria credidit*, *Felix sanctorum chorus*, *Sumer is icumen in* and *Perspice christicola*, and *Ante thronum regentis omnia*), as are the instrumental estampies. The remaining songs, *Regina clemencie* and *Ave gloriosa mater/ Duce creature*, are both found here in versions that differ substantially from their concordances. Taken together, this pattern of preservation suggests that the compilers of **GB-Lbl Harley 978**'s musical materials were able to tap into international networks of song, as well as gaining access to items less widely distributed. Additionally, a high proportion of unique and musically reworked items might lead us to infer some local compositional activity by the compilers or their institutional companions, a suggestion that is lent more weight by the evidence of the list of lost polyphony at the back of the volume, which seems to confirm that musical composition was being engaged in by Reading monks in the thirteenth century.

GB-Lbl Harley 978 seems to have been the product of a small group of educated enthusiasts, with interests in collecting and preserving literature and in recording and cultivating music. The various revisions made to the musical notation of the songs in the first portion point to their continued, practical use by musicians, and additions made throughout the book indicate that the collection as a whole continued to be read. If, as seems likely, the book was assembled at Reading, it speaks of the ready communication between the abbey and the outside world, and combines with the evidence of many other musical miscellanies, both those referred to in this

---

[53] www.bl.uk/manuscripts/Viewer.aspx?ref=harley_ms_978_f160v.

[54] Some have nonetheless attempted to draw conclusions about the musical content of these lost pieces by speculating that they may be identical with polyphonic settings of the same texts found in other English manuscripts; see in particular Ernest H. Sanders 'Burgate, R.de' and 'Wycombe, W.de' via GMO.

[55] For fuller references to concordances, see Deeming 2013, 204–9 and Stevens 1996, *passim*.

chapter and others, to attest to the commonplace circulation of monks, scribes, and books between connected religious houses through which habitual transmission of texts and music took place.

GB-Lbl Harley 978 is perhaps the most extensively studied of any English musical miscellany, not least because it appeals to scholars of so many different disciplines. The tendency to view the book as unique, rather than in the context of other musical miscellanies, however, has been a recurring problem with previous accounts of the manuscript. Lacking more closely-related comparisons, the book has been viewed through the lens of later commonplace-books that reflect the interests of specific individuals, even though its mode of production suggests that efforts to read the whole collection as 'intentional' may be ill-founded. Nevertheless, the multiple contents of the book formed part of the reading experience for the medieval reader, so that – even without inferring a guiding intelligence behind their selection – it is nonetheless vital to consider the ways in which each text's readerly reception may have been inflected by the materials that form its partners on the manuscript page. If we look, as previous musicological generations have done, only at *Sumer is icumen in*, we relinquish the multivalent textual and musical experience that medieval readers and singers would have appreciated.

As simultaneously one of the best known and possibly least understood sources of medieval song, **GB-Lbl Harley 978** has warranted reconsideration here. Still of profound interest, as witness to a tri-lingual, Anglo-French ecclesiastical culture, the manuscript's neglected context – in the form of other miscellanies – casts light on the networks of interchange in which music and other forms of knowledge moved around. The surviving traces of English music before 1300, so many of them preserved in manuscripts of principally non-musical contents, have been described as 'isolated jottings', and contrasted (unfavourably) with the grand and extensive collections of Latin and vernacular song made at the same time on the Continent.[56] But the fuller reconsideration of these traces brings to light a rich culture, not only of music and poetry, but also of the collecting of texts into manuscript compendia.

---

[56] For 'isolated jottings', see Sanders 1979, xi.

6 │ Preserving and recycling: functional multiplicity
and shifting priorities in the compilation and
continued use of London, British Library,
Egerton 274

HELEN DEEMING

The manuscript London, British Library, Egerton 274 (hereafter **GB-Lbl Egerton 274**), known as 'LoB' by scholars of polyphony (following Ludwig) and 'chansonnier *F*' among scholars of Old French song (following Schwan and Gennrich) has long been considered an important manuscript witness of several genres of thirteenth-century music.[1] Comprising a curious mélange of musical and some non-musical works, and juxtaposing items that scholarship (following the genre-based organization of many of the 'central' *ars antiqua* manuscripts) has tended to view separately, the manuscript invites us to reconsider the boundaries between those genres as perceived by thirteenth-century readers. Moreover, it was subject to several layers of accretion and revision by its later thirteenth- and fourteenth-century owners, and thus provides a rare and precious insight into how a thirteenth-century music-book continued to be used later in the Middle Ages. Drawing on methodologies from codicology, in which a recent focus on viewing medieval manuscripts as 'whole books' – however disparate they may appear to us – has yielded fresh perspectives on medieval habits of reading and collecting, this chapter seeks to peel back the layers of **GB-Lbl Egerton 274** and its modern reception in order to cast new light on the cultural values assigned to the manuscript at different stages in its complex history.

Mixed contents and uneven reception

Ludwig and other early scholars working on the manuscript identified six fascicles, defined partly by the manuscript's construction, and partly its

---

[1] Ludwig 1910–61, Schwan 1886, Gennrich 1921.

Table 6.1 The contents of **GB-Lbl Egerton 274**

Fascicle	Quires	Folios	Contents
I	1–7	3–57v	**28 Latin songs, with attribution to Philip the Chancellor** (20 monophonic and 2 polyphonic conducti, 6 motets)
II	8–12	58–93v	**3 troped Kyries, 2 untroped Glorias, 6 sequences**
III	13	94–7v	**Further Latin songs** (3 short Easter lyrics plus one further song erased and replaced with 2 responsories)
IV	14–16	98–118v	**18 French chansons** (marginal attributions to 5 trouvères. 11 chansons have had text and sometimes music erased and overwritten with Latin responsories)
V	17–18	119–30v	**Latin narrative verses without notation** (*Dialogue of Dives & Lazarus*; John Peckham's *Philomena*)
VI	19–23	(131–2v)[2] 133–60v	**Liturgical processions and responsories** (some overwritten above erased items, including a French chanson on ff.131–132)

content (see Table 6.1).[3] This division of the contents into six discrete groups has continued to dominate the manuscript's reception, with many commentators focusing their attention on single fascicles while paying scant attention to the remainder.[4]

- Fascicle I, opening with the rubric 'Incipiunt *dictamin*a [*or dicta*] magis*tri* Phi*lippi* qu*ondam* cancellarii Parisien*sis*' (f.3r),[5] has received the most coverage in the scholarly literature, initially attracting the attention of nineteenth- and early twentieth-century writers because of its polyphonic items (two conducti and six motets, all for two voices).[6] Its conducti (the remaining twenty all monophonic) have been crucial to

---

[2] The bifolium ff.131–2 has usually been linked with Fascicle VI but is in fact separate from it, as described below.

[3] Ludwig 1910–61, 1:251–63.

[4] A notable exception to this trend is Whitcomb 2000, the first study to give a complete inventory of the manuscript's contents and to examine its physical make-up. The present study is much indebted to Whitcomb's work, though it pursues conclusions concerning the medieval afterlife of the manuscript that Whitcomb considered beyond her scope.

[5] http://www.bl.uk/manuscripts/Viewer.aspx?ref=egerton_ms_274_f003r.

[6] Coussemaker 1865, 204; Ludwig 1910–61. See below for exploration of the suggestion that two of the motets were in fact designed to be combined into a single, three-voice piece.

the establishment of Philip the Chancellor's oeuvre, though some of the items included by the Egerton scribe are now deemed doubtful.[7]

- Fascicle II comprises liturgical items,[8] in the form of three troped Kyries, two untroped Glorias and six sequences, mostly widely transmitted, though the sequences are strongly connected to Parisian repertories, especially that of the Abbey of St Victor, and in some other manuscripts have been attributed to its renowned sequence-poet, Adam of St Victor.[9]

- Fascicle III,[10] a single small quire, includes further Latin songs, apparently unique to this manuscript. One of the songs has been erased and overwritten by two fourteenth-century scribes.

- The three-quire fascicle IV comprises eighteen trouvère chansons,[11] and has been referred to as 'trouvère chansonnier *F*': twelve were originally provided with melodies, one of these added in a different hand, and the remaining six texts are laid out beneath blank staves.[12] All but seven of the original eighteen songs have been subject to some sort of revision, most likely during the fourteenth century: their texts erased (and in some cases overwritten with alternative texts), their notation erased and replaced, or new melodies added in those cases where the staves originally remained blank.

- Fascicle V is the only one to contain no musical notation,[13] instead consisting of two long narrative poems, a *Dialogue of Dives and Lazarus*, and John Peckham's allegorical nightingale poem, *Philomena*.[14]

- The final fascicle is largely liturgical in content,[15] and was copied later than the first five fascicles, mostly in the fourteenth century: its processional and responsory chants are linked to Ghent, and one of the fascicle's notators uses the style of Messine notation distinctive to the northern French and Flemish region.[16]

---

[7] The authorial status of the five monophonic rondelli gathered towards the end of the fascicle has been especially called into question; on the question of attribution and this collection of pieces more generally, see Ludwig 1910–61, 1:252–5; Falck 1981, 110–19; Dronke 1987; Payne 1991; and Whitcomb 2000, 46–64.

[8] www.bl.uk/manuscripts/Viewer.aspx?ref=egerton_ms_274_f058r. The illuminated initial opening this fascicle is also reproduced on the cover of the present book.

[9] Fascicles II and III have received almost no attention except that given in Whitcomb 2000, 64–73; Whitcomb also provided transcriptions of these pieces in her Appendix B.

[10] www.bl.uk/manuscripts/Viewer.aspx?ref=egerton_ms_274_f094r.

[11] www.bl.uk/manuscripts/Viewer.aspx?ref=egerton_ms_274_f098r.

[12] P. Meyer 1871, 1:7–13, 34–50; Gennrich 1925.

[13] www.bl.uk/manuscripts/Viewer.aspx?ref=egerton_ms_274_f119r.

[14] Whitcomb 2000, 76–84.

[15] www.bl.uk/manuscripts/Viewer.aspx?ref=egerton_ms_274_f131r.

[16] Whitcomb 2000, 84–92; Huglo 2004, 212–13.

The contents of the different sections of the manuscript have most often been addressed separately (and some hardly at all) in the scholarly literature. Within a modern academic framework that has carved up its subject matter by language and by genre, there has been scarcely any place for holistic discussion of a manuscript that is multi-lingual and encompasses numerous genres of music and poetry. **GB-Lbl Egerton 274**'s author attributions in the first and fourth fascicles have further encouraged a focus on the works of known individuals, to the neglect of the remaining, anonymous contents, and the manuscript's reception has also been affected by a tendency to place Parisian polyphony at the centre of all studies of thirteenth-century music. For these reasons, the conducti of fascicle I have dwarfed the rest of the manuscript in perceived importance, because their attribution to Philip the Chancellor has been seen to connect them intimately to the 'central' polyphonic tradition, even though most of them are in fact monophonic. Since the manuscript is codicologically much less disjointed than its (modern) division into separate fascicles would suggest, the uneven reception of the music of **GB-Lbl Egerton 274** is – as this chapter aims to show – in need of drastic correction in order to advance ways of understanding how the book's mixed contents might have been comprehended collectively, at the various stages of its (medieval) reconfigurations.

The manuscript's construction and modifications

A single ruling-scheme, as well as the same hand or small group of hands, unites fascicles I–III; additionally fascicles I and II have their programme of decorated initials in common (see Table 6.2).[17] These illuminations, which art historian Alison Stones has identified as the work of a Cambrai workshop, coupled with the shared text- and music-scribes and ruling, indicate that these two fascicles were produced in very close chronological and geographical proximity to one another.[18] The illuminated initials are not continued in fascicle III, although its major initials are executed in exactly the same style as the minor initials in fascicles I and II, that is to say alternating blue and gold letters, each with red and blue pen-flourishing. Further evidence that links fascicle III with what comes before has been

[17] For digital images of the manuscript, see www.bl.uk/manuscripts/FullDisplay.aspx?ref= Egerton_MS_274.

[18] Stones 1977, 107; Stones 2011, 182–6.

Table 6.2 The physical make-up of **GB-Lbl Egerton 274**

Fascicle	Quires	Folios	Codicological features
I	1–7	3–57v	
II	8–12	58–93v	Same hands, ruling, and decoration as I
III	13	94–7v	Same hands and ruling as I and II; opens with erased tenor belonging to motet on ff.56v–57v suggesting that III was once intended to follow I
IV	14–16	98–118v	Same hands and decoration as III, but new ruling scheme (designed for alternating staves and plain text, for the extra stanzas of the chansons).
V	17–18	119–30v	New ruling, new hands, new decoration (also thirteenth-century)
inserted bifolium	19	131–2v	New ruling, new hands, new decoration imitating that of IV (thirteenth-century). Notator of chanson here also added a chanson on ff.117–18 – hence this bifolium probably once followed IV.
VI	20–23	133–60v	New ruling, new hands (fourteenth-century). Lacks any significant decoration.

uncovered by Thomas Payne, who has shown that the erased music at the start of fascicle III (f.94r)[19] is the missing tenor belonging to *Venditores labiorum* that closes fascicle I (ff.56v–57v),[20] suggesting that this quire was at one stage intended to follow directly after I.[21] We can only speculate now about how this disruption in the ordering of the first three fascicles came about, and how it was that I and II but not III were given over to the artist for decoration, but it is clear nonetheless that the three units shared a common genesis.

A ruling-scheme designed for five staves plus their underlaid text pre-vails on most of the leaves throughout this section, with the scribe adapting this framework as required by the musical forms. Where strophic pieces occur, whose additional stanzas are written as non-underlaid text, each stave-space was converted into four plain-text lines.[22] For the two-voice conducti notated in score, the scribe switched to six staves per page, but hardly increasing the overall size of the writing-block, because the

---

[19] www.bl.uk/manuscripts/Viewer.aspx?ref=egerton_ms_274_f094r.

[20] www.bl.uk/manuscripts/Viewer.aspx?ref=egerton_ms_274_f056v.

[21] Payne 2011, 80.

[22] See, for example, f.26r: www.bl.uk/manuscripts/Viewer.aspx?ref=egerton_ms_274_f026r.

upper- and lower-voice staves could be placed closer together owing to the lack of text beneath the upper one.[23]

The scribe's approach to the layout may have been partly responsible for a curious feature of the motets in fascicle I: ff.50r–54v preserve what appear to be two two-voice motets, *In salvatoris nomine* and *In veritate comperi*, both supplied with matching tenors, incorrectly labelled *IN SECULUM*.[24] What here are apparently presented as two separate motetus voices for the same tenor are usually transmitted together as the motetus and triplum of a single three-voice motet; it may be that the scribe of **GB-Lbl Egerton 274** had this in mind, but was forced to improvise an unconventional layout for the piece because of the constraints of his ruling-scheme. Nowhere else among the music pages of the manuscript is the two-column format typical among other manuscript witnesses for the upper voices of three-voice motets employed, and the exceptionally small size of the pages would have made this hard to achieve. Nor could the scribe easily have reverted to his earlier score format with six staves per page for this motetus and triplum, because each requires its own underlaid text, unlike the two voices of the polyphonic conducti he copied in this way earlier in the fascicle.[25] Another established layout, involving placing the motetus and triplum voices on facing pages (with the tenor either in a block at the end, or spread along the foot of the opening), would have presented difficulties here, since the piece appears at the start of a new gathering: the scribe would therefore have had to leave the first recto (f.50r) blank or fill it with a particularly short piece.[26] Perhaps, therefore, the Egerton scribe's layout of *In salvatoris nomine* / *In veritate comperi* / *[VERITATEM]* could be viewed as an experimental solution to the problem of how to incorporate a single three-voice piece within his existing ruling-scheme.[27] His copying of the tenor at the end of *both* the triplum and the motetus voices might thus be interpreted not as an

---

[23] See, for example, f.41r: www.bl.uk/manuscripts/Viewer.aspx?ref=egerton_ms_274_f041r.

[24] This tenor is known from other manuscripts to be *VERITATEM* from the Gradual *Propter veritatem V. Audi filia* (M37).

[25] Unlike many double motets, this piece would lend itself to score format for the upper voices, since the two texts *In salvatoris nomine* and *In veritate comperi* have matching poetic structures and their music could readily be presented in vertical alignment. This same feature has led some commentators to regard *In salvatoris nomine* as a subsequent texting of the highest voice of a three-voice conductus-motet, in which configuration the music is found in some other mansucripts; Payne 1991, 338–42.

[26] Most of the songs in fascicle I take up several consecutive folios, with only the five rondelli being sufficiently short to fit on single sides.

[27] See Whitcomb 2000, 53–6, and Payne 2011, xiii–xiv and 176–7, for the alternative view that the **GB-Lbl Egerton 274** copy of this piece represents scribal misunderstanding of the format of his exemplar(s).

indication that he understood them as separate pieces, but rather as a kind of labelling, identifying both as belonging to the same three-voice composition. This suggestion is strengthened by the fact that each copying of the tenor here is incomplete, containing only one statement of the color, so that neither individually nor in combination do they indicate the correct number of repetitions required to complete the piece (three, the third slightly curtailed). The tenors as copied in **GB-Lbl Egerton 274**, therefore, seem to serve more in the manner of prompts than as fully notated parts as such.

Support for the idea of tenor 'prompts' may be found in the scribe's approach to the presentation of the other motets in this fascicle. Though only the *In salvatoris nomine / In veritate comperi / [VERITATEM]* complex of pieces has attracted attention in this respect, 'incomplete' copying of the tenors is the norm in **GB-Lbl Egerton 274**. *In omni fratre tuo / IN SECULUM* (M13) (ff.54v–56v) is also copied with only a single statement of the tenor melody,[28] though five repetitions of it are needed for a complete performance. *Laqueus conteritur / LAQUEUS* (M7) (ff.43r–45r) is based on a single statement of a long tenor color, so the music copied in **GB-Lbl Egerton 274** is complete; however, the text given here for this tenor part is merely the initial word 'Laqueus',[29] whereas the chant portion used sets a longer phrase: 'Laqueus contritus est et nos liberati sumus'.[30] Instead of writing off all of these examples of 'incomplete' copying as error, it seems worth considering them as part of a deliberate strategy on the part of the scribe. Including each tenor color in its full form lies somewhere between an incipit (the first word and a few notes is surely all that would be required to prompt memorial recollection, or to enable it to be found in another source) and a fully notated part (which would write out the correct number of repetitions of the statement needed to perform the piece). The Egerton scribe's approach could be interpreted either as 'archival', preserving the complete tenor melisma as a proper record, or 'pragmatic', writing out the tenor statement only once and leaving the singers to determine through rehearsal the number of repetitions required. In support of the latter possibility, it is worth noting that the two motet tenors that are written out in full in the manuscript both contain musical irregularities that would make a complete performance difficult to extrapolate from a

---

[28] http://www.bl.uk/manuscripts/Viewer.aspx?ref=egerton_ms_274_f056v.

[29] http://www.bl.uk/manuscripts/Viewer.aspx?ref=egerton_ms_274_f045r.

[30] The erased tenor of *Venditores labiorium* at the top of f.94r has left sufficient traces to show that both iterations of the color were written out in this case; however, the 'coda' that ends the part lacks the same two notes that are also missing in one of the concordances of this motet, and only supplied in the one remaining manuscript: see Payne 2011, 78–80.

single color.[31] Whether archival or pragmatic, both approaches imply the work of a literate and discerning musician, rather than a mechanical scribe misunderstanding his exemplars.

The choice of a 'linear' layout for all of the motets, with their tenors presented in a block at the end of the upper voices, and thus sometimes separated by several folios from the start of the piece, merits a similarly sympathetic reading. Such presentations have often been regarded as 'unperformable', since it is not possible for the singers of each part to read from the manuscript at the same time, but in this case (and in others, for different reasons) the scribe's focus seems not so much geared towards the (modern and anachronistic) notion of 'sight-reading', but instead to concerns that are no less musical, and which reveal different priorities in scribal conceptions of the purpose of notated copies.[32]

A new ruling-scheme distinguishes fascicle IV, though again the same hand or hands appear, and the decoration is comparable to that of fascicle III. The change in ruling can be attributed to the demands of the content: switching to musical material that consistently required the scribe to alternate between first stanzas underlaid to the music and subsequent stanzas written as prose below prompted a new ruling based not around a set number of staves per page but rather on a number of text-lines. Where necessary, text was spaced out on every third ruled line and a staff interposed in the space above. The final song in the fascicle, *Li rousignos chante tant*, was added by a different (though roughly contemporary) scribe and continued onto a single leaf at the end of the last gathering (f.118).[33] The same scribal hand copied the song *Ensi com unicorne sui* found on the bifolium now bound as ff.131–2,[34] though the correspondence of hands and repertory strongly suggest that this bifolium originally followed directly after fascicle IV, and was later reordered to its present position, between fascicles V and VI.[35]

---

[31] The (now erased) tenor of *Venditores labiorum* ends with a 'coda' of several extra notes after the second iteration of the color, whereas the tenor *AGMINA* (O40 or M65) of *Agmina milicie* begins with a three-note 'prelude' before the first color, and – unlike all the other motets here – the patterns of rhythmic and melodic repetition are not synchronized, so the rhythmic realization of each color is different.

[32] See Sean Curran's comments on related issues in relation to the motets of La Clayette in Chapter 8 below.

[33] The song begins on f.117r: www.bl.uk/manuscripts/Viewer.aspx?ref=egerton_ms_274_f117r.

[34] www.bl.uk/manuscripts/Viewer.aspx?ref=egerton_ms_274_f131r.

[35] Whitcomb 2000, 35–6. These two songs are catalogued in Spanke 1955 as RS360 and RS2075 respectively.

The beginning of fascicle V represents a codicological juncture from the preceding sections of the manuscript: a different scribe (though also of the later thirteenth century) has copied unnotated text, using plain, alternating red and blue minor initials with no flourishing, and major initials in the 'puzzle' style.[36] Fascicle VI represents another new codicological unit, and is itself in several distinct sections, both copied in the fourteenth century: the first (ff.133–48) uses square notation and a layout of five staves,[37] but much narrower margins and larger script than the similar layout used in fascicles I–III of the manuscript; the second (ff.149–60) was copied by a notator who used the Messine notational style and a more cramped layout of seven staves per page.[38]

Analysis of the manuscript from a codicological perspective makes a strong case for viewing fascicles I–IV as a single, thirteenth-century book, to which one small and two larger sections, produced under different circumstances, were subsequently added.[39] During the thirteenth century, perhaps not long after the manuscript's initial phase of production, the 'supplement' to the chanson collection (in the form of the added songs on ff.117–18 and the inserted bifolium, ff.131–2, most likely in its original position following f.118) and – probably – the devotional poems of fascicle V were added to the book. In the following century, two further layers of revision took place, the first taking the form of alterations and adaptations of the music of the original corpus, and the second involving erasure and replacement of some items in fascicles III, IV, and the inserted bifolium, the removal of that bifolium to its present position, and the addition of fascicle VI. Thus three stages in the medieval afterlife of **GB-Lbl Egerton 274** can be identified: as I hope to show later, each of these stages reveals a shift in the way the book was perceived, valued, and used by its subsequent owners.

Family ties: the first compiler's interests in songs and their relations

Before returning to these later reconfigurations, some consideration of **GB-Lbl Egerton 274**'s thirteenth-century core, compiled and – presumably – used as a single book, is strongly merited. In the broadest sense, the music

---

[36] www.bl.uk/manuscripts/Viewer.aspx?ref=egerton_ms_274_f119r.
[37] www.bl.uk/manuscripts/Viewer.aspx?ref=egerton_ms_274_f133r.
[38] www.bl.uk/manuscripts/Viewer.aspx?ref=egerton_ms_274_f149r.
[39] Whitcomb 2000, 44–5.

of this original compilation can all be described as 'musica cum littera', and nearly all of it as monophonic settings of rhythmic poetry. Such a description takes in not only the chansons, the conducti and the motets (at least their upper voices), but also the sequences of fascicle II and the shorter Latin songs of III. There is no sign here of the parallel musical culture of the thirteenth century – the 'sine littera' genres of organum and clausula – as even the small number of polyphonic items dotted around fascicle I are strongly text-bound.[40]

More specifically, the compiler of **GB-Lbl Egerton 274** seems to have had an interest not just in different kinds of song, but also in the connections between songs in the form of contrafacta and other reworkings. Fourteen of the twenty-two conducti in fascicle I have contrafacta or are otherwise musically related to other pieces: these include two important examples of conductus prosulae (songs generated by texting the melismatic caudae of pre-existing conducti), and in several other cases, the contrafacta of the Latin songs are in Old French or Occitan.[41] Five of the six sequences in fascicle II belong to densely interconnected families of works whose musical and textual cross-quotations were in many cases forged and exploited by the theologians of St Victor for exegetical purposes.[42] The troped Kyries of fascicle II and the motets in fascicle I very likely originated in processes of texting pre-existent musical works. And in fascicle IV, too, almost half of the original French songs are related – as contrafacts or models – to other chansons, and one served as a model for one of the Latin songs interpolated into Adam de la Bassée's *Ludus super Anticlaudianum*.[43]

The interconnections are not only with songs circulating separately from this collection: in several cases, the Egerton scribe copied two related songs adjacently, or at least within the same fascicle. One such example among the chansons is *La douche vois del rosignuel sauvage* (ff.108v–109v, one of the few chansons to have survived the later obliterations),[44] which is found

---

[40] The 'linear' presentation of the motets here reinforces the sense of these pieces as intimately text-bound: at first glance, there is nothing to distinguish the motetus voices from monophonic conductus, and only when the tenor appears at the end (often several folios after the start of the piece) does it become clear that these voices form part of a polyphonic texture.

[41] The conductus prosulae are *Bulla fulminante* (derived from the cauda of *Dic Christi veritas*) and *Minor natu filius* (derived from *Austro terris influente*): for these, see Payne 2011, 38–42 and 49–51. For listings of the other conducti with musical relations, see G. Anderson 1972–5, nos. K75, K57, K56, K52, K54, K61, K62, L5, L6, F17, F1, N19, and further references in Falck 1981 and Whitcomb 2000. Updated information on all these pieces is now becoming available via the online catalogue of conducti (http://catalogue.conductus.ac.uk).

[42] Whitcomb 2000, 69–71 and the references cited there.   [43] For these see Gennrich 1925.

[44] www.bl.uk/manuscripts/Viewer.aspx?ref=egerton_ms_274_f108v.

here not with the melody that accompanies it in its nine other manuscript witnesses, but with a different one, that normally associated with *Loiaus amors et desirriers de joie* by Colart le Boutellier, a song also preserved in this fascicle (f.100r–v).[45] The melodies of these two songs preserved in **GB-Lbl Egerton 274** are not absolutely identical, but it is interesting that this version of *Loiaus amors* differs significantly from concordant versions of the same song, in ways that bring it closer to the melody preserved here for *La douche vois*. This seems to suggest that the scribe of **GB-Lbl Egerton 274** was either party to an alternative line of transmission of these songs that united them through a shared melody, or was even personally responsible for creating that union by matching the two poetically similar texts to a single suitable melody. Pamela Whitcomb has suggested the latter, noting that *La douche vois* is the only song in its quire (quire 15, the second of three that make up fascicle II) to have been provided with music by the thirteenth-century scribe. If this under-provision of music in this part of the fascicle indicates some failure in or unavailability of his exemplars, the scribe's supply of a suitable melody for *La douche vois* from among the stock to which he did have access could be regarded as conscious and intelligent intervention to make the song performable by the users of **GB-Lbl Egerton 274**.[46]

Musical techniques, such as the double-versicle form usually associated with the sequence or lai but here also occupying a prominent role among the conducti, are also shared, and closer musical analysis reveals many techniques of compositional process, such as motivic patterning to articulate verse structure, found in common between the conducti, sequences, Easter songs and chansons.[47] Observing these connections across the entire original contents of the book goes some way to explaining the features that have been identified as unusual in the conductus collection. Robert Falck has drawn attention to the high number of contrafacta, as well as the prevalence of sequence- and rondellus-forms, and concluded that the manuscript 'would seem to be a very special kind of collection of songs

---

[45] Songs RS40 and RS1730 in Spanke 1955, respectively. For discussion and comparison, see Whitcomb 2000, 121–7.

[46] If this were the case, however, it would imply either that the scribe was drawing on text-only exemplars in copying the complete texts of all the songs throughout the fascicle, and relying on separate music exemplars to supply the melodies where they were available, or alternatively that he copied all the texts from his (notated) exemplar first, then went back to fill in their music, but the exemplar became unavailable when he was only part-way through this phase.

[47] The three conducti that open the collection (*Ave gloriosa virginum regina*, *O Maria virginei* and *Inter membra singula*) all use a version of this form, as does *Veritas equitas largitas*, appearing later in fascicle I. Some examples are analysed in Deeming 2011, 199–202.

which are musically unpretentious and closely related to current vernacular song'.[48] I would add that these features also draw the conductus collection closer to the contents of fascicles II and III, especially the sequences and the short, simple Easter lyrics. The compiler seems to have set out to bring into association pieces that share musical or textual features, while also relishing examples of pieces that existed in alternative forms, or that crossed boundaries between genres. The choice of motets, all of which are found elsewhere in versions for different combinations of voices and upper-voice texts, as well as the conductus prosulae and the many Latin and French contrafacta, are further evidence of this interest in the flexibility of song, which extends right across the four fascicles that made up **GB-Lbl Egerton 274** in its original state.

In its arrangement of contents, the book is neither highly organized nor totally unsystematic: it lacks an original contents list or index, and is not carefully ordered by musical texture or genre as many other thirteenth-century manuscripts are. However, some assembling of content, based on generic, thematic and formal criteria, is apparent. In fascicle I, songs that share similar musical forms are placed adjacently: lais, strophic songs, motets, and rondelli all appear clustered in small groups, and pieces with related subject matter are also put together. But throughout the manuscript, individual pieces disrupt the apparent patterns of arrangement, and regularly no more than two or three related pieces follow one another before a contrasting piece intervenes.[49]

Fascicle II opens with two troped Kyries, followed by two Glorias, and then six sequences, but this genre-based organization is then disrupted by the appearance of a third troped Kyrie after the sequences. It is tempting to speculate that the inclusion of this third Kyrie, apparently out of order, came about through a process similar to that of *La douche vois*, discussed above. *Kyrie celum creans* (ff.92r–93v, Example 6.1),[50] like the melody given for *La douche vois* here, is unique to this manuscript: neither its text nor the melody to which it is set has been traced in this form in other manuscripts.[51]

---

[48] Falck 1981, 111.　　　[49] Whitcomb 2000, 46–57.

[50] www.bl.uk/manuscripts/Viewer.aspx?ref=egerton_ms_274_f092r.

[51] The text is edited in AH 47, 132–3; Whitcomb 2000, 67 notes that the melody does not appear in the standard Kyrie catalogues. As shown by square brackets in Example 6.1, the final melisma of the Kyrie has been erased on f.93v; however, the original notation is still partly visible, and its reading easily verifiable by comparison with the texted version of the same melisma that precedes it. My transcription contains a number of different readings from that of Whitcomb 2000, 273–5.

However, the opening phrase of this Kyrie melody was used as a tenor in two separate (but possibly related) polyphonic pieces (Example 6.2): a three-part motet *Donné ma dame ai mon cuer tres dont* (M620) / *Adiés sunt ces sades brunetes* (M621) / *KYRIE CELUM*, and a three-part conductus *Si membrana esset celum* (where the Kyrie is used as the tenor

Example 6.1: *Kyrie celum creans* (ff.92r–93v)

Example 6.1: *(cont.)*

Lord, creating heaven and earth, making man, have mercy; bestowing life in heaven, life to man on earth, have mercy; [bestowing] the birds of the air, the fish of the sea, the beasts of the dry land, have mercy. Lord, have mercy.

Christ Jesus, unbegotten Word born of the Eternal, have mercy; [Word] made flesh made from a virgin marvellously at [that] time, have mercy; not dying but destroying death you returned strongly, have mercy. Christ, have mercy.

Lord, issuing at once from the one and coeternally equal of either, Spirit, have mercy; assembly, source, fire, love, solace, finger and right hand, giver and gift, Spirit, have mercy; who appeared in the aspect of a dove above the baptized Christ in the Jordan and above the faithful in tongues of fire on the day of Pentecost, Spirit, have mercy. Lord, have mercy.

of a textless cauda on the word 'celum').[52] Given the compiler's interests in musical reworkings, it seems possible that the Kyrie's cross-generic ties were what brought it to his attention, and caused him to add it to fascicle II, either

---

[52] The motet is found uniquely in **F-MO H196** ff.335r–36v, and edited in Rokseth 1935–48, 3:170–71; the conductus is found incompletely in **I-Fl Plut. 29** and **D-DS 3471**, but its text is found in full elsewhere (see G. Anderson 1973a, 293–4). As can be seen in Example 6.2, the rhythm of the tenor melisma is the same in both the motet and the conductus, and the pattern is too unusual for this to be coincidental, hence Rokseth's suggestion that one was a deliberate imitation of the other, or that both pieces shared the same composer (Rokseth 1935–48, 4:188). Though the link to the Kyrie in **GB-Lbl Egerton 274** has been made by Rokseth and others studying the motet, it escaped the notice of Ludwig and Whitcomb in their studies of the manuscript cited above.

Example 6.2: The opening phrase of *Kyrie celum creans* in two polyphonic contexts

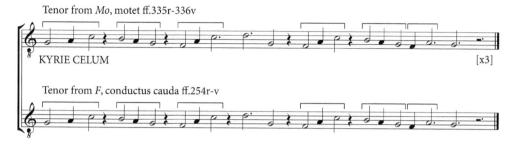

Tenor from *Mo*, motet ff.335r-336v

KYRIE CELUM   [x3]

Tenor from *F*, conductus cauda ff.254r-v

from a different exemplar than the other pieces in this fascicle, or from his own memory. There are no clear codicological grounds to consider this an afterthought, and it may be that the compiler's interests in rare pieces with unusual musical connections were of greater concern to him than maintaining an organizational plan that placed pieces into groups by generic category.

The sense of a partial organizational plan is reinforced by the scribe's provision of rubrics in the first two fascicles. Excluding the initial author attribution on f.3r, twelve of the items in the first fascicle (seven of the conducti, three of the motets, and the two conductus prosulae) and four in the second (one of the Glorias and three of the sequences) are provided with rubrics. Mostly beginning with the descriptive 'de' ('De beata virgine', 'De prelatis', and so on), the rubrics tend to refer to the thematic content of the songs, though two rubrics in the second fascicle resemble liturgical designations: the second Gloria (f.64) is labelled 'In triplici die' ('on triple feasts') and the sequence *Salve mater salvatoris vas electum* (f.69v) is prefaced with 'In purificatione' ('On the Purification'). The pieces with rubrics are not obviously clustered together, nor do the rubrics seem to apply especially to pieces of a particular genre, or those treating particular themes. Consequently, while the use of rubrics at all gives the impression of a planned collection, their incomplete and apparently random provision undercuts that impression.[53] At a later stage in the manuscript's history, author attributions added to the margins in fascicle IV,[54] as well as rubrics

---

[53] A similar point could be made regarding the illuminated initials in the first two fascicles: historiated initials are supplied at the start of some, but not all, pieces, and the scenes they depict bear an obvious relationship to the content of the songs in only some of the cases. Whitcomb 2000, 137–8.

[54] See, for example, f.100r: www.bl.uk/manuscripts/Viewer.aspx?ref=egerton_ms_274_f100r.

appearing in the added fascicle VI,[55] perpetuate the same tension, by following a similar pattern of partial supply.

In its organization of contents and its provision of paratextual apparatus, then, **GB-Lbl Egerton 274** falls far short of the rigorously systematic approach of the compilers of the central Notre-Dame manuscripts, which organize their materials by number of voice parts and genre, and many chansonniers, with their organizational strategies based on author attributions and song forms.[56] At the same time, however, **GB-Lbl Egerton 274** demonstrates distinctive strands of interest that may have lent this songbook a kind of coherence to its thirteenth-century compiler and earliest users, though modern scholarship has done its best to obscure this by treating its contents as distinct and unrelated materials. It is also important not to push the links between the contents too far: the Egerton manuscript would rather seem to be well served by the codicologist Peter Gumbert's description of miscellany manuscripts: 'they have grown much as our own kitchen cupboards [...] grow: there is a plan, but not a very clear or constant plan, and many exceptions and irrationalities, to which we are accustomed and which we like to keep'.[57]

Layers of addition and revision: the changing uses of the manuscript and its music

Encountering **GB-Lbl Egerton 274** within a generation or two of its original production, a later thirteenth-century owner made the first additions to its content. In the state in which he found it, the manuscript was a Latin and French songbook, intended for music throughout, but whose provision thereof tailed off towards the end of the collection: from f.107r to f.118v – the end of the book as he saw it – seven of the nine songs were accompanied by blank staves. The two isolated songs in this final section for which melodies were provided would perhaps have caught this owner's particular attention, standing out prominently from their unnotated environments. The first of these, *La douche vois del rosignuel sauvage*, is – as has already been mentioned – accompanied by an alternative melody, and to a musical reader familiar with chansons, this feature would have made the

---

[55] See, for example, f.135r: www.bl.uk/manuscripts/Viewer.aspx?ref=egerton_ms_274_f135r.

[56] See, for example, Elizabeth Eva Leach's discussion of the chansonnier Douce 308 in Chapter 9 below.

[57] Gumbert 1999, 36.

song stand out even more. This owner (or a scribe commissioned by him) was able to supply the music for the other nightingale song in this fascicle, namely *Li rousignos chante tant* which appears right at the end, on ff.117–18, and the same scribe also wrote the song *Ensi com unicorne sui* on the bifolium that would later become ff.131–2.[58] Both songs – though unattributed here – are the work of Thibaut de Champagne, which perhaps explains their association in either the memory or the exemplar of this scribe. The visual and musical prominence of *La douche vois* and the addition of the music for *Li rousignos chante* invite the speculation that these nightingale songs put the manuscript's new owner in mind of another nightingale work, the devotional narrative poem *Philomena praevia* by John Peckham. This forms the second of two long narrative poems in the two-quire fascicle V, which was also produced in the thirteenth century and was perhaps added to **GB-Lbl Egerton 274** in this same phase of its afterlife. Indeed, we might regard the addition of *Li rousignos chante* as a kind of bridge between the chansonnier and this new fascicle of devotional poetry, particularly as it opens with a description of the nightingale's death, a topic taken up – though in a radically different metaphorical sense – by Peckham in *Philomena praevia*.

Other connections are apparent between the non-musical works in fascicle V and the existing, musical contents of the original corpus. The first poem, a dialogue of the rich man and Lazarus (loosely drawing on the biblical account in Luke 16: 19–31, and introduced in **GB-Lbl Egerton 274** with a short paraphrase of it), corresponds to many of the themes in the conductus collection. Moreover, in departing from the events of the biblical story and instead focusing on 'a rhetorical depiction of the contrasts between worldly travail and heavenly compensation, between the good living of the self-serving sybarite and his punishment in the hereafter', this poem draws very close to the admonitory tone of such songs as *O mens cogita* (ff.20v–22v) and *Homo considera* (ff.22v–24v), and also echoes the dialogic construction of *Inter membra singula* (ff.12r–20r, here labelled 'Disputatio membrorum') and *Quisquis cordis et oculi* (ff.24v–25v), labelled 'Disputatio cordis et oculi').[59] Both *Dives and Lazarus* and *Philomena praevia* originated in the same circles of scholastic poets in which Philip the Chancellor also operated, and in this sense their addition to **GB-Lbl Egerton 274** can be read as responding to the contents already there.[60] At the same time, however, the inclusion of these two pieces not

---

[58] RS360 and RS2075 respectively.

[59] Bolte 1891, 261. On *Homo considera*, see Rankin 2003, 338–41.

[60] See Walther 1920, 124–6; Raby 1951, 435–8; and Baird and Kane 1978, 55.

designed for singing does shift the focus of the book's materials towards a different mode of engagement: the inherently social, public quality of songs and singing is tempered by the more intimate, private sphere of individual silent reading.[61] With *Philomena praevia*, whose nightingale turns away from the song- and love-inspiring bird-performer in vernacular literature (including, implicitly, the chansons *La douche vois* and *Li rousignos chante*), instead becoming an explicit metaphor for the Christian soul meditating privately on the Passion, a gloss, as it were, is placed upon the nightingale songs earlier in the manuscript, and – by extension – the entire collection of songs of which they form part.[62] The moralising conducti of fascicle I, the exegetical tropes and sequences of II and the songs of III and IV could, from the outset, have been used as texts for private contemplation, especially as models of right living in both a devotional and secular-social sense, but the refocusing of **GB-Lbl Egerton 274** through this first phase of additions serves to prioritize and encourage this mode of textual encounter.[63]

The second phase in the manuscript's medieval afterlife, however, shifts the emphasis squarely back towards musical concerns, especially highly practical matters of notation, rhythm and melodic versions. One or more fourteenth-century notators intervened in the music of the original corpus, making revisions to some of the pieces in fascicles I and II. In the latter, minor alterations have been made to the melodies and texts of the two Glorias, one of the Kyrie tropes and one of the sequences. These changes take the form of small pitch adjustments, minor alterations to melismas, and corrections of unconventional spelling; changes, in other words, that suggest these pieces were still deemed current enough to be worth the trouble of altering in fiddly and apparently trivial ways. In fascicle I, the revisions are notational, entailing an attempt to render the rhythmically neutral notation mensural. This involved erasing the stems from *virgae*, so as to make them breves, and replacing some two-note descending ligatures with two minims. In other cases, single notes seem to have been adjusted,

---

[61] Leach 2007a, 101 considers the shift to a singular 'tu' in *Philomena*, as opposed to the plural 'vous' in equivalent vernacular literature, as significant in this respect.

[62] See the discussion of this poem in Leach 2007a, 100–1, and the in-depth analysis of its imagery in Baird and Kane 1978, introduction.

[63] Whitcomb also interprets 'the songbook as a moral and spiritual model', using this as a way of shoring up her proposed identification of the manuscript's first patron. Her interpretation relies heavily on *Philomena praevia*, however, which would imply that she regards fascicle V as integral to the book's original contents rather than added later, as her earlier codicological analysis suggested; Whitcomb 2000, 206–7 and 44.

probably to replace what were originally *virgae* (which would imply breves to someone reading mensurally) with *puncta* (to be read as semibreves). These notational revisions are not applied systematically throughout all the songs, but rather occur mostly in the first song, *Ave gloriosa virginum*, and, after the opening few, only in the first of each repeated versicle:[64] this would seem to suggest that the scribe's intention was not to make a complete revision of the piece but rather to indicate in newer, more familiar notational forms a way of singing the song rhythmically that could be adopted and extended by a singer *ad libitum* for the rest of this song and the others that follow. Late thirteenth-century readers familiar with songs in rhythmically neutral notation may have been more accustomed than their fourteenth-century successors to generating or deducing a rhythmic character for the melody without explicit notational guidance, or indeed have been content to sing it in an unmeasured fashion.[65] It seems probable that neither of these options would be immediately obvious to a later singer accustomed to reading songs from rhythmic notations, and hence the reviser's adjustments to this first song provided guidance that could enable him and his contemporaries to make creative use of a song collection that might otherwise appear to him antiquated.

The addition of custodes to these early fascicles, probably occurring at the same time as the other notational revisions, could be seen in a similar light: not deemed essential by thirteenth-century scribes, they were more routinely expected in the following century, so the reviser supplied them, albeit somewhat sporadically.[66] Most interestingly, the custodes added to the two polyphonic conducti display some inattention to the score format in which they are written: in these pieces, the custos indicates the pitch of the note on the staff immediately below, which in these pieces belongs to the other polyphonic part.[67] The function of the custos in guiding a singer to the next note that must be sung is therefore eliminated in these pieces, suggesting either that the reviser worked carelessly or – more likely, given meticulous modifications to pitches and note-forms elsewhere – was

---

[64] This feature is especially apparent on f.4r: www.bl.uk/manuscripts/Viewer.aspx?ref= egerton_ms_274_f004r; compare the revised versicle beginning 'Cedrus pudicicie' with the unaltered 'Vitis habundancie'.

[65] For the conductus prosulae and motets, thirteenth-century users of the manuscript might also have had access (in the form of notated copies, or forms committed to memory) to the untexted, and therefore rhythmically notated, originals on which they were based; such knowledge is unlikely to have been available to a fourteenth-century singer.

[66] Whitcomb 2000, 107–14.   [67] Whitcomb 2000, 111–12.

relatively unfamiliar with score format, which was much more rarely encountered among the polyphonic manuscripts of the fourteenth century.

In this chapter of **GB-Lbl Egerton 274**'s continuing medieval story, we see musicians engaging actively with the earlier musical contents, grappling with disappearing conventions and finding ways to make the book and its music usable by later generations of musicians. Despite the earlier refocusing of the manuscript towards more contemplative modes of encounter, these revisions point to the manuscript's resurrection as a living and sounding musical repository.

The most drastic interventions by later medieval users of the manuscript were also made in the fourteenth century, and these have left the most obvious traces in the form of mutilated – and in some cases overwritten – songs. Two scribal hands in particular are identifiable as responsible for these erasures and additions (occurring in fascicles III and IV): they are the two main music-scribes of the liturgical materials in fascicle VI, showing that the different parts of the manuscript were united by this point in the fourteenth century. The revisers replaced the song texts and in some cases melodies with those of Latin responsories, chosen on the whole apparently because they share the same first letter as the songs, thus allowing the decorated initials to remain intact. At first glance, one might suppose that their motives for these revisions resulted from pious objection to the amorous content of the chansons, but this explanation is unsatisfactory for a number of reasons. Firstly, at least one of their erasures was a sacred Latin song.[68] Secondly, they left seven of the French chansons fully intact, and some later stanzas of many of the others also remain untouched. Moreover, if deleting content now deemed inappropriate were the only concern, why would they have bothered to insert replacement pieces, which are nearly all complete and performable in both text and melody? This suggests a desire at the very least to preserve these responsories, and to give their preservation higher priority than that of the chansons obliterated beneath them.

The pieces that make up the added fascicle VI are, in many cases, copiously rubricated with details of not only their liturgical occasion, but also their precise processional performance. The care taken to record these details strongly suggests practical use, but at the same time, the fascicle's usefulness as a liturgical processional is limited by its lack of systematic organization and its apparently selective coverage. It is difficult, too, to

---

[68] That is, the song (or perhaps two songs) that originally appeared at the end of fascicle III on ff.96v–97v.

explain why four of the chants that appear in this processional fascicle are duplicated among the items that were added on top of erased songs in the earlier fascicles.[69] Just as in the manuscript's original corpus, some loose groupings of material are apparent in fascicle VI, and there also is a possible connection between these added materials and the original contents. Several chants for the dedication of a church appear in this fascicle, and two of these are duplicated in the additions to fascicle IV (*Terribilis est locus iste*, ff.99r and 154v, and *Benedic Domine domum istam*, ff.100r and 155r). These echo the two interrelated sequences on the same theme found in fascicle II (*Quam dilecta tabernacula*, f.78r, and *Rex Salomon fecit templum*, f.83r), which are especially prominent to the reader flicking through the manuscript, because of the historiated initial depicting a building at the start of the former.[70] Such a link implies a certain attitude to the book as a whole on the part of these fourteenth-century revisers, but in their addition of fascicle VI, as well as in the erasures and additions to fascicles III and IV, there are conflicting indications of the book's purpose, as a store of music for practical use or as an archive of material for silent preservation.

Conclusion

Both in its original state and in the various phases of its later usage **GB-Lbl Egerton 274** hints at multiple functions, testifying to its owners' and compilers' diverse priorities. Aspects of its design – its small size, high level of decoration (at least in its first portion), and some of its musical layouts – initially seem to suggest that it was not a manuscript for practical use by musicians. Yet at the same time, other aspects seem highly geared towards some kind of role in music-making, perhaps sitting alongside more contemplative and archival modes of engagement. The diversity of functions to which it bears witness is matched by a similar diversity of contents, but as we have seen, the first compiler and the manuscript's later owners all seem to have had an interest in forging connections between the

---

[69] These are *Summe trinitate* (added to f.96v and also found in fascicle VI at f.151r), *Homo quidam fecit cenam* (ff.98r and 152r), *Terribilis est locus iste* (ff.99r and 154v) and *Benedic Domine domum istam* (ff.100r and 155r). These chants in fascicle VI are all written in Messine notation, whereas in the additions to fascicle IV, square notation is used. In the case of *Terribilis est locus iste* and *Benedic Domine domum istam*, the revisers who added them to fascicle IV inserted only the texts, leaving the original chanson melodies intact.

[70] www.bl.uk/manuscripts/Viewer.aspx?ref=egerton_ms_274_f078r.

different materials, selecting for inclusion pieces that bridge the generic, textural, and linguistic divides by which medieval music is often classified. This careful selection of pieces implies the existence of a larger stock of music from which the compiler could draw, although there are also clear suggestions of imperfections or gaps in that stock: where possible, it seems, the first and later compilers intervened creatively to remedy these deficiencies of supply. Though the superimposition of new pieces on top of the originals can be seen on one level as an act of vandalism, it is also possible to interpret it as a marker of value: wishing to leave as little as possible of the book in the 'unfinished' state in which they found it, the later owners added their own materials as a way of preserving the book as a usable resource. Standing on the periphery – in both a geographical and conceptual sense – of the 'central' tradition of music in thirteenth-century France, **GB-Lbl Egerton 274** challenges us to rethink the parameters set up by our scholarly forebears of the nineteenth and twentieth centuries, and to view the manuscript and its music on their own terms.

7 | Miniatures, Minnesänger, music: the Codex Manesse

HENRY HOPE

Laconically titled *Minnesang*, Günther Schweikle's 1989 monograph is one of today's seminal handbook studies of medieval German poetry.[1] This volume's final conclusion is telling of Schweikle's overarching understanding of this repertory: 'Minnesang is a language-bound art. Beyond all issues of textual criticism and content-oriented analyses it should never be forgotten that Minnelieder are, essentially, linguistic art works of a high quality, in which the artistry of form and rhyme, the sound of language and sensual dimensions are ligated into an artistic unit.'[2] Apart from the brief admission that these songs were, in fact, performed, Minnesang's musical identity finds no reflection in Schweikle's conclusion beyond his repeated assertion that the melodies of this repertory had been lost in written transmission.[3]

The downplaying of music's importance is a common phenomenon in recent Minnesang scholarship. Beate Kellner, for example, argues in her 2004 publication on Minnesang's medial representation that the 'all but entire lack of musical notation in the German countries further underlines the impression of the Minnelieder as written texts whose artistic and complex forms – at least concerning some of their strategies – can apparently be comprehended only in writing'.[4] Thomas Cramer, too, has stressed the secondary nature and relevance of music and oral performance for all medieval repertories of vernacular song, using the scarce melodic transmission to postulate instead the repertories' primary status as written, literate art.[5] His disregard of music is particularly noteworthy since Cramer makes these claims in the *Handbuch der musikalischen Gattungen*, a standard reference work for (German) musicologists.

This chapter is the result of doctoral research generously funded by the AHRC, the German Academic Exchange Service (DAAD), and Merton College Oxford.

[1] Schweikle 1989, 2nd edn. Schweikle 1995. In a review, Albrecht Classen judged that 'without doubt this book represents the essential study guide to Minnesang of the twelfth and thirteenth centuries, and it will surely see many more print-runs'; see Classen 1993, 250.

[2] Schweikle 1989, 218.

[3] Earlier in the monograph, Schweikle does include a chapter which lists the extant melodies of the Minnesang repertory and outlines some fundamental musical issues without, however, attempting to discuss these. Schweikle 1989, 34–59.

[4] Kellner 2004, 109.   [5] Cramer 2004, 136.

Both Kellner and Cramer justify their neglect of Minnesang's musical aspects with reference to the design of the repertory's extant manuscript sources. The Codex Manesse is possibly the single Minnesang manuscript that has attracted most attention from scholars and lay audiences alike. Held at the Universitätsbibliothek Heidelberg under the shelfmark Cod. Pal. germ. 848 and also known as the 'Große Heidelberger Liederhandschrift' (commonly abbreviated as *C*),[6] this manuscript (hereafter **D-HEu Cod.Pal.germ.848**) is thought to have been commissioned and compiled by a circle of high-standing personalities surrounding the patrician Rüdiger Manesse in Zurich around 1300, with some additions being made as late as 1330/40.[7] The codex is ordered by poet, ranked according to social status, and all but three of the corpora open with a full-folio miniature of their respective poet. In addition to its large corpus of Minnesang poetry, the 137 full-folio miniatures have been essential in establishing **D-HEu Cod.Pal.germ.848**'s prominence.[8] This observation is reinforced by Lothar Voetz, who claims that it was not the poetry but the images that were responsible for the codex's fame.[9] The validity of this bold claim, and its applicability not only to the manuscript's reception in scholarship, but also by the wider public, is exemplarily demonstrated by the Wikipedia entry on Minnesang: the online encyclopaedia makes prominent use of the manuscript's miniature of Walther von der Vogelweide in the top right-hand corner of the web-page – and the Codex Manesse itself receives its own Wikipedia entry, insisting with the words of Ingeborg Glier that the manuscript is 'the most beautifully illumined German manuscript in centuries'.[10]

In contrast to the lavish illustrations, the representation of music in **D-HEu Cod.Pal.germ.848** provides an ample basis for the attitudes explored above. Most notably, the manuscript does not contain any musical notation. Even though Karl-Heinz Schirmer has called attention to a peculiar dash-like sign notated above some of the texts (for example on f.127v),[11] asserting that 'this can be understood only as a musical sign' and discussing its possible interpretation as the indication of a melisma or a rest, the Codex Manesse does not contain any conventional musical notation that can be recognized and understood by modern scholars.[12] Consequently, Schirmer notes, the sign has gone largely unnoticed by

---

[6] A digitized version is available at http://digi.ub.uniheidelberg.de/diglit/cpg848.
[7] Holznagel 1995, 144–70.   [8] Walther and Siebert 1988, viii.
[9] Voetz 1988, 224.   [10] See http://en.wikipedia.org/wiki/Minnesang.
[11] http://digi.ub.uni-heidelberg.de/diglit/cpg848/0250.   [12] Schirmer 1956, 154.

scholars due, in part, to their disinterest in music and prevailing concern for producing new *text* editions.[13] This lack of musical notation is not unique to **D-HEu Cod.Pal.germ.848** but is a constitutional feature of an entire group of manuscripts which together transmit the main corpus of Minnesang, the so-called 'Manesse group'.[14] It is also mirrored by the lack of explicit references to music in the manuscript's miniatures.[15] Of the 137 miniatures, Ewald Jammers has shown that only 20 depict instruments; none explicitly represent singing.[16] In a similar study, Lorenz Welker has identified 19 miniatures that contain musical instruments.[17] Yet even discussions supposedly concerned primarily with the study of music in **D-HEu Cod.Pal.germ.848**, such as Jammers's eighteen-page commentary titled 'Die Manessische Handschrift und die Musik', fail to study the impact of musical practice on this manuscript. After only two pages Jammers leaves his immediate topic behind and decides, instead, to reflect upon the theoretical relationship between music and text in Minnesang, as well as on the musical design of individual genres – without, however, relating these considerations back to the manuscript in question.[18]

Albrecht Classen's contribution to the *Companion to Middle High German Literature to the Fourteenth Century*, published in 2002 by Francis G. Gentry, provides another case in point, demonstrating how the neglect of music in detailed case studies has found its reflection in present-day handbooks.[19] In the final sentence of the section titled 'Musical Performance and Reading', Classen highlights the representation of music in **D-HEu Cod.Pal.germ.848**, noting that Meister Heinrich Frauenlob 'is depicted instructing a group of students who are equipped with a whole array of instruments: fiddles, drum, flute, shawm, bagpipes, and a plucked instrument called a "psalterium"'.[20] Only two sentences later, now under the heading of 'Text versus Melody', Classen stresses that 'the patrons who

---

[13] Ibid.

[14] For a detailed discussion of this group of manuscripts, see Peters 2000 and Roland 2001.

[15] Table 7.2 at the end of this chapter lists all miniatures in the Codex Manesse and their features of musicality.

[16] Jammers 1981, 170.

[17] Welker 1988, 122. In contrast to Jammers, Welker excludes the unfinished drawing on f.196r from his count. Jammers omits the image of Bruno von Hornberg (f.251r) in his description of images with instruments, though he includes it in his total count of twenty. See Table 7.2.

[18] Jammers 1981, 171–3, 181. On pages 182–6, Jammers lists the available musical concordances for the songs in the Codex Manesse in other notated manuscripts. The majority of these melodies is contained in the Jenaer Liederhandschrift (**D-Ju Ms.El.f.101**) or relies on Romance melodies as models of contrafacture.

[19] Classen 2002.   [20] Classen 2002, 145.

commissioned the manuscripts certainly did not demonstrate any interest in the [melodies]. They considered the preservation of the words the most important task at hand'.[21] Like Jammers, Classen deems the lack of melodies and the absence of musical notation more important than the representation of instruments, and both scholars' off-hand dismissal of manuscript evidence is striking. The present discussion suggests that the practice of conflating the absence of musical notation with the absence of music as a whole is closely tied up with the modern ontology of music and argues that the latter's application to this repertory is highly problematic.

Although it may appear very surprising when viewed against the earlier observation that the Codex Manesse has gained its prominence through its miniatures, the offhand rejection of these manuscript illuminations as objects of musical interest is common among music scholars. Elizabeth Teviotdale's consideration of music iconography in medieval manuscripts – included in the pedagogically prominent *Companion to Medieval and Renaissance Music* co-edited by Tess Knighton and David Fallows – voices the conviction that illuminations can provide only very limited information to music historians, and that they should not be part of a closely limited framework of musicological study: 'because they [the miniatures] are works of art, their study is essentially an art historical enterprise [and] their evidential value for the history of music cannot begin to be judged until their integrity as pictures is considered'.[22] Her fundamental scepticism towards pictorial art and the evidence it can provide perpetuates the view held by one of the most influential German and Romance philologists of the first half of the twentieth century, Ernst Robert Curtius. The latter postulated that 'works of art I have to contemplate in museums. The book is far more real than the picture. Here we have a truly ontological relationship and real participation in an intellectual entity. [...] To understand Pindar's poems requires severe mental effort – to understand the Parthenon frieze does not'.[23] Preceding Curtius's polemic remark by almost half a century, Fritz Traugott Schulz had already put into practice these ideals in his study of the Codex Manesse miniatures in 1901, remarking that one must first consider critically the manuscript's texts in order to be able to understand correctly the meaning of the images.[24]

The antagonism between valuing and deploring the miniatures in **D-HEu Cod.Pal.germ.848** had been in play as early as the mid-eighteenth century, when Johann Jacob Bodmer was one of the first scholars to make

---

[21] Ibid.   [22] Teviotdale 1992, 188.
[23] Curtius 1990 [1948], 14–15.   [24] Schulz 1901, 56.

the Codex Manesse known to a wider academic audience.[25] His comments on the manuscript's miniatures encapsulate the dichotomy between considering them as valuable for the manuscript as a whole while at the same time disregarding their content value: 'the magnificent paintings which precede each poet make the work especially valuable and beautiful. Although the drawings follow the appalling contemporary taste and are extremely poor, the colours are very bright and vivid'.[26]

Despite this plethora of reasons not to study the miniatures of the Codex Manesse, Eckhard Grunewald's prosaic observation that they have 'become part of the common, visual heritage' of today provides sufficient justification for scrutinizing them nonetheless.[27] The present discussion heeds Norbert Ott's call to look at manuscript illuminations and to *listen* to their texts, combining the two aspects: it argues that the Codex Manesse's pictorial representations of the Minnesänger can be sounded out and heard as embodiments of their identity as musicians.[28] In order to do so, this chapter examines (1) the manuscript's explicit representation of music-making and the lack thereof, (2) the implicit representation of music through allusions to orality and ownership, and concludes (3) by reconsidering the common academic conceptualization of the Minnesänger as 'part of literary rather than music history', and 'as word-artists rather than musicians'.[29]

Contextualizing musical performance

The only instance in the Codex Manesse that shows a Minnesänger playing an instrument is that of Reinmar der Fiedler (f.312r; see Figure 7.1).[30] His miniature features as many as three fiddles: one on his shield, one on his helm, and one being played by Reinmar himself. These instruments are, however, not intended as realistic depictions: while the three golden fiddles all bear a very close resemblance to each other – notably the tailpieces, the sound holes, and the overall form – the one held by Reinmar clearly shows four strings, while the ones depicted on the shield and helm have only three. On close inspection, the hair of Reinmar's bow is curved and not tightly strung, making it unsuitable for playing; also, Ingo Walther and Gisela Siebert have pointed out that the vertical manner in which

---

[25] Bodmer 1748.   [26] Bodmer 1748, v.   [27] Grunewald 1986, 446.
[28] Ott 1997, 38.   [29] Schweikle 1989, 53.
[30] The Codex Manesse is now available online in its entirety. see http://digi.ub.uni-heidelberg.de/diglit/cpg848.

Figure 7.1: Reinmar der Fiedler in **D-HEu Cod.Pal.germ.848**, f.312r. Reproduced by kind permission of the Universitätsbibliothek Heidelberg.

Reinmar holds the instrument in front of his breast would have rendered it unplayable.[31] Even though this instrument cannot actually emit music, a young girl dances in the background of the image, suggesting that

---

[31] Walther and Siebert 1988, 212.

accuracy and playability are not essential in the instrument's allusion to musical practice.

Music, as embodied by the fiddle, dominates the miniature. All three characters have their eyes fixed towards one of the three fiddles: Reinmar is intent on his 'real' fiddle, the dancing girl looks up towards the fiddle on the helm, and the lady sitting to the right looks up to the fiddle on the shield.[32] The importance of music is further stressed by the over-sized proportions of the fiddle held by Reinmar. If the miniature is divided into four roughly equal segments, then the only one that does not contain a fiddle is the one on the lower right. The lady seated here, however, draws attention back to music by pointing across the image towards Reinmar's fiddle. The image's colour scheme, too, captures music's prevalence. The miniature is embedded in a tri-colour frame. Its two outer colours, red and blue, refer to the clothes worn by the dancing girl and Reinmar (the two characters in the picture which are immediately associated with music). These colours frame a slightly broader stripe of gold, reemphasizing the fiddles' dominance in the image as a whole.

A second miniature with a strong emphasis on music-making is that of Meister Heinrich Frauenlob (f.399r; see Figure 7.2a).[33] While this image presents a total of seven instruments – a drum, flute, shawm, two fiddles, a psaltery, and a set of bagpipes – as in the case of Reinmar der Fiedler, only one of these is played, and none is directly associated with the Minnesänger. In this image, both fiddles are depicted with four strings (though they have five tuning pegs), a tailpiece, and two sound holes. Both bows are strung correctly, but again the fiddle played by the musician at the centre of the image is held too vertically to be played. Here, however, the fiddler's playing seems not to produce any sound as none of the bystanders are dancing or taking note of this music. Walther and Siebert have posited a number of starting points for the interpretation of this setting, viewing Frauenlob as a 'duke of minstrels' or 'king of minstrels'.

He holds in his left hand a wooden rod with which he seems to be conducting the musicians at his feet, while he points towards the shield with his right hand. [...] Teaching, competition, and adoration are united in the language of this poet's image.[34]

---

[32] Walther and Siebert 1988, 212, suggest that the lady who points towards the dancing girl may be her mother or dancing teacher. The attention drawn to the direction of the characters' eyes above, however, questions this interpretation.

[33] See also http://digi.ub.uni-heidelberg.de/diglit/cpg848/0793.

[34] Walther and Siebert 1988, 264.

Figure 7.2: a) Image of Meister Heinrich Frauenlob in **D-HEu Cod.Pal.germ.848**, f.399r; reproduced by kind permission of the Universitätsbibliothek Heidelberg; b) image from **I-Fl Plut.29.1**, f.1v; on concession of the MiBACT. Further reproduction by any means is forbidden.

A study of the characters' gestures and glances affords a different and more nuanced interpretation of this miniature. On closer inspection, Frauenlob's right hand points not towards the shield as suggested by Walther and Siebert, but to the helm and the crest placed just above it.

Figure 7.2: (*cont.*)

This observation is supported by the Minnesänger's gaze which is directed straight at the female figure on top of the helm. This figure, in turn, has turned her eyes towards the poet to meet his gaze. Occupied with the lady, Frauenlob cannot be 'conducting' the musicians below. The rod in his left hand is directed downwards in a nonchalant fashion and does not point towards any one musician in particular; supporting this argument, the hand which clasps the rod does not use its fingers to point downward. The fiddle player amongst the ranks of the minstrels, in contrast, holds his bow up with his left hand while also using the index finger of the same hand to point towards Frauenlob. Together with the three other minstrels standing around him, the fiddle player's gaze follows Frauenlob's rod upwards to look at the master musician. Frauenlob uses his right hand, it seems, to point to the lady on his left, so as to redirect the minstrels' gazes, and the musicians standing beneath Frauenlob's throne do direct their eyes towards the lady on the helm. There are, in fact, only two figures in the miniature that do not look up to either Frauenlob or the female character on top of the helm: the lady on the shield, and the performing fiddler standing amongst the group of minstrels. While the latter is concerned only with his fiddle playing, looking intently at the fingerboard, the portrait on the shield is looking out of the picture towards the manuscript's users, suggesting that the miniature may have a message of relevance to the viewer.

As Walther and Siebert have suggested, the lady on the helm seems to allude to the Minnesänger's name 'which he received either for his advocacy of the term "frouwe" instead of "wîp" in his contest with Regenbogen [. . .] or as a reference to his "Frauenleich" in honour of the Virgin Mary'.[35] If the miniature, like the poet's name, was indeed intended to allude to Frauenlob's poetry, then the female figure on the helm could be understood as the allegorical depiction either of Frau Minne or of the Virgin Mary. While the image's overall secular context might strengthen an understanding of the lady as Frau Minne, the figure's wimple and crown support an interpretation as the Virgin Mary. Turning the leaf to the first of Frauenlob's poems recorded in **D-HEu Cod.Pal.germ.848** provides further support for the Marian interpretation. The text notated here, *Ey ich sach in dem trone*, tells of the lyric persona's encounter of a pregnant woman wearing a crown: the Marienleich (Frauenleich) mentioned by Walther and Siebert. 'Around [the text's] initial E an artist has drawn a

---

[35] Walther and Siebert 1988, 264.

charming indication of the poem's subject [. . .]: Mary, holding the Christ Child, appears above the initial as "mulier amicta sole" with the moon beneath her feet, while below, the poet-seer stands gazing with his hand to his eyes, to show that he is seeing a vision'.[36]

There are, however, two points which make this interpretation less convincing than it would otherwise appear. Frauenlob's song speaks explicitly of twelve gemstones which are set into the Virgin's crown, yet both images in the miniature wear a three-pronged crown with no gemstones (and it would be hard to imagine twelve stones fitting onto these crowns). Secondly, three of the minstrels point not only to the Virgin, but also to the fiddling musician in the centre of their circle. Two of them stand underneath Frauenlob's throne, and thus escape the full influence of the master's guiding rod which attempts to redirect the musicians' attention entirely: away from the worldly musician towards the divine presence of the Virgin.

This contrast between references to the secular and the sacred, to the world of sound and the world of silence, as well as its mitigation through the figure of Frauenlob proposes a third interpretation of the female figure in this miniature. Tilman Seebass has called attention to the title folio of **I-Fl Plut.29.1**, which presents music as a lady, symbolized by the three Boethian categories of music: *musica humana, mundana,* and *instrumentalis*; and Marc Lewon has suggested that the miniature preceding Frauenlob's songs in the Codex Manesse shares a number of striking similarities with this illustration of the Boethian Lady Music in **I-Fl Plut.29.1** (compare examples 7.2a and 7.2b).[37] Indeed, the ladies bear a crown with three prongs and have covered their heads and shoulders with a wimple in both manuscripts. While the prongs allude to the three Boethian categories of music, the wimple emphasizes Lady Music's divine status. The second point of note is that in **I-Fl Plut.29.1** Lady Music uses a rod to admonish and instruct an instrumental musician. As is the case in **D-HEu Cod.Pal.germ.848**, the additionally raised index finger could be seen both as another admonishing gesture and as a literal pointer towards the 'higher' categories of music. For the interpretation of the miniature in **D-HEu Cod.Pal.germ.848** this suggests that the female figure on the shield represents Lady Music, while the figure presiding over the image on top of the helm embodies Lady Music in the Boethian category of *musica mundana*.

---

[36] Newman 2006, 141.

[37] Seebass 1988, 27–31, and Lewon 2011, 110. Lewon has reiterated these observations in a recent blogpost: http://mlewon.wordpress.com/2012/11/05/frauenlob-miniature/.

The musicians in the lower half of the image, and the lone fiddle player in their midst, represent the sphere of *musica instrumentalis*. While it could also be argued that Frauenlob is the representative of *musica mundana*, his placement within the miniature as a mirror image of *musica mundana* instead presents him as the representative of its worldly counterpart. Though his use of admonishing gestures aligns him with the depiction of Lady Music in **I-Fl Plut.29.1**, as do his enthronement and his ermine crown, his upward gaze and reverence of the lady on the helm suggest that he is not Lady Music himself, but an emblem of *musica humana*. Instead, the image on the shield might be understood as the depiction of Lady Music as it draws the onlooker into the miniature through its outward gaze, underlining the importance of the three-fold concept of *musica* as a whole.

As these two case studies demonstrate, the commissioners and scribes of the Codex Manesse were acutely aware of its repertory's musical nature. Yet the observation that only 20 of the manuscript's 137 miniatures depict musical instruments remains. The following paragraphs therefore discuss some alternative aspects of the representations in **D-HEu Cod.Pal. germ.848**, tracing possible reasons for the absence of musicianship in the majority of the manuscript's miniatures.

Courtliness and the absence of music

Two of the Minnesänger best known to modern audiences are Tannhäuser and Wolfram von Eschenbach. Thanks to Richard Wagner's musical exploration of Tannhäuser's adventure at the Venusberg and his ensuing quest for redemption, as well as the same composer's operatic adaptation of Eschenbach's romance *Parzival* (Wolfram also appears as a singing character in Wagner's *Tannhäuser*), both Minnesänger have been familiar to modern audiences since the mid-nineteenth century, not only as poets but also as musicians. Their illustrations in the Codex Manesse, however, make explicit reference neither to music nor to their status as poets in a more broadly conceived sense. While Tannhäuser is shown as a member of the Teutonic Knights (f.264r),[38] Wolfram is shown as a fully garbed knight, ready for battle (f.149v):[39] the latter wears chainmail and a helmet, carries with him shield and sword, and a caparisoned steed and page await his departure on the next quest.[40] Both miniatures present their poets as

[38] http://digi.ub.uni-heidelberg.de/diglit/cpg848/0523.
[39] http://digi.ub.uni-heidelberg.de/diglit/cpg848/0294.   [40] Walther and Siebert 1988, 97.

figures of high social status. The poets' rank in society appears to have been more important to the illuminators than their artistic identities.

One of the images which bridges the gap between closely aligning the Minnesänger with music-making (as in the case of Reinmar and Frauenlob) and dissociating him from music entirely is that of Margrave Otto von Brandenburg (f.13r).[41] Placed in sixth position in the manuscript – with only the corpus of Duke Heinrich von Breslau separating it from the songs of kings and Emperor Heinrich VI – Otto's miniature is an exception: it is the only image of an Earl, Margrave, or Duke within **D-HEu Cod.Pal. germ.848** to feature instruments. Perhaps aware of this, the illuminators strove to separate the instruments – two buisines, a drum, and a set of bagpipes – and the act of musical performance from the noble poet through a number of visual devices. The Minnesänger is engaged in a game of chess with a lady; both players are seated on a cushioned bench which is placed on two ornamented beams, firmly locating the game of chess in the chambers at court and creating a barrier between the upper and lower sections of the image. The four musicians presented in the lower part of the picture, on the other hand, stand on a green, uneven surface, which presumably represents grass. This indoor–outdoor dichotomy is emphasized by further markers of social status: the Minnesänger and the lady are seated, while the musicians stand; the former are presented about twice the size of the latter; the chess players have their hair covered while two of the instrumentalists show their hair openly, and the third has his head covered by a tightly wrapped chaperone; whereas the nobles wear monochrome kirtles and long surcoats, the outer two musicians wear bi-chrome, patterned, knee-length tunics, and all of them wear only a single main piece of clothing; the bag of the bagpipes played by the musician to the right has an animal-like face, with the chanter protruding out of its mouth and the drone and mouthpiece attached to its head like horns, while the upper part of the image is overshadowed by the large representation of an imperial eagle on a shield (and its feathers on the crest of the helm). Socially and physically, the two spheres are clearly distinguished, and indeed, 'to assume the simultaneity of noisy instrumental music and a game of chess would be absurd'.[42]

The instruments themselves, however, break down these barriers. The two buisines played by the musicians to the left extend beyond the 'walls' of the room; one of the two even partly covers a corner of the chess board. Both

[41] http://digi.ub.uni-heidelberg.de/diglit/cpg848/0021.   [42] Welker 1988, 122.

players direct their instruments and gazes towards the lady, suggesting that their music is intended to be heard by the chess players. The bagpipe's drone to the right similarly extends up into the courtly part of the image. Conversely, Otto's right foot reaches down into the outdoor scene. These moments of interaction between the two spheres support Dagmar Hoffmann-Axthelm's suggestion that the instruments were used to bridge the dichotomy between Otto's image as a warrior and an unmanly poet.[43] While Lorenz Welker has claimed that the inclusion of the *haute musique* ensemble symbolizes Otto's sovereignty in general, Hoffmann-Axthelm argues that this role is taken on specifically by the two military buisines.[44] They are contrasted by the bagpipes, which 'belong primarily to the world of dance and the stylized, rural revelry of noble-women and men'.[45] Hoffmann-Axthelm's argument is strengthened by the animalistic features of the set of bagpipes. If one takes into account the vertical alignment of the buisines, Otto, and the helm on the one side, and the bagpipes and the lady on the other, the conclusion that the two ideals of the manly warrior and the effeminate lover-poet are mediated in this image through music and the game of chess, an embodiment of Minne-sang, becomes very convincing.[46]

Emphasized in the images of Wolfram, Tannhäuser, and Otto, the import-ance of courtliness and social status is also reflected in the miniature of Reinmar (discussed at the beginning of the previous section; see Figure 7.1). Seemingly preoccupied with the representation of music-making, this image takes great care to situate its act of performance within a courtly context. The scene is located indoors by the two pointed arches which span the top of the image. Reinmar and the lady are both seated on yellow thrones which, in turn, are placed on two beams with windows or doors, further emphasizing the indoor, courtly setting of this scene. All three figures wear monochrome surcoats; Reinmar and the dancer wear coronets of white beads, and the lady has covered her hair with a white bonnet. The assertion of social rank through the clothes is supported by the inclusion of Reinmar's shield and helm. From the observation that the shield overlaps the arch slightly, Walther and Siebert have concluded that 'the shields may not always have been part of the images' original design, but were often added only at a later stage, possibly on the request of the commissioning patron'.[47] If this was indeed the case, then it may be suggested that the

---

[43] Hoffmann-Axthelm 1994, 162. [44] Hoffmann-Axthelm 1994, 165; and Welker 1988, 122.
[45] Hoffmann-Axthelm 1994, 165. [46] Hoffmann-Axthelm 1994, 165–6.
[47] Walther and Siebert 1988, 212.

patron may have felt Reinmar's miniature to have been too exclusively musical in its original form, and consequently requested the addition of a shield (and helm) in order to ground the image more firmly in a courtly context.

The notion that the representation of the Minnesänger in a context of elevated social status was important to a manuscript's patron is not unlikely. A collection of poetry by noblemen and knights would have been inherently authoritative and, as a result, of greater value to a commissioner of noble birth than a collection of poetry by non-noble performers. Even if the poets whose works were collected within a manuscript may have been of lower rank, their *representation* as established authorities would have put their value beyond question for a medieval audience. In the particular case of the Codex Manesse, the representation of the Minnesänger as noblemen may have even served the poets' own aims. Scholars have suggested that Johannes Hadlaub, whose poetry is collected towards the end of **D-HEu Cod.Pal.germ.848** (ff.371r–380v), was involved with the Manesse circle in Zurich and may have played a role in the compilation of the manuscript.[48] He may have hoped that his inclusion alongside other poets of noble rank and socially elevated status would have reflected positively on his own identity as an ordinary Zurich citizen. Michael Curschmann has emphasized that other poets such as Wolfram von Eschenbach and Hartmann von Aue, too, repeatedly tried to construct their identity as knights and courtiers.[49]

While these considerations provide a background to the endeavour of presenting the Minnesänger as courtly noblemen, Maria Dobozy has pointed towards a reason why their representation as musicians, on the other hand, may have been consciously avoided. Seeking to reinstate the identity of German minstrels as 'poet-singer-composer-musicians', Dobozy points out that minstrels – among whom she includes Minnesänger such as Walther von der Vogelweide and Konrad von Würzburg – inhabited the interstices of medieval German society: 'members of secular society often suspected them of criminality, and official Church records turned the minstrel into the very image of dissolute conduct'.[50] Konrad von Megenberg's *Yconomica* gives testimony to this disrespect of musicians and is crucial for the present argument, as it was voiced around 1350 while Megenberg was living in Regensburg, situating these comments only a few years after the inception of the Codex Manesse,

[48] Renk 1974.   [49] Curschmann 1984, 232.   [50] Dobozy 2005, 3; 26.

around 1300, roughly 450 kilometres further south-west. As Christopher
Page has shown, even of professional musicians Konrad 'has an extremely
low opinion[;] they command no respect because "ability exercised for
gain is beggarly"'.[51] Thomas of Cobham's *Summa Confessorum*, moreover, shows that Konrad was not alone in the fourteenth century in
deploring musicians, asserting that only those musicians who sing for
princes and saints in order to give their patrons solace should be saved
from eternal purgatory.[52] As Franz-Josef Holznagel has demonstrated,
this scepticism also found its way into medieval song anthologies. He has
shown that the Weingartner Liederhandschrift (commonly referred to as
B, here **D-Sl HB XIII 1**) – a manuscript closely related to **D-HEu Cod.
Pal.germ.848** – depicts only unambiguously non-noble poets with
instruments.[53]

While this evidence suggests that the Minnesänger were not portrayed
as musicians, but as courtiers, in the Codex Manesse in order to avoid the
contempt with which musicians were often regarded in the Middle Ages,
it also needs to be considered that the Minnesänger may not have
required any representation as musicians. As an essential part of its
performance, the musical nature of the manuscript's song repertory
would have been apparent to its audience, many of whose members
may have been poets themselves. Supporting this line of argumentation,
a number of scholars have proposed that only those features which
transcended the realm of the ordinary were incorporated in manuscripts
and their illuminations.[54] For the study of manuscripts, this claim would
suggest that anything not notated therein may have been commonly
known by the recipients – or irrelevant.[55] Teviotdale's observation that
'only a tiny percentage of extant manuscript art with musical subject
matter is contained in music manuscripts' provides further evidence to
this assertion. Musical performance, it appears, needed to be referenced
explicitly only once its authors had disappeared from collective
memory.[56] As long as active Minnesänger such as Johannes Hadlaub
were involved in the production of manuscripts, there was no need to
overly emphasize the poets' musicianship; instead, their courtliness
could be stressed in order to strengthen their authority and their valu-
ation by audiences.[57]

---

[51] Page 1982, 195–6.   [52] Curschmann 1984, 230.   [53] Holznagel 1995, 82–3.
[54] See, for example, Unzeitig-Herzog 1996, 135.   [55] Huber 1996, 96.
[56] Teviotdale 1992, 186.   [57] Frühmorgen-Voss 1975, 58.

Orality and ownership

Limiting the study of music in the Codex Manesse to the depiction/
suppression of instruments is problematic: not only because it fails to
address the *reasons* for both the inclusion and the lack of explicit musical
depiction, but also because it turns away from the implicit ways in which
music is present in the manuscripts as, for example, in the image of
Frauenlob, in which Lady Music herself neither performs nor carries an
instrument. In order to avoid such a one-sided interrogation, the following
paragraphs trace the ways in which music is present in **D-HEu Cod.Pal.
germ.848** through allusions to orality, non-instrumental performance, and
authorship.

In her discussion of the manuscript transmission of medieval French
song repertories, Sylvia Huot has repeatedly argued that 'song is first of all
an oral, musical medium'.[58] Worded differently, music is always conceived
orally, and orality is understood as a crucial facet of music. Any reference
to orality, therefore, may also be understood, by its very nature, as a
potential reference to music.

It is possible to discern two main ways in which the images in the Codex
Manesse visualize orality: the pointing index finger and the depiction of
scrolls. While Norbert Ott has proposed an understanding of all scrolls in
D-Sl HB XIII 1 and **D-HEu Cod.Pal.germ.848** as representations of
orality in general, Sylvia Huot and Horst Wenzel have provided more
specific interpretations.[59] In the case of French manuscripts, Huot has
argued that scrolls reference 'song as such', deriving their 'connotations
of orality from [their] use as the medieval equivalent of the "voice
balloon"'; and in his discussion of the miniature of Rudolf von Fenis on
the fourth page of the Weingartner Liederhandschrift, Wenzel has even
gone as far as to argue that the curvaceousness of the scroll resembles sonic
wave-forms which would have been emitted in an oral performance.[60]

Within the Codex Manesse, Michael Curschmann distinguishes between
three types of scroll: the scroll as the attribute of poets, the scroll as the
representation of written literature, and the scroll as the emblem of a
(private) letter.[61] The image of Otto von Botenlauben (f.27r)

---

[58] Huot 1987, 54.   [59] Ott 1997, 41; Huot 1987; H. Wenzel 2006.
[60] Huot 1987, 78–9; H. Wenzel 2006, 31. Although medieval illuminators and onlookers would
  not have conceived of sounds as wave-forms, the medieval concept of *motus vocum* might be an
  appropriate term to describe the curvaceousness of the unfurled scroll. See Fuller 1981, 69–73.
[61] Curschmann 1992, 222.

characteristically combines all three types of scroll distinguished by Curschmann.[62] Otto is seated with his left leg crossed over the right, the left elbow rests on the left knee, and the head is slightly inclined – a posture found also in other images, such as that of Walther von der Vogelweide (f.124r);[63] the poet's right arm crosses in front of his body and holds the end of a scroll in its fingertips. The scroll unfolds downwards, seeming to flow from the poet's inclined head and mirroring the outline of the poet's body. One could argue that the scroll resembles a capital letter 'A' together with Otto's own shape and with the throne on which the poet is seated. The scroll characterizes Otto as a poet. Another, smaller figure on the right-hand side of the picture, however, also holds on to the scroll with both hands. The fact that this figure grasps the scroll firmly with both hands – not only with its fingertips like Otto – highlights the scroll as an actual physical object. The smaller figure to the right, moreover, is depicted as a messenger, ready to deliver the poetry just received from Otto, who is seated on his throne indoors: illustrated by the fact that he stands on a little field of brown earth, suggesting an outdoor setting, and by the round box he carries around the girdle, ideal to keep safe the scrolls which he has been asked to deliver.

Significantly, these scrolls remain empty and without text. Wenzel has proposed that the manuscript's empty scrolls are to be filled by the readers with the text contained on the following folios, and examples such as that of Rudolf von Fenis in the Weingartner Liederhandschrift support this idea: here, the scroll flows from the miniature itself, literally pointing towards the text contained on the following folios.[64] The case of Otto's miniature in the Manesse manuscript, on the other hand, which places the scroll at the centre of the miniature – even more central than the poet himself – suggests a more general and broad application to lyric poetry. In this vein, Ursula Peters has proposed that the scrolls refer to an author's oeuvre, not a particular piece of poetry transmitted in any one particular form.[65] That almost all of the scrolls do not contain any written text, underlines that the songs in the Codex Manesse can be heard and under-stood only in oral performance.[66]

---

[62] http://digi.ub.uni-heidelberg.de/diglit/cpg848/0049.

[63] http://digi.ub.uni-heidelberg.de/diglit/cpg848/0243.   [64] H. Wenzel 2006, 31.

[65] Peters 2001, 398.

[66] A notable exception to this textless depiction is found in the image of Eberhard von Sax (f.48v), whose scroll is inscribed with a dedication to the Virgin Mary. Other exceptions are found in the images of Von Buchheim (f.271r), Herr Alram von Gresten (f.311r), and Meister Konrad von Würzburg (f.383r).

'A universal sign of acoustical performance', the second commonly used referent of orality in the Codex Manesse is the pointing index finger.[67] Michael Camille's explanation of the raised index finger presents an alternative to an earlier interpretation of this gesture proposed by Fritz Traugott Schulz. According to Schulz, the raised fingers depicted the poets counting the syllables of their lyric lines.[68] A striking example which highlights the problematic nature of this interpretation is the miniature of the Duke of Anhalt in the Codex Manesse (f.17r).[69] In this miniature, it is not the Duke who is portrayed with pointing fingers, but the four ladies who watch him in battle from the safety of the battlements. Rather than counting syllables (or anything else), the ladies' raised and pointing fingers seem to refer to their lively verbal discourse about the battle below. A similar case can be made for the illustration that precedes the works of Earl Konrad von Kirchberg (f.24r):[70] the poet exchanges a scroll with a lady, who has raised her right hand and gestures to the poet with her raised thumb, index, and middle finger. Again, any construction of a plausible reason for the lady to count to three will remain highly speculative. Arguing, however, that this exchange of poetry does not take place in silence but is accompanied by a verbal exchange between the poet and the lady seems reasonable, at least from a present-day point of view. Another example in which this gesture is emphatically used to represent oral interaction between characters can be seen in the game of chess in the miniature of Otto von Brandenburg discussed above.

In addition to alluding to orality through scrolls and pointing fingers, the Codex Manesse seeks to establish the Minnesänger as the authors of their poetry. This concept of authorship, however, is broader than the present-day understanding of an author as someone who has produced a work, replacing it with one of personal ownership. Ownership is here not understood as the definition of a legal status or as the precursor of modern copyright concepts, but in an experiential sense: the Minnesänger owns his song because he has experienced the events it retells. Denis Dechant has observed that **D-HEu Cod.Pal.germ.848** presents the authors as perceiving and experiencing characters rather than as creators.[71] Huot has noted a similar tendency in French manuscripts, drawing attention to the fact that poets are represented as lovers and performers.[72] In the wake of recent

---

[67] Camille 1985, 28.   [68] Schulz 1901, 67.
[69] http://digi.ub.uni-heidelberg.de/diglit/cpg848/0029.
[70] http://digi.ub.uni-heidelberg.de/diglit/cpg848/0043.
[71] Dechant 2010, 44.   [72] Huot 1987, 54.

scholarly concern for the performative aspects of Minnesang (as opposed to the songs' performance), Jan-Dirk Müller has further elaborated this distinction between various personae, arguing that there was no strict separation between the performer and the lyric voice/experiencing persona in performance.[73] Viewed from the perspective of the audience, Michael Schilling has claimed that 'Minnesang was considered the expression of experienced feelings, and its statements were able to be related directly to the performer and the present audience, without any further distinction of implicit, explicit and real author, or between implicit, explicit and real audience'.[74] Holznagel's claim that, in Minnesang, 'the presenting and presented personae are identical, and consequently the recipients were interested in the poets not only in their role as authors, but also as humans with a special experience in love', may also be understood to be valid vice versa: the recipients were interested in the poets as experiencing characters, and inferred from their role as lovers their role as performers and, ultimately, as musicians.[75]

The present scrutiny of the miniatures in the Codex Manesse has revealed that they situate the Minnesänger's songs within a musical context in at least three ways. The illuminations present the Minnesänger themselves as musicians or within the context of explicit musical performance, represented through the depiction of instruments. They allude to the orality of the poetry either by depicting it through scrolls, or by showing the poets in communication with other figures. As demonstrated here, the orality of poetry is closely bound up with its conception as music. By presenting the Minnesänger as experiencing characters within their poetry, as its owners, the miniatures simultaneously assert the Minnesänger's role as performers – and the concept of performance was inherently oral and, hence, musical. The indirect channels of music representation expressed in the two latter points may have been preferred to more explicit forms by the manuscript's commissioners in order to avoid a negative stigmatization of the poets. Instead, the illustrators took great care to emphasize the Minnesänger's high social status.

If one takes on board these diverse ways of exploring the musical nature of Minnesang by visual means, and returns to the Codex Manesse as a whole, one may be inclined to disagree with Tilman Seebass's claim that

---

[73] J.-D. Müller 1994, 4. Significantly, the current interest by philologists in performative aspects of Minnesang has not led to a rediscovery of this repertory by musicologists.
[74] Schilling 1996, 108.   [75] Holznagel 1995, 57.

Table 7.1 Orality in **D-HEu Cod.Pal.germ.848**[76]

Total images	137
With (without) scrolls	41 (96)
% with (without) scrolls	~30 (~70)
With (without) reference to orality, through scrolls, pointing fingers, other communicative gestures	127 (10)
% with (without) reference to orality, through scrolls, pointing fingers, other communicative gestures	~93 (~7)

'the subject of inventing, writing, composing, or performing [. . .] is by far not the only, or even the ruling, theme of the illustrations'.[77] Thus, roughly one in three of the manuscript's images contain scrolls, and all but ten images (*c*.93 per cent) reference orality through scrolls, pointing fingers, or other communicative gestures (see Table 7.1 and Table 7.2). Even if one does not agree to consider all of the above elements as representations of music, the fact that there was no necessity to present the Minnesänger as musicians explicitly, since this aspect of their artistry was commonly known to contemporary audiences, retains its validity.

Minnesang and music: a question of ontology?

Considering that the preceding discussion has presented a breadth of arguments for the potential fecundity of considering the Codex Manesse from a musical perspective, it may be wondered why this and other manuscripts of medieval German song have not been studied more closely by musicologists in the past. The closing section of this chapter proposes that two defining features of modern scholarship in particular have – to varying degrees – hindered present-day academics in considering the musical nature of the Minnesänger as presented in the miniatures of **D-HEu Cod.Pal.germ.848**: the ontology of music and the disciplinary separation of the modern academy.

The first conviction concerns definitions of music. Precisely because modern scholars expect music to be explicitly represented, for example through musical notation, they often fail to understand the significance of

---

[76] The figures in this table exclude the unfinished miniature on f.196r.
[77] Seebass 1988, 38.

Table 7.2 Features of musicality in the miniatures of **D-HEu Cod.Pal.germ.848**

Key: M: Minnesänger, L: Lady, O: Other, s: shield, h: helm, t: with text, []: addition/ unfinished, <>: name found with text on following folio. Capital letters in the instruments column denote instruments that are being played.

#	Folio	Minnesänger	Instruments	Scroll	Communicative gestures	Other communication
1	6r	Keiser Heinrich		M		
2	7r	Kiunig Chuonrat der Junge				Bird hunt
3	8r	Kiunig Tyro von Schotten und Fridebrant sin sun			M	Debate
4	10r	Kiunig Wenzel von Behein	o		O	M acclaimed by musicians
5	11v	Herzoge Heinrich von Pressela	O		M;O	M receives laurels
6	13r	Margrave Otte von Brandenburg mit dem Pfile	O		M;L	Game of chess
7	14v	Margrave Heinrich von Misen			M;O	Bird hunt
8	17r	Der Herzoge von Anhalte			O	Commentary from battlements
9	18r	Herzoge Johans von Brabant				
10	20r	Grave Ruodolf von Niuwenburg		M	M	
11	22v	Grave Kraft von Toggenburg			M;L	M receives laurels from L
12	24r	Grave Chuonrat von Kilchberg		M;L	M;L	M receives/gives (?) scroll to L
13	26r	Grave Friderich von Liningen			O	Commentary from battlements
14	27r	Grave Otto von Bottenloube		M;O		M gives scroll to messenger
15	29r	Der Marggrave von Hohenburg		M	M	M performs poetry?
16	30r	Her Heinrich von Veldig		M	M	
17	32v	Her Goetfrit von Nifen	S	M	L	L refuses scroll
18	42r	Graf Albrecht von Heigerlou	H		O	Commentary from battlements

Table 7.2 *(cont.)*

#	Folio	Minnesänger	Instruments	Scroll	Communicative gestures	Other communication
19	43v	Grave Wernher von Honberg			O	Commentary from battlements
20	46v	Her Jacob von Warte			M;O	M receives laurels and cup while bathing
21	48v	Bruoder Eberhart von Sax		Mt	M;O	M venerates Christ-child
22	52r	Her Walther von Klingen			O	Commentary from battlements
23	54r	Her Ruodolf von Rotenburg			M;L	M receives laurels from L
24	59v	Her Heinrich von Sax			L	L caresses stag
25	61v	Her Heinrich von Frowenberg				
26	63r	Der von Kiurenberg		[M; L]	M;L	[Exchange of scrolls between M and L]
27	64r	Her Dietmar von Ast			M;L	M presents gift to L
28	66v	Der von Gliers		M		M holds tablet
29	69r	Her Wernher von Tiufen			M	M woos L
30	70v	Her Heinrich von Stretlingin			M;L	M dances with L
31	71v	Her Kristan von Hamle				L pulls M up into castle
32	73r	Her Uolrich von Guotenburg				
33	75v	Her Heinrich von der Muore		M	M;O	M sings poetry to O
34	76v	Her Heinrich von Morunge		M	L	M gives scroll to L
35	82v	Der Schenke von Limpurg			M	M receives h from L
36	84v	Schenk Uolrich von Winterstetten		M	O	M gives scroll to messenger
37	98r	Her Reinmar der Alte		M	M;L	M sings poetry to L
38	110r	Her Burkart von Hohenvels		M;L	M;L	Exchange of letter between M and L
39	113v	Her Hesso von Rinach			M	M heals afflicted
40	115r	Der Burggrave von Luenz			M;O	Gaming

Table 7.2 *(cont.)*

#	Folio	Minnesänger	Instruments	Scroll	Communicative gestures	Other communication
41	116v	Her Friderich von Husen		[M]	M;O	M narrates battle of sirens (?)
42	119v	Der Burggrave von Rietenburg		M;O		M gives scroll to messenger
43	120v	Her Milon von Sevelingin		M	M;L	M sings poetry to L
44	122r	Her Heinrich von Rugge		M		
45	124r	Her Walther von der Vogelweide		M		
46	146r	Her Hiltbolt von Schwangoei	O		L	M dances with Ls
47	149v	Her Wolfran von Eschilbach				
48	151r	Von Singenberg Truchseze ze Sant Gallen			M;L	M receives laurels from L
49	158r	Der von Sachsendorf				M ministers to fellow M
50	160v	Wachsmuot von Kiunzingen				
51	162v	Her Willeheln von Heinzenburg		M;L		Exchange of letter between M and L
52	164v	Her Liutolt von Seven		M;L	L	Exchange of letter between M and L
53	166v	Her Walther von Mezze				
54	169v	Her Rubin		M	L;O	M shoots letter to L
55	178r	Her Bernge von Horhein				M dances with L
56	179v	Der von Johansdorf				M embraces L
57	181v	Endilhart von Adelburg			L	M shows wounded heart to L
58	182v	Her Bligge von Steinach	s	O	M	M dictates to scribe
59	183v	Her Wachsmuot von Miulnhusen				L pierces M's heart
60	184v	Her Hartman von Owe				

Table 7.2 *(cont.)*

#	Folio	Minnesänger	Instruments	Scroll	Communicative gestures	Other communication
61	188r	Her Reinman von Brennenberg			O	M is slaughtered
62	190v	<Johans von Ringgenberg>			O	Commentary from battlements
63	192v	<Albrecht Marschal von Raprechtswile>	O		O	Commentary from battlements
64	194r	Her Otto vom Turne				M receives h and s from Ls
[138*]	[196r]	[unknown]	[O]			[Battle with music]
65	197v	Her Goesli von Ehenhein			O	Commentary from battlements
66	201r	Der von Wildonie		M;L	L	Exchange of letter between M and L
67	202v	Von Suonegge	M;O			Stag hunt
68	204r	Von Scharpfenberg			O	Commentary from battlements
69	205r	Her Chuonrat der Schenke von Landegge			O	M offers gift to O
70	213r	Der Winsbeke			O	Didactic exchange
71	217r	Diu Winsbekin			M;O	Didactic exchange
72	219v	Klingesor von Ungerlant			M;L;O	Wartburgkrieg
73	226v	<Kristan von Luppin ein Diuring>			O	Commentary from battlements
74	228r	Her Heinrich Hetzbolt von Wissense	o			Hog hunt
75	229v	<Der Diuring>				Siege of castle
76	231r	Winli			M	M given ring and h by Ls
77	237r	Her Uolrich von Liechtenstein				
78	247v	Von Munegiur		M		M gives scroll to messenger
79	248v	Von Raute		O	M	M sends out messenger
80	249v	Her Chuonrat von Altstetten				M and L embrace
81	251r	Her Bruno von Hornberg	s;h	L(?)		Exchange of letter between M and L(?)

Table 7.2 *(cont.)*

#	Folio	Minnesänger	Instruments	Scroll	Communicative gestures	Other communication
82	252r	Her Hug von Werbenwag				M and L embrace
83	253v	Der Piuller				
84	255r	Von Trosberg		M;O		Exchange of letter between M and O
85	256v	Hartman von Starkenberg				M forges h; L offers food
86	257v	Von Stadegge			L	M gropes L
87	258v	Her Brunwart von Oughein				M and L hold hands
88	261r	Von Stamhein		M;L		Exchange of letter between M and L
89	262v	Her Goeli			M;O	Game of backgammon
90	264r	Der Tanhuser			M	Hand raised in blessing gesture
91	271r	Von Buochein	O	st	L	M offers gift to L; book on shield
92	273r	Her Nithart			M;O	M attacked by/ dancing with O (?)
93	281v	\<Meister Heinrich Teschler\>			M;L;O	M woos L (naked in bed)
94	285r	Rost Kilcherre ze Sarne			M;O	L tonsures M; M gropes L
95	290r	Der Hardegger			O	Debate
96	292v	\<Der Schuolmeister von Esselingen\>		M;O	M;O	Debate/lecture
97	299r	Von Wissenlo			M;O	Sending of messenger
98	300r	Von Wengen			O	M and L embrace
99	302r	Her Pfeffel			L	M fishes and is heralded by L
100	303r	Der Taler		M;O	O	M receives letter from O
101	305r	Der tuginthafte Schriber			M;O	Debate
102	308v	Steinmar			O	M serves food to Os
103	311r	Her Alram von Gresten		Lt	M;L	Reading/debate
104	312r	Her Reinmar der Vidiller	M;s;h		L	M plays for dancing L

Table 7.2 *(cont.)*

#	Folio	Minnesänger	Instruments	Scroll	Communicative gestures	Other communication
105	313r	Her Hawart				
106	314v	Her Giunther von dem Vorste			L	M offers gift to L
107	316v	Her Friderich der Knecht			L	M protects L from pursuers
108	318r	Der Burggrave von Regensburg			M;O	Debate
109	319r	Her Niuniu			M;L	Debate
110	320v	Her Geltar	M			Hare/fox hunt
111	321v	Her Dietmar der Sezzer			O	Commentary from battlements
112	323r	Her Reinmar von Zweter		O	M	M dictates to scribes (in 'trance')
113	339r	<Der iung Misner>			O	Gaming and drinking
114	342v	Von Obernburg		M;L	M	Exchange of letter between M and L
115	344v	Bruoder Wernher			M;L;O	Debate
116	349r	Der Marner			O	Food preparation
117	355r	Sueskint der Jude von Trimperg	M		O	Debate
118	359r	Von Buwenburg			O	Hunting party
119	361r	Heinrich von Tettingen				M is taken prisoner
120	362r	Ruodolf der Schriber		M;O		M gives letters to messengers; dictates
121	364r	Meister Goetfrit von Strasburg	M		M;O	Debate
122	371r	Meister Johans Hadloub	M		L;O	M gives letter to L; debate
123	381r	<Regenbog>			M;O	Discussion in smithy
124	383r	Meister Chuonrat von Wiurzburg	Ot		M	M dictates to scribe
125	394r	<Chuonze von Rosenhein>			M	Harvesting
126	395r	<Rubin von Ruedeger>			M	M sets out on adventure?
127	396r	<Der Kol von Niussen>			O	Bird hunt

Table 7.2 *(cont.)*

#	Folio	Minnesänger	Instruments	Scroll	Communicative gestures	Other communication
128	397v	\<Der Diurner\>			O	Commentary from battlements
129	399r	Meister Heinrich Wrouwenlob	O;o		M;O	Instruction in music?
130	407r	Meister Friderich von Suonenburg			O	Blessing
131	410r	Meister Sigeher	O		M;O	M gives/receives cloak (?); commentary from battlements
132	412r	Der wilde Alexander	O		M;O	M hails onlookers on battlements
133	413v	Meister Rumslant	O		M	Preparation for departure; dancing on battlements
134	415v	Spervogil			M;L;O	Debate
135	418r	Boppo	m?		O	Debate; instrument in M's hand?
136	422r	Der Litschower			O	Presentation of children
137	423v	Chanzler	O			Musical performance

music's absence in the construction of a musical presence. This fundamental ontological problem may be understood as a remnant of positivist thought: only what can be factually grasped is a valid object of scholarly scrutiny.

There are, however, plenty of examples in modern musical culture which demonstrate that present-day audiences, too, do not require the explicit presentation of music in order to be able to understand any given object as music or its owner as musician. For example, the cover image on a CD might portray a vocal performer not in the act of singing but rather as the experiencing persona of the songs which the disc records. The explicit representation of the performer as a musician is apparently unnecessary, since audiences will consider this image that of a musician for three reasons. First, the performer may be a household name, and therefore known to be a musician before the disc is purchased. Any representation of the performer will consequently be a reminder of their musicianship. Secondly, when listening to the recorded songs, audiences will realize that the figure on the cover is depicted as the experiencing persona of the song lyrics. This observation, in turn, suggests that the figure is also the songs' narrator and performer. Thirdly, by its very nature, the very medium of the CD will suggest music to its audiences.

Like a modern recording artist, the Minnesänger would have already been familiar as musical performers to the audiences of the Codex Manesse; like modern audiences, medieval listeners would have conflated experiencing and performing personae; and like the CD, an anthology of Minnesang may have been considered by medieval audiences as an inherently musical medium. In her review of Mary Atchison's study of the chansonnier **GB-Ob Douce 308**, Elizabeth Eva Leach has given voice to this conviction, claiming that 'it might [...] be the case that these songs were well enough "notated" for the purpose of singing simply by having their texts copied. Their audience would have known the tunes (which were most likely simple, syllabic, and monophonic), or they would easily have learnt them aurally from those who already knew them'.[78]

Ewald Jammers's lament that it comes as a surprise to the modern scholar that a large-scale anthology of vernacular song such as the Codex Manesse should contain no musical notation adds another dimension to scholars' reluctance to see the Minnesänger as musicians.[79] Scholars have considered neither the manuscript's texts nor its miniatures as musical, for the present ontology of music considers only explicit references to the production of sound, such as the depiction of instruments or musical notation, as instances of musical visualization. In order to understand medieval song manuscripts as musical, however, scholars need to reconsider this modern, narrowly delimited ontology of music and adapt a wider understanding of music that includes its performative, textual, and especially its non-sounding components, defining and guiding their (historical) understanding of music through the medieval concept of a three-fold *musica*.

The strict disciplinary separation within the modern academy has hindered a fruitful interaction between art historians, philologists, and musicologists, making a study of Minnesang as song (including music) increasingly difficult. Scholars such as Friedrich Gennrich, interdisciplinary 'by profession', have found only few successors among today's academics.[80] Wolfgang Harms has pointed out that, instead, 'the research tasks

---

[78] Leach 2006, 417; and see Chapter 9 below.   [79] Jammers 1981, 169.
[80] See, for example, Gennrich's early publication on musicology and its relationship with philology (Gennrich 1918).

which the modern academic disciplines had marked out confidently had disciplinary boundaries potentially running right through the heart of these very research objects, and they were thus studied and interpreted in their entirety by no single discipline'.[81] Musicologists' particular interest in the rhythmical properties of medieval song during the first half of the twentieth century, for example, produced a wealth of complex terminology and arguments, making it exceedingly difficult for non-musicologists to contribute to and benefit from this debate.[82] Conversely, philologists' interest in textual criticism and hermeneutics added to musicologists' latent alienation from the Minnesang repertory because of its unfamiliar Middle High German language.

Leaving behind the disciplinary separation of the modern academy – often hidden behind the commonplace camouflage of *multi*disciplinary research – today's scholars are faced with the challenge of *inter*disciplinarity. A recent interdisciplinary publication on the Jenaer Liederhandschrift, **D-Ju Ms.El.f.101**, co-edited by the philologist Jens Haustein and the musicologist Franz Körndle, demonstrates how the two disciplines can fruitfully engage with each other.[83] The present chapter emphatically argues that, if musicologists heed this call to understanding the Minnesänger from various disciplinary perspectives and reconsider their ontology of music, the songs of the Minnesänger are ready for fresh musicological scrutiny, and the Codex Manesse and other unnotated songbooks may be fruitfully understood as music manuscripts.

---

[81] Harms 1988, 141.   [82] See Kippenberg 1960, 3–4.   [83] Haustein and Körndle 2010.

8 | Writing, performance, and devotion in the thirteenth-century motet: the 'La Clayette' manuscript

SEAN CURRAN

Music, writing, and the motet in thirteenth-century France: a historical sketch

The thirteenth century saw a vast increase in the number and kinds of manuscripts into which music was copied, and in the types of music which entered into writing. Two repertories loom particularly large: the polyphony associated with the Cathedral of Notre-Dame, Paris; and the Old French lyric tradition associated with the trouvères. Both traditions – the one pre-eminently ecclesiastical and polyphonic, the other supposedly courtly, vernacular, and monophonic – enjoyed and stimulated a burgeoning enthusiasm for beholding music in the book. Anthologies of Notre-Dame polyphony (now typified by the manuscripts **D-W Guelf.628 Helmst.**, **I-Fl Plut.29.1**, and **D-W Guelf.1099 Helmst.**) found place in many of the most important libraries of the late thirteenth and fourteenth centuries. They have been considered among the most prized fruits of the book trade growing in the roads around the Cathedral and on Paris's Left Bank.[1] The so-called chansonniers (of which more examples survive than for Notre-Dame polyphony) found home in the collections of many noble families; Arras seems to have had bookmakers specializing in their production.[2] In both kinds of manuscript, scribes busily retransmitted musical materials which were, in large measure, old by the second half of the thirteenth century. Those codices register an awareness that song had a history, and one that could be found in books.

In thirteenth-century compositional practice, old and new music met most spectacularly in the motet, and especially in the polytextual motet of the later thirteenth century. The genre seems to have been born when the skilled singer-liturgists of Notre-Dame prosulated (that is, added text to) passages of discant in their expansive polyphonic settings of Proper chants.[3] Above rhythmic ostinati formed from the pitches of the chant they wove

---

[1] Baltzer 1987; Everist 1989.

[2] Huot 1987, 46–80; Butterfield 2002, 123–68; and Symes 2007.

[3] For a recent re-evaluation of the processes involved, see Bradley 2012 and Bradley 2013b.

threads of melody whose design varies from the highly regularized to the highly and artfully irregular. A style of melody which relied on a kaleidoscopic array of phrase lengths could become, when texted, a formally irregular kind of poetry: often dense in rhyme and alliteration, but with verse lengths that are unruly. Motet texts may treat themes of contemporaneous love poetry or satirical invective, prayer and petition, but their forms are *sui generis*.[4] Thus a motet may look like several different kinds of song, but not one kind exclusively, and this is surely related to the variety and kinds of book into which motets or their texts were copied – from poetic anthologies to devotional texts, chansonniers to prayerbooks.[5] To make matters more complicated, the voices of a motet sometimes travel separately from one another, through a variety of polyphonic or monophonic versions, and we do not yet have a firm critical purchase on the musical principles that allowed some voices to travel while the transmission of others was more narrowly circumscribed. In the second half of the thirteenth century, voluminous collections of motets are put into manuscripts of their own, but scholarship has not got far in working out for whom those volumes were made, and for what they were used.[6] Some have clear relation to the Notre-Dame manuscripts from which the repertory first grew (such as **F-MO H196**, whose first fascicle contains latter-day organum settings), but others (such as **D-BAs Lit.115** and **I-Tr vari 42**) do not. They represent a new kind of anthology book, in some respects as placeless as the ubiquitous but itinerant kind of music the motet itself contains.

Scholarship on the La Clayette manuscript

Polyphonic music of the thirteenth century has enjoyed extensive research from music bibliographers, and the cornerstone of all subsequent work on the repertory remains the *catalogue raisonné* produced by Friedrich Ludwig in the early decades of the twentieth century.[7] Ludwig described all manuscript sources known to him, dividing them into groups according to his understanding of their notation: among many other manuscripts, the

---

[4] On the genre's thematics, see especially Huot 1997; on its compositional dynamics, see Everist 1994.

[5] On motets in chansonniers, see Wolinksi 1996 and Peraino 2011, 186–234. On prayerbooks as a context for motets, see Dillon 2012, 174–328. On devotional texts and music, see the essays collected in Krause and Stones 2007.

[6] For a ready overview of the anthologies, see Ernest H. Sanders and Peter M. Lefferts, 'Sources, MS; Early Motet: Principal Individual Sources' via GMO.

[7] Ludwig 1910–61.

'Notre-Dame' books fell into the group of manuscript sources in 'Quadrat-notation', while **F-MO H196**, **D-BAs Lit.115**, and **I-Tr vari 42** were placed among the manuscripts in 'Mensuralnotation'. Within these groupings, manuscripts were placed in broadly chronological order, and also in order of the size of the repertory they contained. Ludwig indexed networks of pieces according to the liturgical order of organa, then the position of the clausula's tenor segment within its parent chant. He then ordered motets according to his chronological understanding of the manuscript sources in which they were contained, moving progressively from those with textless concordances in the clausula repertories of **I-Fl Plut. 29** and **D-W Guelf.1099 Helmst.** through to those pieces with no known early concordances, composed on tenors not found in the Notre-Dame repertory and witnessed by the latest motet anthologies of the tradition. His work articulates an assumption that the best way to understand a piece was from the liturgical origins of its tenor.[8] This stems in turn from a belief in the fundamentally institutionalized (ecclesiastical, scholastic) milieu for the composition, circulation and consumption of the genre.[9]

The 'La Clayette' manuscript (henceforth **F-Pn n.a.f.13521**) was considered lost when Ludwig compiled the *Repertorium*, and was not 'redis-covered' until 1952, when it surfaced at the Château at La Clayette in Sâone-et-Loire where it seems likely it had been since its suspicious 'disappearance' from that place in the eighteenth century.[10] Involved somehow in its purported disappearance was its loan by the Marquis de Noblet of La Clayette to the celebrated eighteenth-century antiquarian and bibliophile Jean-Baptiste de La Curne de Sainte-Palaye, who in 1773 had a copy made of all the book's literary texts that he had not already found in other sources.[11] He also copied the French texts from the motet fascicle – but not their notation, nor any of the Latin texts – in their own volume as a collection of 'chansons françoises'.[12] Ludwig used the copied texts to demonstrate that the original manuscript had included a volume of motets, to infer that it had once included bilingual pieces as well as Latin ones (which are mentioned in Sainte-Palaye's volume but not copied), and to reconstruct the contents of

---

[8] The updated directory of sources in Van der Werf 1989 still more clearly articulates this liturgical conception.

[9] Busse Berger 2005, 9–44 gives a detailed historiographical critique of Ludwig's work.

[10] For a more detailed account of **F-Pn n.a.f.13521**'s place in scholarship, see Curran 2013a, 219–25 and Curran 2013b, 1–12. The manuscript was apparently 'rediscovered' by Albi Rosenthal. See Rosenthal 2000, 2–4.

[11] The eighteenth-century history of the manuscript is told by Solente 1953, 226–8. Sainte-Palaye's copy survives, and the literary portions are now **F-Pn Moreau 1715–1719**.

[12] This volume is **F-Pa 6361**, this quotation at f.1r.

the missing source with astonishing accuracy.[13] The manuscript's rediscovery ratified Ludwig's hypothesis that it contained pieces almost entirely present in Fascicles 2–5 of **F-MO H196**, and none from Fascicle 6. In his posited chronology of *ars antiqua* manuscript sources, Ludwig placed **F-Pn n.a.f.13521** immediately after the Old Corpus of **F-MO H196**, and before Fascicle 7, though this hypothesis seems less secure.[14] **F-Pn n.a.f.13521**'s motets are most readily accessed in the edition by Gordon Athol Anderson, which also lists all concordances then known for the pieces, compiling data from Ludwig's account and from the work of scholars who had continued his bibliographical labour.[15]

No less monumental a philological feat than Ludwig's was Paul Meyer's description of the lost manuscript's literary materials.[16] The musical section constitutes entries 30 and 31 of his inventory, each entry described as 'chansons', the first in Latin and the second in French. Suzanne Solente inaccurately retained the designation 'chansons' in her account of the book published shortly after the manuscript entered the Bibliothèque nationale de France in 1952.[17] The manuscript's fifty-five *ars antiqua* motets are surrounded by thirty-five literary texts, entirely in Old French, almost all devotional or didactic in purpose, which include the *Conception de Nostre Dame* of Wace, an incomplete copy of the *Miracles de Nostre Dame* by Gautier de Coinci, and three collections of stories from the *Vie des pères*. They are vernacular literary materials of precisely the kind used in the cultivation of lay piety, to be read by or to the lay devout, which were circulated and consumed ever more enthusiastically in the decades after the Fourth Lateran Council of 1215.[18] Table 8.1 lists the complete contents of the book in manuscript order, while Table 8.2 provides a handlist of its motets.[19]

---

[13] His account of **F-Pn n.a.f.13521** is 'Der Motettenfaszikel der verschollenen Handschrift La Clayette', in Ludwig 1910–61, 1: 408–21.

[14] Ludwig 1910–61, 1:420.

[15] G. Anderson 1975. See also the two substantial articles on the manuscript that accompany his edition, G. Anderson 1973b and G. Anderson 1974.

[16] P. Meyer 1890.   [17] Solente 1953, 231.

[18] The literature on this is vast. On the changing lay pieties of the later Middle Ages, see Swanson 1995. For a conspectus of recent critical approaches, see the essays in Kullman 2009.

[19] While the collations in Table 8.1 are my own, the titles of the various literary works have been decided in consultation with the notices held on file at the Institut de Recherche et d'Histoire des Textes, Paris and being incorporated into their online database *Jonas*, and the description given in the online catalogue by the Bibliothèque nationale de France. I am grateful once again to Dr. Marie-Laure Savoye and to the librarians of the IRHT for making their resources available to me. The URL for La Clayette's entry in *Jonas* is http://jonas.irht.cnrs.fr/manuscrit/manuscrit.php?projet=48152. The Bibliothèque nationale de France's catalogue entry can be found at http://archivesetmanuscrits.bnf.fr/ead.html?id=FRBNFEAD000006266.

Table 8.1 The contents of **F-Pn n.a.f.13521**

Production unit	Texts	Foliation	Binding stage[20]
1	Pierre de Beauvais, *Vie de saint Eustache*	1ra–10rb	I or II/III
	Pierre de Beauvais, *Vie de saint Germer*	10rb–15ra	
	Pierre de Beauvais, *Vie de saint Josse*	15ra–19ra	
	Fouque(?), *Vie de sainte Marguerite*	19rb–21va	
2	Pierre de Beauvais, *Bestiaire*, short prose version	22ra–30va	I
	Guillaume de Conches, *Livre de moralitez*, anonymous prose translation	31ra–37rb	
	Pierre de Beauvais, *Translation et miracles de Saint Jacques*	37rb–42rb	
	Pseudo-Turpin, *Chronique*, anonymous prose translation	43ra–56ra	
	Anonymous, "Rapport du Patriarche de Jérusalem au Pape Innocent III sur l'état des Sarrazins," translation of selected prose from Haymarus Monachus, *Relatio tripartita ad Innocentium III de viribus Agarenorum* (incomplete at the end)	56rb–57vb	
3	Guiot de Provins? *Suite de la Bible* (incomplete at the beginning)	58ra–59va	I
	Pierre de Beauvais, *Mappemonde* (incomplete at the end)	59va–64vb	
	Pierre de Beauvais, *Diète du corps et de l'âme* (incomplete at the beginning)	65ra–65va	
	Pierre de Beauvais, *Oeuvre quotidienne*	65va–66ra	
	Pierre de Beauvais, *Les trois séjours de l'homme*	66rb–67rb	
	Pierre de Beauvais, *Les trois Maries*	67rb–68ra	
	Anonymous, "Doctrinal sauvage"	68ra–69vb	
	Anonymous French paraphrase of "Veni creator"	69vb–70ra	
	Pierre de Beauvais, *L'olympiade*	70ra–70rb	
	Genealogy of the kings of France	70rb–70vb	
4	Wace, *La conception de Nostre Dame*	71ra–93ra	II/III
	French paraphrase of Psalm 44, "Eructavit," following the *Conception* without interruption	93ra–93rb	
	Anonymous, *Vie de sainte Catherine d'Alexandrie*	93va–108ra	
	Anonymous, *Vie de sainte Marie-Madeleine*, prose version	108ra–113va	
	Anonymous, *Vie de sainte Marie l'Egyptienne*, prose version	113vb–120ra	
5	Anonymous, *Vie des pères*, first collection	121ra–203va	II/III
6	Anonymous, *Vie des pères*, second collection	204ra–219vb	II/III
7	Anonymous, *Vie des pères*, third collection	220ra–247va	II/III

Table 8.1 *(cont.)*

Production unit	Texts	Foliation	Binding stage[20]
8	Roger d'Argenteuil, *Bible en français*	248ra–278ra	II/III
	French translation of a passage from Honorius of Autun, *Elucidarium*	278ra–281ra	
9	Anonymous, *Roman des sept sages*, version A	282ra–311ra	II/III
10	Pierre des Vaux-de-Cernay, *Historia Albigensis*, anonymous French translation (incomplete at the beginning and the end)	312r–366v	II
11	Pierre des Vaux-de-Cernay, *Historia Albigensis* (continuation for two folios; incomplete at the end)	367ra–368vb	III
12	Fifty-five *ars antiqua* motets	369r–390v	I
13	Anonymous, "Complainte d'amour"	391ra–395ra	II
	Simon, "Epitre amoureuse"	395rb–396ra	
	Simon, "Salut d'amour"	396rb–397ra	
14	Anonymous, *La Châtelaine de Vergi*	398ra–403vb	II
15	Gautier de Coinci, *Miracles de Nostre Dame*, selections (final tale of the collection incomplete at the end)	404ra–419vb	II

If the early literary scholarship misconstrued the musical pieces as 'chansons', subsequent musicological scholarship has ignored the presence of literary materials almost entirely, and on spurious codicological grounds. Almost all commentators have asserted that the music fascicle was originally a separate manuscript, and that it was only bound with **F-Pn n.a.f.13521**'s other materials by codicological accident, probably later than the thirteenth century. In an observation that can stand for several by other writers, James Heustis Cook claimed that the 'motet collection [...] is a self-sufficient fascicle of three gatherings, showing no characteristics found in the other portions of the manuscript', and later adds that 'the many signs of wear, which do not appear on the other portions of the codex, indicate that the collection of motets was used heavily before it was bound with the non-musical parts'.[21] Perhaps the most striking articulation of the 'separate-fascicle' theory is offered tacitly, in the two 1950s facsimiles of

---

[20] Those gatherings showing redundant sewing holes at the spine constitute the first usage unit (binding stage one). Those sections showing fluid damage must have been present at stage two. Remaining sections that show neither sewing holes nor fluid damage, or not included as an act of recopying occasioned by a rebinding, may have been added at stage two and survived the fluid damage unscathed, or were added at the third and final stage. I have allocated each production unit to stage I, stage II, or stage II/III, according to these criteria.

[21] Cook 1978, 1:4, 5.

Table 8.2 A handlist of motets in **F-Pn n.a.f.13521**, with foliation references

No.	Motet	Starts fol.	Ends fol.
1	Ave virgo regia (MV805) / Ave gloriosa (MV804) / Domino (unidentified)	369r,a,1	369v,a,10
2	O Maria virgo davitica (MV449) / O Maria maris stella (MV448) / In veritate (M37)	369v,a,11	370r,a,2
3	Caro spiritui (unnumbered) / Lis hec racio (MV1055) / Anima iugi (unnumbered)	370r,a,3	370r,b,6
4	L'autrier m'esbatoie (MV83) / Demenant grant joie (MV84) / Manere (M5)	370r,b,7	370v,a,14
5	Mout loiaument (MV407) / Se longuement (MV406) / Benedicta (M32)	370v,b,1	370v,b,12
6	Onques n'ama (MV675) / Molt m'abelist (MV674) / Flos filius eius (O16)	370v,b,13	371r,a,14
7	Quant define la verdour (MV661) / Quant repaire la doucour (MV662) / Flos filius eius (O16)	371r,b,1	371v,a,3
8	Cest quadruble (MV798) / Vos n'i dormirez (MV799) / Biau cuers savereus (MV800) / Fiat (O54)	371v,a,4	371v,b,12
9	Qui voudroit fame (MV639) / Quant naist la flor (MV637) / Tanquam suscipit (MV636) / Tanquam (O2)	371v,b,13	372r,b,13
10	Ave deitatis templum (MV512a) / Cele m'a tolu la vie (MV511) / Lonc tens a (MV512) / Et sperabit (M49)	372r,b,14	372v,b,10
11	Mors a primi patris (MV256) / Mors que stimulo (MV254) / Mors morsu (MV255) / Mors (M18)	372v,b,11	373v,a,2
12	Res nova mirabilis (MV582) / Virgo decus castitatis (MV583) / Alleluia (M78)	373v,a,3	373v,b,4
13	Lonc tens ai mise (MV117) / Au coumencement (MV118) / Hec dies (M13)	373v,b,5	374r,a,8
14	Nonne sanz amor (MV549) / Moine qui a cuer jolif (MV550) / Et super (M66)	374r,a,9	374r,b,8
15	Se j'ai servi longuement (MV396) / Trop longuement (MV397) / Pro patribus (M30)	374r,b,9	374v,a,9
16	Ne sai tant (MV283) / Ja de bone amour (MV282) / Sustinere (M22)	374v,a,10	374v,b,11
17	Par une matinee (MV807) / Mellis stilla (MV808) / Alleluia (unidentified)	374v,b,11	375r,b,6
18	Au douz mois de mai (MV275) / Crux forma penitentie (MV274) / Sustinere (M22)	375r,b,7	375v,a,8
19	Ave lux luminum (MV784) / Salve virgo rubens rosa (MV783) / Neuma (O53a)	375v,a,9	375v,b,4
20	Douz rossignolet (MV541) / Virgo gloriosa (MV542) / Letabitur (M66)	375v,b,5	376r,b,7

Table 8.2 *(cont.)*

No.	Motet	Starts fol.	Ends fol.
21	Mout me fait grief (MV196) / In omni fratre tuo (MV197) / In seculum (M13)	376r,b,8	377r,a,10
22	De la virge Katherine (MV536) / Quant froidure (MV535) / Agmina milicie (MV532) / Agmina (M65)	377r,a,11	377v,b,13
23	Plus bele que flors (MV652) / Quant revient (MV650) / L'autrier jouer m'en alai (MV651) / Flos filius eius (O16)	377v,b,14	378r,b,5
24	Qui la voudroit (MV220) / Qui d'amours (MV218) / Qui longuement (MV219) / Nostrum (M14)	378r,b,6	378v,a,13
25	In salvatoris nomine (MV452) / Ce fu en tres douz tens de mai (MV452a) / In veritate comperi (MV451) / Veritatem (M37)	378v,a,14	379v,b,6
26	Pour renvoisier (MV28) / Mulier omnis peccati (MV30) / Omnes (M1)	379v,b,7	380r,a,12
27	Le premier jor de mai (MV521) / Par un matin me levai (MV522) / Je ne puis plus durer (MV523) / Iustus (M53)	380r,a,12	380v,a,14
28	El mois d'avril (MV318) / O Maria mater pia (MV317a) / O quam sancta (MV317) / Et gaudebit (M24)	380v,b,1	381v,b,3
29	Trois sereus (MV343a) / Trois sereus (MV343b) / Trois sereus (MV343c) / Perlustravit (M25)	381v,b,4	381v,b,14
30	Dame de valour (MV71) / Dame vostre douz regart (MV72) / Manere (M5)	382r,a,1	382r,b,2
31	Amours mi font rejoir (MV99a) / In Bethleem Herodes (MV98) / In Bethleem (M8)	382r,b,3	382v,a,11
32	Quant voi le douz tens (MV235) / En mai quant rose est florie (MV236) / Latus (M14)	382v,a,12	382v,b,12
33	Par matin s'est levee (MV528c) / Tres douce pensee (MV528d) / [Florebit] (M53)	382v,b,13	383r,b,5
34	Mout souvent (MV377) / Mout ai este en doulour (MV378) / Mulierum (M29)	383r,b,6	383v,a,9
35	He Dieu (MV708) / Maubatu (MV707) / Cumque evangilasset (O31)	383v,a,10	384r,a,6
36	Ave beatissima (MV778a) / Ave Maria gracia plena (MV778b) / Ave maris stella (O51)	384r,a,7	384r,b,4
37	Chascuns dist que je foloie (MV149) / Se j'ai ame folement (MV150) / In seculum (M13)	384r,b,5	384v,a,6
38	A ce que dist bien m'acort (MV520) / Bele sanz orgueil (MV519) / Et exaltavi (M51)	384v,a,7	384v,b,5
39	Encontre le tens de Pascour (MV496) / Mens fidem seminat (MV495) / In odorem (M45)	384v,b,6	385v,a,9
40	Li douz maus (MV146) / Trop ai lonc tens (MV148) / Ma loialtez (MV147) / In seculum (M13)	385v,a,10	386r,b,3

Table 8.2 *(cont.)*

No.	Motet	Starts fol.	Ends fol.
41	Cil qui aime (MV281a)/ Quant chantent (MV281b)/ PORTARE (M22)	386r,b,4	386v,a,2
42	J'ai les maus d'amours (MV188) / Que ferai (MV189) / IN SECULUM (M13)	386v,a,3	386v,a,9
43	Joie et soulaz (MV684) / Doucete sui (MV685) / EIUS (O16)	386v,a,10	387r,a,7
44	Ja n'amerai (MV211) / Sire Dieux (MV212) / IN SECULUM (M13)	387r,a,8	387v,a,2
45	Amours mi font soffrir (MV664) / En mai quant rose est florie (MV663) / FLOS FILIUS EIUS (O16)	387v,a,3	387v,b,7
46	En doit fine amour (MV187) / La biaute ma dame (MV186) / IN SECULUM (M13)	387v,b,8	388r,b,2
47	Diex de chanter maintenant (MV176) / Chant d'oiseaus (MV177) / IN SECULUM (M13)	388r,b,3	388v,a,8
48	Pour vos amie (MV362) / He quant je remir (MV361) / AMORIS (M27)	388v,a,9	388v,b,10
49	Quant voi remirant (MV126) / Virgo virginum (MV127) / HEC DIES (M13)	388v,b,11	389r,a,7
50	Mout m'a fait cruieus (MV854d) / He Dieux tant sui de joie eloignez (MV854e) / GENTES (unidentified)	389r,a,8	389r,b,10
51	Par un matinet (MV658) / He sire (MV659) / He berger (MV657) / EIUS (O16)	389r,b,11	389v,b,3
52	Diex je ne m'en partire ja (MV828) / NEUMA (O51)	389v,b,4	389v,b,14
53	Ja pour mal (MV278) / He desloials (MV279) / PORTARE (M22)	390r,a,1	390r,b,4
54	Povre secours (MV265) / Aucuns m'ont par leur envie (MV263) / [ANGELUS] (M20)	390r,b,5	390v,b,5
55	L'autrier jouer m'en alai (MV780) / SECULORUM AMEN (O52)	390v,b,6	390v,b,14

The La Clayette motets are listed here in the order they appear in the manuscript. Each voice part is followed by its designated number in Van der Werf 1989. Folio references are abbreviated in the following format: 369r,a,1 means folio 369 recto, column a, line 1.

F-Pn n.a.f.13521's musical portion.[22] Bound in flimsy card and entirely removed from the original's literary materials, the facsimiles make the music fascicle available for scholarly observation entirely unencumbered by the texts.

---

[22] Gennrich 1958 and Dittmer 1959.

Cook was at a loss to explain how the manuscript sustained its damage, as (echoing Leo Schrade and foreshadowing Patricia Norwood) he considered it musically unusable.[23] The voices of each motet are copied successively down the two columns of each page, from the highest part down to the tenor, without any attempt to keep all parts of a piece on the same opening. Page-turns fall within twenty-two of the fifty-five pieces, with the result that, for those motets at least, a performance method in which each singer was reading their part would have been impossible.[24]

To summarize the historiographical problems: a manuscript of apparently scholastic music seems to have become an accidental cohabiter with vernacular literary materials of a pastoral kind, and which are thought removed from the Latinate literacies of scholasticism. The inscription of the pieces does not live up to scholarly expectations about good scribes and robust musical literacy for this pre-eminently literate repertory. A disciplinary space was allocated to **F-Pn n.a.f.13521** in its physical absence, but since the book was recovered it has become increasingly clear that it fits the space poorly. Rather than continuing to lament the ways in which the book does not fit, it is time to use the book to alter the shape of the conceptual spaces available for it.

Building a vernacular book

As I have argued more fully elsewhere, the current form of **F-Pn n.a. f.13521** represents the last of three identifiable bindings, and music took a place in the collection at the first stage.[25] The music fascicle itself comprises three gatherings (nos. 50–52 of the whole, which has 56 gatherings in total).[26] The heavy staining in evidence on the bottom outer corner of each leaf becomes more pronounced towards the back of the fascicle, and is shared by all remaining literary leaves in the subsequent gatherings to the

---

[23] Cook 1978, 4–5; Schrade 1955, 396 and Norwood 1986, 95.

[24] However, earlier motet manuscripts that do not use primarily mensural notation also lay out the parts of motets successively, and with the same 'unperformable' results. Manuscripts using mensural forms are, by contrast, usually laid out to permit all singers to see their parts. See Parsoneault, 2001, 30–72.

[25] Curran 2013a, 225–37; see also the section-by-section analysis of the manuscript's codicology in Appendix 1.1 of Curran 2013b, 241–75. The vocabulary of 'production units' and 'usage units' I deploy there was developed in Kwakkel 2002.

[26] Full-colour digital images of the whole manuscript are now available online at http://gallica.bnf. fr/ark:/12148/btv1b530121530.

back of the book, again becoming more pronounced towards the back. This is fluid damage, not wear-and-tear from the turning of pages. Far from evidencing the music fascicle's circulation apart from the rest of the codex, it demonstrates its embeddedness within it – and at a prior stage of binding: other portions of the manuscript *also* have this same fluid damage, but are no longer contiguous with the stained portions at the back of the book. They must have been together at an earlier stage.

Palaeographically, gatherings 1–10 represent the earliest layer of literary materials. They comprise the fullest extant compendium of texts attributed to Pierre de Beauvais, and include a genealogy of the kings of France which concludes with the reign of Louis IX, and makes it clear he is still on the throne. These portions of the manuscript are not affected by fluid damage. However, their ruling pattern disposes Pierre's prose texts into two columns of uneven width: 66mm for the outer column, 60mm for the inner. Precisely the same discrepancy of column width is shown by the music fascicle. Moreover, gatherings 4–10 have three sets of redundant sewing holes at the spine, spaced 50mm apart from one another, and with the central set falling 140mm from the top edge of the book; it seems likely that corresponding holes on gatherings 1–3 are now obscured by later restoration work. Three sets of holes are also visible on the music fascicle's three gatherings, also spaced at 50mm from one another (though the holes are now more heavily frayed – in keeping with the heavier damage clearly sustained by this portion of the codex). The common irregularity in the page design, combined with this evidence from the spine, suggests that these sections were once bound together, and constitute **F-Pn n.a.f.13521**'s earliest layer; the genealogy would imply that collecting for this layer was begun before the death of Louis IX in 1270.

The palaeographically later materials which show staining from fluid damage, but which are no longer next to the musical leaves, must have formed a second, intermediary stage of binding, in which the supports were sewn through the holes that were later re-used for the final binding (as no further holes can now be seen at the spine). Even the latest palaeographical styles in the literary portions of the book do not require a date much after 1300. Thus the book would seem to have undergone a period of active growth over at least 30 years at the end of the thirteenth century, and perhaps into the early years of the fourteenth. Table 8.1 includes an annotation for each portion of the book indicating at which of the three hypothesized stages of binding it must have been present.

The literary works, like the motets, also divide into smaller sub-codex fascicles. **F-Pn n.a.f.13521** bears many tell-tale signs of having been collected fascicle by fascicle, as texts became available to or were sought out by whoever was building it. This kind of 'fascicular construction' has been extensively studied by Ralph Hanna in later medieval English contexts, and also by Richard Rouse and Mary Rouse for the very different context of the Parisian book trade.[27] **F-Pn n.a.f.13521**'s compiler(s) copied the texts of the earliest codicological layer part by part, and copying was apparently often begun on a section or fascicle before it was certain what texts would form a part of it – perhaps before those texts had become available. Hanna has documented how in a time before a notion of literary canon, and when access to vernacular literature was irregular but increasing in frequency, collectors and book producers alike developed techniques that permitted them to copy whatever useful text came to hand, as it became available, without delimiting future repertorial choices.[28] It is precisely this feature which makes **F-Pn n.a.f.13521** an 'eloquent object' speaking of the possibility of contexts beyond the highly centralized book trade in Paris or even its ecclesiastical institutions and University, since the kind of ready textual access we imagine Paris to have enjoyed does not seem to match the conditions to which **F-Pn n.a.f.13521**'s patterns of growth responded.[29] That is not to say that **F-Pn n.a.f.13521** – or particular fascicles of the book – could not have been made in Paris. But the manuscript bears hallmarks of kinds of production that themselves developed so that books could be made beyond such obvious centres.

The order of pieces in the music fascicle seems to show no principle: there are no alphabet cycles, no liturgical orderings, there is no apparent desire to group pieces by number of voices or by language. It is also true that no aspect of the internal design of the fascicle – its ruling and layout and so on – requires an ordering principle. Indeed, the layout mandates no order at all: it would have been perfectly possible to copy any one piece after any other. Viewed from this perspective, we might well consider the musical pieces to have fallen into the order they did because it resembles something close to the order in which the pieces became available to their compiler.[30]

Features of the music fascicle also provide evidence that **F-Pn n.a. f.13521** was produced outside of a major music centre, and that it offers a decentralized view of *ars antiqua* music and its practices. Recall that the

---

[27] See Hanna III 1996a, 21–34; Rouse and Rouse 2000.

[28] I paraphrase here from Hanna III 1996a, 22–3.

[29] On eloquent objects, see Daston 2004.

[30] Further work might consider clusters of pieces that appear adjacent to one another in more than one manuscript (including **F-Pn n.a.f.13521**) to learn more about the exemplars in which motets circulated. On the significance of clusters of pieces in **I-Fl Plut.29.1**, see Bradley 2013a.

music fascicle is spaced in two columns, and that parts are copied successively down the page. Texted parts always begin with a filigree initial at the left margin, while tenors may begin in the middle of a line.[31] In order to waste as little space as possible, the end of one part may be copied at the end of a line whose start gives the initialized opening of a new voice.[32] The scribe writes with a highly compressed module, with little space between minim strokes, and with only small spaces between words. Text is justified at both the left and right margins, splitting words across line and page breaks without regard to where the break will fall in the musical sense of a passage. No aspect of poetic versification is pointed, nor do the texts have any punctuation marks, though the scribe makes regular use of abbreviation signs. This highly compressed layout strategy clearly economises on space. Its visual effect is to present the motet texts in just the same way as the prose found in the section of the manuscript that shares the same discrepancy of column width between the two sides of a page. Importantly, the text scribe (if different from the notator, which seems very likely) was the primary designer of the page layout: on every page, text was copied even before staves were drawn.

This had consequences when notation was overlaid, and explains many of the features that scholars have found problematic in **F-Pn n.a.f.13521**'s notation and musical readings.[33] Because the text was spaced so narrowly, the notator regularly encountered insufficient room to write the music: ligatures and *coniuncturae* especially require more horizontal space than a textual syllable, and melismatic flourishes are often very cramped. However, passages such as these are rarely problematic to construe, because ligatures and *coniuncturae* are in themselves a means of specifying how a succession of pitches divides into syllables. Similar in visual effect, but more problematic, are those passages of music laid over texts copied erroneously. Motet texts are rich in assonance and alliteration arrayed in verses of varied and unpredictable lengths; they offer abundant opportunities for scribal error by haplography or dittography, and this kind of error

[31] See, for example, f.369v, with the tenor of motet 1 beginning part-way through line 7 of column 1, and the texted upper parts of motet 2 beginning at the left margin of column 1, line 11 and column 2, line 7 respectively: http://gallica.bnf.fr/ark:/12148/btv1b530121530/f744. image.

[32] See, for example, f.370v, column 1, line 3: http://gallica.bnf.fr/ark:/12148/btv1b530121530/f746. image.

[33] Schrade went so far as to speak of 'disturbing deficiencies' in the musical readings, which he was 'frequently [...] at a loss to explain', though he supposed they were not detected by early users because the book was not used in performance. See Schrade 1955, 396. The following five paragraphs summarize the argument of Curran 2014.

is most frequent in **F-Pn n.a.f.13521**. Syllables, words, and even whole phrases of text are sometimes omitted. In all but the most unsalvageable cases, however, the music scribe consistently copied all the music required for the *correct* version of the passage. A user of the manuscript would have had to supply text for the passage, or decide some other manner of performing it, but in almost all such cases, the music is complete and corresponds properly with the other voice parts. The notator manifests a keen concern to produce an accurate and legible result (and could not have erased and recopied the text in these passages without entailing drastic further recopying, given that all the text for a part – and perhaps for several pieces – had been copied in little space before the work of notating the book began).[34] Most significantly, the vast majority of textual errors occur in Latin texts, which the scribe copied with a minimum of understanding: the text scribe of the **F-Pn n.a.f.13521** motets was a vernacular specialist, who copied the motets for inclusion in a vernacular book.

Allegations have been made that **F-Pn n.a.f.13521**'s notation is unsophisticated or inconsistent in the theoretical principles it embodies.[35] All commentators have rightly noticed that the scribe uses the virga, punctus and rhomb for the mensural values of long, breve, and semibreve respectively.[36] The long and breve are the cornerstones of the rhythmic style of all pieces in the manuscript, a style founded upon the rhythmic modes, albeit with regular departures for rhythmic nuance. Other figures can very readily be construed by their lateral position relative to these consistently mensural forms. **F-Pn n.a.f.13521**'s scribe uses a variety of figures to render semibreve clusters, but statistically prefers one form over all others possible in the same category of melodic motion.[37] This statistical work reveals the cornerstones of his 'house style'.[38]

Nicolas Bell calls the labile scribal use of rhythmic patterns 'modality': describing the slightly later case of the Las Huelgas manuscript, he writes that 'the concept underlying the scribe's process was centred not so much

---

[34] Haines 2004, 64 points out the care manifested by the erasures in **F-Pn n.a.f.13521**.

[35] For instance, Mark Everist describes **F-Pn n.a.f.13521**'s notation as 'crude'; Everist 1989, 153.

[36] This is mentioned, more or less explicitly, in Rosenthal 2000, 105; Dittmer 1959, 3; Gennrich 1958, 10; see also David Hiley and Thomas B. Payne, 'Notation, §III, 2, viii: Mensural Sources Before Franco', via GMO, and Ernest H. Sanders and Peter M. Lefferts, 'Sources, MS, §V, 2, Early Motet: Principle Individual Sources', via GMO.

[37] See Curran 2014, 140–1.

[38] Roesner 1981, 393–9 outlines a conception of 'house style' for thirteenth-century manuscripts. The notion is developed with comprehensive reference to the palaeographical literature, and worked out in practice on the much more complicated notation of Las Huelgas (**E-BUlh** without shelfmark), in N. Bell 2003.

on an abstract modal system as on the idea of what we call the perfection, which is notionally a regular pulse lasting a perfect long and divisible into three breves'.[39] To adapt Bell's formulation for **F-Pn n.a.f.13521**, I would observe further that **F-Pn n.a.f.13521**'s scribe wrote with a modal conception of the perfection, understanding that it would produce two unequal parts if subdivided, equivalent to long-breve or breve-long. The scribe then rendered this as a principle of digraphic contrast in the notation: the succession of perfections is visually articulated by pairs of figures, each component of which corresponds to one or other of the two unequal parts. Given the style, one never has to read far before reaching an unambiguous single note that delimits the modal context in which remaining figures must be interpreted. The exact delineation of sub-breve flourishes matters less within this context anyway, because the grammar of discant proceeds at the level of the perfection.[40] As detailed above, the number of perfections almost always matches between the parts, regardless of textual errors.

So the manuscript is legible, its notation rhythmically construable, and with far fewer substantive errors musically than textually. Within what kind of reading practice could the manuscript have been used? This requires some thought. It is true that twenty-two of the fifty-five motets are copied with simultaneous parts on different openings; but that leaves thirty-three pieces whose copying presents no barrier to simultaneous reading by all required singers – if that is the kind of literate practice we think most appropriate for the motet as a genre. All previous work on 'performance manuscripts' from the high or later Middle Ages has required panoptic layout for a manuscript to be so designated, on the unexamined – indeed, unarticulated – assumption that the only kind of literate musical practice is one where all singers read all of the time.[41] That such an assumption has been operative in scholarship has left us with a monochrome and undifferentiated sense of the many manuscripts that cannot hope to fit its bill, few critical models to understand changes in music writing occurring in the thirteenth century, and fewer ways to understand how and where music writing could have been distributed in the social world. The only way to tackle this problem will be to study all of the smaller, fragmentary, or 'peripheral' manuscripts palaeographically and inductively, to see what can be learned from them of the literacy each

[39] N. Bell 2003, 93.

[40] I borrow a notion of the grammar of early polyphony from Bent 1998.

[41] See the study by Norwood cited in note 23 above.

seems to have anticipated, or the range of literate practices in which it might have been used, look for patterns across the repertory, and return to manuscripts of the supposedly central tradition in their light.[42]

For **F-Pn n.a.f.13521**, one solution (doubtless among others) would be to suppose that a single *reader* beheld the manuscript, and taught others from the book, by whatever didactic means proved effective. This would resemble a model of 'praelection', where a single reader performed literature aloud to auditors from the book, anticipated by **F-Pn n.a.f.13521**'s literary texts, and persuasively excavated from the literature of later medieval France and England by Joyce Coleman.[43] It would do justice to the palaeographical quality of the manuscript and the music scribe's care for usable results, would complement the vernacular character of the book and the vernacular specialism of the music fascicle's text scribe, would explain the discrepancy between its line-by-line care and the lack of concern that parts fall visually together, and would provide a point of formal and practical continuity with the manuscript's literary materials. It also opens an avenue of research to explore with other manuscripts.

Motets as devotional songs

The method by which the pieces were learnt by their singers would, if the hypothesis holds, have been inherently didactic. But beyond this, what might singers have found in the motets that rewarded their labour and made singing worthwhile? I have mentioned that the literary texts in the manuscript's earliest layers were devotional in emphasis. The first indication that the motets participated in the manuscript's devotional purpose comes in the gesture of prayer and praise with which the music fascicle opens, which is answered by the reciprocally prayerful gesture by which it is brought to a close. **F-Pn n.a.f.13521** no.1 and no.2 are both Latin motets in three voices: *Ave virgo regia* (MV805) / *Ave gloriosa mater salvatoris* (MV804) / DOMINO (DOMINO I), and *O Maria virgo davitica* (MV449) / *O Maria maris stilla* (MV448) / IN VERITATE (M37).[44] No.1 serves as the

---

[42] I imagine a study of thirteenth-century polyphonic notations akin to Paul Saenger's cognitive-palaeographical work on early-medieval book scripts. See Saenger 1997.

[43] Coleman 1996. It also resembles Brian Stock's conception of a 'textual community', in which single readers proposed interpretations of written texts to which other, non-reading members of a community would acquiesce. See Stock 1983, 88–240.

[44] For a complete list of concordances of **F-Pn n.a.f.13521**, see G. Anderson 1975, XXXII (for no.1) and XXXII–XXXIII (for no.2); and Van der Werf 1989, 134 (for no.1) and 68 (for no.2).

first piece in **D-BAs Lit.115** (f.1r); while no.1 and no.2 are also near the beginning of the fourth fascicle of **F-MO H196**, where they appear in reversed order as no.2 and no.3 (**F-MO H196**, ff.88v and 89v). Such concordances between the manuscripts suggest that these particular motets participated in a developing notion of genre for books of polyphony by the middle of the thirteenth century. At the other end of the fascicle in **F-Pn n.a. f.13521**, no.55, *L'autrier jouer m'en alai* (MV780) / SECULORUM AMEN (O52) bears traces of more local tailoring.[45] To judge from the *mise-en-page*, the triplum has been omitted here to fit the space available at the end of the gathering, while the tenor's textual incipit has been 'stretched' with extended cross-strokes, and its perfect longs given as single notes distributed along the space remaining to fill the end of the column.[46] The tenor incipit 'Seculorum amen' comprises the final words of the lesser doxology *Gloria Patri*, the prayer with which psalms are brought to a close in the Divine Office. The tenor is thus used as means of aping a liturgical kind of musical closure, as if the whole set of motets had been a *cursus* of psalms. These liturgical words reply affirmatively to the exuberant songs of Marian praise with which the fascicle had opened, and retroactively bring their echo to mind. In so doing, they place a devotional frame around the collection as a whole, as if to assert the prayerful continuity of all the pieces in between.[47]

Prayer – and especially Marian prayer – forms the cornerstone of a great number of motet texts, especially those in Latin, like **F-Pn n.a.f.13521** no.1.[48] A transcription, text, and translation of this motet is given in Example 8.1. The first pitch *cursus* of the tenor is built on a fifth-mode rhythmic pattern which is one of the oldest of the Notre-Dame repertory. The motetus part above the old chant has even phrases that consistently elaborate complete syntactic units, constituting a litany of popular Marian

---

[45] **F-Pn n.a.f.13521** is the only witness of this two-part version of the piece, though the tenor and motetus are also found in **F-MO H196**, where they appear with the triplum *Pour escouter le chant du roussignol* (MV779), at f.154v. That triplum's text is also found in **F-Pn fr. 12786**, f.76r, which was planned for notation it never received. G. Anderson 1975, 68 gives **F-MO H196**'s triplum in his edition of **F-Pn n.a.f.13521**'s version, apparently finding the piece incomplete without it. He notes the discrepancy on p. LIV of the critical commentary.

[46] http://gallica.bnf.fr/ark:/12148/btv1b530121530/f786.item.

[47] Which is not to say that all the pieces within the fascicle are equally amenable to devotional interpretation. Indeed, one way to understand the addition of 'courtly' literature at subsequent stages of compilation is to see it as a response to vernacularities brought into the codex with the motets that their devotional frame did not fully contain. See Curran 2013b, 155–62.

[48] For an overview of music in honour of Mary in the later Middle Ages, see Rothenberg 2011, especially 24–91.

Example 8.1: Transcription, text, and translation of **F-Pn n.a.f.13521** no.1, *Ave virgo regia* (MV805) / *Ave gloriosa mater salvatoris* (MV804) / DOMINO (DOMINO I)*

* Edition after Anderson 1975, pp. 1–3. Cl's notational figures are given as a superscript line above each staff, so that the rhythmic choices in my transcription may be compared with the manuscript's testimony. Cl's orthography is preserved, but abbreviations are expanded and given in italics. Text in square brackets corrects a clear scribal error to the version reconstructed in Anderson 1975, pp. 1–3 (for the score) and XXXII (for the critical notes, including collations). There are no musical errors in the Cl copy of this piece.

Example 8.1: (*cont.*)

Example 8.1: (*cont.*)

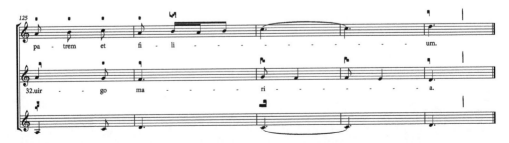

The manuscript's orthography is preserved, but abbreviations are expanded and given in italics. Text in square brackets corrects a clear scribal error to the version reconstructed in Anderson 1975, pp. 1–3 (for the score) and XXXII (for the critical notes, including collations); I have supplied Cl's erroneous readings in footnotes. The translation is adapted from that given in Anderson 1975, pp. LV–LVI.

Triplum

	A Ue uirgo regia	7A	Hail royal Virgin,
	mater clemencie	6B	Mother of clemency,
	uirgo plena gracia	7A	Virgin full of grace,
	regina glorie	6B	queen of glory,
5.	genitrix egregia	7A	singular bearer
	prolis eximie	6B	of an extraordinary offspring;
	que sedes in gloria	7A	you who sit in the glory
	celestis patrie	6B	of the heavenly homeland,
	regis celi regie	7A	of heaven's king the queenly
10.	mater *et* filia	6A	mother and daughter,
	cast[rum][1] pudicicie	7B	fortress of chastity
	stella que preuia	7A	and guiding star;
	in trono iusticie	7B	on the throne of justice
	resides obuia	6A	you firmly take your place.
15.	agmina milicie	7B	All the troops
	celestis omnia	6A	of the heavenly army
	occurrunt leticie	7B	are rushing joyfully forward,
	tibi que preuia	6A	singing unto you
	cantica simphonie	7B	harmonious songs
20.	tam multipharia	6A	So manifold;
	tu tant[e][2] potencie	7B	You of so much power,
	tante uictorie	6B	such victory,
	forme tam egregie	7B	such exceptional beauty,
	mater ecclesie	6B	Mother of the Church,
25.	lux mundicie	5B	light of cleanliness,
	genitrix[que][3] pia	6A	virtuous begetter,
	obediunt tibi celestia	10A	the heavenly bodies are obedient unto you;
	celi luminaria	7A	the sky's lights
	stupefiunt de tua specie	10B	are astounded by your countenance:
30.	sol *et* luna cu*n*cta q*ue*	7B'	the Sun and Moon together with all
	polorum sydera	6A	the constellations of the celestial vault.
	uirgo regens supera	7A	Virgin reigning supernal,

[1] Cl: casta.

[2] Cl: tanta.

[3] Cl: genitrix.

Triplum

	te laudant angeli super ethera	11A	the angels praise you above the heavens.
	aue dei tutum presidium	10C	Hail, God's secure garrison,
35.	pauperis que uerum subsidium	10C	And the poor man's true help.
	tu es pura [lima]⁴ malicie	10B	You are the unblemished tool filing sin away,
	tu genitrix gracie	7B	You, the begetter of grace,
	peccatorum mitte refugium	10C	The soothing refuge of sinners,
	egrotancium	5C	of the afflicted
40.	solabile solatium	8C	A comforting solace.
	nobis [assis]⁵ post obitum	8C'	Be with us after death,
	post istius seculi	7D	After the passing of this age,
	uite [ui]lis⁶ transitum	7C'	of this vile life;
	per gratiam non per meritum	8C'	through grace, not through our merit,
45.	ducas nos ad patrem et filium.	10C	may you lead us to the Father and Son.

Motetus

	A Ue gloriosa	6A	Hail glorious
	mater saluatoris	6B	Mother of the Savior!
	[a]ue⁷ speciosa	6A	Hail splendid
	uirgo flos pudoris	6B	Virgin, flower of modesty!
5.	aue lux iocosa	6A	Hail joyful light,
	thalamus splendoris	6B	Nuptial bed of brilliance!
	aue preciosa	6A	Hail precious
	salus peccatoris	6B	Salvation of the sinner!
	aue uite uia	6A	Hail way of life!
10.	casta munda pura	6A	chaste, refined, pure,
	dulcis mitis pia	6A	Sweet, meek, holy;
	felix creatura	6A	Happy creature,
	parens modo miro	6C	Bearing, in a wondrous way,
	noua paritura	6A	An extraordinary birth,
15.	uirum sine uiro	6C	A man, yet without the touch of man,
	contra legis iura	6A	Against the judgments of law.
	uirgo uirginum	5D	Virgin of virgins,
	expers criminum	5D	Without sin,
	decus luminum	5D	Splendor of lights,

---

⁴ Cl: luna.
⁵ Cl: nobis post (word 'assis' omitted entirely).
⁶ Cl: tulis.
⁷ Cl: que.

Motetus

20.	celi domina	5A	Mistress of heaven,
	salus gentium	5D	Salvation of the people,
	spes fidelium	5D	Hope of the faithful,
	lumen cordium	5D	light of hearts,
	nos illumina	5A	Shine upon us;
25.	nos *que* filio	5C	and to your son
	tuo tam pio	5C	so holy,
	tam propicio	5C	So benevolent,
	reconcilia	5A	Reconcile us,
	et ad gaudia	5A	And lead us into eternal joy
30.	nos per[henni]a[8]	5A	
	duc prece pia	5A	through prayer,
	uirgo maria	5A	O holy Virgin Mary.

[8] Cl: per cupina.

attributes whose string of vocatives becomes a prayer only at l.24, with the imperative request that Mary 'Light of Hearts' shine upon the singers.[49] Its directness of effect is matched by the tune, whose phrases are at once kaleidoscopically varied and always familiar, like the textual appellations they set into motion. The effect of familiarity – of each phrase being like the others, although it is actually different – is produced out of the phrase's shared textual and musical rhythm. In the first half, each pair of 6-syllable lines is set to a single phrase of 8 perfect longs (henceforth 8L), while in the second half (from bar 65 of the transcription) the shorter, 5-syllable lines are set separately from one another, each as its own phrase of 3L followed by a rest of 1L. Especially as the melody is seldom decorated by breaking the modal rhythmic patterns into smaller notes, and then only lightly so as to produce note-values no shorter than a breve, *Ave gloriosa*'s phrase structure might well be called isorhythmic, and lays plain its text's design. Moreover, the 16 lines can be understood to divide into 8 groups of 4, articulated by grouped rhymes: abab abab aaaa caca ddda ddda accc aaaa. There can be no doubt whom the text addresses, but she is only named by the final word. And because her name, 'Maria', has the a-rhyme which has been heard throughout, in retrospect, the Virgin is heard to have lent the sound of her name to the text of the prayer that invokes her. As the prayer

[49] M. Anderson 2010, 57 observes that the Marian antiphons provided a ready fund of appellations that entered into motet texts.

unfolds in time, Mary is literally called into presence. In its elegantly simple style, the motetus addresses the Virgin lovingly.

Against the unassuming motetus, a faster triplum in the sixth rhythmic mode takes audible flight. This song spins less familiar topoi than those heard in the motetus, woven into a more complicated syntax whose difficulty is heightened by the haste with which the syllables pass. Its text invokes a more strident Virgin than the 'precious saviour of the sinner' hailed in *Ave gloriosa*. The Mary of the triplum 'sit[s] in the glory of the heavenly homeland' (ll.7–8) where the things of the sky are obedient unto her ('obediunt tibi celestia', ll.27–8), and where all the luminary bodies are astounded by the brilliance of her beauty – Sun, Moon and stars all ('celi luminaria / stupefiunt de tua specie / sol et luna cunctaque polorum sydera', ll.28–9.) Bands of angels sing on high to a Virgin who reigns supernal ('Virgo regens supera / te laudant angeli super ethera', ll.32–3), and the melodic style of the triplum is apt to figure the energy of the heavenly throng. It is in a higher range than the motetus, sounding out praise in the highest; and its syllables pass in rapid fire against the more stately and unhurried motetus – an effect of surge intensified when the breves are fractured into texted semibreves from b.84. Proclaiming their rapid syllables with rhythmic exuberance at the height of the motet's compass, the triplum's melodies thus report the joy with which the 'bands of the heavenly army rush delighted to greet' the Mother of God ('Agmina milicie / celestis omnia / occurrunt leticie', ll.15–17, which falls at bb.36–43).

This textual moment is important. As it presses forward, the military horde of angels sings to the Virgin 'harmonious songs so manifold' ('tibique previa / cantica simphonie / tam multipharia', ll.18–20; I have marked the passage with a rectangle on the score). Multifarious songs sung in miraculous harmony: in this declaration the motet draws attention to its music's most palpable feature – its polytextuality – enlisting it as an *embodiment* of the heavenly chorus and its surge of welcome. As it does so, the poetry takes what would otherwise be merely the default texture of the thirteenth-century motet, and pushes it into a momentary iconicity that invites the motet to be pondered as a revelation to the senses of the realm of heavenly activity it depicts. Thus while the registral stratification of the voices connotes a space extending from earth to heaven, their differentiated rhythmic styles – characteristically produced at different stages in the historical development of the genre – fuse the tenor's audibly old sounds (its mode-5 tenor) with the triplum's audibly new ones (the pyrotechnics of a fractured, texted mode 6) into something approaching Providence. This is not only a representation. In the virtual environment that emerges from the motet, the singers both echo and embody the angelic voices of which they sing.[50] For a moment they inhabit the ritual bodies they have laboured corporately to produce, and fuse with the holy.[51]

This is an aesthetically abundant music, able to afford experiences of intimacy and celestial grandeur simultaneously. It raises many issues, of which only a few may be adumbrated here. First: the piece draws attention to polytextuality, making it no longer the neutral background of the genre's style, but itself a figuration of plenitude. The transition from ground to figure is triggered by a moment of textual self-referentiality, and the devotional demeanour struck by the whole texture invites a 'monaural' attitude to its polytextuality, that is, a unity of listening stance achieved in a moment when all voices conspire to reveal a common interpretative purpose.[52] The monaural effect reciprocally acknowledges that the stylistic fundament of the polytextual motet is a perceptually opaque, difficult one, and it rewards the close attention that difficulty demands.

This is significant because of the emphasis placed in modern scholarship on the polytextual motet's perceptual difficulty.[53] It has proven complicated to distinguish the *historical* difficulty of the genre from the *historiographical* difficulty of reconstructing old music; but the musico-poetic logic of this motet demands that difficulty be understood as an aesthetic category available to medieval composers and listeners. Emma Dillon has recently construed the polytextual motet as a 'supermusical' genre, 'the most exaggerated example of a kind of music in which sound asserts itself through and beyond words'.[54] In her account, the supermusical responds to the changing soundscapes of later medieval France, and first among these is the 'sonic environment of prayer', which Dillon's study excavates by examining the representation of sound in many prayerbooks of the period.[55] Much as ribald images in the margins heighten the labour of prayer by drawing the eye's attention away from the holy words sanctioned by the centre, so the supermusical effect of polytextuality puts attention into peril, in order that a listener who successfully works with the resistance will hone the discipline of their prayer practice.

---

[50] I borrow the notion of a virtual environment from Clarke 2005, and discuss it in greater detail below.

[51] On ritual bodies, see C. Bell 1992, 94–117.

[52] For an exploration of the several means by which monaurality is achieved, see Curran 2013b, 105–59.

[53] For overviews of these debates, see Clark 2007, 31–5; and (primarily concentrating on the fourteenth-century repertory, but also reviewing scholarship on earlier motets) Zayaruznaya 2010, 73–105.

[54] Dillon 2012, 327.   [55] Dillon 2012, 174–328; this quotation from 293.

Echoing Dillon's approach, I have suggested here that there could also be a meaningful vacillation between sonic opacity and interpretative clarity over the time-span of a motet, available to be heard from outside the piece.[56] There are internal properties available primarily to singers as well. At another moment in *Ave gloriosa*, the imperative 'reconcilia' becomes an impassioned cry to the Virgin as the motetus' melodic height forces the singer's voice out of the range to which it has become accustomed (bb.109–11, also boxed on the score). The twenty-seven lines preparing the gesture have enumerated the Virgin's attributes at great length, rendering her as a complex mental fixture – pictorial, sensory and affective. After this mental work, her Son, to whom the singer will be reconciled, is introduced as '*tam* pio, / *tam* propicio', so holy and *so* benevolent, that the 'reconcilia' seems an almost ineluctable consequence of the wondering tone the intensifiers are calculated to produce. Nested within the prayer is what Sarah McNamer describes (in medieval literary contexts) as an 'intimate script': a structure delineated by the text that seeks to produce affect.[57] It is enhanced by the melody whose literally heightened phrase both describes the motion of an imploring voice and intensifies the singer's physical labour to emotive ends.[58]

Eric Clarke's ecological theory of musical perception offers a useful way to bring all these observations together, and to describe the devotional utility of a motet. Clarke attends to 'the perceptual meaning of sounds, understood as the way in which sounds specify their sources and in so doing afford actions for the perceiver'.[59] A piece of music may afford information about both its empirical sources and about a virtual environment: 'just as spatial patterns of pigment in a painting can create a perceptual effect analogous to that produced by reflection, texture, and shadow in the real world, so music may create perceptual effects with temporal patterns of discrete pitches that reproduce, or approximate, those that we experience with the continuous acoustical transformations that are characteristic of real-world events'.[60] The elegance of the Providential

---

[56] It is true that the 'monaural' moment here is not articulated by a simplification of the texture. Nor could it be: it is precisely *complexity* that the musico-poetic gambit is drawing attention to.

[57] McNamer 2010, 1–57.

[58] Leach 2010 has examined how notation is thematized as a means of controlling the labour of performers in a late fourteenth-century song by Senleches. Like Leach, I am interested here in the kinds of distributed cognition songs require, but the means by which that distribution is achieved is different in **F-Pn n.a.f.13521** than in Senleches's song, because the latter relies upon all singers to be reading their parts, but La Clayette does not.

[59] Clarke 2005, 126.   [60] Clarke 2005, 73.

revelation set up by **F-Pn n.a.f.13521** no.1 is that it furnishes a virtual environment whose celestial sound is actually unknowable; but the piece's fiction proposes that the empirical performance of the motet partakes of the heavenly throng that lies beyond hearing.

Among the invariants of a musical signal must always be information about the empirical body producing the sound. Parts of a motet, always (but not only) scripts for action, sometimes intensify a performer's physical labour (such as with the upward shift in range here) to affective ends and to make interpretive points. One devotional utility of the genre rests in its ability to blur the empirical and virtual environments linked by the performing body in ways the piece's texts describe theologically. The prayerful 'reconcilia' achieves this neatly: in it, the singer's voice is both at one with virtual angels, and intensely present in the real world of human action, and all at once. Clearly the co-ordination of action required to perform a motet produces a structure of distinction separating musicking bodies from their everyday manifestation in the world, and it is in this marking off that I understand a motet to be a ritualizing event in Catherine Bell's terms.[61] As the labouring empirical bodies are invited to fuse imaginatively with the holy ones of which they sing, another, more obviously religious ritualization is also at work. Both kinds of ritualization are properties available in the piece, regardless of where it is performed, because they are produced out of a motet's most basic properties of rhythmic fixity. The ability to intervene in the musical body in these determined and reproducible ways is new to the precisely measured polyphony of the late twelfth and thirteenth centuries. Such ritualizations may, but need not, have been complemented by performing the motet as part of a particular liturgy. This is of crucial importance: the ritualization of the event produced in and through music creates its potentially devotional character – a character over which ecclesiastical liturgy would have no unique purchase, and which could serve with equal efficacy in vernacular devotional practice. The motet has the potential to structure ritualization wherever it goes.

In the thirteenth-century motet, musical effects are thus produced by specifying the labour of mind and body in time, and those specifications

---

[61] C. Bell 1992, 7–8 'propose[s] a focus on "ritualization" as a strategic way of acting' and 'explore[s] how and why this way of acting differentiates itself from other practices. When analyzed as ritualization, acting ritually emerges as a particular cultural strategy of differentiation linked to particular social effects and rooted in a distinctive interplay of a socialized body and the environment it structures'.

are recorded in writing. Writing was used as a tool of composition, and emerging mensural notations made those effects iterable, transmitting them to new bodies to be inhabited again beyond the time and place in which they were first written down.[62] Considered against the repertory of Notre-Dame organa, which was surely informed by oral-mnemotechnic processes of extemporization, possibly based on the memorization of written examples, there is historical change here.[63] Indeed, there is a changed historical character in music; this is a poetics of music that writes it in the future-perfect tense. The testimony of **F-Pn n.a.f.13521** suggests that these effects of writing might have found their way into new singers by means other than by singers' *reading*, while the book opens wide the field of possibilities for who might have used it, and where. Several categories of writing, reading, and *writtenness* are involved in all this, and they will require subtle distinction as scholarship on thirteenth-century music history, and on musical historicism, progresses.

---

[62] I am in dialogue here with Maura Nolan, who draws attention to the '*writtenness* of the past, to its production of textual forms of representation', urging that 'medieval people [...] *did* create artifacts they hoped would speak to the future'. See Nolan 2009, 69 (emphasis original).

[63] See Treitler 2003, 68–83 and Busse Berger 2005, 161–97.

9 | A courtly compilation: the Douce Chansonnier

ELIZABETH EVA LEACH

Oxford, Bodleian Library, Douce 308 (hereafter **GB-Ob Douce 308**) is a large book with a complex mixture of contents, including Old French narratives in verse and prose, and a section of over 500 lyrics arranged by genre into seven sections. The lyrics make it one of the most extensive trouvère collections, although its place in scholarship dealing with courtly song does not reflect this importance, as will be discussed below. The manuscript's initial description by Paul Meyer in 1868 has been superseded both by the Bodleian's own description in 1984 and by the 2005 study of Mary Atchison, which incorporates a later collation report by the Bodleian.[1] The latest scholarship places the manuscript's copying in Lorraine, probably in Metz, in the early part of the fourteenth century, where it remained for a considerable part of its history.[2]

The basic contents of the whole book as it now stands are given in Table 9.1. The items preceding the lyrics (section D) all relate to those lyrics, as will be detailed further below. With the exception of the section of unique *sottes chansons*, the individual lyric genre sections within section D also relate to one another and/or to songs, refrains, and motets outside this particular source. Section D offers a transition between what some have called a courtly, secular first half of the book and a more religious second part, which has eschatological themes. The central place of song within this courtly-religious spectrum shows the power and potential of music to mediate important existential realities of court life, and to focus contemplation of the here-and-now on both itself and its future in the hereafter.

The opening item, section A, Jacques de Longuyon's *Voeux du paon* (here called the 'Romance of Cassamus', after the central character), written in nearly 9,000 twelve-syllable lines arranged in mono-rhymed *laisses*, is a continuation of a sequence of Old French texts on the

---

[1] See P. Meyer 1868, 154–5; Bodleian Library 1984, 60; and Atchison 2005. Most of the images of the miniatures in the manuscript are available via http://bodley30.bodley.ox.ac.uk:8180/luna/servlet/view/search/what/MS.+Douce+308/?&q==%22MS.%20Douce%20308%22. See also the listing at www.arlima.net/mss/united_kingdom/oxford/bodleian_library/douce/00308.html.

[2] See Doss-Quinby, Rosenberg, and Aubrey 2006, XLV–XLVII.

Table 9.1 The overall contents of **GB-Ob Douce 308** in its present state

Fascicle	Item	Hand	Illuminator	Folios	Title	Author	Date/Patron	Broad literary format
I	A	1–3[3]	1 (146 miniatures)	2–85	Li romans de Cassamus [i.e. Les voeux du Paon]	Jacques de Longuyon	Dedicated to Thibaut de Bar, bishop of Liège (1303–12)	narrative verse
II	B	4[4]	2 (40 miniatures)	86d–106v	Li arriere bans damor [i.e. Li bestiaire d'amour]	Richard de Fournival	c.1250	prose (refrain text at end)
III	C	5	1 (15 miniatures)	107–39v	Le Tournoi de Chauvency	Jacques Bretel	Tournament organized by Louis de Looz, count of Chiny in 1285; text from around 1300	narrative verse with refrain interpolations
	D	6	1 (7 miniatures)	140r–250	[Chansonnier]	various	late 12th–early 14thC	lyric verse (organized in 8 genre sections)
IV	E	8	2[5]	250cr [final folio only]	Le Prophetie Sebile	anonymous	13thC	prose
	F	9	2 (3 miniatures; 36 historiated initials)	250cv–282v	Le Tornoiement Antecrist	Huon de Méri	after 1234 (Orgeur, 1995)	narrative verse

[3] ff.1–24v, ff.25–32v, and 33–85 respectively.

[4] Names himself as 'Bretons', f.106v.

[5] Apocalypse extracted to **GB-Lbl Harley 4972**, ff.1–43v, line 24 = copyist 7 and illuminator 1 (79 miniatures); *Prophetie Sebile* follows there on 43v, line 24 and is completed on f.250cr of **GB-Ob Douce 308** = copyist 8 and illuminator 1 (2 miniatures).

Alexander legend; the text can be found in over forty surviving manuscripts.[6] The work's dedication to Thibaut de Bar, bishop of Liège, has been read as making this poem an *admonitio* to Henri VII, in part because of Thibaut's reappearance in section D, where he debates with Roland de Reims in one of the jeux-partis, supporting the idea that a rich and powerful prince should follow his Lord to Rome.[7] Studies of the poem in its various manuscript versions show that while Jacques tried to excise Lotharingisms from his rhymes, the **GB-Ob Douce 308** scribes have put them back in, possibly because the manuscript was copied for the Le gronnais (Le Gournaix) family, patrons from Lorraine.[8] In its other manuscript copies, the *Voeux du paon* is mainly copied alongside other poems in the Alexander cycle, including the slightly later *Parfait du paon*, by the poet-composer Jehan de le Mote.[9]

Item B, Richard de Fournival's *Bestiaire d'amour* ('The Bestiary of Love'), is another widely copied work, existing in more than twenty other manuscripts. Richard was born on 10 October 1201 and was successively canon, deacon, and chancellor of the cathedral chapter of Notre-Dame of Amiens. His other known works include a catalogue of his own books and various notated monophonic lyrics, some of which were used as the upper voices of polyphonic motets.[10] The *Bestiaire* is a parody of a traditional bestiary, in which rather than explaining and moralizing the animals as part of God's universe, the first person lover compares them to himself and his lady and moralizes critically his lady's rejection of his suit. The work cites the opening sentences of Aristotle's *Metaphysics* at its own opening to justify amalgamating an *ars amandi* and a bestiary. While lyric poetry uses animal similes, and satire uses animals, their combination in this fashion is new; the work has been called 'one of the most cynical and misogynistic analyses of love that had yet appeared in any European vernacular'.[11]

---

[6] See www.arlima.net/il/jacques_de_longuyon.html# for a listing of manuscripts and bibliography. The standard edition is Casey 1956.

[7] See Margue 2012, especially 118–19. Thibaut, the dedicatee, is from Bar-le-Duc, on the western edge of Lorraine; the author, Jacques, was probably from Meurthe-et-Moselle.

[8] See the discussion in Busby 2002, 538–9 citing F. Fletcher 1924.

[9] As in **F-Pn fr.12565** and **GB-Ob Douce 165**; in **F-Pn fr.2165-66** (Machaut MS *P*) it is followed by an early, good copy of Machaut's *Judgement of the King of Bohemia*; See the listings for these manuscripts on www.arlima.net/ and http://gallica.bnf.fr/.

[10] See the notes in the edition of the lyrics Lepage 1981. On the other manuscript witnesses of the *Bestiaire*, and for further bibliography, see www.arlima.net/qt/richard_de_fournival.html#bes. The standard edition is Segre 1957. Richard also held a canonry in Rouen, was chaplain to cardinal Robert de Sommercote, and licensed as a surgeon (by Gregory XI and Innocent IV).

[11] Beer 1986, ix.

The *Bestiaire* is often copied in musical sources for the trouvère repertory: it is found in **F-Pn fr.25566**, alongside notated works by Adam de la Halle (for whose grands chants **GB-Ob Douce 308** is a significant source), and in **F-Pn fr.12786**, which was designed for polyphonic rondeaux similar to Adam's and which has concordances with the rondeaux in section D of **GB-Ob Douce 308**.[12]

Sylvia Huot has stressed the importance of Fournival's *Bestiaire* to French literature in general, but draws particular attention to **GB-Ob Douce 308**'s opening double miniature of the scribe at work and of the book being presented to a group of people.[13] There is no hint either of the two lovers of the poem, nor of the doors to memory with eye and ear often shown to illustrate the opening in other manuscripts. The picture in **GB-Ob Douce 308** instead depicts the transmission of knowledge through books and Richard discusses directly the power of books to re-create the presence of events distant in time or space, using Troy as example. Uniquely in **GB-Ob Douce 308** the miniatures showing the animals often do have the lovers illustrated, discussing them to show the book concretizing communication and making the illuminated text of lyrical writing into a 'privileged space within which lover and lady, author and reader, come together in the presence of, and through the means of, the allegorical material'.[14]

Significantly here, **GB-Ob Douce 308**'s is also one of only two copies of the *Bestiaire* to cite a lyric refrain to sign off from the work, and this refrain links the *Bestiaire* to the citation of the same refrain in a motet in Section D of **GB-Ob Douce 308** itself (motet no.20 on f.244v) which is found with musical notation in four other manuscripts.[15] As will be seen further

[12] It is also found in **F-Pn fr.24406**, where it follows notated works by many other trouvères but appears in a section of the manuscript whose illuminations were not completed, and whose text is in a different hand. It appears in **F-Pn fr.12786** with another copy of **GB-Ob Douce 308**'s item F and only one other item; see www.arlima.net/mss/france/paris/bibliotheque_nationale_de_france/francais/12469.html. It is listed in inventories from the Louvre in 1373 and 1411 as being part of a now-lost manuscript which also contained **GB-Ob Douce 308**'s item F and 'pluseurs chansons notees'; see Segre 1957.

[13] Huot 1987, 170–3; **GB-Ob Douce 308**, 86r: http://bodley30.bodley.ox.ac.uk:8180/luna/servlet/s/484k4w.

[14] See Huot 1987, Chapter 5.

[15] The refrain is vdB1308; refrains mentioned here will carry their vdB numbers, referring to their numbering in Boogaard 1969. The other copy of the *Bestiary* with this refrain appended to it is in **F-Pn fr.412**, starting f.226r. The motet which opens with this refrain is *Merci de qui j'atendoie secours et aie / FIAT* and has a tenor drawn from the Office responsory (*Benedictus dominus. Replebitur majestate eius omnia terra fiat fiat*) for which no organum survives. As a two-voice French motet it is transmitted in **D-W Guelf.1099 Helmst.**, f.239v, **F-MO H196**, f.238v (no.192), **F-Pn lat.15139**, f.290, and **F-Pn fr.845**, f.193v. The same melody is texted with the Latin text 'Unum deum in Sinai trinum in personis' in **D-W Guelf.1099 Helmst.**, f.187. This tenor also

below, refrains and motets have an enormous significance both in linking different items within **GB-Ob Douce 308** and in pointing to the manuscript's place within a broader culture of musico-poetic quotation.

Item C is Jacques Bretel's intriguing account, in over 4,500 lines of octosyllabic rhymed couplets, of several days of courtly festivities at Chauvency-le-Château (Meuse) organized by Louis de Looz, Count of Chiny in 1285.[16] The text names a large number of known historical figures, identified often by name and a description of the figure's heraldry, which is even more accurately depicted in **GB-Ob Douce 308**'s extensive programme of illuminations. The poem gives an account not only of tourneying and mêlée fighting, but also of game-playing, masquerade, dancing, and singing. As a poem, *Chauvency* is the least widely copied item in **GB-Ob Douce 308**, appearing in whole or part in only three other manuscripts. Nonetheless it is carefully integrated within **GB-Ob Douce 308** through its use of refrain citation. These refrain texts not only relate to some of the songs and motets in section D of **GB-Ob Douce 308** itself, but also to musical items known from other manuscripts.[17] The relation of item C to the 'chansonnier' in section D will be dealt with further below.

The majority of item E, the *Prophetie Sebile*, of which only the final folio is now present in **GB-Ob Douce 308**, is contained in **GB-Lbl Harley 4972**, where it is preceded by an Apocalypse. Atchison hypothesizes that the Apocalypse and *Sebile* were either originally part of an earlier binding, together with all the present contents of **GB-Ob Douce 308**, or that they were part of a separate volume of three items, on slightly different quality parchment, that would have included the *Tornoiement Antecrist*, item F from the current state of **GB-Ob Douce 308**. The former theory involves a single step to get the present state of the manuscript and would seem to be preferable for that reason. In either case, the two works now in **GB-Lbl Harley 4972** were removed to a separate volume before **GB-Ob Douce 308** entered its current binding state and will not be further discussed here.[18]

The final item in **GB-Ob Douce 308**, F, retained whenever it was decided to extract the Apocalypse and the Sibylline Prophecy, is Huon de Méry's *Tornoiement Antecrist*.[19] This moralizing dream vision transmutes

---

serves for three other French-texted, two-voice motets, one of which has a trouvère melody as the entire upper voice in **I-Rvat Reg.1490**, a significant source for Richard's lyrics.

[16] The standard edition is Delbouille 1932; see also www.arlima.net/il/jacques_bretel.html for further manuscript sources and bibliography.

[17] See Butterfield 2012 and Table 9.3 below.   [18] On *Sebille*, see Baroin and Haffen 1987.

[19] See www.arlima.net/eh/huon_de_mery.html for bibliography and manuscripts sources, including details of editions.

the historical, courtly kind of tournament recounted in Jacques Bretel's *Chauvency* into a dream-vision battle between the vices and virtues in the presence of Christ. *Antecrist* is preserved in seven other manuscripts, some of which contain songs, once again including **F-Pn fr.25566**.[20] The idea of the tournament therefore connects both halves of the manuscript book as it now stands.

The Bodleian catalogue notes that the individual sections are linked closely by their decoration, with one illuminator having a hand in items A, C, and D, while sections B and E share a second illuminator, who is known to have worked with the first on another manuscript.[21] The scribes, however, are different in each section, suggesting that the component parts of the manuscript were prepared separately in the initial stages and then brought together at the point of decoration. That this bringing together was planned, however, is clear. Atchison's representation of the collation structures report undertaken by Martin Kauffmann of the Bodleian Library notes that only the first two of the six books of the manuscript 'are separate codicological units'.[22] Not only are sections C and D part of the same fascicle, but these two sections in particular share many refrains between them and the action in *Chauvency* describes a realistic social context for the performance of the songs of section D.[23] The songs connect the part of the manuscript that comprises courtly themes involving cultural activities such as tourneying, dancing, games, and singing, and the second part of the manuscript, which elaborates moral issues through prophetic themes and apocalyptic imagery. The motet subsection of section D is particularly notable in this regard since the texts there are linked in their forms attested elsewhere to liturgical moments that inform their 'courtly' upper texts; but the other subsections are nearly all linked through motet and refrain citation too. Song thus links and separates the twin aims of cultural and moral education that make **GB-Ob Douce 308** a 'complete kit of secular chivalry'.[24]

---

[20] *Antecrist* is copied in **F-RS 1275**, which contains various similar moralizing 'ways to hell', as well as various song texts; in the large collection in **F-Pn fr. 24432** *Antecrist* follows next but one after Nicole de Gavrelle's *Panthere d'amours* and is itself followed by a *Lai d'amours*, both unnotated. As mentioned above, in **F-Pn fr.12469** it is one of four items among which is a copy of Richard's *Bestiaire* (that is, **GB-Ob Douce 308** item B). The contents of these manuscripts are listed at www.arlima.net.

[21] Stones 2012, 164 situates the two artists of **GB-Ob Douce 308** within the heart of the cultural milieu of extraordinary richness which flourished in Metz during nearly half a century.

[22] Atchison 2005, 25. See also Stones 2012, 165, Appendix A.

[23] See Butterfield 2012.　　[24] Regalado 2006, 343.

The songs of GB-Ob Douce 308 in scholarship

Section D, the 'chansonnier' section of **GB-Ob Douce 308**, is organized by genre and prefaced by an internal index (see Table 9.2). The first six sections are represented both in the index and in situ: sections 1–5 are rubricated with genre names matching those of the index, and sections 2–6 have initial miniatures. The rest of the chansonnier is usually treated as a mixed seventh section of rondeaux and motets, but is not heralded in the index and is unmarked in situ by either rubric or miniature. I depart from earlier writers in considering that this in fact constitutes two further sections, a motet section (items 1–63, ff.243v–247v) and a rondeau section (items 64–101, ff.247v–250r).[25]

Organization by genre has been thought of as a late feature of lyric songbooks, anticipating the organization seen in the single-author collections of Guillaume de Machaut. Robert Lug, however, has argued that since it is a feature shared by one of the earliest trouvère manuscripts, **F-Pn fr.20050**, also copied in Lorraine, generic organization is more likely to represent a geographically specifically organization feature than a chronological one.[26] Eglal Doss-Quinby notes that seventeen trouvère collections arrange their content by genre to some degree, but **GB-Ob Douce 308** uniquely applies only this principle.[27] **GB-Ob Douce 308**'s chansonnier overall has common linguistic features and concordances with trouvère manuscripts **CH-BEb 389** (the so-called Bern chansonnier, or 'trouvère *C*', a manuscript that was designed for musical notation, with staves provided), and **F-Pn fr.20050** (largely with musical notation, although with some empty staves and some blank spaces for staves that were never entered, as well as some text-only copying). **GB-Ob Douce 308** shares 35 songs with **CH-BEb 389** alone, 8 songs with **F-Pn fr.20050** alone, and 20 with both **CH-BEb 389** and **F-Pn fr.20050**, while **CH-BEb 389** and **F-Pn fr.20050** share with each other 211 songs in total.[28] These links, in tandem with its late date, have meant that **GB-Ob Douce 308** is typically regarded as an unnotated trouvère manuscript of little importance, geographically isolated in the far east of francophone Europe with little to offer scholars of text and nothing to offer musicologists. This chapter

---

[25] While it might be objected that this leaves one motet mixed in among the rondeaux, motet texts and texts that are not formally part of the genre type of a given subsection of section D are found in most other subsections: motet texts appear among the section of grands chants; the pastourelle section includes both motets and estampie texts.

[26] See Lug 2012.   [27] Doss-Quinby 2012.

[28] Doss-Quinby, Rosenberg, and Aubrey 2006, LVII. See also Unlandt 2011, XV.

Table 9.2 The contents of the 'chansonnier' (section D) of **GB-Ob Douce 308**

	Folio	Rubric / [Contents]	Miniature	Comments
		INDEX		
1	140r	vez ci labecelaire des grans chans		
2	140v	vesci labecellaire des estampies		
3	141r	vesci labecelaire des ieus partis		
4	141r	vesci labecelaire des pastorelles		
5	141v	vesci labecelaire des ballettes		
6	143v	vesci labecelaire des sottes chansons contre amours		
		SONGS		
1	144br–170v	Ci comancent li grant chant.		
2	171r–177v	vesci labecelaire des estampies		
3	178r–195v	cesci labecelaire des ieus partis	three seated female characters clapping while another directs seated female character and standing male character, hands raised in debate	original first folio of gathering
4	196cr–209v	vez ci la becesllaire des pastorelles	knight on horseback with shepherdess and her sheep	first folio of gathering
5	210vr–237v	Ci encomancet les balletes	three figures, two with hands joined as if dancing and third beating tabor	first folio of gathering
6	239br–243v	[sottes chansons]	two seated female figures ridiculing third female figure	first folio of gathering
7	243v–247v	[motets]		
8	247v–250r	[rondeaux]		

has been planned specifically to challenge such a view and demonstrate the significance of this manuscript witness.

GB-Ob Douce 308's 'generic' organization shows an understanding of genre that is more topical rather than formal, or at least all sections have formal types that do not strictly 'fit': the grands chants include at least two motet texts; the jeu-parti section has songs sung to melodies from the *canso* tradition of the troubadours; the pastourelles include pieces that are in the form of balades as well as another motet text; and the ballettes include two related formal types that correspond effectively to the virelai (that is, with the refrain before the first stanza and after each stanza) and the balade (that is, with the refrain after each stanza).[29] Most significantly, nearly every genre section includes songs with refrains, not in the sense of having a repeating refrain (although many of the ballettes have this) but in the sense of containing text that is quoted in other songs and/or diagnosed as part of the refrain corpus in the standard catalogue of Nico H. J. van den Boogaard.[30] Nearly all the sections actually also include texts found – in whole or in part – in motet voices.

As the section of song lyrics occupies a significant part of the book as a whole, the manuscript is sometimes known as the 'Lorraine chansonnier' or the 'Oxford chansonnier', and has been accorded a siglum as trouvère chansonnier *I*, even though all these designations strictly refer only to the fourth section of the whole manuscript book. Indicative of how the contents of the manuscript have been divided up within musical scholarship, it is also known as motet manuscript *D*. And **GB-Ob Douce 308** not only suffers because of the scholarly dividing line *within* thirteenth-century scholarship (between monophonic trouvère repertories on one hand and thirteenth-century motets on the other). Because of its late dating (after 1309 on account of a name in one of the jeux-partis), it is also awkwardly positioned in the early fourteenth-century gap between Adam de la Halle as culmination of the thirteenth-century tradition, and Machaut as the start of a new art, complete with minims, author-centred codices, polyphonic songs, motets with non-liturgical tenors, and the alleged decline of citation practices of the kind seen earlier between rondeaux, motets, and secular songs).[31] **GB-Ob Douce 308** looks forward and back: back to the grands chants of the trouvères and forward to the motets and songs of the

---

29 See Page 1998.   30 Boogaard 1969.
31 My scepticism about this 'division' should be evident. On musicology's problems with the tricky period around 1300, see Everist 2007.

mid-fourteenth century, some of which use individual poems from **GB-Ob Douce 308** in full as motet tenors or in part as refrains.[32] The teleological drive of music history has meant that **GB-Ob Douce 308** has been more often appreciated as the source or origin for something later and newer than as a significant repository of older music. Virtually no one has discussed its significant status as a document of reception and synthesis of an older tradition that it recasts within a specific geographical and social milieu.

Most importantly, the lack of musical notation in **GB-Ob Douce 308** means that it has not been fully incorporated within any of the musico-logical scholarship, whether on monophony or polyphony, and whether on thirteenth- or fourteenth-century music. At the time of writing there is no online listing or inventory of the manuscript on DIAMM or Musicologie médiévale, but only on the literary resource Arlima, which does not list the lyrics individually. My response to the dismissal of **GB-Ob Douce 308** for being an unnotated witness is twofold. First, the implication that without music *notation* there is nothing musicological to be said is itself question-able, as if musicology is still tightly bound to only literate music-making. Second, I argue that staves or separate notation for musical melodies would be superfluous for the readers of this book because the music is already effectively notated for the purposes of its (musically informed) readers by means of its 'notation' of the songs' verbal texts.

The lyric section of the manuscript had to wait until the 2005 publication of Atchison's PhD thesis before it was treated to a complete modern edition.[33] The closest the chansonnier had come before this was the piecemeal publication of the first six genre sections in order by Georg Steffens in *Archiv für das Studium der neueren Sprachen und Literaturen* between 1896 and 1900.[34] These articles present a diplomatic transcription, with the lyrics rendered as prose and without differentiation between u and v , or i and j; no translations are offered. The final part of section D, the unindexed, unillustrated, and un-rubricated mixed section of the motets and rondeaux at the end of the chansonnier, was not edited by Steffens.

---

[32] One of the texts in the pastourelle subsection, Pastourelle no. 6, topically a *chanson de mal mariée*, was used by Machaut as a motet tenor; the full text of his tenor is known only from **GB-Ob Douce 308** and the melody from the several Machaut manuscripts; no witness survives that transmits both. Machaut cites several items now known only through **GB-Ob Douce 308**. See, for example, Leach 2003a and 2003b.

[33] Atchison 2005.

[34] Steffens, 1896, 1897a, 1897b, 1898a, 1898b, 1900. Many of the pastourelles had already appeared in Bartsch 1870.

Atchison's edition of the complete chansonnier section is, like Steffens', largely diplomatic: it replicates manuscript spelling and punctuation, retains i and j as well as u and v, and also represents the presence and visual extent of large capitals. In addition, however, it adds editorial layout showing poetic structure, although unfortunately this is not always competently handled. Again, no translation is offered and the mis-transcription of words and the misapprehension of versification suggest that the texts are not fully understood at the level of structure or content by their editor.[35] Nonetheless, Atchison's edition remains the most complete representation of the songs of **GB-Ob Douce 308** yet published and the vital starting point for any study.

Better than Atchison's edition but far less complete, covering only the subsection of ballettes, is the exemplary edition of Eglal Doss-Quinby, Samuel N. Rosenberg, and Elizabeth Aubrey, which includes English facing-page translations and an extensive introduction by the interdisciplinary three-person editorial team. Significantly this publication also attempts to re-musicalize the manuscript, supplying music from other sources for songs or parts of songs (for the latter, typically refrains) in **GB-Ob Douce 308**.[36] While similar attempts had been made before, these had not been done in the context of a consideration of entire songs in an entire subsection of the manuscript.[37]

Many of the songs in **GB-Ob Douce 308**, especially the grands chants, jeux-partis, pastourelles, motets, and rondeaux, have concordances, often to musically notated author-attributed sources, in multiple other versions, from the repertory of monophonic trouvère song. The grands chants, for example, open with a widely copied song by the early trouvère Blondel to which is appended a poem by one of the most recent trouvères, Adam de la Halle.[38] Of the 93 songs in that subsection (92 discrete texts, since one text is copied twice), 55 have concordances in other manuscripts, of which 44 have specifically musical notation in at least one other manuscript.[39]

Attending to **GB-Ob Douce 308**'s representation of older repertory yields some unexpected results, of which one example must suffice. Jeu-parti no.27a, 'Amins ke est li muez vaillans' (RS365; ff.190v–191r) discusses whether the best way to combat desire is to satisfy it or abstain from

---

[35] See the comments in Leach 2006.

[36] See Doss-Quinby, Rosenberg, and Aubrey 2006; see also my review in Leach 2007b.

[37] See, for example, Gennrich 1927.

[38] Adam's song is not given the usual pen-flourished capital and is not listed in the index.

[39] And of the 10 whose melodies cannot now be reconstructed, all are concordant with C, which was designed for music that was never entered.

satisfaction. The woman who sings first puts it more specifically: is it better for a man to lie the whole night with a lady without accomplishing all of his desire, or to lie with many women and flee immediately he has finished with each? Ultimately, the lady argues for the former and the man the latter. The seven-stanza version of this text is found in **GB-Ob Douce 308** and **CH-BEb 389**, but **F-Pn fr.846** has the melody, which turns out to be that of troubadour Bernart de Ventadorn's *Can vei la lauzeter mover*, a very famous song which was subject to multiple contrafact texts (including at least one other in debate form), and which itself exemplifies a 'je' whose subjectivity is divided against itself with the desire to love his lady in so far as she is his lord (*domna*) but rail against her as a woman (*femna*).[40] Here, not only can the melody of this song be realized readily by anyone who knows Bernart's famous tune, but **GB-Ob Douce 308**'s more careful attention to a fully notated *verbal* text supplies additional complexities to the debate in its later stanzas that **F-Pn fr.846**'s lacks.[41]

The relatively small number of complete concordances among the ballettes, and total lack of concordances for the estampies and sottes chansons, has led to the conclusion 'either that the manuscript records relatively recent compositions or that these songs represent a contained tradition, fostered in Lorraine, which was not known to compilers of mainstream trouvère manuscripts'.[42] For the ballettes, at least, this may be an overstatement once one adds to the *full* concordances with known notated songs music that is notated at least in part by shared refrains, as the tables in the preface to the edition detail.[43] Despite their general isolation, even one of the 19 estampies cites a widely transmitted refrain. Only the sottes chansons remain completely without concordant material, either within **GB-Ob Douce 308** or outside it.[44]

The chansonnier section represents in microcosm the holistic and intertextual moves taking place at the larger level of the overall contents

---

[40] See Gaunt 1995, 127–31.

[41] Although it is possible that these stanzas might be later addition, this would not invalidate the point, which is that **GB-Ob Douce 308** represents a sustained reinterpretation of earlier melodies and earlier texts within a new context whose narrative setting is outlined in *Chauvency*.

[42] Doss-Quinby, Rosenberg, and Aubrey 2006, LVIII.

[43] See Doss-Quinby, Rosenberg, and Aubrey 2006, Table XII (pp. CXXXVIII–CXL) and Table XIII (p. CXLI).

[44] Despite the lack of further refrain citation, the estampie texts read like pastiches of citation and might be later and/or improvised texting of dance song versions without text. The sottes chansons represent a rare survival of a genre possibly considered too risqué for frequent literate collection; see Doss-Quinby, Grossel, and Rosenberg 2010.

of the manuscript. Taken as a whole (as per Table 9.1), and as discussed above, the manuscript integrates a fairly local literary work, *Chauvency*, within more widely transmitted works. Taken as a section (as per Table 9.2), the chansonnier integrates songs that may be new and/or local within traditions that are far older. And beyond this, the whole manuscript is girded round with a profusion of refrains, which reach out from the manuscript's individual texts, linking between pieces in the same section of the manuscript, items in different sections, and items that are known from other manuscript witnesses. The overall impression, to me at least, is of a manuscript whose contents are deeply plugged into wider practices of both contrafaction and refrain usage (both in the sense of citation and in the sense of formal-repetition type).[45] The manuscript seeks to integrate the new and/or local within wider practices; the fact that we can realize the melodies of some of the ballettes not from their earlier instances but because they were later cited in turn by fourteenth-century composers suggests that this strategy of integration had some success.

The musical nature of the songbook

As already noted, the lack of musical notation in **GB-Ob Douce 308** has effectively prevented its serious treatment as a music book, leading to its relative neglect by musicology compared to other trouvère manuscripts. This view is based on the assumption that verbal and musical notation are two discrete systems and that musical manuscripts signal this through musical notation and that 'songs' without musical notation might be songs only in the allusive sense of 'lyrics', for reading aloud or silently, but not for real singing. But anyone who has ever sung hymns from a standard text-only hymn book, or sung along to popular music from words in a CD booklet, text under a YouTube video, or lyrics on a karaoke video will attest that even today, verbal notation (that is, the written words of a song) is a sufficient way to notate a sung performance when the song is familiar or can be heard from the singing of those to whom it is familiar. In short, one can even learn a song one does not know and whose words are difficult to hear from the sound of a YouTube video, provided one has the verbal text and the sung song in combination.

---

[45] On this distinction, see Doss-Quinby 1984 on repeated refrains vs cited refrains; see also the discussion in Saltzstein 2013.

In many cases, concordances with manuscripts that have musical notation make it clear that the songs of **GB-Ob Douce 308** were sung to
melodies. But doubt can still linger: how did someone who only had access
to the unnotated **GB-Ob Douce 308** know that these songs were anything
other than simply poetry? The answer to this is suggested by the two
central sections of the manuscript, D and C.

The genre sections of the chansonnier in section D are illustrated with
miniatures that show dancing and singing. In addition, the songs themselves make copious reference to their own status as sung songs and to the
je singing, especially when introducing refrain texts. For example, Ballette
no.46, ll.1.1–2, 'De grant volantei jolie / Chanterai jolïement [. . .] / an ceste
chanson dirai: / E, ai! ke ferai?' (With great merry willingness I shall sing
merrily [. . .] in this song I shall say: 'Ah, oh, what shall I do'). In Ballette
no.49 (=Ballette no.92), l.4 has 'S'an chanterai' (so I'll sing of it) to
introduce the refrain. Ballette no.50 starts the first stanza (l.1.1) with 'Bone
amor me fait chanter' and the third with 'A ma chanson defineir' (Good
Love makes me sing [. . .] To conclude my song). *Chansons avec des
refrains*, with a changing refrain citation every stanza, make the sung
nature of their refrains particularly clear. For example, Ballette no.52 starts
'Je ne chantai onkes mais / De si bone volantei' (ll.1.1–2; I have never sung
before with such a good will), telling how his lady 'ait comandeit [. . .] /
Novelle chanson a faire, / S'an di por faire son grei / Iceste chansonete /
Doucette' (ll.1.5, 7–11; has commanded [me] to do a new song, so I will
perform, in order to please her, this sweet little song); then follows the first
refrain. The second is introduced with the phrase 's'an di sans mantir'
(l.2.9; so without lying I perform), with the refrain being that which is
performed ('dire' in this case is performing the song aloud, *pronunciatio*).
The last refrain follows another invocation of 'S'an vuel dire' (l.3.8; so
I wish to perform) and identifies itself as 'Cis virelis ke j'ai trouveit' (l.3.10;
this virelai that I've invented).

The clearest description of the songs of **GB-Ob Douce 308** as songs is
indirectly though the narrative action in *Chauvency* and through verbal
and personal links between the two sections.[46] A short synopsis of *Chauvency* is necessary to provide the context for this, in conjunction with
consulting the list of the poem's refrains in Table 9.3.

---

[46] While most of the illuminations of *Chauvency* are about the heraldry of the participants, f.113r
has an illustration of a lady dancing between two men; a bird perches on rose bushes and a man
to the left plays a bowed string instrument (rebec), not specifically illustrating anything in the
text, but merely signalling the importance of song.

Table 9.3 The refrains of the *Tournoi de Chauvency* (section C) in **GB-Ob Douce 308**

	Line	vdB	Text	Refrain concordances	Singer(s) in context of *Chauvency*
				TUESDAY	
1	2350	765	Trai toi arriere, fai me voie, Par ci pascent gens de joie	1. Motet voice no.33 (in **F-MO H196; *F-Pn fr.25566*) 2. Motet voice no.1115 (= motet no.39 in **GB-Ob Douce 308**) 3. In narrative poem *Cour d'Amour* (in **F-Pn n.a. f.1731**)	a group at the end of the jousts
2	2454	872	Hé, tres douce Jehannette Vos m'avéz mon cuer emblé!	NONE	Renaut de Trie
3	2462	1422	Onques mais n'amai! Hé Diex, bone estrainne: Encommencié l'ai!	1. Song by Lescurel (in **F-Pn fr.146*).	Jeanne d'Avillers
4	2478	374	Clere blondete sui, a mi Lassette, et si n'ai point d'ami!	1. Song RS1991 I (= pastourelle no.32 in **GB-Ob Douce 308**)	Aëlys de Louppy
5	2490	116	Améz moi, blondete, améz, Et je n'amerai se vos non!	NONE	Jean d'Oiselay
6	2498	513	Diex, donéz a mon ami Pris d'armes, joie d'amours!	1. In narrative poem *Renart le Nouvel* (in **F-Pn fr.372*; +**F-Pn fr.1581**; **F-Pn fr.1593*; **F-Pn fr.25566*), sung by Orgueilleuse the lioness	Hable de Boinville

Table 9.3 (*cont.*)

	Line	vdB	Text	Refrain concordances	Singer(s) in context of *Chauvency*
7	2518	977	Ai tout mon cuer mis en bien amer	NONE	Joffroi d'Asprement
8	2524	1165	Jolietement m'en vois! Jolietement!	1. Motet voice no.1076a (In *F-MO H196) 2. Motet voice no.1095 (= motet no.8 in **GB-Ob Douce 308**) 3. In narrative poem *Le Chastelaine de Saint Gille* (in **F-Pn fr.837**)	Aëlys de la Neuve Vile
				THURSDAY MORNING	
9	3118	200	An si bone conpaignie Doit on bien joie mener!	1. In narrative poem *Renart le Nouvel* (in *F-Pn fr.372; +F-Pn fr.1581; *F-Pn 1593; *F-Pn fr.25566), sung by Noble the lion 2. In *Le Jeu de Robin et Marion* (in *F-Pn fr.25566; °F-Pn fr.1569; *F-AIXm 166), sung by Marion 3. In *Salut d'Amours I* (F-Pn fr.837)	Countess of Luxembourg (Beatrice)
10	3186	65	Ainsi doit on aler a son ami!	1. VdB rondeau no.168 (in °F-Pn fr.12786) 2. Song RS584, stanza V (in F-Pn fr.20050; +CH-BEb 389; I-MOe R4,4) 3. Motet voice no.435 (in *F-Pn fr.844; *F-Pn fr.845)	Margot de Luxembourg (sister of the Countess)

4. Motet voice no.1143a (in +**I-Rvat Reg.1490** attributed to Richard de Fournival)

5. In narrative poem *Le court de Paradis* (in **F-Pn fr.837**; ***F-Pn fr.25532**; **F-Pn fr.1802**)

No.	RS	Incipit	Concordances	Character
11	3256	Diex qui dirai en mon païs / Que j'ai amour novelle?	NONE	Agnes de Commercy
12	3316	Hareu, comment mi mainterai? / Amors ne mi laissent durer	1. vdB rondeau no.89 (in °**F-Pn fr.12786**; +**I-Rvat Reg.1490** attributed to Guillaume d'Amiens) 2. Song RS816, stanza no.I (***F-Pn fr.846**) 3. In narrative poem *Cour d'Amour* (in **F-Pn n.a. f.1731**)	Renaut de Trie
13	3328	Ja mauvais n'avera bele amie / Li prous lez enmaigne dous et dous	1. In French prose translation of Ovid *Ars Amandi* (in **F-Pn fr.881; F-Pa 2741**)[47]	a group of ladies

THURSDAY AFTERNOON

No.	RS	Incipit	Concordances	Character
14	4130	Je taig par le doi m'amie / Viagne avant cui je en fas tort!	NONE	knights returning from the mêlée
15	4220	Si n'a plus joliete de mi	NONE	Countess of Luxembourg
16	4233–4	Douce dame, parléz a nous! / Que quiert vostres gens cors li dous?	NONE	a minstrel (fiddle player)

Table 9.3 (*cont.*)

	Line	vdB	Text	Refrain concordances	Singer(s) in context of *Chauvency*
17	4235–6	1739a	Sire, qu'an afiert il a vos? Ne vos voi pas bien, saige. J'ai fait mon chapelet jolif La jus en cel boscage!	NONE	Countess of Luxembourg
18	4248	612a	Douce dame, voléz baron?	NONE	minstrel (fiddle player)
19	4249–50	690	N'ai! Se je ne lai tres bon, je i avroie damaige! J'ain miex mon chapelet de flors qu malvais mariaige!		Countess of Luxembourg
20	5251–2	1796a	Trez douce dame, il est trovéz Si fait com vos le demandéz	NONE	minstrel (fiddle player)
21	4253–4	227a	Biaus sire, et car le m'amenéz la jus en cel herbaige! Je m'en vois; vos m'i troverés seant sor le rivaige!	NONE	Countess of Luxembourg
22	4282	577	Diex, trop demoure! Quant venra? Sa demoree m'occira!	1. In narrative poem *Méliacin* (in **F-Pn fr.1455**; °**F-Pn fr.1589**; **F-Pn fr.1633**; **I-Fr 2757**; **B-Br IV-319**)[48]	Countess of Luxembourg

23	4289–92	445a	Dame, ves ci le bacheler; De proesce ne sai son per. Tenéz, dame, je le vos baille, Et a millor de lui trover Fauriéz vos bien sans faille.	2. In narrative poem *Renart le Nouvel* (in ***F-Pn fr.372**; **+F-Pn fr.1581**; ***F-Pn fr.1593**; ***F-Pn fr.25566**), sung by Harouge the leopardess 3. *L'abeïe dou chastel Amoureus* (in **F-AN 403**)[49] NONE	minstrel (fiddle player)
24	4296	1191	La merci Deu j'ai ataint Se que je voloie	1. vdB rondeau no.147 (= rondeau no.98 in **GB-Ob Douce 308**)	Countess of Luxembourg
25	4450	507	Dex, doneis amors a sous Qui amors maintienent muez!	1. song RS1103 (= ballette no.100 in **GB-Ob Douce 308**)	Simon de Lalaing

* = with musical notation; + = with blank staves but no notation entered; 0 = with space for staves but no staves or notation

[47] Arsenal library manuscript not examined.

[48] Manuscripts not examined.

[49] Manuscript not examined.

As the gathering for the Tournament starts on Sunday 1 October at the castle of Chauvency, the herald Bruiant helps the narrator identify the lords present.[50] The Sunday can be considered a 'preliminary evening' for the Tournament proper, whose first day is Monday, when a series of one-to-one jousts take place between historically verifiable figures, who are depicted in illuminations with their correct heraldry. The version of *Chauvency* in another manuscript, **B-Mbu 330-215**, includes the praise of these figures from the minstrel Henri de Laon as well as a description of the evening's refrain-rich musical entertainment back at the castle, although both are omitted in the copy in **GB-Ob Douce 308**.[51]

Day two, Tuesday, is much the same but with a longer series of jousts. As night falls the company retires singing (refrain no.1 in Table 9.3; vdB765), an activity they resume after supper (refrains nos. 2–8 in Table 9.3). Of these initial eight refrains in the copy of *Chauvency* in **GB-Ob Douce 308**, nos. 1 (vdB765), 4 (vdB374), and 8 (vdB1165) have concordances with the motet subsection of the chansonnier (Section D) of the same manuscript.[52] Refrains nos.2 (vdB872) and 7 (vdB977) are unique to *Chauvency*; the others have concordances with works in the motet repertory and with refrains cited in narrative works (see Table 9.3 for details).

After the initial set of refrains, performed by the group (refrain no.1) and then a wide variety of individuals (nos.2–8), the musical proceedings of Tuesday evening are closed when two of the ladies, Agnès de Florenville and Perrine d'Esch, perform the 'jeu du robardel' while fruit is served (ll.2533–2613). This event is treated to one of only two non-tournament illuminations in **GB-Ob Douce 308**'s copy of *Chauvency*: f.123r illustrates the robardel dance, with Agnès de Florenville on the left in a scarlet gown and floral crown, looking into a mirror while Jehannette de Boinville, cross-dressed as a shepherd, wears a folded hood as a hat; a male figure on the right plays a drum.[53] This incident suggests that pastourelles could be performed by noble women voicing peasant women and men – a

---

[50] Given the significant number of refrains shared with *Renart le Nouvel*, the name of the herald provides a further reference to that poem, in which Bruiant the bull sings three refrains. See Haines 2010b, 54, table 2.1.

[51] See Delbouille 1932, introduction; Butterfield 2012; Atchison 2012.

[52] Motets nos. 8, 32, and 39. In addition, motets no.3, 27, 32=51, and 46 share refrains with the part of *Chauvency* that is omitted from **GB-Ob Douce 308** itself, but present in other manuscripts of the poem.

[53] See http://bodley30.bodley.ox.ac.uk:8180/luna/servlet/detail/ODLodl~1~1~41648~110272:Les-tournois-de-Chauvenci-?sort=Shelfmark.

performance practice that evokes as yet unexplored possibilities for the dynamics of class and gender in this genre.

On Wednesday, after a sung Mass, the day is spent organizing the mêlée, which is due to take place on Thursday. By evening the organization gives way to various social games. On Thursday after matins, the nobles once more hear sung Mass and then, a little before midday, the knights head to the field. The ladies staying behind at the castle begin to dance, led by the Countess of Luxembourg singing refrain no.9 (vdB200) until a herald bids them haste to watch the action on the field. The mêlée takes place at vespers and Bretel describes various historical personages leaving the castle and singing songs and refrains on their way there (refrains nos.10–13); the majority of the refrains sung on the Thursday morning of *Chauvency* have multiple concordances with a mixture of songs, motets, and interpolated narratives.

During the mêlée itself the men fight, while the narrator describes both the action and the comments of the women about it. The violent part of the festivities ends when night falls and the combatants can no longer recognize each other. The entire company, men and women, return to the castle, again singing as they go (refrain no.14; vdB1143). They once more spend the evening in dances and games, including the 'jeu du chapelet', in which the Countess of Luxembourg exchanges refrains with a minstrel and André d'Amance (refrains nos.15–24) and then a final mixed-sex dance to close the evening's entertainments (refrain no.25; vdB507). The majority of these refrains are unique; Nancy Freeman Regalado has suggested they were specially composed for the poem.[54] And while the last two of these refrains have concordances, they are only (but significantly) with other subsections in section D of **GB-Ob Douce 308** itself: the ballettes and rondeaux.

On Friday morning the knights and ladies hear Mass, dance, and dine, while their valets prepare for their departure. Finally, they take leave of one another and the narrator offers a prayer to God on behalf of lovers and of the author.

GB-Ob Douce 308 is a book whose various parts and various media within those parts work together. It has been remarked that the illuminations in the **GB-Ob Douce 308** copy of *Chauvency* provide a more accurate record of the heraldry identifying the historical participants than the descriptions in the text.[55] The poem is thus an under-prescriptive performance of the heraldry, which cues its fuller performance on the

---

[54] Regalado 2006.   [55] Ibid.

manuscript page. Similarly, the songs in section D provide a more accurate account of the singing and dancing described in *Chauvency* because they contain full texts of genres that are referenced explicitly or through refrain citation in the narrative work. As described above, several of the songs cited in *Chauvency* are identifiable because the refrain in question is shared with a song in the chansonnier section of the manuscript.[56] In addition, one of the biggest clues to the use of the song book is the description of courtly singing in *Chauvency*, where it is an important part of the four-day event.

Butterfield notes the high instance of motet refrain citation within *Chauvency* and it is noticeable that reference to refrains found in motets permeates nearly all parts of **GB-Ob Douce 308**. Refrains that appear also in motets are used not only in the *Bestiaire* (section B; see above) and *Chauvency* (section C; see Table 9.3), but throughout most of the subsections of Section D, arguably suggesting that the motet is more of a practice than a genre and that its audience might be more courtly than the clerical audience usually posited for the motet.[57] This suggestion is furthered by the presence of entire motet texts among the grands chants, jeux-partis, pastourelles, and ballettes, four contrasting but equally courtly song genres. In most cases **GB-Ob Douce 308** transmits a longer version of the text used by the motet voice when it is transmitted in its polyphonic motet context, perhaps offering a clue to the diminutive ending in 'motet'.[58]

There are a number of songs in **GB-Ob Douce 308** that represent longer versions of entire refrains (in the sense of repeating refrains in refrain forms, rather than in the sense of cited textual tag) or entire stanzas found in motets. Space precludes a full enumeration and discussion of these items here; their concordances are complex and they are quite varied in their specifics. Instead, *Quant la saisons desiree est entree* (RS505; **GB-Ob Douce 308** grand chant no.56) will serve as a case-study, but this is not to claim that the details of its case are replicated exactly in the other examples. Nonetheless, some of the issues raised can be seen as indicative.

The section of grands chants has two motets within it, both of them copied polyphonically in **I-Tr vari 42**.[59] In both cases the voice in **GB-Ob Douce 308** is the tenor part of **I-Tr vari 42**.[60] *Quant la saisons*

---

[56] See also Butterfield 2012.

[57] On the audience for the motet, see Page 1993, Page 2000, and Saltzstein 2013.

[58] A similar suggestion was made by Hofmann 1970.   [59] The other is grand chant no.67.

[60] Grand chant no.34 is copied in the position on the page in **I-Tr vari 42**, f.21r of the triplum voice and is often so labelled in the secondary musicological literature; it takes the bottom of the texture musically, however, and is thus functionally the tenor part.

desiree est entree has a suggestive feature in its concordances, which are detailed in Table 9.4. Only the first stanza, the only stanza transmitted by the motet version, very closely agrees between all copies in both text and music (where musical staff notation is present). The monophonic witnesses **F-Pn fr.846** and **F-Pn fr.24406** even copy this song in mensural notation, akin to that in the motet manuscript **I-Tr vari 42**, despite not ordinarily using such notation for song.[61] But the later stanzas have quite different texts between manuscripts. **GB-Ob Douce 308** has three further stanzas; **F-Pn fr.20050**, which has two further stanzas, is closest to **GB-Ob Douce 308** in text, although the difference increases until stanza three is really quite a different stanza in the two manuscripts.[62] **F-Pn fr.846** only ventures a single residuum stanza, and except for the last two lines it is completely different from any other manuscript.[63] Similarly **F-Pn fr.24406** has five further stanzas, all substantially different again. Were it not for the provision of mensural notation of the same melody in the trouvère manuscripts, it might be suggested that the first stanza base had been provided by the copy of the first stanza only, which is interpolated as a lyric insertion into the narrative poem *Méliacin*, but the agreement of such different versions of the poem in their musical details, right down to the notational style used, denies this.[64] It might be hypothesized instead that the motet tenor pre-dated any of the surviving versions of the song, each of which has extracted the motet voice and provided new later stanzas to turn the whole into a monophonic song.[65]

Aspects of the wider transmission of both motet and song versions of individual texts like *Quant la saisons desiree est entree* suggests either that some of the songs of **GB-Ob Douce 308** originated in motets or, at the very least, that there was an avid use of motets by the same kinds of audiences that practised song. *Chauvency* suggests the nature of this audience: noble men and women with their servants, clerics, and minstrels. The material trace and varied generic situations for text and music also suggest that this

---

[61] Compare **F-Pn fr.846**, f.124v, http://gallica.bnf.fr/ark:/12148/btv1b6000950p/f278.item, **F-Pn fr.24406**, f.60r; http://gallica.bnf.fr/ark:/12148/btv1b84386028/f133.item, and **I-Tr vari 42**, f.21r.

[62] For **F-Pn fr.20050**, f.124v see http://gallica.bnf.fr/ark:/12148/btv1b60009580/f256.item.

[63] These last two lines resemble the equivalent lines in **GB-Ob Douce 308** and **F-Pn fr.20050**, but reversed.

[64] See Saly 1990, ll.16,878–88.

[65] This accords with the composition of new, mensurally notated songs around 1300 seen in **F-Pn fr.844**.

Table 9.4 Handlist of sources for *Quant la saisons desiree est entree* (RS505; **GB-Ob Douce 308** grand chant no.56)

Source	Notation?	Total number of stanzas	Context
I-Tr vari 42	staff notation (mensural)	1	tenor voice of three-part motet (MV891)
GB-Ob Douce 308	verbal text only	4	chansonnier section D; grand chant no.34
F-Pn fr.24406	staff notation (mensural)	5	song in large chansonnier
F-Pn fr.846	staff notation (mensural)	2	song in large chansonnier
F-Pn fr.20050	space for staves above first stanza (but staves and music not entered)	3	song in large chansonnier
F-Pn fr.1589	space for staves (but staves and music not entered)	1	lyric insertion into Girart d'Amiens, *Méliacin* ll. 16878–88
F-Pn fr.1455	not examined	1	lyric insertion into Girart d'Amiens, *Méliacin* ll. 16878–88
F-Pn fr.1633	not examined	1	lyric insertion into Girart d'Amiens, *Méliacin* ll. 16878–88
I-Fr 2757	not examined	1	lyric insertion into Girart d'Amiens, *Méliacin* ll. 16878–88
B-Br IV-319	not examined	1	lyric insertion into Girart d'Amiens, *Méliacin* ll. 16878–88

audience performed these songs and knew their text and music. Such knowledge can be imagined to inform motet performance, cutting a swathe through the musicology that rejects intellectual readings of motets as a bookish intellectualism more akin to the preoccupations of modern scholars than medieval musical culture.[66]

Conclusion: reconsidering gender, reconsidering genre

The present chapter has only scratched the surface of the musical nature of this manuscript as a whole and its song collection in particular but has sought to make a number of key points. First, it has stressed that **GB-Ob Douce 308** is an important *music* manuscript, recording the 'part-literate' practice of music making at court that is far more fully described in one of its other contents, *Chauvency*. The term part-literate describes the fact that the songs' notation depicts in writing only their verbal texts and not their musical ones, but **GB-Ob Douce 308** should nonetheless be considered a music manuscript: the description of singing in *Chauvency*, and the sharing of refrain material with the chansonniers' songs and with songs and motets in other manuscripts, makes the sung nature of **GB-Ob Douce 308**'s songs abundantly clear. The pitches of song are not figured in musical notation here because it is not necessary in order to fully notate them within the cultural practice of which they are a record. The users of **GB-Ob Douce 308** knew the tunes, which are cued by the opening words and are stanzaic; they just could not remember all the words, so they wrote them down.

The other genre sections with musical concordances need to be treated to the same quality of editing and translation as the ballettes, which are already well served by Doss-Quinby, Rosenberg, and Aubrey.[67] The manuscript as a whole should now be reintegrated into the history of the motet, which might need to be re-imagined for the later thirteenth century within a more distinctly courtly, even *al fresco* setting.

The second finding of this chapter's brief brush of the surface of song in **GB-Ob Douce 308** is that the new history of thirteenth-century song will

---

[66] Space constraints prevent presentation of the specifics of this argument, which, together with detailed discussion of the motets outside the motet subsection in **GB-Ob Douce 308**, I intend to pursue elsewhere.

[67] See Doss-Quinby, Rosenberg, and Aubrey 2006.

trace intertextual networking, with no holds barred between musically notated and musically unnotated, between polyphony and monophony, in order to gain a fuller picture of the cultural reach of musical perform-ances. The songs of **GB-Ob Douce 308** seem to draw together genres typically separated in musicology, showing a clear interaction between, for instance, courtly song, refrains, or pastourelle, and the motet. Although this interaction has been noted in musicology, the focus has been on the clerical absorption, appropriation, re-use, re-working of, and commentary on more courtly forms and topics. In some cases this Christianizing – or, more often, Marian – reworking of courtly love texts is explicit, as for example, in Gautier de Coinci's *Miracles*. But **GB-Ob Douce 308** suggests that motets may have provided material for courtly songs as well as vice versa, offering the possibility that motets themselves were part of a courtly repertory and underwent a process similar to the reinterpretation of Boethius' theologically focused *Consolation of Philosophy*, a text with which francophone readers were obsessed in the 'long fourteenth century' as writers sought to evade Philosophy's dismissal of the muses of poetry and song as whores.[68]

Given Boethius' depiction of singing women as both muses and pros-titutes, a third point to be noted is the centrality of women to the culture of song in **GB-Ob Douce 308**. Not only does **GB-Ob Douce 308** contain a large body of lyrics in the feminine voice per se and a large number of pastourelles in which a woman's voice is ventriloquized by the male narrator, but *Chauvency* shows a woman impersonating a man, singing as a male 'je', thereby making the entire repertory of courtly song potentially women's song.[69] Given the challenge this poses to already sophisticated readings of gender and (male) homosociability in courtly love song, **GB-Ob Douce 308** needs to be more fully integrated into the discussion.[70]

---

[68] See Kay 2008 and Leach 2012.

[69] Doss-Quinby 2012 notes that 'the ballette section of manuscript I [**GB-Ob Douce 308**] contains more *chansons de femme* than any other source', listing 15 *chansons d'ami* and 2 *chansons de mal mariée*. It should be noted, however, that the idea of 'any other source' observes the deleterious disjunction between Machaut and pre-Machaut noted above, since the Machaut **F-Pn fr.1586** has more feminine-voiced songs than the number Doss-Quinby lists for **GB-Ob Douce 308**.

[70] On the significance of **GB-Ob Douce 308** for performance of women's 'part in the story of chivalry', see also Regalado 2006, 341ff.

10 | Machaut's first single-author compilation

ELIZABETH EVA LEACH

Introduction: reception history

For most of the twentieth century, fonds français 1586 of what is now the Bibliothèque nationale de France, a book known to Machaut scholars by the siglum *C*, was not a top ranking Machaut manuscript: its school report might have read, '*C*, could do better'.[1] The nineteenth-century description in the catalogue of the Imperial Library had dated this manuscript (hereafter **F-Pn fr.1586**) to the late fifteenth century, and since it only included around half the items contained in the manuscript with Machaut's authorial index, **F-Pn fr.1584**, scholars concluded that **F-Pn fr.1586** was a late copy of an early redaction of Machaut's collection, a witness thereby doubly worth ignoring.[2]

In the early 1970s, however, the history of **F-Pn fr.1586** changed when François Avril re-dated it on art-historical grounds.[3] As Avril's work became widely known, Machaut manuscript **F-Pn fr.1586** should have been promoted to nearer the top of the class, since it became the earliest copied collected manuscript witness of Machaut's music to have survived and probably the earliest ever to have existed.[4] But by 1971 it was too late. In the other disciplines dealing with Machaut – literary and musical studies – the historiographical writing was already on the wall: complete

---

[1] The Machaut manuscripts tend to be known by standard sigla, detailed in Earp 1995, although here RISM sigla will be used. The large collected manuscripts with musical notation are *A* (**F-Pn fr.1584**); *B* (**F-Pn fr.1585**); *C* (**F-Pn fr.1586**); *E* (**F-Pn fr.9221**); *F-G* (**F-Pn fr.22545-6**); *Vg* (**GB-Cccc Ferrell 1**). Other Machaut manuscripts referenced in the present chapter are *D* (**F-Pn fr.1587**); *H* (**F-Pn fr.881**); *P* (**F-Pn fr.2165-6**); *Pe* (**GB-Cmc 1594**). Readers are directed to an aggregated list of links to online surrogates of the manuscript witnesses for Machaut found at www.stanford.edu/group/dmstech/cgi-bin/drupal/machautmss.

[2] See Earp 1995, 77–9 and Bibliothèque Impériale 1868, 259. Ludwig 1926–54, 2: 10* refers to it as a fifteenth-century manuscript and gives its complete order, noting the stark deviation in ordering compared to the other manuscripts both overall and at the level of individual items.

[3] Avril 1973. The late date in the Imperial catalogue was questioned as early as Guelliot 1914, 312, but the error was live as late as Gallica's twenty-first-century online digital proxy of the manuscript, http://gallica.bnf.fr/ark:/12148/btv1b8449043q, although in response to feedback they now list the date correctly as *c*.1350–55.

[4] See Earp 2011, 227.

modern editions of text and music had already appeared in the early twentieth century, their editors accepting the erroneous fifteenth-century dating of **F-Pn fr.1586** and thus largely ignoring it.

When Ernst Hoepffner edited Machaut's narrative poetry for three volumes published by the Société des anciens textes français between 1908 and 1921, he listed seventeen manuscripts. For Hoepffner, **F-Pn fr.1586** fitted into neither of his two groups of Machaut manuscripts, according partly with one, partly with the other, and with neither in its overall ordering: **F-Pn fr.1586** 'does not seem to have been copied from a single source, but has instead been compiled from isolated sources that must have existed alongside the complete Machaut sources [...] and which were gathered together by a lover of poetry into a collection [...] from which C derives'.[5]

Working simultaneously with, and independently of Hoepffner, Russian romanist Vladimir Chichmaref published an edition of Machaut's lyric poetry in 1909, listing 21 manuscripts.[6] Chichmaref conducts his discussion from the perspective that the most authoritative collected works manuscript is **F-Pn fr.1584** on account of the authorial rubric in the index.[7] He notes **F-Pn fr.1586** as the most incomplete manuscript, which is above all a collection of Machaut's lyric poetry, notated and non-notated, containing fewer items in all corresponding sections compared with the manuscripts to whose family it belongs.[8] Examination of the variants in the lyrics led Chichmaref to group **F-Pn fr.1586** most closely with **F-Pn fr.9221**, whose closeness to the text-only manuscript **F-Pn fr.881** he had already argued earlier in the introduction, with both **F-Pn fr.9221** and **F-Pn fr.881** being more broadly linked with **F-Pn fr.1585**, **F-Pn fr.1587**, and **GB-Cccc Ferrell 1**.[9]

---

[5] Hoepffner 1908–22, 1:xlvii–xlviii.

[6] See Chichmaref 1909, LXXIII–LXXIV. He used different sigla: **F-Pn fr.1586** is his *E*. See also Earp 1995, 74.

[7] Chichmaref 1909, LXXVI–LXXVII.

[8] See Chichmaref 1909, CV, CVIII.

[9] Chichmaref 1909, CIX–CX. For the lais, Chichmaref found manuscript **F-Pn fr.1586** closest in its variants to **F-Pn fr.9221**, while for the other notated pieces, variants ally it more closely with **F-Pn fr.1585** and **GB-Cccc Ferrell 1**. Since **F-Pn fr.1586**'s re-dating, the variants tell us more about the sources for these other, later manuscripts; **GB-Cccc Ferrell 1** is the second earliest surviving complete manuscript and its nearness to **F-Pn fr.1586** might therefore be expected; **F-Pn fr.1585** is an almost complete copy of **GB-Cccc Ferrell 1** and **F-Pn fr.9221** is partly drawn from **F-Pn fr.1585** and partly from other sources, which seem to link it to early copies that might have been circulating before **F-Pn fr.1586** and on which **F-Pn fr.1586** might have drawn. See Leach 1997, chapter 1.

In his notes to the earliest collected modern edition of Machaut's music, Friedrich Ludwig lists forty-one surviving manuscript sources, together with five lost ones.[10] Ludwig's agreement with Hoepffner's 'growing collection' theory of the narrative poems led him to adopt Hoepffner's sigla for these manuscripts (while recording those of Chichmaref), which effectively made Hoepffner's sigla the standard for Machaut scholars today, regardless of disciplinary affiliation. Ludwig's edition remains the better of the two modern collected editions (Leo Schrade's, which appeared in 1956, more conveniently uses modern clefs but is inferior in philological detail).[11] Ludwig, swayed it seems by the Imperial Library's dating and description, made only an incipit catalogue from **F-Pn fr.1586**; his edition does not therefore collate the full variants in **F-Pn fr.1586**. And while Schrade's edition does list variants of **F-Pn fr.1586**, it does not do so reliably, and chooses not to adopt **F-Pn fr.1586**'s readings, even when they are clearly preferable.[12]

Given Machaut's continued interest in collecting together his expanding output, it might be assumed that the later, more complete manuscripts represent a later redaction of the works, transmitting not only more of them in a definitive ordering, but also better texts for both words and music. The evidence from studies of literary variants in editions of the narrative poetry that have appeared since **F-Pn fr.1586** was more correctly dated, however, suggests otherwise. In 1988, editors of a new text and translation of the *Remede de Fortune* and the *Jugement dou Roy de Behaigne* found the earliest texts to be significantly better at the level of line-by-line textual detail than later texts from more complete collected Machaut manuscript sources.[13] While earlier editors had chosen **F-Pn fr.1584** as their base text because it seemed most authorial on account of its index rubric declaring that 'this is the order that Guillaume de Machaut wants there to be in his book', text editors James I. Wimsatt and William W. Kibler choose **F-Pn fr.1586** as the base text for their edition of *Remede*, and **F-Pn fr.2165-6**, a

---

[10] Ludwig 1926–54, 4 vols. The commentary to the edition is in volume 2, which dates from 1928; the last volume was published posthumously.

[11] Schrade 1956. See Earp 1995, 281.

[12] It will be interesting to see what attitude to **F-Pn fr.1586** is adopted in the projected new complete Machaut edition to be produced by the project The Works of Guillaume de Machaut: Music, Image, Text in the Middle Ages; see http://machaut.exeter.ac.uk/?q=node/1510.

[13] Wimsatt, Kibler, and Baltzer 1988.

manuscript closely grouped with **F-Pn fr.1586**, for *Behaigne*. Manuscript **F-Pn fr.2165-6** is part of a double-volume anthology in which Machaut's *Behaigne* is the only work by him.[14] It seems that Machaut's works entered circulation outside his collected works efforts in an earlier and textually better form than is exhibited by the later, more complete codices for which evidence of direct authorial input is more usually adduced.[15]

A similar conclusion has been advanced for musical readings as for the reading of the poetry. At the level of the variants in a given individual musical piece, Lawrence Earp has shown for specific pieces that where Machaut's works are copied in manuscripts containing only musical pieces by a mixture of authors (the more usual type of transmission for fourteenth-century songs by composers other than Machaut) the readings are sometimes better and, despite the later copying date of the physical manuscripts, probably earlier and therefore closer to the composer than the versions in the collected Machaut manuscripts.[16] Earp's work suggests that Machaut's music, like his poems, entered broader circulation before being collected into the author's complete-works manuscripts. It implies, moreover, that Machaut's oversight of the compilation of the collected works manuscripts focused each time on large-scale issues of ordering rather than on redacting the details of individual poems or songs. Although **F-Pn fr.1586** is a redaction that shows an interest in order, given the suggestion that earlier copies (or late copies of earlier transmissions) are more reliable, its earliness means that it has better readings of certain musical and textual details than the later collected manuscript sources, as shown in **F-Pn fr.1586**'s rather better reading of the tenor at the start of the B section of *N'en fait, n'en dit* (Machaut balade no.11; see Example 10.1), where the tenor in **F-Pn fr.1586** both provides a

---

[14] See the comments in Wimsatt, Kibler, and Baltzer 1988, 18–19.

[15] The pairing of *Behaigne* (featuring John of Luxembourg) with the *Voeux du Paon* (an *admonitio* to John's father, Henry VII, the Holy Roman Emperor) might, however, make it possible that **F-Pn fr.2165-6** is a later copy of a now-lost witness contemporary with Machaut's service to John, prepared for the house of Luxembourg from originals closer to Machaut's purview.

[16] Earp 1989. Schrade introduced the term 'repertory manuscript' for these kinds of witnesses, which he viewed as documents of musical reception, but Earp 2011, 225ff. has convincingly argued conversely that there is 'no central manuscript of repertory around which to write our history' (227) for this period.

Example 10.1: Opening of the B section of *N'en fait, n'en dit* (Balade no.11), comparing **F-Pn fr.1586**'s reading with that in the other manuscripts

directed progression to the octave between the first and second notes of the cantus (something typical of opening sections in the early balades), and also avoids the dissonance of a fourth created by the other manuscripts' tenor *d*.

Contents, patrons, owners

Manuscript **F-Pn fr.1586** is now known to be the earliest of several surviving larger manuscripts that transmit exclusively the works of Machaut, organized by genre. The precedents for scribal (and/or authorial) control over an authorial corpus lie in the authorial organization of earlier secular song repertories, in particular the manuscript that contains the complete works of Adam de la Halle, **F-Pn fr.25566** and, before that, various manuscript sources for Gautier de Coinci's *Miracles de Nostre Dame*.[17] Precedents for ordering song collections by genre can be seen in trouvère manuscripts, both early and late.[18]

Table 10.1 outlines the major sections of **F-Pn fr.1586** and gives details of their contents, gathering structure, artists, and text scribes. The order of **F-Pn fr.1586** seems to show that the plan for it changed abruptly before the copying was completed. Musicologists, following Ludwig, have referred to these sections as *CI* and *CII*. The order and emphasis in this book, together with its revised dating, have prompted suggestions that it was prepared for Bonne of Luxembourg, possibly as a commission by her

---

[17] See Huot 1987, 64–74 and Okubo 2005. A list including links to the manuscripts can be found at http://eeleach.wordpress.com/2013/03/15/gautier-de-coincis-miracles-de-nostre-dame/.

[18] See Lug 2012, 455, for **F-Pn fr.20050** and Chapter 9 above for **GB-Ob Douce 308**.

husband (the future King John II of France).[27] The manuscript's illuminations make it a 'codicological pair' with the *Jeu des echecs moralisés* in **US-NYpm Glazier 52**, allowing an association with an atelier that had royal patronage for a translation that was ordered around the time from which both manuscripts date.[28]

Machaut's only known employment is as almoner, notary, and finally secretary in the administration of Bonne's father, John of Luxembourg, King of Bohemia, who died in 1346.[29] Bonne's own death in 1349, probably from plague, has been thought to provide a possible explanation for the final state of the manuscript, in which a rather disordered section of new work – including rondeaux set to music, a genre not present in the original manuscript at all – was simply inserted between the lais and a closed (and ordered) motet section, which had already been prepared.[30] If Roger Bowers is right that Machaut's reference in the Prologue of the *Jugement dou roy de Navarre* to sitting out the plague in 1349 shows that he was already at that time in Pamplona in the service of Charles of Navarre, the manuscript was probably finished without its author's oversight.[31]

The manuscript was present in the French Royal Library by the seventeenth century at the latest, but was catalogued until the late eighteenth century as a book of notated songs by the trouvère Thibaut de Champagne, King of Navarre; it might, therefore, have been in the royal collection continuously (but in a way that is unrecognizable from earlier catalogues) since it was completed.[32] All this and other circumstantial evidence has led scholars to speculate that Bonne's husband, who was from 1350 King John II of France, had the manuscript he had originally ordered for her completed after her death.[33]

If Machaut wrote the *Remede* specifically, as has also been suggested, for John of Luxembourg's daughter, Bonne, 'her' poem fittingly follows that presided over by her father, the *Jugement dou roy de Behaigne*, at the head of **F-Pn fr.1586**.[34] The *Remede* is followed by shorter dits treating the

---

[27] See summary and further references in Earp 1995, 78.

[28] Lowden 2000, 234. See also Earp 1995, 79.

[29] Earp 1995, 8–9; see also Leach 2011, chapter 1.

[30] See Earp 1983, 133, 139–41 for a discussion of how this was done, with the opening motets probably recopied, resulting in the omission of *De bon espoir / Puis que la douce / SPERAVI* (Motet no.4).

[31] Bowers 2004.   [32] Earp 1995, 78.   [33] See Earp 1995, 78.

[34] Bonne as dedicatee was suggested as early as Poirion 1965, 201n28; see details in Earp 1995, 213.

theme of courtly love: the *Dit de l'Alerion* (whose emphasis on training for those wanting to use hawks or women is fitting for both the ladies of court and their young male children; see below), the *Dit du Vergier* (a dream-vision, in which the lover is instructed by a blind god of Love, who some have seen as representing the blind John of Luxembourg), and finally the *Dit du Lyon* (a poem that internally dates its action to 1342 on an island ruled by an unnamed noble lady).

F-Pn fr.1586 contains the highest quality illuminations of any Machaut manuscript; art historians have named the artist who illuminated the *Remede* after his work here as 'The Master of the *Remede de Fortune*'.[35] His second assistant is identified with the artist who would later become the Master of the Coronation Book of Charles V, an artist prominent throughout the reign of Bonne's son, the future Charles V of France (r.1365–1380).[36] In four of its five dits, **F-Pn fr.1586** has a higher density of illuminations than any other manuscript, and those dits provide ample didactic material suitable for Bonne, her husband, and her children. Especially illuminated are those dits that can be interpreted, as mentioned above, as having presiding characters that are explicitly or implicitly John of Luxembourg (*Behaigne*, *Vergier*, the lady's ancestor in *Lyon*) or Bonne (the perfect bird in *Alerion*, Esperance in *Remede*, the lady of *Lyon*).[37] *Vergier* has 6 illuminations (other copies have 4 or 1), *Behaigne* 9 (others have 4, 3, or 1), *Remede* 34 (others have at most 12), and *Alerion* 18 (the next most illuminated, **GB-Cccc Ferrell 1**, has 8; most have only 1).[38] And although *Lyon* has more illuminations in other manuscripts (**F-Pn fr.1584** has 26, **GB-Cccc Ferrell 1** has 31), the 24 in **F-Pn fr.1586** are hardly few, and are of a higher quality than in the more illustrated manuscript sources.[39]

Some of the pictures in **F-Pn fr.1586** specifically depict children, a feature which has led Domenic Leo to suggest that the book as a whole might have served a didactic purpose within the royal household, aimed specifically at the young princes.[40] While speculative and inductive, Leo's

---

[35] See Earp 1995, chapter 4 and references there; see also Leo 2005.

[36] This artist also worked on **GB-Cccc Ferrell 1**; see Earp 1995, 133.

[37] Not only did John become John II of France (r.1350–1365), but his three most important children with Bonne were Charles (1338–1380, r. as King Charles V of France, 1365–1380), Jean, Duke of Berry (1340–1416), and Philippe, Duke of Burgundy (1342–1404).

[38] See Earp 1995, 147–50, 152–65.

[39] Images of the entire manuscript can be viewed online at http://gallica.bnf.fr/ark:/12148/btv1b8449043q.

[40] Leo 2005, 131–5.

Table 10.1 The major sections of **F-Pn fr.1586**, showing contents, gathering structure, artists, and text scribes

Section CI

	Folios	Content	Gatherings	Text scribe	Artist
POETRY(*narrative*)	**1r**–22v	*Le temps pascour* [*Behaigne*][19]	I–III	A	Y[20]
	23r–58v	*Remede* (with music in situ)[21]	IV–VIII	B	X[22]
	59r–92v	*Alerion*[23]	IX–XII	B	Z[24]
	93r–102v	*Vergier*[25]	XIII	A	Y
	103r–120v	*Lyon*[26]	XIV–XV	A	Y
(*lyric*)	**121r**–148v	*Loange* (198 texts)	XVI–XVII	B (**121r**–136v)	Z
			XVIII	A (**137r**–146v)	
			XIX (part)	B (from **147r**)	
			XIX–XXIII		
MUSIC	**148v**–157v	Virelais (1–15, 17–20, 23, 21–2, 24)		B	–
	157v–165r	Balades (1–16)		B	–
	165r–186v	Lais (1–3, 4*, 5–7, 10–12)		A	Z
	186v	B19 (ADDED WITH **CII**)		A	–

Section CII

	Folios	Content	Gatherings	Text scribe	Artist
	187r–197v	L22, L14, L11*, L13*, L8*, L9*	XXIV-XXVIII	A	Z
	197v–198r	V25, V28			–
	198r–201r	B17, B18, B20, B23, B21			–
	201v–202r	R2, B24			–
	202r–203v	R7 [blank triplum], R5, R9, R1, R6			–
	203v–204r	V16			–

204r–204v	B22	—
204v	R3, R4	—
205r–205v	V30, V29	—
205v–206r	R10 (with unique second contratenor)	—
(prepared before CII) 206v–225r	motets (1–3, 5–20)	A
225v–[226r]	blank	—

underlined = shares folio with next or preceding item
bold = starts a new gathering
⋆ not set to music

[19] 2 blank lines and explicit in ordinary ink colour.
[20] First assistant to the Master of the *Remede de Fortune*; see Earp 1995, 132, table 4.1, and the bibliographic references on p.133.
[21] Amen at end; blue explicit; b-column blank.
[22] Master of the *Remede de Fortune*; see Earp 1995, 132, table 4.1.
[23] Intra-textual explicit; last 6 lines of a-column and entire b-column blank.
[24] Second assistant to the Master of the *Remede de Fortune* = Master of the Coronation Book of Charles V; see Earp 1995, 132, table 4.1.
[25] 2 lines blank and explicit in ordinary ink colour.
[26] 4 lines blank and explicit in ordinary ink colour.

arguments are persuasive. *Alerion* opens with a miniature in which three boys play in an outdoor setting, attended by a servant.[41] The youngest is catching butterflies with a net and the assistance of a servant, while the older two have graduated to the more grown-up princely sport of hawking. Three male children similarly sit on and cling to Fortune's mechanically sophisticated wheel in the *Remede*, which forms the lower register of a large double-register illumination, illustrating the narrator composing his complaint to the fickle goddess.[42] If the copying of **F-Pn fr.1586** were interrupted by Bonne's death in 1349, as has been argued, her three oldest children – Charles, Louis, and Jean – would have been eleven, ten, and eight – approximately the same age as the three children in both the *Remede* and *Alerion* illustrations at the period when they were executed.[43] All three boys were destined to be important figures in the French Royal House; their education would have been of the utmost importance. Machaut was perhaps in the service of Bonne in the period between the death of John of Luxembourg in 1346 and the start of his possible service with Charles of Navarre late in 1349, following Bonne's death in September of that year.[44] The lower register of the complaint picture is presented as the product of the imagination of the poet-lover-narrator who sits writing in the top half of the illumination.[45] If the boys on the wheel are meant to symbolize Bonne's sons, the narrator qua lover imagines his own subjection to Fortune in the dit, but the narrator qua author and court administrator draws attention to the subjection to Fortune of his patrons and their children – the likely readers and owners of his book.

Contexts: order and subjectivity

Music provides the culmination of manuscript **F-Pn fr.1586**, which comprises narrative, unnotated lyrics, and lyrics set to music. Music also

---

[41] See http://gallica.bnf.fr/ark:/12148/btv1b8449043q/f124.item.

[42] See http://gallica.bnf.fr/ark:/12148/btv1b8449043q/f67.item.

[43] Domenic Leo makes a convincing case for the importance of children more widely in the iconography of **F-Pn fr.1586** (see Leo 2005, 131ff.). Alternative datings for *Remede* of before 1342 or before 1357 have been posited; see Earp 1995, 213–14 for a synopsis of views. The reigning boy king even resembles the symbolic iconography of the blond wavy-haired Charles seen in his Coronation Book. See the plates in O'Meara 2001.

[44] Bonne died on 3 or 11 September 1349; Charles d'Evreux became King of Navarre on 7 October that year, but was not crowned until the following May because of the level of plague in Pamplona. See Bowers 2004, 12n32.

[45] Huot 1987, 252.

penetrates both other large sections – visually in the *Remede*, where it is copied in situ, and verbally in the *Loange*, where the duplication of lyrics that are also in the music section sets up dialogue between these two sections in the manuscript.[46] A thoroughgoing use of ordering, and the integration of a discussion of music at the outset, as seen in the *Prologue* of the far better studied manuscript **F-Pn fr.1584**, is not a feature of **F-Pn fr.1586**. I will argue below that the experience of collecting his works (or seeing them collected) as they are presented in **F-Pn fr.1586** affected Machaut's subsequent output, concerning both the future attention to peri- and para-textual features (the *Prologue* miniatures and authorial index in **F-Pn fr.1584**), and also the kinds of poems he wrote (notably the *Voir dit*, which is centrally concerned with authorship, varieties of textuality, and music).

Manuscript **F-Pn fr.1586** can be read as an initial attempt to exploit a scribal poetics of authorship and in particular to integrate music within this project.[47] The book opens with five narrative poems, each physically separate from the other. This physical separation allowed the division of labour between two scribes and three artists, and also meant that the ordering of the items could be freely accomplished. The order of these narrative items differs significantly from that found in the later manu- scripts. Given **F-Pn fr.1586**'s very different order from the explicitly authorial **F-Pn fr.1584** ordering, it is tempting to see it as belonging to a period before Machaut developed an interest in order, or indicating a lack of closeness to Machaut's authority. But evidence of an interest in order can be seen clearly in the music section: in the iconographic programme for the lais, and in the preservation of the order internal to most of the genre sections (especially the balades and motets) in the later manuscripts. It is possible that the ordering of the narrative poems was finalized at a later stage, when *CII* was added, which was arguably after authorial involvement in the manuscript had ceased (see above). As the narrative poems are self-contained physical units, they could be bound in any order.

---

[46] On this idea, see Leach 2011, 78n173 and *passim*.

[47] Huot 1987 and Peraino 2011 have seen precedents in the possibly authorial *libelli* of Thibaut de Champagne and Adam de la Halle included within manuscripts of trouvère works from the thirteenth century (**F-Pn fr.844** and **F-Pn fr.25566**, respectively). In both cases, however, the *libelli* are still part of multi-author manuscripts, which do not integrate music, unnotated lyric, and narrative by the same author. Gautier de Coinci's *Miracles* survive in single-author manuscripts that integrate music and narrative poetry, although it is difficult to date any surviving witness from Gautier's lifetime; on Gautier as a significant precedent for Machaut's preoccupation with bookmaking, see Butterfield 2006, 3–8.

The order currently present appears to respond directly to the demands of patronage for the manuscript: the longest and most important of the narrative poems appear in the first two places.

Sylvia Huot has noted that the large-scale articulations of **F-Pn fr.1586** – from narrative to lyric to musical lyric – which could offer potential discontinuities, are smoothed over by the ongoing iconographical presence of the poet-compiler figure. Although in *Remede* the younger alter ego of the poet is depicted as a noble (with a beard and tight-fitting clothing), he is engaged explicitly in the work of a trouvère – a poet-composer – often depicted in the act of writing on a scroll, which stands at once for the textualization of music and poetry that the manuscript itself represents but also provides an image ultimately symbolic of sonic performance, as when the narrator is forced to perform his lai to the lady.[48] This poet-composer figure is also present at the outset of the unnotated lyrics.[49]

Huot notes the similarity with some of the later trouvère chansonniers, 'where the poetic "I" appears in a variety of poses that encompass private meditation, making songs, performing them, and interacting with the lady' and, moreover, notes that **F-Pn fr.1586** 'is the only one that maintains this trouvère iconography'.[50] Later Machaut manuscripts separate the author from the lover or performer and depict the poet much more as a figure writing at a desk with a book (rather than a lover with scrolls). Huot logically shows that the early codification of Machaut's works in **F-Pn fr.1586** relied on the trouvère model; I would argue that paradoxically this retrospective activity also had forward momentum, effectively prompting the departure from **F-Pn fr.1586**'s iconography in later Machaut manuscripts by promoting ideas of ordering and care for layout. In collecting his works therefore, **F-Pn fr.1586** not only reflects Machaut's interest in himself as an author figure, but seems also to have further entrenched and developed that interest. While Machaut's precise level of authorial involvement in most of his manuscripts' planning is unknowable, the consistent attention to this aspect in the collected manuscripts from the last twenty-five years of his life, together with the evidence of **F-Pn fr.1584**, is highly suggestive. Without the collection of **F-Pn fr.1586**, it is doubtful whether the degree of cross-referencing within and between narrative and lyric poems, particularly as found in the multi-media complexity of the *Voir dit*, would have been

---

[48] Huot 1987, 246.   [49] See http://gallica.bnf.fr/ark:/12148/btv1b8449043q/f248.item.
[50] Huot 1987, 247.

possible.[51] Thus **F-Pn fr.1586** not only provided a logical culmination of the trouvère chansonniers of the early fourteenth century, but also prompted Machaut to further copying and collecting. It seems to have stimulated a poetic mindset that integrated scribal function not only into the material presentation of a body of work but also into the very subjectivity of the narrative and lyric subjects that its poems projected (for example in the *Voir dit*'s thematization of the *je*'s book-making).[52]

The lais in **F-Pn fr.1586** are the only other musical items outside those in the *Remede* to be illuminated in this manuscript. They start with a miniature and a musical piece for which the text has been underlaid but no notes are entered in the staves above.[53] *Loyauté* (Lai no.1) is a somewhat unusual lai in that the same music is used for all stanzas (all other lais have different melodies for each stanza, with that of the final stanza sometimes being that of the first written at a different pitch level).[54] Only the first versicle of the first stanza is underlaid; the second appears in the residuum (as also in **GB-Cccc Ferrell 1**, **F-Pn fr.1584**, and **F-Pn fr.22546**; only **F-Pn fr.9221** writes both versicles out in full).[55] The staves maintain the double-column layout found in the preceding music and pervasive in the narrative poetry as do the second versicle and the following eleven double-versicle stanzas copied after the staves stop. The next item, however, *J'aim la flour* (Lai no.2; f.168v),[56] recognizing that no other lais have a textual residuum, switches to a single-column layout: an initial miniature occupies half the width of the page for the first two staff lines and then the music adopts a single-column layout for the remainder of the notated lais, using double-column layout only for the text-only lai, *Aus amans* (Lai no.4; starts at the bottom of 173r and runs to 174r).[57] Each time thereafter that a notated lai follows a text-only lai, the transition back to the single-column format is assisted by a miniature that takes up the left-hand column for at least a couple of staff lines.

---

[51] See 'Related Machaut Works' in Earp 1995, 230; *Remede* is referenced explicitly in *Confort*, see Earp 1995, 214.

[52] The influence of this aspect of Machaut's work on other poets is traced in the later chapters of Huot 1987.

[53] http://gallica.bnf.fr/ark:/12148/btv1b8449043q/f336.image.

[54] For a summary, see Albritton 2009 and 2012. Twelve-stanza lais are standard in Machaut's works, but contemporary poets vary this; see Bétemps 2002, 103 and Sinnreich-Levi 1994, 52fn53.

[55] **F-Pn fr.1585** is missing the folio that would have had the underlaid text and starts at l.125; see Earp 1983, 338. **F-Pn fr.1584** has the omission of an entire phrase which is squeezed in beneath the initial and cued into the first stanza.

[56] http://gallica.bnf.fr/ark:/12148/btv1b8449043q/f343.image.

[57] http://gallica.bnf.fr/ark:/12148/btv1b8449043q/f352.image.

Case-studies

The vast amount of music in **F-Pn fr.1586** makes selection of case-studies difficult, but the rest of this chapter will focus on three parts of the manuscript containing music. The first section considers the lai in the *Remede*, which thus covers the copying of music into a predominantly non-musical part of the manuscript. Section two looks at the copying of the virelais in the ordered music section, *CI*, and the last case-study briefly considers the apparently unordered collection of music in *CII*. One focus common to all these sections is the planning of space under staves for text, which requires scribes to anticipate the musico-textual form of not only a given genre, but of specific variants within that genre. In particular, leaving space under staves for double text-underlay in the correct places requires that a scribe know where this typically happens in a given formal type, but also where it atypically might occur. The provision of a stacked, double text-underlay to show repeated music seems to begin with this manuscript; although trouvère song typically begins with two couplets, each to the same melody, they are invariably copied out twice.

To follow the case-studies more closely, the reader is urged to follow the footnote links to the specific folios in the digital surrogate of **F-Pn fr.1586** found on Gallica.[58]

The lai in *Remede*

In all the collected manuscripts of Machaut's works except **F-Pn fr.1586**, the lais sit at the head of the notated music section of each manuscript, mirroring the placement of this form as the first musical item copied in the *Remede*.[59] In **F-Pn fr.1586**, as seen above, their importance is indicated instead by the fact that the lais alone of the music outside the *Remede* merit a series of illuminations that add 'an important theatrical dimension to the written text' by picturing the voices of the individual lais.[60] Despite **F-Pn fr.1586**'s placement of the virelais at the head of its section of notated music, the first musical item in the manuscript is still a lai. Although it is a narrative poem, the *Remede* always hosts the first copying of music in the notated Machaut manuscripts: the first interpolated lyric of the poem is the lai *Qui n'aroit* (*Remede* musical item no.1;

---

[58] http://gallica.bnf.fr/ark:/12148/btv1b8449043q
[59] See Fallows 1977. A fuller bibliography can be found in Earp 1995, 286–7.
[60] On these see Huot 1987, 260–72.

Table 10.2 The basic plot of *Remede de Fortune*, showing position of musical interpolations and their folio number in **F-Pn fr.1586**

PROLOGUE (ll.1–44)

Clerkly-didactic voice of older narrator proposes to relate his own youthful love apprenticeship.

I (ll.45–782): AT COURT (lover and lady = lover's failure)

1. ll.45–134	Presentation of the narrator as courtly lover in the first person;
2. ll.135–66	Love as a teacher;
3. ll.167–356	The lady as a teacher;
4. ll.357–681	Lover's service to his lady; secret composition of poems (ll.357–430) including:
	▪ his lai (ll.431–680), *Qui n'aroit autre deport* (RF1; ff.26r–28r);
5. ll.681–782	Lady discovers the lai; lover flees in despair.

II (ll.783-3044): THE PARK OF HESDIN (lover and Hope = instruction)

1. ll.783–1480	The lover enters the park (ll.783–904) and bewails his state to Fortune in:
	▪ his complaint (ll.905–1480), *Tels rit au main qui au soir pleure* (RF2; 30r–35r).
2. ll.1481–2125	Hope's arrival as a mysterious figure; her defence of Love argued in part in:
	▪ her chanson roial (ll.1985–2032), *Joie, plaisence et douce norriture* (RF3; 39r–39v)
3. ll.2126–2347	After the lover asks her, Hope reveals her identity.
4. ll.2348–2892	Hope explains the nature of Fortune; before departing she sings:
	▪ her baladelle [=duplex balade] (ll.2857–2892), *En amer a douce vie* (RF4; 46r–46v)
5. ll.2893–3044	The lover, now happy, leaves the park after singing:
	▪ his balade (ll.3013–36), *Dame, de qui toute ma joie vient* (RF5; 47v–48r)

III (ll.3045–4258): BACK AT COURT (lover, lady, Hope = lover's 'success')

1. ll.3045–3348	Sight of the lady's chateau paralyzes the lover with fear; Hope returns to support him; the lover performs an unnotated Prière, *Amours, je te lo et graci* (ll. 3205–3348) addressed to Hope and Love.
2. ll.3349–3516	At an outdoor courtly festivity, with dancing and singing, the lover sings to the lady:
	▪ his chanson baladée [virelai] (ll.3451–96), *Dame, a vous sans retollir* (RF6; 51r–51v)
3. ll.3517–3872	At the lady's chateau the lover declares his love; the lady accepts it.
4. ll.3873–4116	Dinner at the lady's chateau; exchange of rings in presence of Hope; lover sings:
	▪ his rondelet [rondeau] (ll.4109–16), *Dame, mon cuer en vous remaint* (RF7; 57r)
5. ll.4117–4258	After brief absence, lady treats lover with indifference; ambiguous reassurances.

EPILOGUE (ll.4259–4300)

f.26r),[61] which, as with all of *Remede*'s musical items, is presented at the point in the narrative where it takes place diegetically.

One of Machaut's most explicitly didactic dits, the *Remede de Fortune* is at once an art of love and an art of musical poetry. The basic plot is outlined in Table 10.2, which also notes the position of the musical interpolations, giving their folio number in **F-Pn fr.1586**. At the outset of the dit, the heart of the young narrator causes him to delight in composing and singing a lai in honour of his lady, but he is not singing directly to her. Instead, the audience reads or overhears this lai as an example of one of the compositions resulting from the lover's fluctuating *sentement*. Here he claims it results from happiness, which gives birth to song because he has Sweet Thought, *Souvenir*, Loyalty, and Hope enclosed in his heart. Like the other lyric items in the dit, *Qui n'aroit* is exemplary as a musico-poetic item, as well as offering insight into the mental state of the protagonist and undercutting the youthful narrator's claims to self-knowledge (something further undercut by the framing of the poem as having happened in the overall narrator's youthful past).[62]

Musically, the lai comes closest of all forms at this period to being through-composed, in contrast to the strophic forms with refrains used in the balade, rondeau, and virelai. With the exception of the final stanza, which has the same melody (usually at a different pitch) as the opening one, each of a lai's twelve stanzas has its own versification, rhymes, and music. The poetry and music of each stanza are subdivided into two identical 'versicles', with each half of the stanza sung to the same music. The manuscript presentation copies these two halves of each stanza's text under one another, beneath the music that will be sung twice. Writing slightly later than Machaut, Eustache Deschamps describes the complete lai as effectively having twenty-four stanzas ('couples') on account of this subdivision.[63] In many of the stanzas of Machaut's lais these two halves are themselves musically subdivided so that there are effectively four versicles with basically the same melody, differing only in that versicles 1 and 3 have a tonally 'open' ending, and 2 and 4 a tonally 'closed' cadence. David Fallows has described this 'quadrupled versicle' structure as making each stanza of the lai into an almost self-contained four-stanza song.[64] Despite

---

[61] http://gallica.bnf.fr/ark:/12148/btv1b8449043q/f58.image.

[62] For a fuller exposition of my reading of the lai, see Leach 2011, 160–73.

[63] The twenty-four stanzas are most readily visible in the case of Lai no.1, above, since each double versicle is the same. See Sinnreich-Levi 1994, 96, l.584; the translation makes a distinction between strophe and stanza (the subdivision), although the French text uses *couple* for both parts. I will use stanza for the large unit and versicle for subdivisions of the stanza.

[64] The entire lai effectively becomes a twelve-song song cycle; see Fallows 1977, 482.

the prevalence of this quadruple versicle structure, the copying layout of lais does not usually abbreviate the melodic repeats further than the basic bipartite division; this sacrifices economy of space for keeping the fundamental double-versicle structure clear. In fact, the only two examples of the medieval layout resembling that of the efficient, modern abbreviated layout is found in the copies of *Qui n'aroit* in **F-Pn fr.1586** (see ff.26v-28r on the digital facsimile)[65] and **GB-Cmc 1594**, another 'early' version of the text.[66] *Qui n'aroit* has a quadrupled versicle structure for all stanzas except I and XII (which share the same versification); stanza XI has a very long closed ending for the second and fourth of its quadruple versicles, which allows the scribe to segue seamlessly from a layout that involved leaving four lines of text space for each musical staff line to one requiring only two (this transition occurs on the first two staves of f.28r).[67]

    F-Pn fr.1586 thus shows a degree of layout reflection of musical repetition structure for the lai of the *Remede* that is not present in later copies. The manuscripts **F-Pn fr.22545** and **F-Pn fr.1584**, for example, start *Qui n'aroit* within the two-column format that they use for the narrative poem, only switching to a single-column format when they get onto the next complete page. In **F-Pn fr.1584** the music remains in single-column format with the text reverting to two-column layout when it resumes towards the bottom of f.54r. In **F-Pn fr.22545**'s case, the switch back to two-column format is made within the copying of the music, a whole folio in advance of the resumption of the text (43v when the text itself resumes on 44r), although it means that each opening has a single kind of layout showing across it (single-column in 42v–43r and two columns for 41v–42r and 43v–44r). The manuscript **GB-Cccc Ferrell 1** and its copy **F-Pn fr.1585** present the lai entirely within their regular two-column text layout for the dit. The large-format book **F-Pn fr.9221** copies the text in three columns, starting the music in a single column partway into f.23r and resuming the three-column format for the text after one staff line on f.24v. In addition, none of these manuscripts uses anything other than double

---

[65] http://gallica.bnf.fr/ark:/12148/btv1b8449043q/f59.image.

[66] For the status of **GB-Cmc 1594**'s text, see Wimsatt, Kibler, and Baltzer 1988, Introduction. The lais in *Fauvel* (**F-Pn fr.146**), for example, are through-copied with no text stacking, even though all have double-versicle structures and the French ones all have some stanzas with quadruple versicle structure. The lais in the trouvère manuscript **F-Pn fr.12615** also eschew text stacking and either write both versicles out, or place the second versicle as a residuum after the underlaid first versicle (see, for example, f.68v ff.). On the sporadic use of text stacking in earlier English manuscripts, see Helen Deeming, Chapter 5 above.

[67] http://gallica.bnf.fr/ark:/12148/btv1b8449043q/f62.image.

text-underlay for any of the stanzas, thereby taking up far more parchment to copy the song than is the case in **F-Pn fr.1586**.

In such a luxury book, **F-Pn fr.1586**'s economy can hardly be motivated by the cost of parchment. It can be surmised, therefore, that **F-Pn fr.1586** reflects an understanding of the repetition structure of the lai more visually than is the case in later manuscripts of the same piece. Perhaps it relates to a piece of authorial notational ephemera in which this format was used as economical, although there was a reversion to the Machaut manuscript default of double text-underlay as the maximum in later manuscripts.

Virelais in *CI*

While all other collected manuscripts for Machaut's music and poetry place the lais first, the section of notated musical lyrics in **F-Pn fr.1586** uniquely starts with the virelais. It is possible to argue that the pre-eminence of the lai was a backwards rationalization that followed from its premier position within the didactic *Remede de Fortune*. Once Machaut had thought about presenting genres in the order given in the *Remede*, it subsequently influenced his choice for the larger order within the music section. But the virelai is also 'first' in *Remede* in that it is the first song that the narrator of *Remede* composes once he re-enters court society (and the company of his lady, specifically), after his instruction by Hope. Either the newness of *Remede* meant that its ordering had not had time to percolate through the overall codex ordering when *CI* was planned, or Machaut's first thoughts about the implications of the order of the genres in the *Remede* was to start with the genre that opens the lover's new life, after gaining Hope: on this reading the virelai represents the most modern, most socially acceptable, high status form.

Its importance and novelty seems borne out by the positioning and careful copying of the virelai collection in *CI*. Unlike all the music in the *Remede*, which breaks into single-column layout, the virelais use the same two-column layout used for the narrative texts.[68] There is a careful distinction between staves with space for double text-underlay beneath them and those with single text-underlay, correctly (in most cases) anticipating what is needed. The virelai form opens with the refrain text and music, which requires single text underlay. The refrain is followed by two verses, which form a double versicle structure, sometimes with open and closed

---

[68] http://gallica.bnf.fr/ark:/12148/btv168449043q/f303.image.

endings, sometimes not; these need double-height text-underlay and even for the separate endings the second text will generally retain its inferior heighting to make clear the length of the open and closed endings. In most cases, the layout then reverts to single-height text-underlay for the *tierce* text and music; although the melody for this section is the same as the refrain, the *tierce* text is never stacked under the refrain text as it is typically in modern editions, although it is sometimes not underlaid to the music (see the example of *Foy porter* (Virelai no.25) below). If the complete *tierce* music is given it is sometimes followed by a short musico-textual cue of the refrain repeat.

He! Dame de vaillance (Virelai no.1; ff.148v–149r) provides an example of the standard layout.[69] Four staves with single-text space are followed by one with space for double text – there seems to have been an effort to start the text of the verses at the beginning of a staff line. These four staves complete f.148v, and the next page, f.149r, has one staff line with space for double text; the *tierce* text starts towards the end of this line and there are then four further staves with single underlay space, giving a fully underlaid *tierce* and a refrain cue with three syllables (four notes); the last staff is nearly half blank.

Despite being one of what are known as the formes fixes, the virelai's text-music relations admit a great deal of variation in the length of sections and their music-textual form. This occasionally gave the scribe trouble, even in *CI*. One example is when the refrain/*tierce* music is itself, like the verses, in a double versicle format. The first of these is *Dame, a qui* (Virelai no.12) on f.153r.[70] It starts at the bottom of the left-hand column, but there is insufficient space for the entire refrain unless it were to be written with double text underlay, for which the layout has not left space, since it has the normal single-line underlay space at the outset of the refrain. The text scribe thus gets as far as 'Dame qui m'ottri de' at the base of the left-hand column, with only the notes for 'Dame qui m'ottri' entered above them (and then an erasure of two notes above 'de') before ceasing to enter text in the new right-hand column. Where there is no text, there are no notes entered. The music and text resume in the last part of the third staff in the right-hand column, which normatively deploys the double text underlay spacing to take the text of the verses. The last two staves are able to take the double

[69] http://gallica.bnf.fr/ark:/12148/btv1b8449043q/f303.image. Albeit in double-column format its text layout compares closely with the layout of *Dame, a vous* (*Remede* musical item no.6; ff.51r–v), the first virelai in the order of the bound manuscript.

[70] http://gallica.bnf.fr/ark:/12148/btv168449043q/f312.image. *De bonte, de valour* (Virelai no.10) is laid out as a double versicle refrain in modern editions, but only the first three breves of the repeated six-breve phrase are actually the same, so it is not surprising that it was not laid out as ouvert/clos in the manuscript.

text-underlay of the *tierce*, although the closed ending bleeds off the staves and into the margin. In total, then, *Dame, a qui* (V12) has all the *music* for the refrain because it has the *tierce*, but it lacks the full refrain text; the later stanzas just have the textual cue 'Dame etc'. As it stands, the complete piece is not performable from **F-Pn fr.1586**. The following scenario may be imagined: the scribe started copying the refrain; discovered there was not enough staff space for the entire refrain if written out in full, but also not enough space to double up the text-underlay. The text scribe skipped to the parts of the virelai that were possible to copy and left the refrain unresolved, perhaps intending to go back later, possibly after seeking help; just maybe the double text-underlay provided for the *tierce* was only prompted once the scribe had hit this snag. In any case, it is possible that this example implies that the same scribe was simultaneously copying text and music; it at least undermines the usual pattern of entering text first, then staves, then notes, since here the staves exist without text or notes.

Evidence from later examples of virelais with the same feature (a double versicle refrain structure with a relatively short ouvert/clos cadence) suggests that the entire manuscript was being copied with a relatively short amount of forward planning for the entire ensemble of page elements, so that the problematic encounter with *Dame, a qui* (V12) was able to be fed into the planning of later pages. For *Diex, Biauté* (Virelai no.19; f.155v) the scribe leaves space for double text underlay from the outset of the refrain as well as for the *tierce* staff lines.[71] For both *Dame vostre doulz viaire* (Virelai no.17; f.154v) and *Se d'amer* (Virelai no.20; f.156r) the situation shows even greater planning.[72] Both these virelais have a double versicle refrain, again with correctly anticipated double text underlay spacing below the staff of the refrain and *tierce* sections. But the two different endings of their refrains are relatively lengthy and thus sport a partial reversion to single text-underlay. In the former, for example, the relatively long ouvert/clos structure in the refrain and *tierce* permit a single staff of single underlay for each of those sections (see second and fifth staves in the right-hand column on f.154v: the last word under the second staff is the start of the 'second-time-bar' for the refrain; the last two words under the fifth staff are the start of the 'second-time-bar' for the verses). In order to anticipate this, the person planning the page must have had a very good idea of these pieces and their musico-poetic structure.

---

[71] http://gallica.bnf.fr/ark:/12148/btv1b8449043q/f317.image.

[72] f.154v: http://gallica.bnf.fr/ark:/12148/btv1b8449043q/f315.image; f.156r: http://gallica.bnf.fr/ark:/12148/btv1b8449043q/f318.image.

Mixed music in *CII*

Un mortel lay (Lai no.12 in Ludwig's numbering; no.8 in Schrade's), the ninth lai copied in *CI*, finishes on f.186v,[73] two-thirds of the way across the first staff ruled on the page, ending the section that scholars have termed *CI*. Although the new gathering of *CII* continues with another lai, space below *Un mortel lay* (L12/8) on f.186v was filled in at the time *CII* was added with the duplex balade *Amours me fait* (Balade no.19). The spacing of its last two staves is narrowed so as to allow the residuum text to fit below the tenor part, and the lineation of Balade 19's second heterometric stanza in the text residuum has been compacted. The correct lineation in stanza 3 shows that the scribe knows what it is, but copied the residuum as compactly as possible at first, relaxing back into displaying the heterometric verse form visually through correct lineation only in the final stanza when it was clear that there would be sufficient remaining space.[74]

The next gathering – the first of *CII* – opens with the *Lay de Plour* (Lai no.22/16) on 187r.[75] Like the earlier lais, the *Lay de Plour* (L22/16) has an initial miniature, which takes up half the width of the writing block; the first two musical staff lines are thus only in the right-hand part of the page. The lai seems well planned until the final stanza, when the music stops early in the first quarter of the stanza. Realizing there would not be sufficient space to copy all of the final stanza underlaid to the music in the remaining space on f.188v,[76] the scribe copies the text as a residuum in two columns at the base of the page instead of one staff line and its double text-underlay. Even this space was not enough for all the text, however, so the final part of the stanza is in the right-hand column at the top of f.189r, on the right of the half-width miniature that opens L22/16;[77] this means that the decision had already been taken not to draw two half-width staves in that space (compare the presence of these on 187r).[78] This confirms, then, that the text was entered before anything else and that the musical staves were red-inked in only after the miniatures were planned. In any case, it implies a very close working relationship between all the individuals involved in the production of this section. In particular, the scribe of the lai

[73] http://gallica.bnf.fr/ark:/12148/btv1b8449043q/f379.image.

[74] Alternatively it is possible that the exemplar for the notated new pieces in the new gathering, starting with Lai no.22/16, only had an incipit with musical notation for their final stanza, where notated.

[75] http://gallica.bnf.fr/ark:/12148/btv1b8449043q/f380.image.

[76] http://gallica.bnf.fr/ark:/12148/btv1b8449043q/f383.image.

[77] http://gallica.bnf.fr/ark:/12148/btv1b8449043q/f384.image.

[78] http://gallica.bnf.fr/ark:/12148/btv1b8449043q/f380.image.

text must have known that abandoning the musical notation was a legitimate option: the final stanza's melody is merely that of the opening stanza a fifth higher, so the piece can be completely performed from what might seem an incomplete copy.

The notated and unnotated lais that occupy 188r–197v preserve the same format as in *CI*: double text underlay for notated lais, copied in single-column format; double-column format for the unnotated texts.[79] Despite the lack of genre ordering in *CII*, there is a similar care in copying and layout for this. The main layout switch is that not just the lais, but all musical items in *CII* are copied in single-column layout, with residuum text still in double-column format in verse, with the exception of the relatively small amount of residuum text required for the rondeaux, which is copied as prose in a small block set aside to the right of the last staff (see the first example on f.201v,[80] where uniquely there is rather too much space left for the tenor, a slip not made for the later rondeaux).

The first virelai in *CII*, and thus the first virelai in the music section to have single-column layout for the staves, starts after *Amours, se plus* (Lai no.9) ends on f.197v.[81] The scribe carefully copies the last nine poetic lines of the lai in two, short, five-line columns at the top of the page; after these the entire width is used for the three staves of *Foy porter* (Virelai no.25), whose text and music entirely fills the rest of the verso. The text residuum of *Foy porter* (V25) resumes the two-column format.

In *Foy porter* (V25) the first staff has space for single-line text-underlay (the refrain) but the second and third staves have double-text-underlay spacing. Nonetheless the refrain text extends well past the midpoint of the second staff so that the double space is only needed towards the end of the line. In the final staff line, the double text-underlay extends less than halfway across the page, since the verses have a first and second time ending, so that the text-underlay for these is offset, although the closed ending's text is at the same height as the second line of the text-underlay. Only the music for the refrain and verses is given; copying the *tierce* would have required another staff and pushed the text residuum onto the next recto. The fairly wide spacing of the verses of the B section, and a little bit of blank staff left at the end, together suggest that the scribe took this decision early. As the entire *tierce* text is copied in the left-hand column below the staff at the start of residuum, and as it is sung to the same music

---

[79]   http://gallica.bnf.fr/ark:/12148/btv1b8449043q/f382.image.

[80]   http://gallica.bnf.fr/ark:/12148/btv1b8449043q/f409.image.

[81]   http://gallica.bnf.fr/ark:/12148/btv1b8449043q/f401.image.

as the refrain, as with the *Lay de Plour* (L22/16) above, the musical copy is effectively complete for a singer or reader who knows the form, implicitly knowledge assumed by the scribe.

Conclusion: after *CII*

CII shows scribes planning and adapting quickly to a new virelai layout (single-column) and to the new genre of the rondeau. Some of the polyphonic pieces that are contained in this section also gave them layout and copying problems too intricate to detail here. The previous norm of the two-column music forms resumes on f.206v where a closed series of motets starts,[82] in an order that remains pretty stable in later manuscripts, all features that attest that the motet section existed before the copying of *CII*.[83] These polyphonic pieces conform to what Earp has termed the 'polyphonic norm', a standard way of copying polyphonic music after the period of the earliest motet manuscripts, in which page turns were arranged so that simultaneously sounding voices were visually present on a single page. To this end, the motets are copied at the rate of one per opening, the triplum in both verso columns and extending into the left-hand column of the recto page; the tenor (and, for *Aucune gent / Qui plus* (Motet no.5),[84] the contratenor) follows in the left-hand column of the recto and the motetus starts at the top of the right-hand column; sometimes the triplum runs so far down the left-hand recto column that the tenor's tiny part of the last left-hand staff is joined to the last staff in the right-hand staff, below the motetus (as in *Helas!/Corde mesto/LIBERA ME*; Motet no.12).[85] When a tenor is short and a motetus long, the two-column format can give way to single columns below the tenor part into which the end of the motetus extends.[86]

---

[82] http://gallica.bnf.fr/ark:/12148/btv1b8449043q/f419.image.

[83] The first gathering of the motet section had to be recopied in order to fit after the later-copied *CII*; see Earp 1983, 141.

[84] http://gallica.bnf.fr/ark:/12148/btv1b8449043q/f425.image and http://gallica.bnf.fr/ark:/12148/btv1b8449043q/f426.image.

[85] http://gallica.bnf.fr/ark:/12148/btv1b8449043q/f439.image and http://gallica.bnf.fr/ark:/12148/btv1b8449043q/f440.image.

[86] This is true of *J'ay tant/Lasse!/EGO MORIAR PRO TE* (Motet no.7; ff.211v–212r), *Qui es/Ha! Fortune/ET NON EST QUI ADJUVET* (Motet no.8; ff.212v–213r), *Hareu!/Helas!/OBEDIENS USQUE AD MORTEM* (Motet no.10; ff.214v–215r), *Maugré mon cuer/De ma dolour/QUIA AMORE LANGUEO* (Motet no.14; ff.218v–219r), and *Trop plus/Biauté/JE NE SUI MIE CERTEINS* (Motet no.20; 224v–225r).

Even in *CI*, this polyphonic norm does not pertain for the songs. Earp has commented that various polyphonic pieces in both *CI* and *CII* break with the 'polyphonic norm' for copying and speculates that this might point either to the relative newness of polyphonic song (as opposed to the motet) or show that order was a higher priority than visual simultaneity.[87] The former would indicate a relative dating for the start of polyphonic song.[88] The latter would fit with Machaut's later authorial-scribal poetics, in the form that they are represented in the *Prologue* and Index of **F-Pn fr.1584**. But a third reading is possible since it fits with the generic norms for monophonic song manuscripts: it is common in the trouvère repertory for the text of later stanzas to be found visually separated from the notation of the melody to which it is set. Bits of the monophonic song that must be performed together – the melody of stanza 1 and the words of stanza 3 – are not able to be viewed at the same time. This feature, together with the kind of 'part-literate' (and, for our purposes, woefully incomplete) notation of songs seen in the manuscript witnesses considered in Chapters 7 and 9, leads to the question of the function and use of these kinds of songbooks, something that will be taken up in Chapter 11 of the present volume.

---

[87] Earp 2011, 233–4; 233fn45 notes *Helas! tant* (Balade no.2; 158r–v) and *Se je me plaing* (Balade no.15; 164r–v) from *CI* and *De Fortune* (Balade no.23; 200r–v), *Quant j'ay l'espart* (Rondeau no.5; 202r–v) and *Cinc, un* (Rondeau no.6; 203r–v) from *CII*.

[88] See Arlt 2002.

11 | Songs, scattered and gathered

HELEN DEEMING AND ELIZABETH EVA LEACH

The fresh perspectives taken to the manuscripts considered in this book have repeatedly catalogued and challenged previous scholarly tendencies both to scatter and also to gather songs according to criteria that are at odds with those of medieval scribes: by language, by anachronistic binaries like monophony/polyphony or sacred/secular, and by formal categories that seem unrelated to manuscript content. Instead, the new approaches to the manuscripts considered in this book attempt to bring out the manifest multi-layered processes of scattering and gathering songs reflected in the manuscript sources themselves. Scattered – geographically and chronologically – are the ten case-studies, which are representatives of a very broad and diverse base of materials for the study of medieval song; and the songs found within the manuscripts the preceding ten chapters consider are the scattered traces of rich oral song traditions, large parts of which are now lost through the destruction of manuscripts or because they were never written down at all. Manuscripts containing medieval songs are, however, the products of diverse processes of gathering. The case-studies here have demonstrated the value of close attention to the varied ways in which songs were gathered: alongside other songs, in combination with other kinds of written material, and varied in their written presentation and distribution on the page and in the book.

Despite the undeniable diversity of the manuscripts chosen for inclusion here, the long chronological separation between the earliest and the latest, their geographic dispersal (in both original provenance and current location), and their different linguistic, generic, and repertorial emphases, particular themes have emerged from their juxtaposition in this volume. In justifying the choice of the manuscripts treated here, our introduction noted that the idea of the medieval song tradition has been predicated on a small subset of witnesses from within a few sub-repertories. Through a focus on important manuscripts that for various reasons had all previously been considered to some extent 'peripheral', that is, by broadening the scope of the song tradition and explicitly seeking to draw parallels across repertories and manuscripts normally considered in isolation, our book has opened up the possibility for wholesale reconsideration of the nature of

271

the medieval song tradition. Surprising points of comparison that speak to shared or similar concerns among the manuscripts' first writers and readers will be drawn out in this concluding chapter. These are grouped under the three headings of our subtitle, 'inscription', 'performance', and 'context', but, as will become abundantly clear in what follows, the three themes are almost inseparable.

Inscription

One of the most significant new perspectives to emerge from the case-studies in this book is a wider, more inclusive view of the nature of musical inscription and musical reading. Modern preconceptions concerning the ways in which musical notation operates as an agent of communication have skewed understanding of the sheer range of purposes for which music was written down and subsequently encountered in visual form in the Middle Ages. Any kind of teleological progression – from unnotated to notated, via ever more specific and prescriptive ways of fixing musical information in writing – is not a reality of the medieval manuscripts we have examined. Instead, they suggest that a more fruitful approach is to remain open to a wide domain of communicative situations in which specific kinds of notations may have been used. Deliberately provocative in this sense has been our choice to include as case-studies two manuscripts that lack any 'explicit' musical notation (see Chapters 7 and 9), but which invite us, as Henry Hope notes, to consider the significance of 'music's absence in the construction of a musical presence' (p.190). Moreover, these two witnesses, both profoundly musical, should not be placed on one side of an imagined barrier between the 'notated' and the 'unnotated', but rather can be shown to form part of a spectrum of denotation, in which music and song are inscribed in various ways and to varying degrees, according to the functions which their inscribers envisaged that they would fulfil.

In addition to those inscriptions traditionally labelled as musical notation (including neumatic, diastematic, and staff notations, both unmeasured and rhythmic), the manuscripts considered here also inscribe music pictorially, verbally, and contextually. In **D-HEu Cod.Pal.germ.848**, the musical element of the Minnelieder is present in spite of the lack of musical notation, by means of the iconographic attributes that identify their authors as musicians, as oral performers, and as active owners of the materials presented in the manuscript. Hope argues that the musicality of the songs, and the status of their creators as musical inventors and performers, could not have been doubted by the readers of the manuscript, given the contexts in which it circulated; music's explicit denotation in the form of musical notation would thus have been a redundant signifier of this musicality. Whether the melodies of the songs themselves were familiar to the readers of the book, or whether their access to the music came through listening to sung performances, it seems very likely that the first readers of **D-HEu Cod.Pal.germ.848** (and those who compiled the volume for their use) aurally encountered the Minnelieder *as song*, in situations that may have been before, during, or after their visual encounter with the book. A similar case was made by Elizabeth Eva Leach for **GB-Ob Douce 308**, in which a narrative description of courtly music making signals a possible performance context for the songs which follow it, 'notated' only as verbal texts. Coupled with their organization by generic categories, which relies – at least in part – on an understanding of the specifically musical factors that differentiate them, the musicality of the songs of **GB-Ob Douce 308** is likewise clearly inscribed, albeit in ways that do not rely on an explicitly musical form of notation.

These manuscript witnesses both strongly suggest that the gatherers of song took care to avoid redundancy in the form and extent of their musical inscriptions, and were acutely aware of the degree of musical knowledge (or foreknowledge) they could expect of those using the books that they assembled. Such awareness is not limited to these two, but is also apparent across the manuscripts examined here. Numerous other cases of musical notations that seem – from our perspective – to be incomplete, partial, or inadequate, can be shown instead to represent scribes inscribing only so much as was required for a given purpose. Neumatic notations, such as those found in **F-Pn lat.1154** (Chapter 1), **GB-Cu Gg.V.35** (Chapter 2), and **D-Mbs Clm.4660** (Chapter 4), require by their very nature the musical user to have foreknowledge of the melodies they inscribe. They serve, in other words, not as materials suited to a singer's initial learning of a song, or as arbiters of musical correctness when dispute arose, but as aides-mémoires for music already encountered through aural means. Two of these three witnesses were written at a time when staff notation was – at least theoretically – available. One must conclude that those who produced the notations in those two manuscripts had uses in mind for them that did not require staff notation's capacity for transmitting musical information previously unfamiliar to those reading it. Instead they envisaged situations in which songs were already known to their readers, such that the prompt to melodic shape and contour provided by neumatic notation was all that was necessary; the inscribers of **GB-Cu Gg.V.35** and **D-Mbs Clm 4660** inscribed music sufficiently for precisely those purposes. Just as verbal notation (that is, the inscription of the song texts alone) sufficed for the denotation of music in **GB-Ob Douce 308** and **D-HEu Cod.Pal.germ.848**, neumatically notated manuscripts were likewise adequate for the kinds of visual encounter with song that they presupposed.

This line of argument applies not just to entire categories of musical notation (neumatic, diastematic, and so on), but also to scribes' approaches to the quantity of musical denotation required for any given song. In **GB-Cu Gg.V.35**, Jeremy Llewellyn considers the highly abbreviated verbal texts along with the copying of only parts of their melodies to be mnemonics that cue the reactivation of the songs as wholes: in these cases, the scribes could be confident that this amount of verbal and musical notation would suffice for the uses they envisaged. In **D-Mbs Clm 4660**, the amount of neumatic musical notation varies between songs, ranging from none at all, through notation for the opening gesture or the first stanza of a strophic text only, right up to the provision of melodic information for the entirety of the text. The entire collection hence defies simple classification along notational lines, and demonstrates a nuanced understanding on the part of its compilers of the varying requirements of the manuscripts' users in relation to particular pieces.

Similar observations about the extent of explicit notation can be made of the highly sophisticated and apparently musically prescriptive notations to be found in later thirteenth-century song manuscripts and in the authorial compilations of Guillaume de Machaut. Helen Deeming has drawn attention to a pattern of 'incomplete' copying of the tenors in the motets preserved in **GB-Lbl Egerton 274** (Chapter 6), and interpreted these not as failures on the part of the scribe or the scribe's exemplars, but as prompts designed to record and transmit the full melodic and rhythmic information encoded within the tenors, empowering singers to generate complete and accurate performances once the number of required repetitions had been worked out through a rehearsal process. In both this manuscript and in **F-Pn n.a.f.13521** (Chapter 8), numerous indicators of special care taken by the music scribes in other respects make it unlikely that their decisions to eschew a panoptic layout, with all polyphonic parts visible simultaneously, should be read as faults, or even as evidence that they were not intended for use in musical performance. Instead, both manuscripts suggest an environment in which multi-voiced pieces were learned collectively or taught by one singer to a group of others. Careful prior consideration of their musical and textual components – which Sean

Curran, borrowing terminology from Joyce Coleman, terms 'praelection' (p.208) – formed part of the process of encountering the music in the books.

The panoptic layout, labelled by Lawrence Earp as the 'polyphonic norm' after the earliest motet witnesses, is in fact far from the norm among the multi-voiced songs preserved in the manuscripts examined here, and is not even used consistently in **F-Pn fr.1586** (Chapter 10).[1] A view of musical reading that limits it, in effect, to 'sight-reading', is a prevailing but demonstrably anachronistic perspective that has problematized these kinds of musical inscription without considering other possible ways in which visual encounter with music in the book could ultimately lead to sounding performances (or indeed to non-sounding forms of musical appreciation).

Further clear suggestions of the use of these manuscripts as aids to the performance of song, though not in the moment of performance itself, are found in the Aquitanian book, **GB-Lbl Add.36881** (Chapter 3). Its tiny physical dimensions render this volume highly unsuited to use as a resource for singers to read from as they sang, while at the same time its copious annotations relating to such practical matters as voice coordination and proper phrasing rule out the possibility that it was drawn upon only as an archival reference point. The manuscript's employment of notational features that mark it out – against the backdrop of its time – as emblematic of an especially textual or literate approach to music writing further suggest a heightened awareness of the increasing amounts and qualities of musical information that could be transmitted in written form, though Rachel May Golden suggested that these notational advances were likely to have been appreciated by musical readers during 'pre-performance preparation or [...] post-performance reflection' (p.70). **GB-Lbl Add.36881** and many other manuscripts examined here call into question the notion that musical witnesses can be divided into simple categories of 'practical' and 'non-practical' (for example, reference or presentation copies), since many betray features that seem to point to several different functions, as well as a wider range of practical or performance uses than the narrow conception usually inferred by modern scholars.

In the ways outlined above, various kinds of musical 'absence' or 'lack' (at least in relation to more recent expectations of musical inscription) can be construed as purposeful and instructive in the light of the manuscripts' specific goals and contexts. And while the inclusion of musical notation for

---

[1] See Earp 2011, 233–4.

specific items within a manuscript collection was sometimes a marker of the special esteem in which certain texts were held, equally the absence of any form of musical denotation for an item need not imply the opposite. Both **GB-Lbl Add.36881** and **D-Mbs Clm 4660** include, within otherwise musically notated sections of the manuscripts, individual unnotated pieces that were clearly never intended to receive any explicit musical notation. Gundela Bobeth has contended that such instances may exemplify 'the wide-spread fame and firm knowledge of any given song, making its written transmission superfluous' (p.92), a reading that is confirmed by the unusually heavy abbreviation of the texts of this kind in **GB-Lbl Add.36881**.

Just as knowledge of, or alternative access to, the melodies of songs could be assumed by the compilers of **D-HEu Cod.Pal.germ.848** and **GB-Ob Douce 308**, numerous other instances of melodies not explicitly denoted but contextually implied may be traced among the manuscripts considered here. Sam Barrett points to the litany, penitential psalms, and antiphon preserved without explicit notation in **F-Pn lat.1154** as being items that are very likely to have been sung in the contexts for which the manuscript was designed. This suggests that the boundaries between what was and was not considered 'song' do not correspond to the provision or non-provision of musical notation for items in this manuscript.

In a different way, contrafacta, too, contextually imply the presence of music, especially prominently in **D-Mbs Clm 4660**, in which stanzas of German song are appended to copies of Latin songs sharing the same poetic form. Though there is no single explanation that accounts for either the genesis of these examples (Latin text created in response to pre-existing German, or vice versa, or both jointly conceived), or for the performance practices that may be implied by their disposition in the manuscript, they are nonetheless instances in which music is denoted for one piece by means of contextual transfer from another.

In a few cases, evidence preserved in the manuscripts permits specific insights into the musical knowledge assumed of their readers, in the form of alterations made in the books to accommodate the different expectations of later users. **GB-Lbl Egerton 274**, perhaps the most drastically revised of all the manuscripts studied here, offers a particularly rich testimony in this respect. It shows, for example, that indications of rhythm absent from the notation in its original, thirteenth-century form were desirable for fourteenth-century users (though for their purposes, it was apparently not necessary to rhythmicize the entirety of the music but only to show indicatively, through a few examples, how rhythm might be applied to the songs). The custodes added to the songs at the same time are also examples of inscribed information that was apparently superfluous to the thirteenth-century reader but more necessary to later musicians; their misapplication in the score-format polyphonic pieces further implies that this form of musical inscription had served one set of users adequately but was not aligned to the musical foreknowledge of another generation.

The musical revisions made to **GB-Lbl Harley 978** (Chapter 5) have usually been interpreted as altering the songs as originally inscribed, by rendering their notation rhythmic (as in **GB-Lbl Egerton 274**), but close examination instead reveals that the revisions nearly always preserve the written information but re-write it in an alternative (presumably more familiar) way. **GB-Lbl Harley 978** provides an example, therefore, not of later users re-composing song to align with their own aesthetic priorities, but rather re-inscribing it so as to prolong the useful life of the song in its original musical state.

Two further observations on the nature of inscription in these medieval manuscripts remain to be made. The first is that musical inscription could, in some cases, be an end in itself, either didactically or creatively. The preparation of a musical book as a site for teaching the skill of music-writing is apparent in **F-Pn lat.1154**, where the inscribing of musical notation by a writing-master and pupils can be traced in the alternation of higher- and lower-quality script. This practice, along with the related phenomena of erasure and correction of musical inscriptions, has only recently begun to be investigated critically and much work still remains to be done.[2] A related practice is the use of a music book to experiment with policies for the layout and organization of songs on the page.[3] Far from being limited to written ephemera or 'informal' book contexts, Leach has documented this very process in one of the most luxurious productions considered in this book, **F-Pn fr.1586** (Chapter 10). Despite the highest quality of the planning for the book, which attests to Machaut's 'initial attempt to exploit a scribal poetics of authorship' (p.257) and thus bring about a fundamental shift in the nature of song-gathering in medieval manuscripts, its material manifestations – such as the changing approach to the use of columns and to the indication of musical repetition through the stacking of two lines of text below a repeated melody – are conceptually

---

[2] Grier 1992, Haines 2004; some recent publications in literary studies that could serve as useful points of departure for further musicological investigations along these lines include the essays by Pearsall, Fisher, Beadle, Wakelin, Morrison, Powell, and Allen in Gillespie and Hudson 2013.
[3] Deeming 2006.

analogous to earlier scribes' use of the inscription process to test out, practise, and refine their methods for inscribing song.

Further hints that the moment of inscription was aligned with a moment of musical creation also appear in other manuscripts considered here. The scribe's unusual choice to interleave the stanzas of the two songs *Dic Christi veritas* and *Bulla fulminante* in **D-Mbs Clm 4660** amounts at the very least to a creative decision to draw attention through layout to the pieces' musical kinship, and may even be understood as a recomposition that generates a new work drawing on the musical possibilities of the materials. Similarly, the use of a melody drawn from another song for the text of *La douche vois del rosignuel sauvage* in **GB-Lbl Egerton 274** shows the later scribe actively drawing upon the resources of the book itself to create something musico-poetically new.

The final aspect of musical inscription to be explored here is the range of attitudes towards the relative fixity or variability of song revealed by different scribal approaches. A complex interaction between sounding and written practice is apparent in the songs with repetitive structures, whose scribes wrote out all the repetitions in full, typically preserving multiple minor variations between the repetitions as they did so (this phenomenon is apparent in the manuscripts considered in Chapters 4, 5, and 6). In song forms such as the sequence, lai, virelai, rondeau, and balade, the opportunity to economize on both space and effort by copying out the music of repeated sections only once, with the corresponding lines of text stacked multiply beneath, was taken up only rarely towards the end of the period spanned by the manuscripts in this book (it occurs for one of the sequences in **GB-Lbl Harley 978**, and more pervasively for forms with repetition in **F-Pn fr.1586**, although even there quadruple versicle structures in many lai stanzas are usually given double text underlay and the repetition thus partly written out with the capacity for minor variants, except for the lai in the *Remede de Fortune* discussed in Chapter 10).

The variations between two different written-out versions of what is essentially a repeated melodic statement usually involve nuances, such as the use of a 'full' note versus a liquescence, or the filling-in of an interval of a third with a passing note, that strongly imply an origin in performance practice: that is, they are the sorts of musical modification that tend to come about in the act of singing. Scribes' desire to preserve these performative variations in writing implies an apparently oxymoronic attitude, which both recognizes the inherent variability of a musical phrase, but at the same time commits a set number of permutations of it (usually two) to writing. That the same scribes routinely inscribed strophic songs by writing out the music for the first stanza only, seemingly content to leave the subsequent stanzas entirely open to the variations that singers might introduce, suggests that their careful preservation of two different versions of repeated phrases in sequences and lais should not be interpreted as a desire to fix those particular versions as the only permissible options for future performances. Instead, they could be usefully read as exemplifying the fluidity of the song as sung, and inviting the musical reader to engage in creative dialogue with the inscribed text. Modern editorial practices in music and poetry range from the rigorously philological approaches of the early twentieth century to the ascendancy of the Zumthorian idea of *mouvance* as medieval lyric's fundamental aesthetic from the 1970s onwards.[4] The manuscript witnesses, however, suggest that even *mouvance* was subject to *mouvance* and that a notion of fixity could be used to construct powerful ideas of variation.

Performance

All manners of musical inscription can figure performance, although – as the chapters above have aimed to show – this is not all that they accomplish. But just as modern perspectives have too narrowly circumscribed the roles and interpretations of musical inscription, similar assumptions have placed implicit limits on the kinds of musical practice deemed to constitute performance. The manuscripts studied here point to a wide range of performative activities, including (but not necessarily limited to) singing aloud to an audience, singing aloud alongside companions, singing pieces but not necessarily straight through from beginning to end, and singing in a low voice – or even silently – to oneself. All of these activities could involve the book either before, during, or after the performance, and the person or people with visual access to the book might be all of the performers, only some of them, or not the performers at all, but listeners following along or appreciating the music at a different time. Though suggestions to this effect have occasionally been made in recent scholarship, Curran aptly remarks that the general 'unexamined – indeed unarticulated – assumption that the only kind of literate musical practice is one where all singers read all of the time' has left us with 'few critical models [...] to understand how and where music writing could have been distributed in the social world' (p.207).

---

[4] See, for example, Gennrich 1932. Zumthor 1972.

Aspects of the assumptions about literate musical practice pertaining to the ways in which music was inscribed in the manuscripts have been alluded to above, and further remarks concerning the implications for social activities will be made in the third section of this chapter. One often underestimated dimension of performance that has been apparent in several of the case-studies in this book, however, is that of music's capacity to perform text, specifically those qualities that a musically vocalized reading can bring to the semantic world of a text, which are not available in an unsung rendering. These specific qualities operate on the level of individual compositions, such as the opening motet in **F-Pn n.a.f.13521**, *Ave virgo regia / Ave gloriosa mater salvatoris / DOMINO*, exposed in Chapter 8 as a dazzlingly virtuosic exploitation of the motet's characteristic polytextuality and the ways in which the musical attributes of the genre can be harnessed to specific hermeneutic ends. Medieval polytextual genres, especially the thirteenth-century motet, have been examined from such perspectives more than other kinds of medieval song, but the musical analyses carried out in the chapters above demonstrate the value of considering the specific meanings achieved through musicalization across the spectrum of forms, textures and registers of song they represent. Several of the chapters have drawn attention to the special nature of contrafacta as representatives of music's capacity to bring two (or more) texts into creative association in ways that are more laborious to achieve without the agency of music. Bobeth, for example, demonstrates that the singing of *Alte clamat Epicurus* to the melody of Walther von der Vogelweide's *Palästinalied* could constitute a 'grotesque re-contextualisation of the familiar melody' (p.100) to enhance the comic effect of the text; similar phenomena of music inflecting the performance of one text on account of its original association with another likewise lie behind the Latin–French, French–Latin and English–Latin contrafacta in **GB-Lbl Egerton 274** and **GB-Lbl Harley 978**.

A highly significant performance-related theme throughout several chapters has been the use of song in the enactment of prayer. By drawing out the implications of **F-Pn lat.1154**'s combination of texts, and comparing them to contemporary instructions for personal devotion, Barrett builds a convincing case for viewing the *versus* in the manuscript as integral to its prayerful function, even arguing that the boundary between song and prayer is explicitly blurred in the book's contents and directional rubrics. The contemplation of the book's contents as a whole also lay behind Curran's reading of **F-Pn n.a.f.13521** as a devotional manual, whose musical contents – far from being at odds with that reading – in fact contribute actively to the manuscript's programme of prayerful contemplation. In **GB-Lbl Egerton 274**, the later addition of a fascicle of narrative, devotional verse can be shown to shore up the identification of private prayerful reading as one of the manuscript's multiple functions, and in many other cases considered in this book, traces in the form of rubrics of the use of books or individual songs within them in acts of prayer and worship may be found. A perceived boundary between the official liturgical *cursus* and more informal devotional practice is repeatedly undercut in the examples examined here, with materials extracted from the authorized liturgy juxtaposed with those that had no clearly defined liturgical use, suggesting a fluid and probably two-way traffic of songs from one context to another.

Especially striking among the manuscripts we have examined in this book is the variety of means by which performance and sounding expression are figured, over and above the more obvious tactics of musical inscription and rubrication. These include the signs of the cross that appear among the charms preserved in **GB-Lbl Add.36881**, which prompt the devotional user to enact this reverential gesture as part of an active performance of the charms' texts. That the well-known prayers incorporated within the sequence of charms are radically abbreviated, often including only the first letter of each word, likewise points to a performative act, in signalling their re-expansion by the performer as the sequence is carried out. This written strategy is analogous to the abbreviation in medieval liturgical books of the doxology to 'evovae' (the vowels of its closing words, 'seculorum amen'), something that musical readers would have had no difficulty in interpreting as a prompt to sound out the indicated melodic tone for the psalm- or canticle-text required. Golden regards the performance indications of the charms as reinforcing the functions of the *versus* and **GB-Lbl Add.36881** as a whole, an interpretation that is likely to hold true of other collections in which music and items geared to private devotional practice are found together.[5]

Pictorial means for portraying performance, and thus linking these manuscripts to a sounding practice, have also been revealed in the chapters above. In **D-HEu Cod.Pal.germ.848**, the appearances of scrolls in the miniatures fulfil several performance-related goals because of the strong iconographic associations of the scroll (or banderole) with sounding, dynamic speech or song. In some illustrations, the scrolls serve to link

---

[5] For an examination of a very similar phenomenon in a thirteenth-century English collection, see Deeming 2009, 256–9 and 264–5.

the following song with the portrait of its author, causing it to be read as an individual utterance, most likely based on the personal experiences of the poet-musician. The same iconographic intention can be read in **F-Pn fr.1586**, in which the use of scrolls is linked both to sounding performance and to textualization, but in which – in contrast to the later Machaut codices – the author is clearly conflated with the poetic 'I', collapsing the subjectivity of the composer, performer and lover into one. Another iconographic feature relating to performance in **D-HEu Cod.Pal.germ.848** is the pointing index finger, described by Michael Camille as 'the universal sign of acoustical performance', and used in the miniatures as a signifier of verbal (or sung) dialogue. Though not so straightforward to interpret using iconographic conventions, the (disembodied) hand with its finger pointing to the proem *Caute cane, cantor care* in **GB-Cu Gg.V.35** may serve a similarly dynamic function, since it points to a piece which encapsulates the ideals of right living and right performance to be espoused by the singer of the songs.

Context

An assumption that the social contexts in which medieval songs were created and performed are irretrievably lost to us has shaped their study in modern academic disciplines. Lacking knowledge of their functional environments, much scholarship has been directed instead towards the language and poetics of the songs as a hermetic system of formal elements, isolated from the environment that engendered them.[6] One of this book's principal contentions has been that the material traces of song, in the form of the manuscripts that house them, can supply – at least implicitly – a good deal of information about these lost social contexts, as well as providing, in and of themselves, a direct written context for song that has not been fully acknowledged. Influenced by more recent trends in scholarship that have sometimes been labelled 'new historicism' and 'new philology', as well as by the idea of 'the whole book', our examination of medieval songs in context acts as a corrective to earlier approaches that underestimated the significance of their material, mediating traces in manuscripts.

To focus on just one of the social contexts that is revealed by several of the manuscripts considered in this book, attention has repeatedly been

---

[6] See Zumthor 1972. See also Kay 1999, 212.

drawn to didactic situations as locations for song. A role for song in the education of children is hinted at by the references to them within the texts of **GB-Cu Gg.V.35** and – this time in a courtly rather than ecclesiastical setting – in their pictorial representation in **F-Pn fr.1586**. Songs and other theoretical materials geared towards musical instruction also appear, especially in **GB-Lbl Harley 978,** whose practical guides to the musical intervals very probably found a use in the training of those destined for a life of sung liturgical observance. Less explicitly, several of the manuscripts suggest their possible employment as personal manuals of good conduct: these include **F-Pn lat.1154**, whose materials chime with those prescribed for individual religious observance in contemporary instructions for both lay and monastic readers, and **F-Pn n.a.f.13521** and **GB-Lbl Egerton 274**, both of whose non-musical materials imply a pastoral function that was likely extended to the ways in which their songs were read and used. The didactic value of books as sites for the teaching and learning of script – both textual and musical – has already been mentioned in this chapter, and those books that classify their songs by form or genre (**GB-Ob Douce 308** and **F-Pn fr.1586**) might also have served an instructional purpose to readers familiarizing themselves with the distinctions between different kinds of song.

The most obvious context for medieval song, namely the parchment pages on which they are inscribed and the other textual, diagrammatic, and graphic materials with which they are partnered there, has been all too often overlooked or underplayed for reasons that have more to do with the disciplinary preoccupations and organization of the modern academy than with any reality of the manuscript witnesses themselves. Attention to this very real context has repeatedly posed challenges to the binaries which have often been posited in relation to medieval song. Even 'song' itself, as a circumscribed category, is called into question by the manuscripts studied in this book, all of which include items that fall outside that category as more recently understood in both musicology and literary studies, and several of which present evidence that suggests their medieval compilers and readers regarded some items as both 'song' and 'not song' depending on context. Many of the manuscripts considered here place monophonic and polyphonic items together, sometimes separately grouped and classi-fied, but equally often intermingled, and some blur this apparent distinc-tion even further by paying particular attention to pieces that exist in multiple versions, both single- and multi-voiced. Some of the manuscripts are mono-lingual (Latin, German or French), but others present a com-bination of texts in two or three languages, representing a cultural situation (especially later in the Middle Ages) in which the notion of literacy presupposed familiarity – in written and spoken forms – with both Latin and at least one vernacular language. Once again, certain manuscripts suggest a particular interest in cross-linguistic interplay on the part of their compilers, drawing texts in different languages into dialogue with one another through musical settings and reworkings, and by their arrangement on the manuscript page. An explicit consciousness of the author figure is apparent in only a minority of cases, both among the manuscripts included in this book, and more generally across witnesses to medieval song, and close adherence to generic categories likewise forms a significant organizing principle in only a few instances.

Several of the manuscripts hint at a mode of production that incorporated materials as they came to hand, rather than according to a rigidly preconceived plan, and investigation – such as has been recently initiated in literary studies – of what we can learn from music manuscripts of the nature and circulation of exemplars, as well as related selection and copying processes, suggests itself as a potentially fruitful area of further study.[7] Whether they display thoroughgoing anthologizing principles or not, however, all manuscripts containing song came about as the result of a gathering process in which a wider stock is implied. For each song chosen for inclusion in one of these witnesses, a much greater number must have been left out, and while we can speculate – sometimes quite confidently – about the reasons why some songs were included in them, we cannot know on what grounds other songs, unknown to us, were omitted. Nevertheless, a notion that some manuscripts are 'ordered' whereas others are 'random', in their assembly of sung materials, barely holds true for any of the case-studies in this book, which repeatedly exemplify partial anthologizing tendencies that were abandoned, interrupted or set aside in favour of other concerns.

Considering the codex in the ways that we have attempted in this book has been more constructive than destructive. Though it has not shied away from problematizing interpretative binaries that misrepresent the manuscripts and their music, or from breaking down the barriers that have artificially separated and demarcated medieval songs, such revisionism has been merely the starting point from which to open up newer perspectives. Reading songs through the manuscript books that preserve them – a task made ever more achievable by the increasing availability of high-quality

---

[7] The literary work in this area includes Hanna III 1996a, Hanna III 1996b, and Pearsall 2005.

digital surrogates – brings us much closer to the social worlds they once inhabited, even though we acknowledge that much of the detail of those worlds is inevitably irrecoverable. Encountering medieval song through its manuscripts confronts the twenty-first-century reader with the jarring disjuncture between the ways in which songs were gathered for readerly consumption in their own time, and the ways in which they have been presented to modern scholars and performers, through editions and his-toriographical endeavour. Viewing the manuscripts as whole books, and the songs within them not as contextless forms, but as traces of living musical practice, allows us access to the multiplicity of their functions and meanings, and – crucially – enables us to make meaningful comparisons across regions, languages, and centuries in the era of the manuscript book.

Bibliography

Albritton, Benjamin L. 2009. 'Citation and Allusion in the Lays of Guillaume de Machaut'. PhD dissertation. University of Washington.

2012. 'Moving Across Media: Machaut's Lais and the Judgement Tradition'. In *A Companion to Guillaume de Machaut,* ed. Deborah McGrady and Jennifer Bain. Leiden: Brill, 119–39.

Anderson, Gordon A. 1972–5. 'Notre Dame and Related Conductus: A Catalogue Raisonné'. *Miscellanea Musicologica* 6: 153–229 and 7: 1–81.

1973a. 'The Rhythm of "cum littera" Sections of Polyphonic Conductus in Mensural Sources'. *Journal of the American Musicological Society* 26: 288–304.

1973b. 'Motets of the Thirteenth Century Manuscript La Clayette: The Repertory and Its Historical Significance'. *Musica Disciplina* 27: 11–40.

1974. 'Motets of the Thirteenth-Century Manuscript La Clayette: A Stylistic Study of the Repertory'. *Musica Disciplina* 28: 5–37.

1975, ed. *Motets of the Manuscript La Clayette: Paris, Bibliothèque nationale, nouv. acq. f. fr. 13521.* Corpus mensurabilis musicae 68. [Rome]: American Institute of Musicology.

1979, ed. *Notre Dame and Related Conductus: Opera Omnia. Part 5: 2pt. Conductus, Unica in the Four Central Sources.* Henryville PA: Institute of Medieval Music.

1986, ed. *Notre Dame and Related Conductus: Opera Omnia. Part 1: Four- and Three-Part Conductus in the Central Sources.* Henryville PA: Institute of Medieval Music.

Anderson, Michael. 2010. 'Enhancing the *Ave Maria* in the *Ars antiqua*'. *Plainsong and Medieval Music* 19: 35–65.

Arlt, Wulf. 1986. '*Nova Cantica*: Grundsätlziches und Spezielles zur Interpretation musikalischer Texte des Mittelalters'. *Basler Jahrbuch für historische Musikpraxis* 10: 13–62.

1992. 'Sequence and "Neues Lied"'. In *La Sequenza medievale: Atti del Convegno Internazionale Milano, 7–8 Aprile 1984,* ed. Agostino Ziino. Lucca: Libreria musicale italiana, 3–18.

2000. 'The Office of the Feast of the Circumcision from Le Puy'. In *The Divine Office in the Latin Middle Ages,* ed. Margot E. Fassler and Rebecca A. Baltzer. Oxford University Press, 324–43.

2002. 'Machaut in Context'. In *Guillaume de Machaut: 1300–2000. Actes du Colloque de la Sorbonne 28–29 septembre 2000*, ed. Jacqueline Cerquiglini-Toulet and Nigel Wilkins. Paris: Presses de l'Université de Paris–Sorbonne, 147–62.

Arlt, Wulf and Mathias Stauffacher, eds. 1986. *Engelberg Stiftsbibliothek 314* [Facsimile]. Winterthur: Amadeus.

Arnaud, Leonard E. 1944. 'The Sottes chansons in MS. Douce 308 of the Bodleian Library at Oxford'. *Speculum* 19: 68–88.

Arndt, Wilhelm, ed. 1887. *Vita Alcuini*. MGH Scriptores 15.1. Hannover: Hahn.

Astell, Ann W. 1990. *The Song of Songs in the Middle Ages*. Ithaca: Cornell University Press.

Atchison, Mary. 2005. *The Chansonnier of Oxford Bodleian MS Douce 308: Essays and Complete Edition of Texts*. Aldershot: Ashgate.

2012. 'Two versions of the *Tournoi de Chauvency* and their connections to the Chansonnier of Oxford, Bodleian MS Douce 308'. In *Lettres, musique et société en Lorraine médiévale: Autour du Tournoi de Chauvency (Ms. Oxford Bodleian Douce 308)*, ed. Mireille Chazan and Nancy Freeman Regalado. Geneva: Droz, 71–104.

Aubert, Eduardo Henrik. 2011. 'Écrire, chanter, agir: les Graduels et Missels notés en notation aquitaine avant 1100'. PhD dissertation. 4 vols. École des Hautes Études en Sciences Sociales, Paris.

Aubrey, Elizabeth. 1993. 'Literacy, Orality, and the Preservation of French and Occitan Medieval Songs'. *Revista de Musicología* 16: 2355–66.

Aubrun, Michel. 1981. *L'Ancien diocèse de Limoges des origines au milieu du Xie siècle*. Clermont-Ferrand: Institut d'études du Massif central.

Avril, François. 1970. Review of Gaborit–Chopin 1969. *La Décoration: Bulletin Monumental* 128: 259–62.

1973. 'Un Chef-d'oeuvre de l'enluminure sous le règne de Jean le Bon: La Bible Moralisée manuscrit français 167 de la Bibliothèque Nationale', Monuments et mémoires de la Fondation Eugène Piot. Paris: Presses Universitaires de France, 91–125.

Bagby, Benjamin, with Mark Amodio, Karl Reichl, and John Miles Foley. 2012. 'Performance I: Beowulf (A Roundtable Discussion)'. In *Beowulf at Kalamazoo: Essays on Translation and Performance*, ed. Jana K. Schulman and Paul E. Szarmach. Kalamazoo: Medieval Institute Publications, 209–34.

Baird, J.L. and John R. Kane, eds. 1978. *Rossignol: An Edition and Translation*. Kent OH: Kent State University Press.

Baltzer, Rebecca. 1987. 'Notre Dame Manuscripts and Their Owners: Lost and Found', *Journal of Musicology* 5: 380–99.

Barezzani, Maria Teresa R. 2000. 'Guido d'Arezzo fra tradizione e innovazione'. In *Guido d'Arezzo, monaco pomposiano*, ed. Angelo Rusconi. Florence: Olschki, 134–49.

Baroin, Jeanne and Josiane Haffen, eds. 1987. *La Prophétie de la Sibylle tiburtine: édition des MSS B.N. Fr. 375 et Rennes B.M. Fr. 593*. Paris: Belles lettres.

Barrett, Sam. 1997. 'Music and Writing: On the Compilation of Paris Bibliothèque Nationale lat. 1154'. *Early Music History* 16: 55–96.

2000. '*Notated Verse in Ninth- and Tenth-Century Poetic Collections*'. PhD dissertation. 2 vols. University of Cambridge.

2012. 'The Sponsorship of Early Medieval Latin Song: The Musical Evidence of Two Carolingian Poetic Collections'. In *Patrons and Professionals in the Middle Ages*, ed. Paul Binski and Elizabeth A. New. Donington: Shaun Tyas, 122–40.

2013. *The Melodic Tradition of Boethius'* De consolatione philosophiae *in the Middle Ages*. 2 vols. Monumenta Monodica Medii Aevi. Subsidia 7. Kassel: Bärenreiter.

Bartsch, Karl. 1870. *Altfranzösische Romanzen und Pastourellen*. Leipzig: F. C. W. Vogel.

Bayless, Martha. 2005. 'Simulation and Dissimulation in the Snow Child Sequence ("Modus Liebinc")'. *Mittellateinisches Jahrbuch* 40: 75–84.

Beatie, Bruce A. 1965. 'Carmina Burana 48–48a: A Case of "Irregular Contrafacture"'. *Modern Language Notes* 80: 470–78.

Becquet, Jean. 1979. 'Les Premiers abbés de Saint-Martin de Limoges (XIe–XIIe siècles)'. *Revue Mabillon* 59: 375–92.

Beer, Jeanette. 1986. *Master Richard's Bestiary of Love and Response*. Berkeley: University of California Press.

Bell, Catherine. 1992. *Ritual Theory, Ritual Practice*. New York: Oxford University Press.

Bell, Nicolas. 2003. *The Las Huelgas Music Codex: A Companion Study to the Facsimile*. Madrid: Testimonio Compañia Editorial.

2008. 'Music'. In *The Cambridge History of the Book in Britain: 1100–1400*. Vol. 2, ed. Nigel Morgan and Rodney M. Thomson. Cambridge University Press, 463–73.

Bent, Margaret. 1998. 'The Grammar of Early Music: Preconditions for Analysis'. In *Tonal Structures in Early Music*, ed. Cristle Collins Judd. New York: Garland Publishing, 15–59.

Bent, Margaret and Andrew Wathey, eds. 1998. *Fauvel Studies: Allegory, Chronicle, Music, and Image in Paris, Bibliothèque Nationale de France, MS Français 146*. Oxford University Press.

Bernhard, Michael. 1989. 'Parallelüberlieferung zu vier Cambridger Liedern'. In *Tradition und Wertung: Festschrift für Franz Brunhözl zum 65. Geburtstag*, ed. Günter Bernt, Fidel Rädle, and Gabriel Silagi. Sigmaringen: Jan Thorbecke, 141–5.

Bernt, Günter 1979. *Carmina Burana: Die Lieder der Benediktbeurer Handschrift. Zweisprachige Ausgabe [Latin–German]*. 6th edition. Munich: Amadeus.

1999. 'Vagantendichtung'. In *Lexikon des Mittelalters*, vol. VIII. Stuttgart: Metzler, 1366–8.

Berschin, Walter and Angelika Häse, eds. 1993. *Gerhard von Augsburg: Vita Sancti Uodarici. Die älteste Lebensbeschreibung des heiligen Ulrich. Lateinisch-deutsch*. Heidelberg: Winter.

Bétemps, Isabelle. 2002. 'Les *Lais de plour*: Guillaume de Machaut et Oton de Granson'. In *Guillaume de Machaut: 1300–2000. Actes du Colloque de la Sorbonne 28–29 septembre 2000*, ed. Jacqueline Cerquiglini-Toulet and Nigel Wilkins. Paris: Presses de l'Université de Paris–Sorbonne, 95–106.

Bibliothèque Impériale. 1868. *Anciens fonds. Vol. I of Département des manuscrits: Catalogue des manuscrits français*. Paris: Firmin–Didot.

Binkley, Thomas. 1983. 'The Greater Passion Play from *Carmina Burana*: An Introduction'. In *Alte Musik: Praxis und Reflexion: Sonderband der Reihe Basler Jahrbuch für Historische Musikpraxis zum 50. Jubiläum der Schola Cantorum Basiliensis*, ed. Peter Reidemeister and Veronika Gutmann. Winterthur: Amadeus, 144–57.

Bischoff, Bernhard. 1951. 'Die lateinischen Übersetzungen und Bearbeitungen aus den Oracula Sibyllina'. In *Mélanges Joseph de Ghellinck, S.J.*, vol. I. Gembloux: J. Duculot, 121–47. Reprinted in Bischoff 1966–81, 1: 150–70.

   1960. 'Gottschalks Lied für den Reichenauer Freund'. In *Medium Aevum Vivum: Festschrift für Walther Bulst*, ed. Hans Robert Jauss and Dieter Schaller. Heidelberg: Winter, 61–8. Reprinted in Bischoff 1966–81, 2: 26–34.

   1965. [Item no.] '361', *Karl der Grosse: Werk und Wirkung*, ed. Wolfgang Braunfels. Aachen, [n.p.], 361.

   1966–81. *Mittelalterliche Studien*. 3 vols. Stuttgart: Hiersemann.

   1970. *Carmina Burana. Einführung zur Faksimile-Ausgabe der Benediktbeurer Handschrift*. Munich: Peter Lang.

   1980. *Die vorwiegend österreichischen Diözesen*. Vol. II of *Die südöstdeutschen Schreibschulen und Bibliotheken in der Karolingerzeit*. Wiesbaden: Harrassowitz.

   2004. *Laon-Paderborn*. Vol. 2 of *Katalog der festländischen Handschriften des neunten Jahrhunderts (mit Ausnahme der wisigotischen)*. Wiesbaden: Harrassowitz.

Black, Jonathan. 2002. 'Psalm Uses in Carolingian Prayerbooks: Alcuin and the Preface to *De psalmorum usu*'. *Mediaeval Studies* 64: 1–60.

   2005. 'Divine Office and Private Devotion in the Latin West'. In *The Liturgy of the Medieval Church*, ed. Thomas J. Heffernan and E. Ann Miller. Rev. ed. Kalamazoo: Medieval Institute Publications, 45–71.

   2008. Review of Waldhoff 2003. *Speculum* 83: 772–4.

Bobeth, Gundela. 2002. 'Conductus sub pelle tropi'. *Schweizer Jahrbuch für Musikwissenschaft*, new series 22: 253–75.

   2012. 'Zum Transfer von Conducti des Notre-Dame-Repertoires'. In *Musik und kulturelle Identität: Bericht über den XIII. internationalen Kongress der Gesellschaft für Musikforschung Weimar 2004*, ed. Detlev Altenburg and Rainer Bayreuther. Kassel: Bärenreiter, 476–88.

Bodleian Library. 1984. *The Douce Legacy: An Exhibition to Commemorate the 150th Anniversary of the Bequest of Francis Douce (1757–1834)*. Oxford: Bodleian Library.

Bodmer, Johann Jacob. 1748. *Proben der alten schwäbischen Poesie des dreyzehnten Jahrhunderts: aus der Maneßischen Sammlung.* Zurich: Heidegger.

Bolte, Johannes. 1891. 'Dyalogus de Divite et Lazaro'. *Zeitschrift für deutsches Alterthum* 35: 257–61.

Bonderup, Jens. 1982. *The Saint Martial Polyphony, Texture and Tonality: A Contribution to Research in the Development of Polyphonic Style in the Middle Ages.* Trans. Stephanie Olsen and Jean McVeigh. Copenhagen: Dan Fog Musikforlag.

Boogaard, Nico H. J. van den. 1969. *Rondeaux et Refrains du XIIe siècle au début du XIVe.* Paris: Klincksieck.

Bowers, Roger. 2004. 'Guillaume de Machaut and His Canonry of Reims, 1338–1377'. *Early Music History* 23: 1–48.

Boynton, Susan. 2007. 'Prayer as Liturgical Performance in Eleventh- and Twelfth-century Monastic Psalters'. *Speculum* 82: 896–931.

Bradley, Catherine. 2012. 'New Texts for Old Music: Three Early Thirteenth-Century Motets'. *Music & Letters* 93: 149–69.

    2013a. 'Ordering in the Motet Fascicles of the Florence Manuscript'. *Plainsong and Medieval Music* 22: 1–35.

    2013b. 'Contrafacta and Transcribed Motets: Vernacular Influences on Latin Motets and Clausulae in the Florence Manuscript'. *Early Music History* 32: 1–70.

Breul, Karl. 1915. *The Cambridge Songs. A Goliard's Songbook of the Eleventh Century.* Cambridge University Press.

Brewer, Charles E. 2012. 'The Web of Sources for *Planctus ante nescia*'. In *Cantus Planus: Study Group of the International Musicological Society: Papers Read at the 16th Meeting, Vienna, Austria, 2011*, ed. Robert Klugseder. Vienna: Brüder Hollinek, 72–7.

Brown, Catherine. 2000. 'In the Middle'. *Journal of Medieval and Early Modern Studies* 30: 547–74.

Bullough, Donald A. 1991. 'Alcuin and the Kingdom of Heaven'. In *Carolingian Renewal: Sources and Heritage.* Manchester University Press, 161–240.

Bulst, Walther. 1950. *Carmina Cantabrigiensia.* Heidelberg: Carl Winter.

Busby, Keith. 2002. *Codex and Context: Reading Old French Verse Narrative in Manuscript.* 2 vols. Amsterdam: Rodopi.

Busse Berger, Anna Maria. 2005. *Medieval Music and the Art of Memory.* Berkeley: University of California Press.

Butterfield, Ardis. 2002. *Poetry and Music in Medieval France From Jean Renart to Guillaume de Machaut.* Cambridge University Press.

    2006. 'Introduction. Gautier de Coinci, Miracles de Nostre Dame: Texts and Manuscripts'. In *Gautier de Coinci: Miracles, Music, and Manuscripts*, ed. Kathy M. Krause and Alison Stones. Turnhout: Brepols, 1–18.

    2012. 'The Musical Contexts of *Le Tournoi de Chauvency* in Oxford, Bodleian MS Douce 308'. In *Lettres, musique et société en Lorraine médiévale: Autour du Tournoi de Chauvency (Ms. Oxford Bodleian Douce 308)*, ed. Mireille Chazan and Nancy Freeman Regalado. Geneva: Droz, 399–422.

Camille, Michael. 1985. 'Seeing and Reading: Some Visual Implications of Medieval Literacy and Illiteracy'. *Art History* 8: 26–49.

Carruthers, Mary. 1998. *The Craft of Thought: Meditation, Rhetoric, and the Making of Images, 400–1200*. Cambridge University Press.

2008. *The Book of Memory: A Study of Memory in Medieval Culture*. 2nd ed. Cambridge University Press.

Casey, Camillus. 1956. '"Les Voeux du Paon" by Jacques de Longuyon: An Edition of the Manuscripts of the P Redaction'. PhD dissertation. Columbia University.

Cerquiglini, Bernard. 1989. *Éloge de la variante: Histoire critique de la philologie*. Paris: Seuil.

Chailley, Jacques. 1955. 'Les premieres troubadours et les versus de l'école d'Aquitaine'. *Romania* 76: 212–39.

1960. *L'école musicale de Saint Martial de Limoges, jusqu'à la fin du XIe siècle*. Paris, Les livres essentiels.

Chichmaref [Shishmarev], Vladimir Feodorovich. 1909. *Guillaume de Machaut: Poésies lyriques*, 2 vols. Zapiski istoriko-filologicheskago fakul'teta imperatorskago S.-Peterburgskago Universiteta, 92. St. Petersburg: Imperial Faculty of Historical Philology.

Clark, Suzannah. 2007. '"S'en dirai chançonete": Hearing Text and Music in a Medieval Motet'. *Plainsong and Medieval Music* 16: 31–59.

Clarke, Eric. 2005. *Ways of Listening: An Ecological Approach to the Perception of Musical Meaning*. Oxford University Press.

Classen, Albrecht. 1993. Review of Schweikle 1989. *Studia neophilologica* 65: 250.

2002. 'Courtly Love Lyric'. In *A Companion to Middle High German Literature to the 14th Century*, ed. Francis G. Gentry. Leiden: Brill, 117–50.

Clemencic, René and Michael Korth. 1979. *Carmina Burana Lateinisch–deutsch: Gesamtausgabe der mittelalterlichen Melodien mit den dazugehörigen Texten. Übertragen, kommentiert und erprobt von René Clemencic; Textkommentar von Ulrich Müller; Übersetzung von René Clemencic und Michael Korth; herausgegeben von Michael Korth*. Munich: Heimeram.

Coates, Alan. 1999. *English Medieval Books: The Reading Abbey Collections from Foundation to Dispersal*. New York: Oxford University Press.

Coleman, Joyce. 1996. *Public Reading and the Reading Public in Late Medieval England and France*. Cambridge University Press.

Cook, James Heustis. 1978. 'Manuscript Transmission of Thirteenth-Century Motets'. PhD dissertation. University of Texas at Austin.

Corbin, Solange. 1973. 'Paléographie Musicale'. *École pratique des Hautes Études: IVe section, Sciences historiques et philologiques. Annuaire 1972–3*: 385–92.

Coussemaker, Edmond de. 1852. *Histoire de l'harmonie au moyen âge*. Paris: V. Didron.

1865. *L'Art harmonique aux XIIe et XIIIe siècles*. Paris: A. Durand.

Cramer, Thomas. 2004. 'Die Lieder der Trobadors, Trouvères und Minnesänger: literarhistorische Probleme'. In *Musikalische Lyrik*, ed. Hermann Danuser. Laaber: Laaber, 130–6.

Crocker, Richard. 1994. 'Two Recent Editions of Aquitanian Polyphony'. *Plainsong and Medieval Music* 3: 57–101.

Curran, Sean. 2013a. 'Composing a Codex: The Motets in the 'La Clayette' Manuscript'. In *Medieval Music in Practice: Studies in Honor of Richard Crocker*, ed. Judith A. Peraino. Middleton WI: American Institute of Musicology, 219–54.

2013b. 'Vernacular Book Production, Vernacular Polyphony, and the Motets of the "La Clayette" Manuscript (Paris, Bibliothèque nationale de France, nouvelles acquisitions françaises 13521)'. PhD dissertation. University of California, Berkeley.

2014. 'Reading and Rhythm in the "La Clayette" Manuscript'. *Plainsong and Medieval Music* 23: 125–51.

Curschmann, Michael. 1984. 'Hören, Lesen, Sehen: Buch und Schriftlichkeit im Selbstverständnis der volkssprachlichen literarischen Kultur Deutschlands um 1200'. *Beiträge zur Geschichte der deutschen Sprache und Literatur* 106: 218–57.

1992. '"Pictura laicorum litteratura?" Überlegungen zum Verhältnis von Bild und volkssprachlicher Schriftlichkeit im Hoch- und Spätmittelalter bis zum Codex Manesse'. In *Pragmatische Schriftlichkeit im Mittelalter: Erscheinungsformen und Entwicklungsstufen*, ed. Hagen Keller, Klaus Grubmüller, and Nikolaus Staubach. Munich: Wilhelm Fink, 211–29.

Curtius, Ernst Robert. 1990 [1948]. *European Literature and the Latin Middle Ages*. Trans. Willard R. Trask. Princeton University Press, 1990. Originally published as *Europäische Literatur und Lateinisches Mittelalter*. Bern: Francke, 1948.

Dangel-Hofmann, Frohmut, ed. 1990. *Carl Orff – Michel Hofmann: Briefe zur Entstehung der Carmina Burana*. Tutzing: Hans Schneider.

Daston, Lorraine, ed. 2004. *Things that Talk: Object Lessons From Art and Science*. New York: Zone Books.

Dechant, Denis Lyle. 2010. 'Transformations of Authorial Representation in the Manesse Codex'. MA dissertation. University of Oregon. Available via https://scholarsbank.uoregon.edu/x mlui/bitstream/handle/1794/10625/Dechant_Dennis%20_Lyle_ma2010s p.pdf?sequence=1

Deeming, Helen. 2005. 'Music in English Miscellanies of the Twelfth and Thirteenth Centuries'. PhD dissertation, Cambridge.

2006. 'The Song and the Page: Experiments with Form and Layout in Manuscripts of Medieval Latin Song'. *Plainsong and Medieval Music* 15: 1–27.

2009. 'French Devotional Texts in Thirteenth-Century Preachers' Anthologies'. In *Language and Culture in Medieval Britain: The French of England, c.1100–c.1500*, ed. Jocelyn Wogan-Browne, with Carolyn Collette, Maryanne

Kowaleski, Linne Mooney, Ad Putter, and David Trotter. Woodbridge: York Medieval Press, 254–65.

2011. 'Words and Music in a Thirteenth-Century Songbook'. In *Ars musica septentrionalis: De l'interprétation du patrimoine musical à l'historiographie*, ed. Barbara Haggh and Frédéric Billiet. Paris: Presses de l'université Paris–Sorbonne, 189–205.

2013, ed. *Songs in British Sources, c.1150–1300*. Musica Britannica 95. London: Stainer & Bell.

Forthcoming. 'Songs and Sermons in Thirteenth-Century England'. In *Pastoral Care in the Middle Ages*, ed. Peter Clarke and Sarah James. Farnham: Ashgate.

Delbouille, Maurice, ed. 1932. *Jacques Bretel: Le Tournoi de Chauvency*. Liège: H. Vaillant-Carmanne.

Delisle, Léopold. 1895. 'Les manuscrits de Saint-Martial de Limoges: Réimpression textuelle du catalogue de 1730'. *Bulletin de la Société archéologique et historique du Limousin* 43: 1–60.

Deshusses, Jean. 1979. 'Les anciens sacramentaires de Tours'. *Revue bénédictine* 89: 281–302.

Dillon, Emma. 2012. *The Sense of Sound: Musical Meaning in France, 1260–1330*. New York: Oxford University Press.

Dittmer, Luther. ed. 1959. *Paris 13521 & 11411*, Publications of Mediaeval Music Manuscripts 4. Brooklyn: Institute of Mediaeval Music.

Dobozy, Maria. 2005. *Re-Membering the Present: The Medieval German Poet-Minstrel in Cultural Context*. Turnhout: Brepols.

Doss-Quinby, Eglal. 1984. *Les Refrains chez les trouvères du XIIe siècle au debut du XVIe*. New York: Peter Lang.

2012. 'The Douce 308 Chansonnier within the Corpus of Trouvère Songbooks'. In *Lettres, musique et société en Lorraine médiévale: Autour du Tournoi de Chauvency (Ms. Oxford Bodleian Douce 308)*, ed. Mireille Chazan and Nancy Freeman Regalado. Geneva: Droz, 435–50.

Doss-Quinby, Eglal, Marie-Geneviève Grossel, and Samuel N. Rosenberg, eds. 2010. *'Sottes chansons contre Amours': parodie et burlesque au Moyen Âge*. Paris: Honoré Champion.

Doss-Quinby, Eglal, Samuel N. Rosenberg, and Elizabeth Aubrey, eds. 2006. *The Old French Ballette: Oxford, Bodleian Library, MS Douce 308*. Geneva: Droz.

Dronke, Peter. 1962. 'A Critical Note on Schumann's Dating of the Codex Buranus'. *Beiträge zur Geschichte der deutschen Sprache und Literatur* 84: 173–83.

1968. *Medieval Latin and the Rise of the European Love Lyric*. 2nd ed. 2 vols. Oxford University Press.

1987. 'The Lyrical Compositions of Philip the Chancellor'. *Studi medievali*, 3rd series 28: 563–92.

1996. *The Medieval Lyric*. 3rd ed. Cambridge: Brewer, 1996.

Dronke, Peter, Michael Lapidge, and Peter Stotz. 1982. 'Die unveröffentlichten Gedichte der Cambridger Liederhandschrift (CUL Gg.V.35)'. *Mittellateinisches Jahrbuch* 17: 54–92.

Drumbl, Johann. 2003. 'Studien zum Codex Buranus'. *Aevum: Rassegna di scienze storiche linguistiche e filologiche* 77: 323–56.

Dubois, Véronique. 2012. 'La notation française du tropaire-prosaire de Saint-Martial (Paris, BnF lat. 1240, Xe siècle)'. *Études grégoriennes* 39: 105–23.

Düchting, Reinhard. 2000. 'Sexualität in der Liebeslyrik der *Carmina Burana*'. In *Sexualität im Gedicht: 11. Kolloquium der Forschungsstelle für europäische Lyrik*, ed. Theo Stemmler and Stefan Horlacher. Tübingen: Narr, 51–64.

Duffin, Ross W. 1988. 'The Sumer Canon: A New Revision'. *Speculum* 63: 1–21.

Duggan, Anne J. 2000. 'The World of the *Carmina Burana*'. In *The* Carmina Burana: *Four Essays*, ed. Martin H. Jones. London: King's College, 1–24.

Duine, François. 1923. *Inventaire liturgique de l'hagiographe bretonne*. Paris: Champion.

Dümmler, Ernst, ed. 1895. *Epistolae Karolini aevi (II)*. MGH Epistolarum 4. Berlin: Weidmann.

Duplès-Agier, Henri. 1874. *Chroniques de Saint-Martial de Limoges publiées d'après les manuscrits originaux pour la Société de l'histoire de France*. Paris: Mme. Ve. J. Renouard.

Earp, Lawrence. 1983. 'Scribal Practice, Manuscript Production and the Transmission of Music in Late Medieval France: The Manuscripts of Guillaume de Machaut'. PhD thesis. Princeton.

　　1989. 'Machaut's Role in the production of his works'. *Journal of the American Musicological Society*, 42: 461–503.

　　1995. *Guillaume de Machaut: A Guide to Research*. New York: Garland.

　　2011. 'Interpreting the Deluxe Manuscript: Exigencies of Scribal Practice and Manuscript Production in Machaut'. In *The Calligraphy of Medieval Music*, ed. John Haines. Turnhout: Brepols, 223–40.

Edwards, Cyril. 2000. 'The German Texts in the *Codex Buranus*'. In The Carmina Burana: *Four Essays*, ed. Martin H. Jones. London: King's College, 41–70.

Elfassi, Jacques. 2006. 'Trois aspects inattendus de la postérité des *Synonyma* d'Isidore de Seville: Les prières, les textes hagiographiques et les collections canoniques'. *Revue d'histoire des textes*, new series 1: 109–52.

Emerson, John A. 1965. 'Two Newly Identified Offices for Saints Valeria and Austriclinianus by Adémar de Chabannes (MS Paris, Bibl. Nat., Latin 909, Fols. 79–85v)'. *Speculum* 40: 31–46.

　　1993. 'Neglected Aspects of the Oldest Full Troper (Paris, Bibliothèque nationale, lat. 1240)'. In *Recherches nouvelles sur les tropes liturgiques*, ed. Wulf Arlt and Gunilla Björkvall. Stockholm: Almqvist & Wiksell, 193–218.

Evans, Paul. 1970. 'Northern French Elements in an Early Aquitanian Troper'. In *Speculum Musicae Artis: Festgabe für Heinrich Husmann*, ed. Heinz Becker and Reinhard Gurlach. Munich: Wilhelm Fink, 103–10.

Everist, Mark. 1989. *Polyphonic Music in Thirteenth-Century France: Aspects of Sources and Distribution*. New York: Garland.

    1994. *French Motets in the Thirteenth Century: Music, Poetry, and Genre*. Cambridge University Press.

    2007. 'Motets, French Tenors and the Polyphonic Chanson ca.1300'. *Journal of Musicology* 24: 365–406.

Falck, Robert. 1981. *The Notre Dame Conductus: A Guide to the Repertory*. Henryville PA: Institute of Mediaeval Music.

Fallows, David. 1977. 'Guillaume de Machaut and the Lai: A New Source'. *Early Music* 5: 477–83.

Fassler, Margot. 1993. *Gothic Song: Victorine Sequences and Augustinian Reform in Twelfth-Century Paris*. Cambridge University Press.

Fletcher, Alan J. 1998. *Preaching, Politics and Poetry in Late Medieval England*. Dublin: Four Courts Press.

Fletcher, Frank T. H. 1924. *Étude sur la langue des 'Voeux du paon', roman en vers du XIVe siècle de Jacques de Longuyon*. Paris: Presses universitaires de France.

Flotzinger, Rudolf. 1981. 'Reduzierte Notre-Dame-Conductus im sogenannten Codex Buranus?'. *Muzikološki Zbornik – Musicological Annual* 17: 97–102.

Frühmorgen-Voss, Hella. 1975. *Text und Illustration im Mittelalter: Aufsätze zu den Wechselbeziehungen zwischen Literatur und bildender Kunst*. Munich: C. H. Beck.

Fuller, Sarah. 1969. 'Aquitanian Polyphony of the Eleventh and Twelfth Centuries'. PhD dissertation. 3 vols. University of California, Berkeley.

    1971. 'Hidden Polyphony: A Reappraisal'. *Journal of the American Musicological Society* 24: 169–92.

    1979. 'The Myth of "Saint Martial" Polyphony: A Study of the Sources'. *Musica Disciplina* 33: 5–26.

    1981. 'Theoretical Foundations of Early Organum Theory'. *Acta Musicologica* 53: 52–84.

Fulton, Rachel. 2002. *From Judgment to Passion: Devotion to Christ and the Virgin Mary, 800–1200*. New York: Columbia University Press.

Gaborit-Chopin, Danielle. 1969. *La Décoration des manuscrits à Saint-Martial de Limoges en Limousin du IXe au XIIe siècle*. Paris: Droz.

Galvez, Marisa. 2012. *Songbook: How Lyrics became Poetry in Medieval Europe*. University of Chicago Press.

Gamber, Klaus. 1985. 'Ein Brevier-Fragment aus der 1. Hälfte des 9. Jahrhunderts'. *Revue bénédictine* 95: 232–9.

Gaunt, Simon. 1995. *Gender and Genre in Medieval French Literature*. Cambridge University Press.

Gauthier, Marie-Madeleine. 1955. 'La Légende de sainte Valérie'. *Bulletin de la Société Archéologique et Historique du Limousin* 86: 35–80.

Gennrich, Friedrich. 1918. *Musikwissenschaft und romanische Philologie: ein Beitrag zur Bewertung der Musik als Hilfswissenschaft der romanischen Philologie*. Halle (Saale): Niemeyer.

1921. 'Die beiden neuesten Bibliographien altfranzösischer und altprovenzalischer Lieder'. *Zeitschrift für romanische Philologie* 41: 289–346.

1925. 'Die altfranzösische Liederhandschrift London, British Museum, Egerton 274'. *Zeitschrift für romanische Philologie* 45: 402–44.

1927. *Rondeaux, Virelais, und Balladen aus dem Ende des XII., dem XIII und dem ersten Drittel des XIV. Jahrhunderts mit den überlieferten Melodien*. vol. II: Materialien, Literaturnachweise, Refrainverzeichnis. Göttingen: Gesellschaft für romanische Literatur.

1932. *Grundriss einer Formenlehre des mittelalterlichen Liedes als Grundlage einer musikalischen Formenlehre des Liedes*. Halle (Saale): Niemeyer.

1958, ed. *Ein Altfranzösischer Motettenkodex: Faksimile Ausgabe der Hs La Clayette, Paris, Bibl. nat. nouv. acq. fr. 13521*. Summa musicae medii aevi 6. Darmstadt: [n.publ.].

Gibson, Margaret, Michael Lapidge, and Christopher Page. 1983. 'Neumed Boethian metra from Canterbury: a newly recovered leaf of Cambridge, University Library, Gg. 5. 35 (the 'Cambridge Songs' manuscript)'. *Anglo-Saxon England* 12: 141–52.

Gillespie, Vincent and Anne Hudson. 2013. *Probable Truth: Editing Medieval Texts from Britain in the Twenty-First Century*. Turnhout: Brepols.

Gillingham, Bryan. 1984. *Saint-Martial Mehrstimmigkeit*. Henryville PA: Institute for Mediaeval Studies.

1987, ed. *Paris B.N., fonds latin 3549 and London, B.L., add. 36,881* [facsimile edition]. Ottawa: Institute for Mediaeval Music.

1991. 'A New Etiology and Etymology for the Conductus'. *Musical Quarterly* 75: 59–73.

1993. *Secular Medieval Latin Song: An Anthology*. Ottawa: The Institute of Mediaeval Music.

2004. 'The Transmission of Two Secular Latin Songs'. *Studia Musicologica Academiae Scientiarum Hungaricae* 45: 105–17.

2006. *Music in the Cluniac Ecclesia: A Pilot Project*. Ottawa: Institute of Medieval Music.

Golden Carlson, Rachel. 2000. 'Devotion to the Virgin Mary in Twelfth-Century Aquitanian Versus'. PhD dissertation. University of North Carolina at Chapel Hill.

2003. 'Striking Ornaments: Complexity of Sense and Song in Aquitanian Versus'. *Music & Letters* 84: 527–56.

2006. 'Two Paths to Daniel's Mountain: Poetic-Musical Unity in Aquitanian Versus'. *The Journal of Musicology* 23: 620–46.

Grier, James. 1985. 'Transmission in the Aquitanian Versaria of the Eleventh and Twelfth Centuries'. PhD dissertation. University of Toronto.

1988. 'The Stemma of the Aquitanian Versaria'. *Journal of the American Musicological Society* 41: 250–88.

1990. 'Some Codicological Observations on the Aquitanian Versaria'. *Musical Disciplina* 44: 5–56.

1992. 'Scribal Practices in the Aquitanian Versaria of the Twelfth Century: Towards a Typology of Error and Variant'. *Journal of the American Musicological Society* 45: 373–427.

1994. 'A New Voice in the Monastery: Tropes and Versus from Eleventh- and Twelfth-Century Aquitaine'. *Speculum* 69: 1023–69.

2000. 'The Divine Office at St. Martial in the Early Eleventh Century: Paris, BN lat. 1085'. In *The Divine Office in the Latin Middle Ages: Methodology and Source Studies, Regional Developments, Hagiography*, ed. Margot Fassler and Rebecca Baltzer. Oxford University Press, 179–204.

2006. *The Musical World of a Medieval Monk: Adémar of Chabannes in Eleventh-Century Aquitaine*. Cambridge University Press.

Grunewald, Eckhard. 1986. 'Retuschiertes Mittelalter. Zur Rezeption und Reproduktion der "Manessischen" Liederhandschrift im 18. und frühen 19. Jahrhundert'. In *Mittelalter-Rezeption: Ein Symposion*, ed. Peter Wapnewski. Stuttgart: Metzler, 435–49.

Guelliot, Octave. 1914. 'Guillaume de Machaut'. *Revue historique ardennaise* 21: 297–316.

Gumbert. J. P. 1999. 'One Book with Many Texts: The Latin Tradition'. In *Codices Miscellanearum, Brussels Van Hulthem Colloquium 1999*, ed. R. Jansen-Sieben and H. van Dijk. Brussels: Archives et Bibliothèques de Belgique, 27–36.

Gushee, Lawrence, ed. 1975. *Aureliani Reomensis Musica disciplina*. Rome: American Institute of Musicology.

Haines, John. 2004. 'Erasures in Thirteenth-Century Music'. In *Music and Medieval Manuscripts: Palaeography and Performance*, ed. John Haines and Randall Rosenfeld. Aldershot: Ashgate, 60–88.

2010a. *Medieval Song in Romance Languages*. Cambridge University Press.

2010b. *Satire in the Songs of* Renart le Nouvel. Geneva: Droz.

Hamilton, Sarah. 2001a. '"Most illustrious king of kings": Evidence for Ottonian kingship in the Otto III prayerbook (Munich, Bayerische Staatsbibliothek, Clm 30111)'. *Journal of Medieval History* 27: 257–88.

2001b. *The Practice of Penance, 900–1050*. Woodbridge: Boydell.

Handschin, Jacques. 1930. 'Über Estampie und Sequenz II'. *Zeitschrift für Musikwissenschaft* 13: 113–32.

1949–51. 'The Summer Canon and Its Background'. *Musica Disciplina* 3: 55–94 and 5: 65–113.

Hanna III, Ralph. 1996a. *Pursuing History: Middle English Manuscripts and Their Texts*. Stanford University Press.

1996b. 'Miscellaneity and Vernacularity: Conditions of Literary Production in Late Medieval England'. In *The Whole Book: Cultural Perspectives on the*

Medieval Miscellany, ed. Stephen G. Nichols and Siegfried Wenzel. Ann Arbor: University of Michigan Press, 37–52.

Hardman, Phillipa, Barbara Morris, and Sally Castle. 2006. *Sumer is icumen in: A new edition of Reading's famous medieval round.* Reading: Two Rivers Press.

Harms, Wolfgang. 1988. 'Themenbereich "Zwischen Wort und Bild": Einführung'. In *Bibliographische Probleme im Zeichen eines erweiterten Literaturbegriffs*, ed. Wolfgang Martens. Weinheim: VCH, 141–2.

Hartzell, Karl Drew. 2006. *Catalogue of Manuscripts Written or Owned in England up to 1200 Containing Music.* Woodbridge: Boydell.

Haug, Andreas. 1987. *Gesungene und schriftlich dargestellte sequenz: Beobachtungen zum schriftbild der ältesten ostfränkischen sequenzhandschriften.* Neuhausen/ Stuttgart: Hänssler.

2004. 'Musikalische Lyrik im Mittelalter'. In *Musikalische Lyrik*, ed. Hermann Danuser. Laaber: Laaber, 59–129.

Haustein, Jens and Franz Körndle, eds. 2010. *Die 'Jenaer Liederhandschrift': Codex, Geschichte, Umfeld.* Berlin: De Gruyter.

Heinzle, Joachim. 1978. *Mittelhochdeutsche Dietrichepik: Untersuchungen zur Tradierungsweise, Überlieferungskritik und Gattungsgeschichte später Heldendichtung.* Zürich: Artemus.

Hesbert, René-Jean. 1963–79. *Corpus Antiphonalium Officii.* 6 vols. Herder: Rome.

Hilka, Alfons and Otto Schumann, eds. 1930–1970. *Carmina Burana.* 2 vols. Vol. I. *Text.* 3 vols. Vol I.1 *Die moralisch-satirischen Dichtungen*, ed. Alfons Hilka and Otto Schumann. Heidelberg: Winter, 1930. Vol. I.2: *Die Liebeslieder*, Heidelberg: Winter 1941, ed. Alfons Hilka and Otto Schumann. Vol. I.3: *Die Trink- und Spielerlieder – Die geistlichen Dramen. Nachträge*, ed. Otto Schumann† and Bernhard Bischoff. Heidelberg: Winter 1970. Vol II. *Kommentar.* Vol. II: *Einleitung (Die Handschrift der Carmina Burana); Die moralisch-satirischen Dichtungen*, Alfons Hilka and Otto Schumann. Heidelberg: Winter, 1930.

Hoepffner, Ernest. 1908–22. *Oeuvres de Guillaume de Machaut.* 3 vols. Paris: Firmin-Didot.

Hoffmann-Axthelm, Dagmar. 1994. '"Markgraf Otto von Brandenburg mit dem Pfeile" (Codex Manesse, fol. 13): Zum höfischen Minne-, Schach- und Instrumentalspiel im frühen 14. Jahrhundert'. *Hamburger Jahrbuch für Musikwissenschaft* 12: 157–70.

Hofmann, Klaus. 1970. 'Zur Entstehungs- und Frühgeschichte des Terminus Motette'. *Acta Musicologica* 42: 138–50.

Hohler, Christopher. 1978. 'Reflections on Some Manuscripts Containing Thirteenth-Century Polyphony'. *Journal of the Plainsong and Mediaeval Music Society* 1: 2–38.

Holznagel, Franz-Josef. 1995. *Wege in die Schriftlichkeit: Untersuchungen und Materialien zur Überlieferung der mittelhochdeutschen Lyrik.* Tübingen: Francke.

Hornby, Emma. 2010. 'Interactions between Brittany and Christ Church, Canterbury in the Tenth Century: The Linenthal Leaf'. In *Essays on the History of English Music in Honour of John Caldwell*, ed. Emma Hornby and David Maw. Woodbridge: Boydell, 47–65.

Huber, Martin. 1996. 'Fingierte Performanz: Überlegungen zur Codifizierung spätmittelalterlicher Liedkunst'. In *'Aufführung' und 'Schrift' in Mittelalter und früher Neuzeit*, ed. Jan-Dirk Müller. Stuttgart: Metzler, 93–106.

Hughes, Anselm, ed. 1958–60. *The Portiforium of Saint Wulfstan (Corpus Christi College, Cambridge, MS 391)*. 2 vols. London: Henry Bradshaw Society.

Huglo, Michel. 1988. 'Chant liturgique et chanson profane au moyen-âge'. In *Musique et société: hommages à Robert Wangermée*, ed. Henri Vanhulst and Malou Haine. Brussels: Éditions de l'Université de Bruxelles, 23–6.

   2004. *France à Afrique du Sud*. Vol 2 of *Les Manuscrits du processional*. Répertoire international des sources musicales B XIV/2. Munich: Henle.

   2006. 'Les versus *Salve Festa Dies*, leur dissémination dans les manuscrits du processionnal'. In *Cantus Planus: papers read at the 12th meeting of the IMS study group, Lillafüred/Hungary, 2004, Aug., 23–28*, [ed. László Dobszay]. Budapest: Institute for Musicology of the Hungarian Academy of Sciences, 595–603.

Hunt, Richard. 1961. 'The Collections of a Monk of Bardney: A Dismembered Rawlinson Manuscript'. *Medieval and Renaissance Studies* 5: 28–42.

Huot, Sylvia. 1987. *From Song to Book: The Poetics of Writing in Old French Lyric and Lyrical Narrative Poetry*. Ithaca: Cornell University Press.

   1997. *Allegorical Play in the Old French Motet: The Sacred and the Profane in Thirteenth-Century Polyphony*. Stanford University Press.

Hurry, Jamieson Boyd. 1913. *Sumer is icumen in*. Reading: Poynder & Son.

Hüschen, Heinrich. 1985. 'Vaganten- und Scholarenlieder aus der Frühzeit der Universität'. In *Schnittpunkte Mensch Musik: Beiträge zur Erkenntnis und Vermittlung von Musik. Walter Gieseler zum 65. Geburtstag*, ed. Rudolf Klinkhammer. Regensburg: Gustav Bosse, 46–53.

Irrgang, Stephanie. 2002. *Peregrinatio academia: Wanderungen und Karrieren von Gelehrten der Universitäten Rostock, Greifswald, Trier und Mainz im 15. Jahrhundert*. Stuttgart: Franz Steiner.

Iversen, Gunilla. 2009. 'From *jubilus* to Learned Exegesis: New Liturgical Poetry in Twelfth-Century Nevers'. In *Sapientia et eloquentia: Meaning and Function in Liturgical Poetry, Music, Drama, and Biblical Commentary in the Middle Ages*, ed. Gunilla Iversen and Nicolas Bell. Turnhout: Brepols, 203–58.

Jammers, Ewald. 1981. 'Die Manessische Liederhandschrift und die Musik'. In *Codex Manesse: Die Grosse Heidelberger Liederhandschrift: Kommentar zum Faksimile des Codex Palatinus Germanicus 848 der Universitätsbibliothek Heidelberg*, ed. Walter Koschorreck and Wilfried Werner. Kassel: Graphische Anstalt für Kunst und Wissenschaft, 169–87.

Jubainville, Marie-Henry d'Arbois de. 1876–8. 'Quelques noms de saints bretons dans un texte du XIe siècle'. *Revue celtique* 3: 449–50.

Karp, Theodore. 1992. *The Polyphony of Saint Martial and Santiago de Compostela.* 2 vols. Berkeley: University of California Press.

1999. 'Evaluating Performances and Editions of Aquitanian Polyphony'. *Acta Musicologica* 71: 19–49.

Kay, Sarah. 1990. *Subjectivity in Troubadour Poetry.* Cambridge University Press.

1999. 'Desire and Subjectivity'. In *The Troubadours: An Introduction*, ed. Simon Gaunt and Sarah Kay. Cambridge University Press, 212–27.

2008. 'Touching Singularity: Consolation, Philosophy, and Poetry in the French *dit*'. In *The Erotics of Consolation: Desire and Distance in the Late Middle Ages*, ed. Catherine E. Léglu and Stephen J. Milner. Basingstoke: Palgrave Macmillan, 21–38.

Kellner, Beate. 2004. '"Ich grüeze mit gesange": Mediale Formen und Inszenierungen der Überwindung von Distanz im Minnesang'. In *Text und Handeln: Zum kommunikativen Ort von Minnesang und antiker Lyrik*, ed. Albrecht Hausmann. Heidelberg: Universitätsverlag Winter, 107–37.

Kingsford, C. L. 1890. *The Song of Lewes.* Oxford: Clarendon Press, 1890. Reprinted, Brussels: J. Adam for the Faculty of Modern History, University of Oxford, 1963.

Kippenberg, Burkhard. 1960. *Der Rhythmus im Minnesang: eine Kritik der literar- und musikhistorischen Forschung mit einer Übersicht über die musikalischen Quellen.* Munich: C. H. Beck.

Knapp, Fritz Peter. 1998. 'Die "Carmina Burana" als Ergebnis europäischen Kulturtransfers'. *Beihefte der Francia* 43, 283–301.

Knowles, David. 1951. *The Monastic Constitutions of Lanfranc.* London: Thomas Nelson.

Krause, Kathy M. and Alison Stones, eds. 2007. *Gautier de Coinci: Miracles, Music, and Manuscripts.* Turnhout: Brepols.

Krüger, Astrid. 2007. *Litanei-Handschriften der Karolingerzeit.* Hannover: Hahn.

Kugler, Hartmut. 2012. 'Zum kulturwissenschaftlichen Konzept "Kulturtransfer" im europäischen Mittelalter'. In *Musik und kulturelle Identität*, ed. Detlef Altenburg and Rainer Bayreuther. Kassel: Bärenreiter, 456–65.

Kullman, Dorothea, ed. 2009. *The Church and Vernacular Literature in Medieval France.* Toronto: Pontifical Institute of Mediaeval Studies.

Kwakkel, Erik. 2002. 'Towards a Terminology for the Analysis of Composite Manuscripts'. *Gazette du livre médiéval* 41: 12–19.

Lammers, Heike Sigrid. 2000. 'Carmina Burana: Musik und Aufzeichnung'. PhD dissertation. Ludwig-Maximilians University, Munich.

2004. 'The Planctus Repertory in the *Carmina Burana*'. In *The Echo of Music. Essays in Honor of Marie Louise Göllner*, ed. Blair Sullivan. Warren MI: Harmonie Park Press, 75–99.

Landes, Richard. 1995. *Relics, Apocalypse, and the Deceits of History: Ademar of Chabannes, 989–1034*. Cambridge MA: Harvard University Press.

Lauer, Philippe. 1939. *Catalogue général des manuscrits latins*. Vol I. Paris: Bibliothèque Nationale.

Leach, Elizabeth Eva. 1997 [i.e. 1998]. 'Counterpoint in Guillaume de Machaut's Musical Ballades'. DPhil dissertation. University of Oxford.

 2003a. 'Singing More about Singing Less: Machaut's *Pour ce que tous* (B12)'. In *Machaut's Music: New Interpretations*, ed. Elizabeth Eva Leach. Woodbridge: Boydell, 111–24.

 2003b. 'Love, Hope, and the Nature of *Merci* in Machaut's Musical Balades *Esperance* (B13) and *Je ne cuit pas* (B14)'. *French Forum* 28: 1–27.

 2006. Review of Atchison 2005. *Music & Letters* 87: 416–20.

 2007a. *Sung Birds: Music, Nature and Poetry in the Later Middle Ages*. Ithaca: Cornell University Press.

 2007b. Review of Doss-Quinby, Rosenberg, and Aubrey 2006. *Music & Letters* 88: 673–76.

 2010. 'Nature's Forge and Mechanical Production: Writing, Reading, and Performing Song'. In *Rhetoric Beyond Words: Delight and Persuasion in the Arts of the Middle Ages*, ed. Mary Carruthers. Cambridge University Press, 72–95.

 2011. *Guillaume de Machaut: Secretary, Poet, Musician*. Ithaca: Cornell University Press.

 2012. 'Poet as Musician'. In *A Companion to Guillaume de Machaut*, ed. Deborah McGrady and Jennifer Bain. Leiden: Brill, 49–66.

Leclercq, Jean. 1929. 'Limoges'. In *Dictionnaire d'Archéologie chrétienne et de liturgie*, volume IX.1, ed. Fernand Cabrol et al. Paris: Letouzey & Ané, cols. 1136–7.

 1982. *The Love of Learning and Desire for God: A Study of Monastic Culture*. 3rd ed. Trans. Catherine Misrahi. New York: Fordham University Press.

Leo, Domenic. 2005. 'Authorial Presence in the Illuminated Machaut Manuscripts'. PhD dissertation. New York University.

Lepage, Yvan G., ed. 1981. *L'Oeuvre lyrique de Richard de Fournival*. University of Ottawa.

LeRoux, Mary Protase. 1965. 'The *Harmonica institutione* and *Tonarius* of Regino of Prüm'. PhD dissertation. Catholic University of America.

Lewon, Marc. 2011. 'Wie klang Minnesang? Eine Skizze zum Klangbild an den Höfen der staufischen Epoche'. In *Dichtung und Musik der Stauferzeit: wissenschaftliches Symposium 12. bis 14. November 2010*, ed. Volker Gallé. Worms, 69–124.

Lipphardt, Walther. 1955. 'Unbekannte Weisen zu den Carmina Burana'. *Archiv für Musikwissenschaft* 12: 122–42.

 1961. 'Einige unbekannte Weisen zu den Carmina Burana aus der zweiten Hälfte des 12. Jahrhunderts'. In *Festschrift Heinrich Besseler zum sechzigsten*

Geburtstag, ed. Institut für Musikwissenschaft der Karl-Marx-Universität. Leipzig: Deutscher Verlag für Musik, 101–25.

1982. 'Zur Herkunft der *Carmina Burana*'. In *Literatur und bildende Kunst im Tiroler Mittelalter*, ed. Egon Kühebacher. Innsbruck: Kowatsch, 209–23.

Llewellyn, Jeremy. 2004. 'A Paulinus of Aquileia versus in Eleventh-Century Italy'. In *The Appearances of Medieval Rituals. The Play of Construction and Modification*, ed. Nils Holger Petersen, Mette Birkedal Bruun, Jeremy Llewellyn, and Eyolf Østrem. Turnhout: Brepols, 97–122.

Lo Monaco, Francesco. 2009. *Carmina Cantabrigiensia: Il canzoniere di Cambridge*. Ospedaletto (Pisa): Pacini.

Loth, Joseph. 1890. 'Les anciennes litanies des saints de Bretagne'. *Revue celtique* 11: 135–51.

Lowden, John. 2000. *The Making of the Bibles moralisées*. University Park PA: Pennsylvania State University Press.

Ludwig, Friedrich. 1910–61. *Repertorium organorum recentioris et motetorum vetustissimi stili, vol. I: Catalogue raisonné der Quellen* (Pt. 1: *Handschriften in Quadrat-Notation*. Halle (Saale): Niemeyer, 1910. Reprinted, ed. Luther Dittmer. New York: Institute of Mediaeval Music, and Hildesheim: Georg Olms, 1964. Pt. 2: *Handschriften in Mensuralnotation*, ed Friedrich Gennrich. Summa musicae medii aevi, vol. 7. Langen bei Frankfurt: [n.publ.], 1961.)

1926–54, ed. *Guillaume de Machaut: Musikalische Werke*. Publikationen älterer Musik. Leipzig: Breitkopf & Härtel.

Lug, Robert. 2012. 'Politique et littérature à Metz autour de la Guerre des Amis (1231–1234): Le témoinage du Chansonnier de Saint-Germain-des Prés'. In *Lettres, musique et société en Lorraine médiévale: Autour du Tournoi de Chauvency (Ms. Oxford Bodleian Douce 308)*, ed. Mireille Chazan and Nancy Freeman Regalado. Geneva: Droz, 451–86.

McNamer, Sarah. 2010. *Affective Meditation and the Invention of Medieval Compassion*. Philadelphia: University of Pennsylvania Press.

Madan, Falconer. 1924. 'The Literary Work of a Benedictine Monk at Leominster in the Thirteenth Century'. *Bodleian Quarterly Record* 4: 168–70.

Mahone, Mary Margaret. 1977. 'Latin Liturgical Drama and the Ludus Peregrinus: A Unique Form of Medieval Monastic Worship'. PhD dissertation. University of Miami.

Margue, Michel. 2012. '*Voeux du paon* et *Voeux de l'épervier*: L'empereur et ses 'meilleurs chevaliers' dan la culture courtoise entre Metz, Bar et Luxembourg (début XIVe siècle)'. In *Lettres, musique et société en Lorraine médiévale: Autour du Tournoi de Chauvency (Ms. Oxford Bodleian Douce 308)*, ed. Mireille Chazan and Nancy Freeman Regalado. Geneva: Droz, 105–36.

Meier, Hedwig and Gerhard Lauer. 1996. 'Partitur und Spiel: Die Stimme der Schrift im "Codex Buranus"'. In *'Aufführung' und 'Schrift' in Mittelalter und früher Neuzeit*, ed. Jan-Dirk Müller. Stuttgart: Metzler, 31–47.

Meyer, Paul. 1868. 'Troisième rapport sur un mission littéraire en Angleterre et en Écosse'. *Archives des Missions Scientifiques et Littéraires*, 2nd series 5: 139–272.

———. 1871. *Documents manuscrits de l'ancienne littérature de la France conservés dans les bibliothèques de la Grande-Bretagne*. Paris, Imprimerie nationale.

———. 1890. 'Notice sur deux anciens manuscrits français ayant appartenu au Marquis de La Clayette (Bibliothèque nationale, Moreau 1715–1719)'. *Notices et extraits des manuscrits de la Bibliothèque nationale et autres bibliothèques* 33: 1–90.

Meyer, Wilhelm, ed. 1901. *Fragmenta Burana*. Berlin: Weidmannsche Buchhandlung.

Meyers, Jean, ed. 1991. *Sedulii Scotti Carmina*. Corpus Christianorum. Continuatio Mediaevalis 117. Turnhout, Brepols.

Middell, Matthias. 2001. 'Von der Wechselseitigkeit der Kulturen im Austausch: Das Konzept des Kulturtransfers in verschiedenen Forschungskontexten'. In *Metropolen und Kulturtransfer im 15./16. Jahrhundert: Prag – Krakau – Danzig – Wien*, ed. Andrea Langer and Georg Michels. Stuttgart: Franz Steiner, 7–51.

Mittermüller, Ruppert, ed. 1880. *Expositio Regulae ab Hildemaro tradita*. Regensburg: Pustet.

Montfaucon, Bernardo de. 1789. *Bibliotheca Bibliothecarum manuscriptorum nova*, vol.II Paris: Briasson.

Moser, Dietz-Rüdiger. 1998. 'Vaganten oder Vagabunden? Anmerkungen zu den Dichtern der "Carmina Burana" und ihren literarischen Werken'. In *Die deutsche Literatur des Mittelalters im europäischen Kontext: Tagung Greifswald, 11.–15. September 1995*, ed. Rolf Bräuner. Göppingen: Kümmerle, 9–26.

Müller, Jan-Dirk. 1994. '"Ir sult sprechen willekomen": Sänger, Sprecherrolle und die Anfänge volkssprachiger Lyrik'. *Internationales Archiv für Sozialgeschichte der deutschen Literatur* 19: 1–21.

Müller, Ulrich. 1980. 'Beobachtungen zu den "Carmina Burana": 1. Eine Melodie zur Vaganten-Strophe. 2. Walthers "Palästina-Lied" in "versoffenem" Kontext: eine Parodie'. *Mittellateinisches Jahrbuch* 15: 104–11.

———. 1981. 'Mehrsprachigkeit und Sprachmischung als poetische Technik: Barbarolexis in den *Carmina Burana*'. In *Europäische Mehrsprachigkeit: Festschrift zum 70. Geburtstag von Mario Wandruszka*, ed. Wolfgang Pöckl. Tübingen: Max Niemeyer, 87–104.

———. 1988. '"Carmina Burana" – Carmini Popolari? Zu den mittelalterlichen "Originalmelodien" und den modernen Aufführungsversuchen: Mit zwei Postskripta zu den deutschen Strophen der "Carmina Burana" und zur Melodie der "Vagantenstrophe"'. In *Festschrift für Paul Klopsch*, ed. Udo Kindermann, Wolfgang Maaz, and Fritz Wagner. Göppingen: Kümmerle, 1988, 359–69.

Naumann, Heinrich. 1969. 'Gab es eine Vagantendichtung?'. *Der altsprachliche Unterricht* 12: 69–105.

Nettl, Bruno. 1981. 'Transmission and Form in Oral Traditions'. In *International Musicological Society: Report of the Twelfth Congress, Berkeley, 1977*, ed. Daniel Heartz and Bonnie Wade. Kassel: Bärenreiter, 139–44.

Newman, Barbara. 2006. *Frauenlob's Song of Songs: a Medieval German Poet and His Masterpiece*. University Park PA: Pennsylvania State University Press.

Nichols, Stephen G. and Siegfried Wenzel, eds. 1996. *The Whole Book: Cultural Perspectives on the Medieval Miscellany*. Ann Arbor: University of Michigan Press.

Nicholson, Edward Williams Byron, ed. 1909. *Introduction to the Study of Some of the Oldest Latin Musical Manuscripts in the Bodleian Library, Oxford*. Early Bodleian Music 3. London: Novello.

Nolan, Maura. 2009. 'Historicism After Historicism'. In *The Post-Historical Middle Ages*, ed. Elizabeth Scala and Sylvia Federico. New York: Palgrave Macmillan, 63–86.

Norwood, Patricia. 1986. 'Performance Manuscripts of the Thirteenth-Century?'. *College Music Symposium* 26: 92–6.

Okubo, M. 2005. 'La Formation de la collection des Miracles de Gautier de Coinci'. *Romania* 123: 141–212 and 406–58.

Olsan, Lea. 1989. 'Latin Charms in British Library, MS Royal 12.B.XXV'. *Manuscripta* 33: 119–28.

    1992. 'Latin Charms of Medieval England: Verbal Healing in a Christian Oral Tradition'. *Oral Tradition* 7: 116–42.

O'Meara, Carra Ferguson. 2001. *Monarchy and Consent: The Coronation Book of Charles V of France, British Library MS Cotton Tiberius B. VIII*. London: Harvey Miller.

Ott, Norbert H. 1997. 'Mündlichkeit, Schriftlichkeit, Illustration: Einiges Grundsätzliche zur Handschriftenillustration, insbesondere in der Volkssprache'. In *Buchmalerei im Bodenseeraum: 13. bis 16. Jahrhundert*, ed. Eva Moser. Friedrichshafen: Robert Gessler, 37–51.

Paden, William D. and Frances Freeman Paden. 2010. 'Swollen Woman, Shifting Canon: A Midwife's Charm and the Birth of Secular Romance Lyric'. *Proceedings of the Modern Languages Association* 125: 306–21.

Paden, William D., Tilde Sankovitch, and Patricia H. Stäblein, eds. 1986. *The Poems of the Troubadour Bertran de Born*. Berkeley: University of California Press.

Page, Christopher. 1982. 'German Musicians and Their Instruments: A 14th-Century Account by Konrad of Megenberg'. *Early Music* 10: 192–200.

    1993. 'Johannes Grocheio on Secular Music: A Corrected Text and a New Translation'. *Plainsong and Medieval Music* 2: 17–41.

    1998. 'Tradition and Innovation in BN fr. 146: The Background to the Ballades'. In *Fauvel Studies: Allegory, Chronicle, Music, and Image in Paris, Bibliothèque Nationale de France, MS français 146*, ed. Margaret Bent and Andrew Wathey. Oxford University Press, 353–94.

2000. 'Around the Performance of a Thirteenth-Century Motet'. *Early Music* 28: 343–57.

2010. 'The Carol in Anglo-Saxon Canterbury?'. In *Essays on the History of English Music in Honour of John Caldwell*, ed. Emma Hornby and David Maw. Woodbridge: Boydell, 259–69.

Parsoneault, Catherine. 2001. 'The Montpellier Codex: Royal Influence and Musical Taste in Late Thirteenth-Century Paris'. PhD dissertation. University of Texas at Austin.

Payne, Thomas B. 1991. 'Poetry, Politics, and Polyphony: Philip the Chancellor's Contribution to the Music of the Notre Dame School'. PhD dissertation. University of Chicago.

2007. 'Philip the Chancellor and the conductus prosula: "motettish" works from the School of Notre Dame'. In *Music in Medieval Europe: Studies in Honour of Bryan Gillingham*, ed. Terence Bailey and Alma Santosuosso. Aldershot: Ashgate, 220–38.

2011, ed. *Philip the Chancellor: Motets and Prosulas*. Madison WI: A-R Editions.

Pearsall, Derek. 2005. 'The Whole Book: Late Medieval English Manuscript Miscellanies and their Modern Interpreters'. In *Imagining the Book*, ed. Stephen Kelly and John J. Thompson. Turnhout: Brepols, 17–29.

Pepin, Ronald E. and Jan M. Ziolkowski, eds. and trans. 2011. *Satires: Sextus Amarcius and Eupolemius*. Cambridge MA: Harvard University Press.

Peraino, Judith A. 2011. *Giving Voice to Love: Song and Self-Expression from the Troubadours to Guillaume de Machaut*. New York: Oxford University Press.

Pesce, Dolores. 1999. *Guido d'Arezzo's* Regule rithmice, Prologus in antiphonarium, *and* Epistola ad Michahelem. Ottawa: The Institute of Mediæval Music.

Peters, Ursula. 2000. 'Autorbilder in volkssprachigen Handschriften des Mittelalters: eine Problemskizze'. *Zeitschrift für deutsche Philologie* 119, 321–68.

2001. 'Ordnungsfunktion, Textillustration, Autorenkonstruktion: Zu den Bildern der romanischen und deutschen Liederhandschriften'. *Zeitschrift für deutsches Altertum und deutsche Literatur* 130, 392–430.

Planchart, Alejandro. 1991. Review of Clemencic and Korth 1979. *Notes*. 2nd series 47: 712–15.

Poirion, Daniel. 1965. *Le poète et le prince: l'évolution du lyrisme courtois de Guillaume de Machaut à Charles d'Orléans*. Grenoble: Allier.

Pouzet, Jean-Pascal. 2004. 'Quelques aspects de l'influence des chanoines augustins sur la production et la transmission littéraire vernaculaire en Angleterre (XIIIe–XVe siècles)'. *Comptes rendus de l'académie des inscriptions et belles-lettres* 148: 169–213.

Quiller-Couch, Arthur. 1900. *The Oxford Book of English Verse, 1250–1900*. Oxford University Press.

Raby, F. J. E. 1951. 'Philomena praevia temporis amoeni'. In *Mélanges Joseph de Ghellinck, S.J.*, vol. 2. Gembloux: J. Duculot, 435–48.

Rankin, Susan. 1996. 'Some reflections on liturgical music at late Anglo-Saxon Worcester'. In *St Oswald of Worcester: Life and Influence*, ed. Nicholas Brookes and Catherine Cubbitt. London: Leicester University Press, 325–48.

2000. 'The Study of Medieval Music: Some Thoughts on Past, Present and Future'. In *Musicology and Sister Disciplines: Past, Present, Future*, ed. David Greer. Oxford University Press, 154–68.

2003. 'Some Medieval Songs', *Early Music* 31: 327–42.

2005. 'Music at Wulfstan's Cathedral'. In *St Wulfstan and his World*, ed. Julia S. Barrow and Nicholas P. Brooks. Aldershot: Ashgate, 219–29.

2008. 'Quem quaeritis en voyage'. In *Itinerari e Stratificazioni dei Tropi: San Marco, l'Italia settentrionale e le Regioni Transalpine*, ed. Wulf Arlt and Giulio Cattin. Venezia: Edizioni Fondazione Levi, 177–207.

2011. 'On the Treatment of Pitch in Early Music Writing'. *Early Music History* 30: 105–75.

Regalado, Nancy Freeman. 2006. 'Picturing the Story of Chivalry in Jacques Bretel's *Tournoi de Chauvency* (Oxford, Bodleian Library, MS Douce 308)'. In *Tributes to Jonathan J. G. Alexander: Making and Meaning in the Middle Ages and the Renaissance*, ed. Susan L'Engle and Gerald B. Guest. London: Harvey Miller, 341–52.

Renk, Herta-Elisabeth. 1974. *Der Manessekreis, seine Dichter und die Manessesche Handschrift*. Stuttgart: W. Kohlhammer.

Rigg, Arthur G. and Gernot Wieland. 1975. 'A Canterbury Classbook of the Mid-Eleventh Century (the 'Cambridge Songs' Manuscript)'. *Anglo-Saxon England* 4, 113–30.

Roesner, Edward H. 1981. 'The Problem of Chronology in the Transmission of Organum Purum'. In *Music in Medieval and Early Modern Europe: Patronage, Sources, and Texts*, ed. Iain Fenlon. Cambridge University Press, 365–99.

Rokseth, Yvonne. 1935–48. *Polyphonies du XIIIe siècle: Le manuscrit H.196 de la Faculté de Médecine de Montpellier*. 4 vols. Paris: Editions de l'Oiseau-Lyre.

Roland, Martin. 2001. 'Kunsthistorisches zu den Budapester Fragmenten'. In *Entstehung und Typen mittelalterlicher Lyrikhandschriften: Akten des Grazer Symposiums 13.–17. Oktober 1999*, ed. Anton Schwob and András Vizkelety. Bern: Peter Lang, 207–22.

Rosenthal, Albi. 2000. *Obiter Scripta: Essays, Lectures, Articles, Interviews, and Reviews on Music and Other Subjects*. Oxford: Offox Press.

Rothenberg, David J. 2011. *The Flower of Paradise: Marian Devotion and Secular Song in Medieval and Renaissance Music*. New York: Oxford University Press.

Rouse, Richard and Mary Rouse. 2000. *Manuscripts and their Makers: Commercial Book Producers in Medieval Paris, 1200–1500*. Turnhout: H. Miller.

Rubin, Miri. 2009. *Mother of God: A History of the Virgin Mary*. New Haven: Yale University Press.

Sachs, Klaus-Jürgen. 1989. 'Tradition und Innovation bei Guido von Arezzo'. In *Kontinuität und Transformation der Antike im Mittelalter: Veröffentlichung* der Kongressakten zum Freiburger Symposion des Mediävistenverbandes, ed. Willi Erzgräber. Sigmaringen: Thorbecke, 233–44.

Saenger, Paul. 1997. *Space Between Words: The Origins of Silent Reading.* Stanford University Press.

Saltzstein, Jennifer. 2013. *The Refrain and the Rise of the Vernacular in Medieval French Music and Poetry.* Woodbridge: Boydell.

Saly, Antoinette, ed. 1990. *Girart d'Amiens: Meliacin ou le Cheval de Fust.* Aix-en-Provence: Publications du CUER MA.

Samaran, Charles and Robert Marichal. 1962. *Catalogue des manuscrits en écriture latine portant des indications de date, de lieu ou de copiste.* Vol. II. Paris: Centre national de la recherche scientifique.

Sanders, Ernest H. 1979. *English Music of the Thirteenth and Early Fourteenth Centuries.* Polyphonic Music of the Fourteenth Century 14. Les Remparts, Monaco: Éditions de l'Oiseau-Lyre.

Sannelli, Massimo. 2005. 'Raccolta, Canzoniere, Liederbuch: Ratio e ordo delle raccolte poetiche mediolatine'. In *Poesía latina medieval (siglos V–XV): actas del IV Congreso del Internationales Mittellateinerkomitee, Santiago de Compostela, 12–15 de septiembre de 2002,* ed. Manuel C. Díaz y Díaz and José Maria Díaz de Bustamant. Tavarnuzze: SISMEL edizioni del Galluzzo, 303–7.

Sayce, Olive. 1982. *The Medieval German Lyric 1150–1300: The Development of its Themes and Forms in Their European Context.* Oxford: Clarendon Press.

1992. *Plurilingualism in the Carmina Burana: A Study of Linguistics and Literary Influences on the Codex.* Göppingen: Kümmerle.

Schilling, Michael. 1996. 'Minnesang als Gesellschaftskunst und Privatvergnügen: Gebrauchsformen und Funktionen der Lieder im "Frauendienst" Ulrichs von Liechtenstein'. In *Wechselspiele: Kommunikationsformen und Gattungsinterferenzen mittelhochdeutscher Lyrik,* ed. Michael Schilling and Peter Strohschneider. Heidelberg: Winter, 103–21.

Schirmer, Karl-Heinz. 1956. *Die Strophik Walthers von der Vogelweide: ein Beitrag zu den Aufbauprinzipien in der lyrischen Dichtung des Hochmittelalters.* Halle (Saale): Niemeyer.

Schmeller, Johann Andreas, ed. 1847. *Carmina Burana: Lateinische und Deutsche Lieder und Gedichte einer Handschrift des XIII. Jahrhunderts aus Benedictbeuern auf der K. Hofbibliothek zu München.* Stuttgart; Literarischer Verein.

Schrade, Leo. 1955. 'Unknown Motets in a Recovered Thirteenth-Century Manuscript'. *Speculum* 30: 393–412.

1956, ed. *The Works of Guillaume de Machaut.* 2 vols. Polyphonic Music of the Fourteenth Century. Les Remparts, Monaco: L'Oiseau-Lyre.

Schulman, Nichole M. 2001. *Where Troubadours were Bishops: The Occitania of Folc of Marseille, 1150–1231.* New York: Routledge.

Schulz, Fritz Traugott. 1901. *Typisches der grossen Heidelberger Liederhandschrift und verwandter Handschriften nach Wort und Bild: eine germanistisch-antiquarische Untersuchung.* Göttingen: Vandenhoeck & Ruprecht.

Schwan, Eduard. 1886. *Die altfranzösische Liederhandschriften: ihr Verhältnis, ihre Entstehung und ihre Bestimmung*. Berlin: Weidmann.

Schweikle, Günther. 1989. *Minnesang*. Stuttgart: Metzler.

    1995. *Minnesang*. 2nd ed. Stuttgart: Metzler.

Seebass, Tilman. 1988. 'Lady Music and Her Protégés: From Musical Allegory to Musician's Portraits'. *Musica Disciplina* 42: 23–61.

Segre, Cesare, ed. 1957. *Li Bestiaires d'amours di maistre Richart de Fournival e li response du bestiaire*. Milan: Riccardo Ricciardi.

Sequentia, dir. Benjamin Bagby. 2004. Booklet accompanying *Lost Songs of a Rhineland Harper, X & XI centuries*. Deutsche Harmonia Mundi. Deutsche Harmonia Mundi (BMG) 82876 58939 2 (CD, SACD-H, DSD, NA); Deutsche Harmonia Mundi (BMG) 82876 58940 2 (CD, SACD-H, DSD, Europe)

Sharpe, Richard, J. P. Carley, R. M. Thomson, and A. G. Watson, eds. 1996. *English Benedictine Libraries: The Shorter Catalogues*. London: The British Library.

Sinnreich-Levi, Deborah M., ed. 1994. *Eustache Deschamps' L'Art de dictier*. East Lansing MI: Colleagues Press, 1994.

Solente, Suzanne. 1953. 'Le grand recueil La Clayette à la Bibliothèque nationale'. *Scriptorium* 7: 226–34.

Sollerio, Joanne Bapt., Joanne Pinio, and Guilielmo Cupero. 1723. *Acta sanctorum Julii*, vol. 3. Antwerp: Jacobum du Moulin.

Spanke, Hans. 1928–32. 'Die Londoner St. Martial-Conductushandschrift', *Butlletí de la Biblioteca de Catalunya* 9: 280–301.

    1930–31. 'Der *Codex Buranus* als Liederbuch'. *Zeitschrift für Musikwissenschaft* 13: 241–51.

    1931. 'Rythmen- und Sequenzstudien', *Studi medievali*, 2nd (new) series 4: 286–320.

    1936. *Beziehungen zwischen romanischer und mittellateinischer Lyrik mit besonderer Berücksightigung der Metrik und Musik*. Berlin: Weidmannsche Buchhandlung. Reprinted Nendeln, Liechtenstein: Kraus, 1972.

    1942. 'Ein lateinisches Liederbuch des 11. Jahrhunderts'. *Studi Medievali*, 2nd (new) series 15: 111–42.

    1955, ed. *G. Raynauds Bibliographie des altfranzösischen Liedes*. Leiden: Brill.

Stäblein, Bruno. 1963. 'Modale Rhythmen in Saint Martial-Repertoire?'. In *Festschrift Friedrich Blume zum 70. Geburtstag*, ed. Anna Amalie Abert and Wilhelm Pfannkuch. Kassel: Bärenreiter, 340–62.

    1975. *Schriftbild der einstimmigen Musik*. Musikgeschichte in Bildern III: Musik des Mittelalters und der Renaissance 4. Leipzig: Deutscher Verlag für Musik.

Steffens, Georg. 1896. 'Die altfranzösiche Liederhandschrift der Bodleiana in Oxford, Douce 308'. *Archiv für das Studium der neueren Sprachen und Litteraturen* 97: 283–308.

    1897a. 'Die altfranzösische Liederhandschrift der Bodleiana in Oxford, Douce 308 (1. Fortsetzung)'. *Archiv für das Studium der neueren Sprachen und Litteraturen* 98: 59–80.

1897b. 'Die altfranzösiche Liederhandschrift der Bodleiana in Oxford, Douce 308 (2. Fortsetzung)'. *Archiv für das Studium der neueren Sprachen und Litteraturen* 98: 339–88.

1898a. 'Die altfranzösiche Liederhandschrift der Bodleiana in Oxford, Douce 308 (3. Fortsetzung)'. *Archiv für das Studium der neueren Sprachen und Litteraturen* 99: 77–100.

1898b. 'Die altfranzösiche Liederhandschrift der Bodleiana in Oxford, Douce 308 (4. Fortsetzung. Schlufs)'. *Archiv für das Studium der neueren Sprachen und Litteraturen* 99: 339–88.

1900. 'Die altfranzösiche Liederhandschrift der Bodleiana in Oxford, Douce 308 (5. Fortsetzung. Schlufs)'. *Archiv für das Studium der neueren Sprachen und Litteraturen* 104: 331–54.

Steigemann, Christoph and Matthias Wemhoff. 1999. *Kunst und Kultur der Karolingerzeit: Karl der Große und Papst Leo III. in Paderborn*. Beitragsband zur Katalog der Ausstellung. Mainz: Philipp von Zabern.

Stevens, Denis. 1979. 'Music in Honour of St Thomas of Canterbury'. *Musical Quarterly* 56: 311–48.

Stevens, John. 1986. *Words and Music in the Middle Ages: Song, Narrative, Dance and Drama, 1050–1350*. Cambridge University Press.

1992. '*Samson dux fortissime*: An International Latin Song'. *Plainsong and Medieval Music* 1:1–40.

1996. '"Sumer is icumen in": A Neglected Context'. In *Expedition nach der Wahrheit: Poems, Essays and Papers in Honour of Theo Stemmler*, ed. Stefan Horlacher and Marion Islinger. Heidelberg: Winter, 307–47.

2005, ed. *The Later Cambridge Songs. An English Song Collection of the Twelfth Century*. Oxford University Press.

Stewart, Columba. 2008. 'Prayer among the Benedictines'. In *A History of Prayer: The First to the Fifteenth Century*, ed. Roy Hammerling. Leiden: Brill, 201–21.

Stock, Brian. 1983. *The Implications of Literacy: Written Language and Models of Interpretation in the Eleventh and Twelfth Centuries*. Princeton University Press.

Stones, Alison. 1977. 'Sacred and Profane Art: Secular and Liturgical Book-Illumination in the Thirteenth Century'. In *The Epic in Medieval Society: Aesthetic and Moral Values*, ed. H. Scholler. Tübingen: Niemeyer, 100–112.

2011. 'Some Northern French Chansonniers and their Cultural Context'. In *Ars musica septentrionalis: De l'interprétation du patrimoine musical à l'historiographie*, ed. Barbara Haggh and Frédéric Billiet. Paris: Presses de l'université Paris-Sorbonne, 169–87.

2012. 'Le contexte artistique du *Tournoi de Chauvency*'. In *Lettres, musique et société en Lorraine médiévale: Autour du Tournoi de Chauvency (Ms. Oxford Bodleian Douce 308)*, ed. Mireille Chazan and Nancy Freeman Regalado. Geneva: Droz, 151–204.

Strecker, Karl. 1925. 'Zu den Cambridger Liedern'. *Zeitschrift für deutsches Altertum und Literatur* 62: 209–20.

　1926. *Die Cambridger Lieder*. MGH Scriptores rerum Germanicum in usum scholarum separatim editi 40. Berlin: Weidmann.

Swanson, R. N. 1995. *Religion and Devotion in Europe, c.1200 to c.1515*. Cambridge University Press.

Switten, Margaret. 1999. 'Music and Versification: *Fetz Marcabrus los motz e•l so*'. In *The Troubadours: An Introduction*, ed. Simon Gaunt and Sarah Kay. Cambridge University Press, 141–63.

　2007. 'Versus and Troubadour Around 1100: A Comparative Study of Refrain Technique in the "New Song"'. *Plainsong and Medieval Music* 16: 91–143.

Symes, Carol. 2007. *A Common Stage: Theater and Public Life in Medieval Arras*. Ithaca: Cornell University Press.

Taylor, Andrew. 2002. *Textual Situations: Three Medieval Manuscripts and Their Readers*. Philadelphia: University of Pennsylvania Press.

Taylor, Andrew and Alan Coates. 1998. 'The Dates of the Reading Calendar and the Summer Canon', *Notes and Queries* 243: 22–4.

Teviotdale, Elizabeth C. 1992. 'Music and Pictures in the Middle Ages'. In *Companion to Medieval and Renaissance Music*, ed. Tess Knighton and David Fallows. London: Dent, 179–88.

Traill, David A. 2006. 'A Cluster of Poems by Philip the Chancellor' *Studi Medievali*, 3rd series 47: 267–85.

Traube, Ludwig. 1896. *Poetae Latini aevi Carolini*, vol. III. MGH Antiquitates. Berlin: Weidmann.

Treitler, Leo. 1964. 'The Polyphony of St. Martial'. *Journal of the American Musicological Society* 17: 29–42.

　1965. 'Musical Syntax in the Middle Ages: Background to an Aesthetic Problem'. *Perspectives of New Music* 4: 78–85.

　1967. 'The Aquitanian Repertories of Sacred Monody in the Eleventh and Twelfth Centuries'. PhD dissertation. 3 vols. Princeton University.

　1981. 'Oral, Written, and Literate Process in the Transmission of Medieval Music'. *Speculum* 56: 471–91.

　1995. 'Once More, Music and Language in Mediaeval Song'. In *Essays on Medieval Music in Honor of David Hughes*, ed. Graeme M. Boone. Cambridge MA: Harvard University Press, 441–69.

　2003. *With Voice and Pen: Coming to Know Medieval Song and How It Was Made*. Cambridge University Press.

Unlandt, Nicolaas. 2011. *Le chansonnier français de la Burgerbibliothek de Berne: Analyse et description du manuscrit et édition de 53 unica anonymes*. Berlin: De Gruyter.

Unzeitig-Herzog, Monika. 1996. 'Diskussionsbericht: Vortrag, Abbildung, Handschrift am Beispiel der höfischen Lied-und Sangspruchdichtung'. In

'*Aufführung*' *und* '*Schrift*' *in Mittelalter und früher Neuzeit*, ed. Jan-Dirk Müller. Stuttgart: Metzler, 130–7.

Van der Werf, Hendrik. 1972. *The Chansons of the Troubadours and Trouvères: A Study of the Melodies and Their Relation to the Poems*. Utrecht: A. Oosthoek.

1989. *Integrated Directory of Organa, Clausulae, and Motets of the Thirteenth Century*. Rochester NY: Van der Werf.

1993. *The Oldest Extant Part Music and the Origin of Western Polyphony*. 2 vols. Rochester NY: Van der Werf.

Van Vleck, Amelia. 1991. *Memory and Re-Creation in Troubadour Lyric*. Berkeley: University of California Press.

Voetz, Lothar. 1988. 'Überlieferungsformen mittelhochdeutscher Lyrik'. In *Codex Manesse: Katalog zur Ausstellung vom 12. Juni bis 2. Oktober 1988 Universitätsbibliothek Heidelberg*, ed. Elmar Mittler and Wilfried Werner. Heidelberg: Brauns, 224–74.

Vogel, Cyrille and Reinhard Elze, eds. 1963. *Le Texte*. Vol. 2 of *Le Pontifical romano-germanique du dixième* siècle. Vatican City: Biblioteca apostolica vaticana.

Vogüé, Adalbert de and Jean Neufville, eds. 1972. *La Règle de Saint Benoît*. Vol. 2. Paris: Éditions du Cerf.

Vollmann, Benedikt. 1987, ed. *Carmina Burana: Texte und Übersetzungen*. Frankfurt am Main: Deutscher Klassiker Verlag.

1995. 'Carmina Burana'. In *Die Musik in Geschichte und Gegenwart: Sachteil*. New edition, ed. Ludwig Finscher. Kassel: Bärenreiter, 2: 455–9.

Wachinger, Burghart. 1985. 'Deutsche und lateinische Liebeslieder: Zu den deutschen Strophen der *Carmina Burana*'. In *Der deutsche Minnesang: Aufsätze zu seiner Erforschung*, vol. 2, ed. Hans Fromm. Darmstadt: Wissenschaftliche Buchgesellschaft, 275–308.

Waldhoff, Stephan. 2003. *Alcuins Gebetbuch für Karl den Grossen: Seine Rekonstruktion und seine Stellung in der frühmittelalterlichen Geschichte der Libelli Precum*. Münster: Aschendorff.

Walther, H. 1920. *Das Streitgedicht in der lateinischen Literatur des Mittelalters*. Munich: Oskar Beck.

Walther, Ingo F. and Gisela Siebert, eds. 1988. *Codex Manesse: Die Miniaturen der Großen Heidelberger Liederhandschrift*. Frankfurt am Main: Insel.

Welker, Lorenz. 1988. 'Melodien und Instrumente'. In *Codex Manesse: Katalog zur Ausstellung vom 12. Juni bis 2. Oktober 1988 Universitätsbibliothek Heidelberg*, ed. Elmar Mittler and Wilfried Werner. Heidelberg: Brauns, 113–26.

Wenzel, Horst. 2006. 'Wahrnehmung und Deixis: Zur Poetik der Sichtbarkeit in der höfischen Literatur'. In *Visualisierungsstratiegien in mittelalterlichen Bildern und Texten*, ed. Horst Wenzel and C. Stephen Jaeger. Berlin: Erich Schmidt, 17–43.

Wenzel, Siegfried. 1986. *Preachers, Poets and the Early English Lyric*. Princeton University Press.

Whitcomb, Pamela. 2000. 'The Manuscript London, British Library, Egerton 274: A Study of its Origin, Purpose, and Musical Repertory in Thirteenth-Century France'. PhD dissertation. University of Texas at Austin.

Wibberley, Roger. 1977. 'English polyphonic music of the late thirteenth and early fourteenth centuries: a reconstruction, transcription, and commentary'. DPhil dissertation. Oxford University.

Wilmart, André. 1914. 'Un témoin anglo-saxon du calendrier métrique d'York'. *Revue bénédictine* 46: 41–69.

   1922. 'Lettres de l'époque carolingienne'. *Revue bénédictine* 34: 234–45.

   1936. 'Le Manuel de prières de saint Jean Gualbert'. *Revue bénédictine* 48: 259–99.

   1940. *Precum libelli Quattuor aevi Karolini*. Ephemerides Liturgicae: Rome.

   1941. 'Le florilège mixte de Thomas Bekynton'. *Medieval and Renaissance Studies* 1: 41–84.

Wimsatt, James I., William W. Kibler and Rebecca A. Baltzer, eds. 1988. *Guillaume de Machaut: Le Jugement du Roy de Behaigne and Remede de Fortune*. Athens GA: University of Georgia Press.

Wolinksi, Mary. 1996. 'Tenors Lost and Found: The Reconstruction of Motets in Two Medieval Chansonniers.' In *Critica Musica: Essays in Honor of Paul Brainerd*, ed. John Knowles. Amsterdam: Gordon and Breach, 461–82.

Wright, Craig. 1989. *Music and Ceremony at Notre Dame of Paris, 500–1550*. Cambridge University Press.

Wulstan, David. 2000. '"Sumer is icumen in" – a perpetual puzzle-canon?'. *Plainsong and Medieval Music* 9: 1–17.

Zayaruznaya, Anna. 2010. 'Form and Idea in the *Ars Nova* Motet'. PhD dissertation. Harvard University.

Ziolkowski, Jan M. 1994. *The Cambridge Songs. Carmina Cantabrigiensia*. New York: Garland.

Zumthor, Paul. 1972. *Essai de poétique médiévale*. Paris: Seuil.

   1984. *La poésie et la voix dans la civilisation médiévale*. Paris: Presses universitaires des France.

   1992. *Toward a Medieval Poetics*. Trans. Philip Bennett. Minneapolis: University of Minnesota Press.

Index